YOUNG STUDENTS

Learning Library

VOLUME 22

World War II–Index

WEEKLY READER BOOKS
MIDDLETOWN·CONNECTICUT

PHOTO CREDITS

Young Students Learning Library is a trademark of Field Publications.

ISBN 0-8374-6052-2

CONTENTS

WORLD WAR II

The Great War (World War I) was called "the war to end all wars." When it ended in 1919, people generally believed that nothing so terrible could happen again. But within 20 years, nations around the globe were plunged into another world war that lasted from September 1, 1939, to September 2, 1945, and in which more than 50 million people lost their lives.

As in World War I, the opposing armies of World War II were made up of two groups of nations. The *Axis Powers* included Germany, Italy, and Japan. The *Allied Powers* included Great Britain and other members of the Commonwealth of Nations, the United States, the Soviet Union, France, and China.

The areas of major fighting were in Europe, northern Africa, Asia, and in the Pacific, Atlantic, and Indian oceans. Battles took place on land, sea, and in the air with a power and destructiveness never before experienced in history. Nuclear bombs were developed and used for the first time, as were high-altitude, supersonic rocket missiles and jet planes.

Events Leading to War   At the end of World War I, Europe was in a shambles. The Treaty of Versailles had exacted harsh repayment from Germany, which that country was unable to provide. The United States did not join the League of Nations, preferring to stay out of European affairs. Nations became concerned with their own internal problems. Members of the League of Nations were not enthusiastic about enforcing international agreements made by the League.

In the early 1930's, a great economic depression hit the United

States and Europe. In Germany, as in other countries, prices increased as wages and jobs decreased. The government leadership that had developed in Germany after World War I was unable to cope with the economic conditions. Into this situation stepped Adolf Hitler, head of the Nazi (National Socialist) Party. On January 30, 1933, Hitler became Chancellor of Germany. He promised to make Germany the strongest nation on earth and began increasing production of military supplies. Other countries recognized that Hitler was gaining power, but few people believed he would actually go to war.

Europe was having political as well as economic troubles in the 1920's and 1930's. After World War I, the empire of Austria-Hungary had been broken up into a group of smaller nations—Yugoslavia, Albania, Hungary, Czechoslovakia, and Austria— that were all suspicious of each other. The Soviet Union had gained in industrial and military strength, and most Western powers were fearful of Stalin's dictatorial regime. In 1922, Benito Mussolini came to power as dictator of Italy and set out to build up the Italian military forces. For defense, France fortified the Maginot Line, a series of forts and huge concrete bunkers along their border with Germany. But the Maginot fortifications did not extend along France's Belgian border, where German forces had first invaded France in World War I.

In 1931, Japan attacked China. When the League of Nations ordered Japan to withdraw from China, Japan ignored the order and resigned from the League in 1933. Hitler, noting that the League was powerless to stop Japan's aggression, decided to take over former German lands along the Rhine River. In 1936, Hitler's troops moved into the Rhineland unopposed. In the same year, Mussolini's troops conquered Ethiopia and forced the emperor, Haile Selassie, into ex-

▲ *Germany's leader, Adolf Hitler (right), meets with Britain's peace-seeking prime minister, Neville Chamberlain, in 1938.*

The Allied invasion of France on June 6, 1944, was the greatest naval invasion the world has ever seen. Over 150,000 soldiers from the U.S. and British armies stormed ashore on five beaches. They were supported by about 12,000 airplanes, 350 warships, and 6,100 landing craft.

During World War II, between 55 and 60 million people were killed, the greatest loss of life in any war. Over a third of this number were Russians. About 10 million people had been killed in World War I.

◀ *U.S. Marines in action against the Japanese in the Pacific during World War II. A news cameraman crouches in the foreground.*

▲ *The German Focke-Wulf FW190. Top speed: 410 miles per hour (660 km/h).*

▲ *The American Mustang P-51. Top speed: 435 miles per hour (700 km/h).*

▲ *The American Republic P-47 Thunderbolt. Top speed: 430 miles per hour (690 km/h).*

▲ *The Russian Mikoyan MiG-3. Top speed: 405 miles per hour (650 km/h).*

▲ *The Japanese Nakajima Ki-84. Top speed: 380 miles per hour (610 km/h).*

ile. Throughout 1936 and 1937, Germany and Italy gave military support to Generalissimo Francisco Franco in the Spanish civil war. In 1938, Hitler took over Austria without a battle. He then demanded the Sudetenland, the borderlands of Czechoslovakia. France, Czechoslovakia's main ally, and Britain gave the borderlands to Hitler through negotiations resulting in the Munich Pact of 1938. In March 1939, Hitler moved in and seized all of Czechoslovakia.

Europe was slow to realize Hitler's plan for world domination in spite of his speeches declaring the Germans to be superior to all other people. Most governments felt that Hitler was a reasonable man and could be dealt with by negotiation and *appeasement* (giving in to Hitler's demands in order to maintain peace). But appeasement was not working.

The Fighting EUROPE FROM 1939–1942. On August 23, 1939, Hitler and Joseph Stalin (premier of the Soviet Union) signed a pact agreeing not to attack each other. They also agreed to invade and divide Poland. Great Britain and France warned that if Poland were attacked, they would declare war on Germany. But Hitler knew that neither France nor Britain could seriously attack Germany without help from the Soviet Union. On September 1, 1939, German forces crashed through Poland. On September 3, Britain and France, joined by countries of the Commonwealth of Nations, declared war on Germany. German *blitzkrieg* ("lightning warfare") tactics—a combination of tanks and motor artillery with air support (bombs)—were overwhelming. The Soviet Union attacked from the east, and after one month Poland fell.

Among Hitler's troops was a special S.S. corps. "S.S." stood for *Schutzstaffel*, meaning "protection staff" or "defense corps." The S.S. troops were first organized in the 1920's as Hitler's personal body-

guards. But the corps had since grown to tremendous strength and was under the direction of Heinrich Himmler, Hitler's police chief. The S.S. corps took over and ran a country once it was conquered. In Poland, as in other countries, the S.S. deliberately set out to kill all Jews (whom Hitler blamed for Germany's troubles) and to kill all people capable of leadership.

After Poland, the Soviet Union conquered part of Finland. The German army attacked and occupied Norway and Denmark. The British prime minister, Neville Chamberlain, was forced to resign because of his ineffective policies against Germany.

Winston Churchill was made prime minister on May 10, 1940—the day Germany invaded Belgium and the Netherlands. The confident Germans swept southward into France, as they had in World War I, avoiding the Maginot Line that the French army had been so long preparing. The British tried to help France, but were forced northward to the port of Dunkirk on the English Channel, from which they withdrew back to England. On May 28, King Leopold III of Belgium surrendered to the Germans. The French tried to defend Paris, but the capital was taken on June 14. The French government

▼ *During the air war, Allied bombers, such as these British Stirlings, attacked targets in Germany.*

▲ *Allied military leaders: General Eisenhower (left), supreme commander of Allied forces in Europe, and General Montgomery.*

▲ *U.S. troops man an anti-tank gun positioned to command a beach.*

signed an armistice with Gemany on June 22. The whole northern half of France was now in German hands. The southern half was headed by Marshal Henri Petain with headquarters at the town of Vichy. This Vichy Government, because of its armistice with Hitler, was repudiated by many French people who called themselves the "Free French." The Free French determined to use any means to free France from German domination.

The Germans had built up a powerful *Luftwaffe* (air force), and Marshal Hermann Goering, the Luftwaffe chief, set out to conquer Britain by air. However, the British had also developed a strong air force and an extensive radar warning system. On July 10, the Luftwaffe began bombing British airfields, ports, bridges, factories, and power plants. Later, Goering ordered the Luftwaffe to

bomb the city of London. But this was a mistake because it gave the British air force a chance to repair damaged planes and fit out new aircraft. British planes beat off the German air force, and the Battle of Britain was broken off by the Germans in the autumn of 1940.

Hitler sent a strong army and tank force under General Erwin Rommel into Africa on February 12, 1941. British and Commonwealth troops were forced to spend two years fighting Rommel's Afrika Korps, which kept many Allied troops from defending Asia against Japan.

On October 28, 1940, without telling Hitler, Mussolini sprang a surprise attack on Greece. This attack brought in the British to defend Greece. The British attacked the Italian fleet at Taranto, Italy, and fought Italian troops in Greece. Hitler was furious. British troops were now close to the Romanian oil fields that Hitler planned to use as the fuel supply for Germany's invasion of the Soviet Union. Hitler had to get the British out of Greece, but the Yugoslav government refused to provide the needed railroad transport for Hitler's troops. Hitler decided to utterly destroy Yugoslavia. This meant he had to delay his invasion of the Soviet Union from May 15 until June 22, 1941. This delay was a terrible mistake. The invasion brought the Soviet Union to the Allied Powers' side.

The Germans attacked the Soviet Union along three fronts. But Hitler had delayed the invasion too long, and the terrible Russian winter set in. He had also gravely underestimated the strength of Soviet forces. After months of bitter fighting, especially in Stalingrad (now Volgograd), the German forces had run out of supplies and willpower. They were forced to retreat, and the Soviets began their push toward Germany in 1943.

THE PACIFIC FROM 1940–1942. The fighting in Europe had left many Asian nations with inadequate de-

After the Battle of Britain, Prime Minister Churchill paid a famous tribute to the courageous young pilots of the Royal Air Force. His words were: "Never in the field of human conflict has so much been owed by so many to so few."

ОТСТОИМ ВОЛГУ-МАТУШК

▲ *This Soviet poster proclaims: "We will defend Mother Volga." The Soviet troops prevented the German invaders from crossing the Volga River.*

▼ *The Battle of Britain in 1940 was a crucial struggle. The British victory prevented a German invasion of the British Isles. Among the most famous warplanes was the British Spitfire fighter, shown here.*

◄ *On D-Day, June 6, 1944, the Allies began the liberation of Western Europe. In the first week after the seaborne landing, they poured more than 325,000 troops into northern France.*

MAJOR EVENTS OF WORLD WAR II

Sept. 1939	Germany invades Poland; signs non-aggression pact with Soviet Union. Britain and France declare war on Germany.
April/May 1940	German troops conquer most of Western Europe.
July/Sept. 1940	Battle of Britain.
Oct. 1940	Italy joins war on German side. Axis forces overrun Balkans and North Africa.
June 1941	Germany invades Soviet Union.
Dec. 1941	Pearl Harbor attack. U.S. declares war on Axis powers.
Jan./March 1942	Japanese capture Philippines, Java, Burma.
May/June 1942	U.S. and Japanese fleets in naval battles of Coral Sea and Midway.
July 1942	Battle of El Alamein; British halt Axis advance in North Africa.
Nov. 1942	Allies land in west North Africa.
Feb. 1943	Germans surrender at Stalingrad.
July/Sept. 1943	Allies invade Italy; Italy signs armistice.
June 1944	D-Day landings by Allied armies in France.
Dec. 1944	Battle of the Bulge, last German attack in Western Europe.
Feb. 1945	U.S. forces liberate Philippines; battle for Iwo Jima. Allied leaders meet at Yalta.
April 1945	German leader Hitler commits suicide as Berlin falls to Soviet armies.
May 7, 1945	Germany surrenders.
June 1945	U.S. forces fight for Okinawa, Japan.
Aug. 1945	Atomic bombs dropped on Hiroshima and Nagasaki.
Sept. 2, 1945	Japan surrenders.

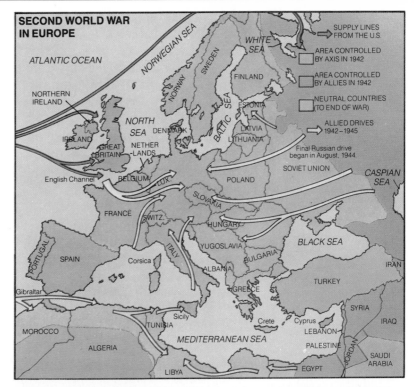

SECOND WORLD WAR IN EUROPE

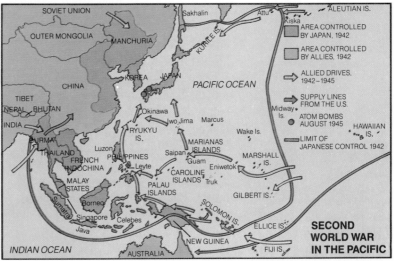

SECOND WORLD WAR IN THE PACIFIC

▶ *U.S. airplanes sink the Japanese aircraft carrier* Shoho *at the Battle of Coral Sea, May 1942 (taken from a painting by Robert Benny).*

The Battle of Leyte Gulf in the Philippines, in October 1944, involved the highest number of ships and aircraft ever to fight in a single air and sea battle. More than 150 U.S. and allied ships took part against Japanese ships, and over 1,200 U.S. aircraft flew in the battle.

▲ *German defeat at Stalingrad. In tattered uniforms, German soldiers march in the bitter cold as they are taken prisoner by the Soviet forces.*

fenses. Japan hungered after the oil and iron ore that were available in other Asian countries. In September 1940, Japan signed a military pact with the Axis powers and immediately took over part of French Indochina (now Vietnam). From there, Japan planned to take the Dutch East Indies, the Philippines, Malaya, Thailand, Burma, and various islands in the Pacific Ocean.

The United States, however, had moved its Pacific fleet closer to Japan—to a base at Pearl Harbor, Hawaii. The U.S. fleet was the only real threat to Japan. Japanese Admiral Isoroku Yamamoto insisted that a war with the United States had to begin with the bombing of Pearl Harbor. Early on December 7, 1941, Japanese planes roared over the Pearl Harbor base. The attack was a complete surprise to the United States, but it failed to destroy the entire U.S. fleet, the repair yards, or the fuel depots. On December 8, President Franklin Roosevelt asked Congress to declare war on Japan. Three days later, Germany and Italy declared war on the United States in support of Japan. Admiral Chester W. Nimitz took command of U.S. naval operations in the Pacific. General Douglas MacArthur became the Pacific army commander.

By the spring of 1942, Japanese forces had conquered most of southeast Asia, the Dutch East Indies, and the Philippines. But the United States was mobilizing quickly. U.S. factories churned out guns, aircraft, tanks, ships, and other supplies for use against the Germans in Europe and the Japanese in the Pacific. The Japanese planned to establish a line of military bases extending from the Aleutian Islands (off the tip of Alaska) across the central Pacific through Wake Island and the Marshall Islands, then westward to New Guinea and Burma. Except for the Aleutian bases, this Japanese defense system was set by May 1942. The Japanese

▲ *The Germans fighting in the snow outside Moscow. The soldiers are dressed in white to act as camouflage against the snow.*

then decided to take Midway Island and Australia.

Early in 1942, the United States broke the Japanese military communications code. From then on, the United States knew Japanese plans in advance. In the Battle of the Coral Sea from May 5 to 8, U.S. ships kept Japan from threatening Australia. Admiral Nimitz next learned of Japan's plan to take Midway Island. In the Battle of Midway from June 3 to 6, the United States destroyed Japan's air superiority in the Pacific.

ALLIED COOPERATION. After U.S. entry into the war, the British and U.S. forces decided to combine their efforts. President Roosevelt and Prime Minister Churchill set up the Anglo-American Combined Chiefs of Staff (CCS) with headquarters in Washington, D.C. The British chief was Field Marshal Sir John Dill; the U.S. chief was General George C. Marshall. The CCS kept contact with Stalin's military advisory group.

In 1942, the Soviet Union was taking the brunt of Hitler's war effort. The CCS promised to aid the Soviets with supplies. They also decided that an Allied invasion force was needed to break into Europe from the Atlantic

coast and drive the Germans eastward. In May 1942, the British started a policy of "saturation bombing." Heavy bombing raids were now started on German industrial cities, disrupting supplies of arms to the Soviet and African fronts.

The Allies invaded North Africa in November 1942. British Field Marshal Bernard Montgomery and U.S. General George S. Patton forced the surrender of the German Africa Korps on May 14, 1943. Montgomery and Patton then invaded the Italian island of Sicily, which was to be used as an Allied air base. On July 25, Italy's King Victor Emmanuel III dismissed Mussolini as prime minister. Hitler sent troops into Italy to fight the invading Allies, but on October 13, the Italian government joined the Allies and declared war on Germany.

In the Pacific, the U.S. Navy was the Allies' only large force to push the Japanese off the many islands they had captured. By June 1943, General Douglas MacArthur had driven the Japanese from New Guinea. U.S. troops soundly defeated a large Japanese force at the Battle of Guadalcanal.

In December 1943, General Dwight D. Eisenhower was appointed to command an Allied invasion of Europe. The first landings would be made on the beaches of Normandy in northern France. At this location, troops could move inland quickly, and air bases in Britain could provide continuous fighter cover. The Pas de Calais, across the English Channel from Dover, was the only other location to fit these characteristics. Eisenhower bluffed the Germans into thinking that the main invasion would take place from Dover and that the Normandy landing farther west would be a fake.

On D-Day (June 6, 1944) the first wave of Allied troops hit the beaches at Normandy under a tremendous cover of naval and air bombardment. Allied aircraft destroyed bridges, railways, and roads leading to Normandy in order to delay the arrival of German reinforcements. The remaining Allied invasion force landed, using artificial harbors towed across from England, and began pushing the Germans out of France, Belgium, and the Netherlands. Germany now had to fight on three fronts—in Italy, in the Soviet Union, and in France. Fast-moving tank forces led by General George Patton encircled and demolished German army groups in France. A Free French division under General Charles de Gaulle moved southward and liberated Paris on August 24. Armies under the command of General Omar Bradley continued to push the Germans back toward the Rhine River.

Meanwhile, Soviet troops were de-

▲ *Cities suffered terrible destruction from air raids. Here, the walls of a bombed building tumble near St. Paul's Cathedral in London during a German air raid on the city. The cathedral itself survived.*

◀ *German U-boats (submarines) preyed on Allied convoys. The escorting warships hunted the U-boats with sonar and depth charges. This painting shows a surfaced U-boat being attacked by an Allied destroyer.*

▲ *U.S. Marines plant the United States flag at the summit of Mount Suribachi on the Pacific island of Iwo Jima, February 23, 1943. A famous picture captured by Joe Rosenthal.*

▼ *Crowds of Parisians, celebrating the liberation of their city by the Allied armies, scatter for cover as a sniper fires from a building on the Place de la Concorde.*

molishing German forces in their move westward through what is now Poland, East Germany, Czechoslovakia, Hungary, Romania, Bulgaria, and Yugoslavia. On June 13, 1944, Hitler began launching V-1 and V-2 missiles—rocket-powered warheads aimed at London. They killed and wounded thousands of British citizens but did not halt the progress of the war.

On September 11, Allied troops crossed the western border of Germany. Germany was being squeezed from all sides, but Hitler had no intention of giving up. He speeded up production of war supplies and especially of his new jet airplanes.

On December 16, Hitler launched a great counterattack on the Allies in the west by taking soldiers and equipment away from the eastern front. At first, Germany was successful in pushing the Allies back—creating a bulge in the Allied line. Hitler's forces fought bitterly to keep their advantage in this Battle of the Bulge. But German losses were so high that they were forced to retreat on January 8, 1945. During March and April, Allied forces took the great German industrial area in the Ruhr Valley. On April 25, U.S. and Soviet patrols met

▲ *The B-17 Flying Fortress was the mainstay of U.S. Army Air Force daylight bombing raids in Europe.*

along the Elbe River. This was the eastern limit of the U.S. advance—75 miles (120 km) short of Berlin—that had been agreed upon between the Soviet Union and the Western Allies. U.S. forces under General Patton crossed to the southeast to take Austria. Germany was completely overrun.

On April 30, 1945, Adolf Hitler committed suicide at his underground headquarters in Berlin. Surrender terms were signed with Germany on May 7, and the war in Europe was officially over on May 8 (V-E Day). Hitler's attempt at world domination had failed, Germany was in ruins, and the German people were prisoners of war in their own country.

VICTORY IN THE PACIFIC. In 1943, the U.S. Pacific command was joined by British Admiral Lord Louis Mountbatten. He directed successful maneuvers to drive the Japanese from Burma, Malaya, the Dutch East Indies, Thailand, and French Indochina. Admiral Nimitz planned to capture certain Pacific islands to be used as bases for attacks on the Japanese home islands. One after another, U.S. forces took Tarawa (now part of Kiribati), Kwajalein (the main island of Japanese defense in the Marshall Islands), and Saipan, Tinian, Rota, and Guam (all part of the Mariana Islands).

Meanwhile, Japanese Admiral Jisa-

buro Ozawa steamed toward the Philippine Sea with orders to destroy the U.S. fleet stationed there. The Battle of the Philippine Sea, on June 19, 1944, was the greatest carrier battle of the war. The Japanese were left with almost nothing. U.S. forces eventually took the Philippines early in 1945. During that operation, severe damage was done by Japanese *kamikaze* pilots—suicide pilots who attacked by sending their planes loaded with bombs directly at a target and blowing themselves up.

On November 24, 1944, U.S. planes based in the Marianas began bombing Tokyo and other Japanese home targets. However, the flying distance was too great. Damaged U.S. planes could not make the long trip back to base. To get closer to Japan, the United States attacked and took the island of Iwo Jima after fierce fighting that lasted from February 19 to March 16, 1945. U.S. bomber attacks from Iwo Jima did tremendous damage to Japanese industry, but the Japanese would not surrender unless their home islands were invaded. U.S. troops began preparing for this invasion by capturing the island of Okinawa on May 31.

Early in August, President Harry S. Truman ordered the use of atomic weapons against Japan. The first atomic bomb ever used in warfare was exploded over the city of Hiroshima on August 6, 1945. The second atomic bomb was exploded over Nagasaki on August 9. On the same day, the Soviet Union declared war on Japan and captured Manchuria. On August 14, 1945, Japanese Emperor Hirohito accepted Allied surrender terms. The surrender became official on September 2 (V-J Day), and World War II was finally ended.

The Terms of Peace As a result of agreements made during the war, Germany was to be demilitarized and occupied by two powers. The Soviets occupied East Germany, which has

since become the German Democratic Republic. The Allies occupied West Germany, which has since become the Federal Republic of Germany. The city of Berlin was split into four sectors, or zones—one each for the Soviet Union, Great Britain, France, and the United States. The former Soviet zone is now East Berlin, the capital of the German Democratic Republic. The other Allied zones were combined, forming the city of West Berlin, which belongs to the Federal Republic of Germany.

Japan was demilitarized and occupied by U.S. troops until 1952. The United States initiated the Marshall Plan, whereby it lent huge sums of money and material to war-torn countries to help them rebuild. The Soviet Union took control in the countries it occupied, and the Communist governments based on the Soviet system were established in Hungary, Czechoslovakia, Bulgaria, Yugoslavia, Poland, and Romania.

On October 24, 1945, the United Nations was established to help ensure peace.

ALSO READ: AIRCRAFT CARRIER; ARMY; CHURCHILL, WINSTON; DE GAULLE, CHARLES; EISENHOWER, DWIGHT D.; HITLER, ADOLF; INTERNATIONAL RELATIONS; MACARTHUR, DOUGLAS; MARINE CORPS; MISSILE; MUSSOLINI, BENITO; NAVY; NUCLEAR ENERGY; PEARL HARBOR; ROOSEVELT, FRANKLIN D.;

▲ *Allied leaders met at Yalta, in the Soviet Union, in 1945. From left to right: Churchill, Roosevelt, and Stalin.*

▼ *The end of the war in Europe, May 7, 1945. Cheering crowds throng the streets of London; among them are U.S. soldiers.*

▲ *The U.S. forces bore the brunt of the Pacific war against the Japanese. To bring about Japan's surrender, President Truman ordered the dropping of atomic bombs on the cities of Hiroshima and Nagasaki. The huge mushroom-shaped cloud of the second explosion, marking the destruction of Nagasaki, heralded the end of the war in the Pacific.*

The soil is full of earthworms. There are so many of them that if all the worms in the soil of the United States were weighed, they would be ten times as heavy as the whole human population.

The largest worm is the Giant Gippsland earthworm of Victoria, Australia. It can be 12 feet (3.7 m) long and ¾ inch (2 cm) thick.

STALIN, JOSEPH; SUBMARINE; TANK; TITO; TREATY; TRUMAN, HARRY S.; UNITED NATIONS; WAR; WORLD WAR I. *See article at name of each country involved.*

WORM Worms are slender animals with soft bodies and no backbones. They vary greatly in their sizes, shapes, and habitats. Some worms, like the common earthworm, are familiar to everyone. Other worms, such as those that live deep in the ocean, are seldom seen. Some worms are so small that they can only be seen under a microscope. All kinds of worms need plenty of moisture to survive. In fact, most of them are water dwellers.

Roundworms, or *nematodes*, live almost anywhere in enormous numbers. They are tiny, thin worms that look something like fine bits of thread. Many roundworms are *parasites*, or animals that must live on, or inside, some other kind of animal or plant. Hookworms and pinworms live in the bodies of mammals, including human beings. Roundworms that are plant parasites inhabit the roots of plants and cause millions of dollars' worth of damage each year to farmers.

Flatworms receive their name from their flattened bodies. Some are less than half an inch (13 mm) long. Tapeworms, which are a kind of flatworm, may grow to be 50 feet (15 m) long in the intestines of large animals. All tapeworms are parasites. Flukes are flatworms that may live in the blood, liver, or other body parts of animals. Some flukes cause serious illness to human beings in Africa and Asia. Planaria are freshwater flatworms. They swim about in lakes and ponds, scavenging for food.

The very long ribbon worms are not parasites. Most ribbon worms live in the ocean. You can find different kinds of ribbon worms under rocks near the seashore. One, the sand-

worm, is often used as fishing bait.

The common earthworm is in the big group of worms called *annelida*, or segmented worms. Annelids are not related to other kinds of worms. The bodies of annelids are divided into sections, or segments. Many annelids live in the ocean. Bloodworms are annelids that live in shallow parts of the ocean. They have bright red bodies. At one end of its body, the bloodworm has a *proboscis*, which looks like a small tube. The proboscis shoots out quickly, attaches itself to food, and then is drawn back into the body.

Clam worms are also common ocean dwellers. Clam worms have

▼ *The fanworm is a marine bristleworm. It uses its feathery tentacles to trap tiny particles of food. It lives inside a protective tube.*

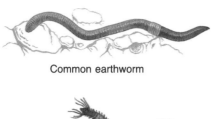

Common earthworm

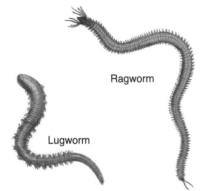

Ragworm

Lugworm

▲ *The earthworm is a land animal, while lugworms and ragworms live on the seabed and shore.*

tiny paddles on each segment of their body. They are active swimmers. They can also burrow in sand and mud. During the breeding season, clam worms swarm in large numbers near the water's surface to mate. Some sea worms are not active swimmers. They spend most of their time in tunnels or burrows. The parchment worm lives in a tunnel in the mud. The tunnel provides a protective covering for the parchment worm's fragile body. Other sea worms build tubes or tunnels with hard, limey material. The *serpula* often covers rocks and seashells with its whitish tunnels.

ALSO READ: ANIMAL KINGDOM, EARTHWORM, PARASITE.

WRESTLING The sport of wrestling is one of the oldest in the world. The art of almost all ancient civilizations showed scenes of people wrestling. There are Egyptian wall paintings over 5,000 years old and ancient Japanese sculptures that show wrestlers in action. The sport was included in the first Olympic Games, which were held by the Greeks in 776 B.C.

Wrestling is basically a test of strength, quickness, and stamina (endurance). A good wrestler must also know how to use a variety of *holds*. A hold is a grip you apply to your opponent's body that makes it difficult for him or her to use any strength and helps you to throw your opponent to the ground. All wrestling matches are fought on a padded canvas mat. There are two main styles of the sport. The first is the *freestyle,* or *catch-as-catch-can,* style which is common in the United States. The *Greco-Roman* style is popular in Europe. Both styles are contested in the Olympic Games. In freestyle wrestling, contestants are allowed to apply holds below the waist of their opponents and to trip and tackle them. In the Greco-Roman style, wrestlers cannot trip or tackle, they cannot apply holds to their opponents' legs, and they cannot use their own legs to grip or squeeze their opponents.

In both styles, wrestlers compete in their own weight classes since it would be unfair for one person to wrestle with a much heavier opponent. The winner of a match either pins the opponent's shoulders to the mat, or scores more points than the opponent. Points are scored for falls, for applying holds, and for ability and aggressiveness. College wrestling matches are divided into three periods of three minutes each. High school matches are divided into three two-

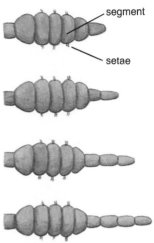

segment

setae

▲ *Each segment of an earthworm's body has four pairs of small bristles, called setae. These bristles dig into the soil as the earthworm burrows. An earthworm moves by contracting (shortening) and lengthening its segments, in a series of wavelike ripples.*

▼ *Sumo wrestlers take guard in a Tokyo wrestling hall. Whichever wrestler is forced out of the ring or down on the floor is the loser.*

▲ *Amateur wrestlers attempt to topple over each other. This style of wrestling is often called the Greco-Roman style, referring to the ancient Olympic games where it was the most popular sport.*

minute periods. In all amateur matches, the contestants are not allowed to use punishing holds, such as a headlock, strangle hold, or a scissors. The scissors hold is one in which the legs are used like a pair of scissors to squeeze any part of an opponent's body.

Professional wrestling used to be much like the amateur sport, but in recent years, it has become a fake exhibition of brutality. Professional wrestlers entertain the spectators by seeming to slug, bounce, and kick each other around. Actually professional wrestling is a well-rehearsed act. It looks savage but the contestants do little harm to each other.

One of the most popular sports in Japan is *sumo* wrestling. Sumo contestants weigh about 300 pounds (136 kg) and have great strength. The matches are held in a large circle and the winner is the one who makes any part of the opponent's body, other than the feet, touch the ground. Sumo champions are national heroes in Japan.

ALSO READ: SPORTS.

▲ *Frank Lloyd Wright, U.S. architect.*

WRIGHT, FRANK LLOYD (1867–1959) Frank Lloyd Wright was one of the most influential architects of modern times. He was born in Richland Center, Wisconsin. He studied under the American architect, Louis Sullivan. Wright set up his own office in Chicago in 1893. Most new buildings at that time were decorated with classical (Greek and Roman) arches and columns. But Wright began to design buildings with simple, bold lines and no fussy decoration. One of his main aims was to give as much freedom and space as possible to the people living or working inside. His "prairie" houses have rooms that open into one another with very few dividing walls. Wright believed that a house should blend with its surrounding landscape. He

▲ *Falling Water, built in Pennsylvania in 1936, was Frank Lloyd Wright's ultimate private house—blending nature and man-made materials into organic architecture.*

called this idea "organic architecture." One of Wright's most spectacular buildings is the Solomon R. Guggenheim Museum in New York City. The galleries are arranged around a huge spiral ramp.

Wright founded the Taliesin Fellowship, a community and school for young architects. The community is now centered at Wright's winter home, Taliesin West, near Scottsdale, Arizona.

ALSO READ: ARCHITECTURE.

WRIGHT, RICHARD (1908–1960) Richard Wright was one of America's most important black writers. He was born near Natchez, Mississippi. His mother was crippled and unable to take care of him for most of his childhood, so he had to live in orphanages or with poor relatives.

Wright went to Chicago, Illinois, in the 1930's, and worked at many jobs while beginning his career as a writer. He joined the Federal Writers Project, a government agency created

to help writers during the economic depression of the 1930's. For a while, Wright believed that the Communist party could offer hope to black Americans, but he later decided that the movement did not live up to its ideals.

Wright's first published work was a collection of four stories, *Uncle Tom's Children*, about racial prejudice in the South. His best-known book, *Native Son*, tells how the pressure of trying to survive in the slums of Chicago drives a young black man to commit murder. In *Black Boy*, which is based on his own unhappy childhood, Wright describes the terrible effects of poverty and racial hatred on a growing child.

Other books by Wright include *Twelve Million Black Voices; The Outsider; Black Power; White Man, Listen!;* and *The Long Dream.* Wright's work is a bitter, unforgiving description of the miseries, discouragement, and hatred brought about by racial prejudice in the United States. Wright left the United States in 1950 and lived in Paris, France, for the rest of his life.

ALSO READ: BLACK AMERICANS, LITERATURE.

WRIGHT BROTHERS Wilbur Wright (1867–1912) and Orville Wright (1871–1948) were U.S. inventors and aviators. They built and piloted the world's first successful power-driven airplane.

Wilbur was born near New Castle, Indiana, and Orville was born in Dayton, Ohio. In 1892, they opened a bicycle repair shop and later designed and manufactured bicycles. They became interested in a type of unpowered airplane, called a *glider*, which was being built in Europe. The brothers taught themselves *aeronautics* (the science of flight) and built their own glider. They made their first glider flight in 1900 at Kitty Hawk, North Carolina. Their glider was a biplane,

with two wings, one above the other. The brothers built two other biplane gliders that they flew at Kill Devil Hill near Kitty Hawk in 1901 and 1902. One glider made a record flight of more than 600 feet (182 m). The brothers also built a wind tunnel to experiment with different air pressures on the wings of their gliders.

In the winter of 1902, they designed a propeller powered by a light-weight gasoline engine, which was fitted onto a large biplane that they named "Flyer I." At Kill Devil Hill on December 17, 1903, Orville Wright piloted the first powered flight. Later that day, Wilbur made a flight of 852 feet (260 m).

The brothers continued to improve their airplane design and built several more biplanes. During 1908, Wilbur gave flying demonstrations in Europe. On one flight, he stayed in the air for 2 hours and 20 minutes. The brothers opened their own airplane company in New York City in 1909.

After Wilbur died of typhoid, Orville continued to design and manufacture airplanes. The site of the Wright brothers' first flight at Kitty Hawk is now preserved as the Wright Brothers National Monument.

ALSO READ: AIRPLANE, AVIATION, GLIDER.

▲ *Richard Wright, U.S. writer.*

▲ *Wilbur (left) and Orville Wright.*

▼ *Orville Wright piloting the "Baby Wright."*

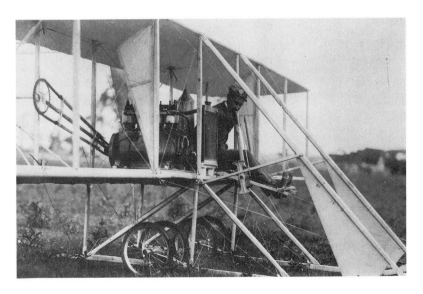

▲ *One of the earliest forms of writing was Egyptian hieroglyphics. Figures or objects were used to represent words or sounds. This example of hieroglyphics is from the wall of an Egyptian pharoah's tomb.*

▲ *The Maya Indians of Central America erected this stone pillar, or stele, about 1,000 years ago in Copan, Honduras. It is covered with carved hieroglyphics.*

WRITTEN LANGUAGE When you speak, you make certain sounds in order to communicate with other people. The speech sounds you make are *word symbols*. A word symbol always stands for, or represents, something. For example, when someone says "dog," you immediately think of a certain type of animal. When someone says "hello," you know this is a greeting. When someone says "happy," you think of a certain type of feeling. If someone said "sobaka," it wouldn't mean anything to you because that word symbol is not part of your language. Languages are simply various systems of spoken word symbols.

Most day-to-day communication among people is done in spoken language—by talking. But much communication is also done in written language—by writing. When people write, they make certain marks on paper or some other material. The written marks are symbols standing for the words of spoken language.

Written language was not invented by any one person at any particular time or place. Writing evolved gradually as people needed ways to keep lasting records. By writing things down, people could communicate in a way more permanent and lasting than speech. Spoken language is not permanent. Once you have said something, that particular communication ends and cannot be heard again unless you keep repeating it over and over.

Drawings on the walls of caves were probably the earliest attempts by human beings to express themselves in writing. The cave paintings were not actually writing as we know it. But like writing, they were created by people in order to express something they had seen or thought about. Pictures eventually became used as written word symbols. In early picture writing, each picture stood for the object it represented. A picture of a sun stood for the sun. A picture of a sheep stood for a sheep.

Additional meanings were gradually assigned to the picture signs. A picture of the sun, for example, might stand for "day," "light," or "warmth." A sheep might stand for "wool" or just "animal." A house might stand for "shelter," "home," "building," or a number of other ideas. Each picture symbol stood for a whole word.

Another important development in written language was the *syllabary*. Syllabaries are writing systems in which syllables, rather than whole words, are represented each by a separate symbol. The Japanese writing system uses a syllabary.

The type of writing used in most Western languages is the alphabetic system. It was developed by the ancient Greeks from earlier symbols used by the Phoenicians. The Greeks assigned one symbol (letter) for each spoken sound. The alphabet you use for writing is made up of 26 symbols that stand for various speech sounds. The symbols B-A-R-N, written in that order, represent four speech sounds that together make up a spoken word. The spoken word, in turn, is a symbol standing for a real barn—a building where farm animals are kept. There are various alphabets in use—Roman, Greek, Hebrew, Ara-

▼ *This beautifully decorated page is from a book that was handwritten in Latin in 1156.*

bic, Cyrillic, Devanagari—but all are based on the idea of letters standing for speech sounds.

ALSO READ: ALPHABET, BRAILLE, COMMUNICATION, CROSSWORD PUZZLE, DICTIONARY, GRAMMAR, HANDWRITING, HIEROGLYPHICS, LANGUAGE ARTS, LANGUAGES, LITERACY, PRINTING, SHORTHAND, SPEECH, SPELLING, WORD GAMES.

WYOMING A visitor to a dude ranch in Wyoming can ride horses over mountain trails, go camping and fishing, and perhaps take a boat ride on a river. In the capital city of Cheyenne during the Frontier Days festival in July, a visitor can see Indian dances and rodeo events, with cowboys and cowgirls riding bucking broncos and wrestling steers. Wyoming is one of the largest states in size and the smallest in population.

The Land and Climate Wyoming belongs to the group of Rocky Mountain States. Other mountain states are north, west, and south of it. Montana is to the north and northwest, and Idaho is to the west. Southwest is Utah, and Colorado is to the south. On the east are South Dakota and Nebraska.

Wide basins lie between the tall ranges of the Rocky Mountains. The Big Horn Basin is in the north central part of the state. The Wyoming Basin is in the south central region. Large river systems start from the Continental Divide in Wyoming. The Snake River flows west to join the Columbia, and the Green River flows south into the Colorado.

In eastern Wyoming, the Great Plains slope toward the east. They are hilly, and they are cut by many rivers. The plains are lower than the mountains, but even so, they are high. The lowest point in the state is more than half a mile above sea level. (It is in the northeast corner.)

There is too little rain for raising crops in the usual way. Some farmers irrigate their fields. Others do dry farming—using the rainfall of *two* years, stored in the soil, to produce *one* crop. The Great Plains are grassy. The basins of the mountain section are sagebrush country.

Winters are long and cold in Wyoming, especially in the mountainous west. The short summers are hot during daylight hours, but night brings rapid cooling.

History Every museum in Wyoming has a collection of Indian arrowheads found in the state. Some of these arrowheads are thousands of years old. The early Indian peoples left things that puzzle Indians as well as others today. On cliffs and in caves are pictures that no one can understand. Some are painted and some are carved. In the Big Horn Mountains, there is the amazing Medicine Wheel. Its center is a hub of stone, and twenty-eight stone spokes go out from the hub. The wheel is 245 feet (75 m) across. Around its edge are the remains of several low stone shelters. In later times, Crow Indians lived in the Big Horn Mountains.

Part of what is now the state was claimed by Spain in the early days. A large part belonged to France. And part was in the Oregon Territory that

▲ *Bronco riders try their luck at the Cheyenne Frontier Days rodeo in Wyoming.*

Wyoming has weathered rock towers called buttes on its treeless basins. The most famous is Devils Tower which became the first national monument in the United States.

Jim Bridger, a Wyoming scout and fur trapper, built a trading post, Fort Bridger, in 1842. It is gone, but the state park at the site has other old, restored buildings to visit. Stables of the Pony Express and the store of a frontier trader are among them.

▲ *The Teton Mountains in western Wyoming are part of the Grand Teton National Park, established in 1929.*

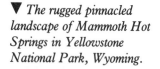

▼ *The rugged pinnacled landscape of Mammoth Hot Springs in Yellowstone National Park, Wyoming.*

Britain and the United States argued over.

The first American exploration in Wyoming was that of John Colter. He had been a member of the Lewis and Clark party of soldier-explorers. The party did not enter Wyoming, but Colter received permission to leave the others and go there.

In 1807, Colter went trapping in the Big Horn Mountains. Later he passed through the Yellowstone country. When he returned to Saint Louis, he described the geysers he had seen shooting from the ground. Not many people believed what he told them.

For some time, trapping was the chief occupation of the white people in Wyoming. Trappers and soldiers helped the "Westward Movement" by discovering the best routes west. A fur-trading post, later named Fort Laramie, became the earliest lasting settlement in Wyoming.

Thousands of wagons crossed the Rockies through the South Pass, which ran through the valley of the Sweetwater River. Many people were going to California for gold. Others were going to Oregon for rich farmland. Only a few wanted to settle in dry Wyoming. But the discovery of gold and coal in Wyoming changed matters, and so did the discovery that plains grass made good grazing. Settlers began to arrive. The Union Pacific Railroad helped them come. The railroad's tracks reached Wyoming in 1867.

The motto of Wyoming is "Equal Rights." Even before Wyoming was a state, it became a leader in the cause of women's rights. The territory was the first to grant women the vote. After 1869, women could also serve on juries. In 1870, South Pass City had the first woman justice of the peace in the United States. The country's first woman governor, Nellie Tayloe Ross, took office in Cheyenne, the capital of Wyoming, in 1925. Mrs. Ross later became director of the U.S. Mint.

Wyoming People at Work Coal lies under much of Wyoming. Only a small part of it has been mined so far. Oil is Wyoming's most important underground resource. The state also has natural gas, iron ore, and uranium. Sand and gravel is extracted for use in construction work. Casper is an oil-refining center. The University of Wyoming is at Laramie.

Ranching is the second biggest business. The main animals bred are cattle and sheep. Since cowboys must ride, horse raising has always been important in Wyoming. The state's leading field crops are wheat, hay, oats, and sugar beets. Manufacturing employs relatively few people.

The mountains and lakes of Grand Teton National Park and the wildlife and geysers of Yellowstone National Park attract many people to Wyoming every year. The nation's first national monument, Devils Tower, is a high volcanic plug in northeastern Wyoming. It can be seen for many miles. National Elk Refuge, covering 25,000 acres (10,000 hectares), is near Jackson and provides winter grazing grounds for thousands of migrating elks.

ALSO READ: GEYSER, GREAT PLAINS, ROCKY MOUNTAINS, SHOSHONE INDIANS, YELLOWSTONE PARK.

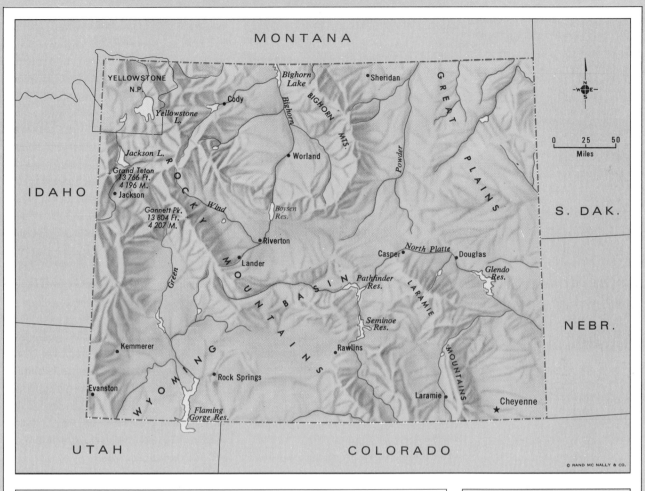

MONTANA

YELLOWSTONE N.P.

Yellowstone L.

IDAHO

Bighorn Lake

Sheridan

Cody

Bighorn

BIGHORN MTS.

Worland

Powder

GREAT PLAINS

Jackson L.

Grand Teton
13 766 Ft.
4 196 M.

Jackson

Gannett Pk.
13 804 Ft.
4 207 M.

Wind

Boysen Res.

Riverton

Lander

ROCKY MOUNTAINS

Green

Casper   North Platte   Douglas

Glendo Res.

Pathfinder Res.

LARAMIE MOUNTAINS

S. DAK.

NEBR.

WYOMING BASIN

Seminoe Res.

Kemmerer

Rock Springs

Rawlins

Laramie

Cheyenne

Evanston

Flaming Gorge Res.

UTAH

COLORADO

0   25   50
Miles

© RAND MC NALLY & CO.

STATE EMBLEMS

Cottonwood

Meadowlark

Indian Paintbrush

WYOMING

Capital
Cheyenne (47,000 people)

Area
97,914 square miles (253,358 sq. km). Rank: 9th

Population
509,000 people
Rank: 50th

Statehood
July 10, 1890
44th state admitted

Principal rivers
Bighorn River
Green River
North Platte River

Highest point
Gannet Peak on the Continental Divide; 13,785 feet (4,202 m)

Largest city
Casper (51,000 people)

Motto
"Equal Rights"

Song
"Wyoming"

Famous people
James Bridger, Buffalo Bill Cody, Nellie Tayloe Ross

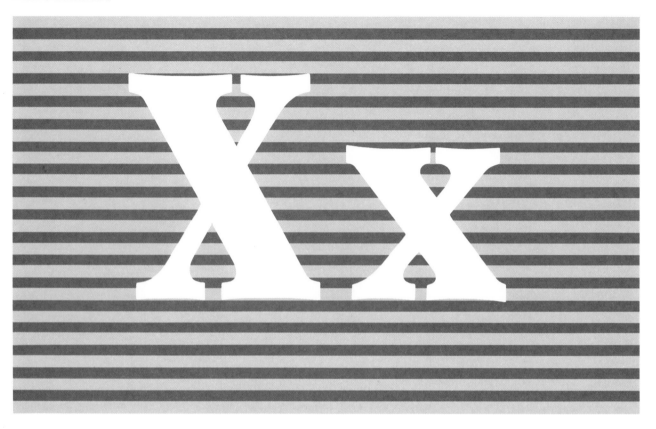

▲ *The Persian king Xerxes I, also called Ahasuerus.*

XEROGRAPHY see PHOTO-COPIER.

XERXES I (about 519–465 B.C.) Xerxes I was a king of the ancient Persian Empire. In the book of Esther in the Bible, Xerxes is the mighty king Ahasuerus, who "reigned from India to Ethiopia over 127 provinces." He was a wise ruler as well as a fearful conqueror of other lands.

Xerxes became king after the death of his father, Darius the Great, in 486 B.C. At that time, the Persians were enemies of the Greeks. During Darius' reign, the Athenians had defeated the Persians at the great Battle of Marathon in 490 B.C. Soon after Xerxes became king, he began to plan an invasion of Greece. He gathered together a great army of over 180,000 men and a very large fleet of ships. He built roads and stored food for his armies along the way. He built two bridges of boats moored end to end across the Hellespont strait (now the Dardanelles). He is also said to have

dug a canal across the peninsula of Mount Athos.

Xerxes set out in 480 B.C. According to the Greek historian Herodotus, the Persian army numbered nearly three million men. (The actual figure was probably nearer 200,000.) Xerxes defeated the people of the Greek city of Sparta at the Battle of Thermopylae, in 480 B.C. He then marched to Athens and burned the city including all the houses and temples.

But at the Battle of Salamis later that year, the Greek fleet, commanded by the Athenian general Themistocles, defeated the much larger Persian fleet. Xerxes watched the battle from his throne, which had been placed on a nearby hilltop. After the defeat, Xerxes returned to Persia. He left his brother-in-law, Mardonius, in charge of the Persian army in Greece. Mardonius was defeated the following year, 479 B.C. Xerxes gave up his ideas of conquest and was later murdered by his palace guard.

ALSO READ: GREECE, ANCIENT; PERSIA.

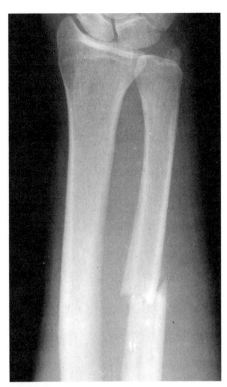

▲ *An X ray of a broken bone. Bone tissue shows up as white or light gray on an X ray.*

X RAY When you go to the dentist, he or she shines a bright light into your mouth. The visible light rays make it possible for the dentist to examine the outside of your teeth. To examine the inside of your teeth, the dentist uses an X-ray machine that sends invisible X rays through your teeth. A piece of photographic film is placed behind the teeth. The X rays make a shadow picture of the teeth on the film.

Light rays and X rays are both forms of electromagnetic radiation. Electromagnetic radiation is caused by the motion of electrical charges. X rays are produced when high-speed electrons (electrically charged bits of matter) strike a solid target. The electrons can produce X rays in two different ways. As electrons are slowed down by the target, their path is bent and energy is given off in the form of X rays. They can also knock other electrons out of the atoms. The remaining electrons jump to fill the gap

and also give off X rays.

The penetrating power of the X rays given off depends on the velocity (speed and direction) of the electrons striking the target. The velocity of the electrons can be changed by changing the voltage (electrical potential) in the X-ray tube. A higher voltage produces faster electrons, and, therefore, more powerful X rays.

A typical X-ray tube is a glass tube that has been *evacuated*—it contains no air or other gases. Inside the glass tube at opposite ends are a *cathode* that gives off electrons and an *anode*, or target, that is hit by the electrons. When the cathode is heated by an electric current to a high temperature, electrons fly off the hot cathode and strike the anode. This action produces X rays and heat.

In medicine, X rays are used both for diagnosis—finding out what is wrong—and treatment. The dentist uses X rays to photograph cavities and other disorders of the teeth. Physicians use X rays to photograph broken bones, tumors, and the effects of certain diseases, such as tuberculosis and pneumonia. The physican may use a fluorescent screen called a *fluoroscope* instead of photographic film. The fluoroscope forms a temporary X-ray image on a screen. Patients who are to be X-rayed sometimes swallow, or are injected with, special dyes or substances that will pass into

▲ *Wilhelm Conrad Roentgen, the German scientist who discovered the X ray.*

▼ *Inside the X-ray machine, a heated filament produces a stream of electrons. These are accelerated toward a metal target. When the electron beam hits the target, X rays are given off by the electrons. The X-ray beam is directed through a window to pass through the patient's body.*

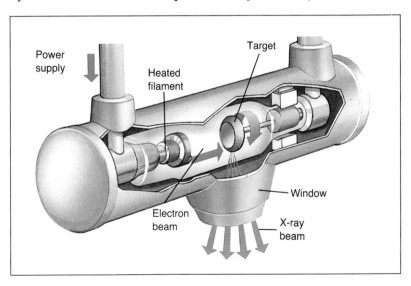

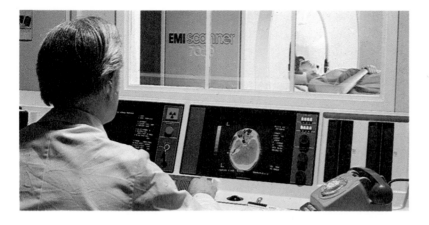

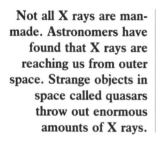

▲ *Ordinary X rays cannot show great internal detail. The X-ray scanner, however, can take a detailed picture of a "slice" through the patient's body. It X-rays the slice from different angles and then uses a computer to calculate tissue thickness within the slice. The result is displayed as a cross-section picture on a screen.*

their bloodstream, digestive tract, or certain organs. The dyes show conditions that would not otherwise be visible on the X rays.

Although X rays can penetrate all parts of the body, they do not pene-

trate them equally well. Bones, teeth, and other hard parts of the body block more X rays than do organs, muscles, and the softer parts of the body. This is what makes X-ray photographs possible. The more X rays that strike the film, the darker the film will be when it is developed. Flesh appears dark in an X-ray photograph, and bones appear light.

X rays can make people sick or make them well. X rays can destroy healthy tissues and cause unhealthy tissue growth. An overexposure to X rays can cause blood diseases, cancer, and damage to reproductive organs. But X rays can also destroy unhealthy tissue. Because of this, they can be used to treat cancer, which is a

Not all X rays are man-made. Astronomers have found that X rays are reaching us from outer space. Strange objects in space called quasars throw out enormous amounts of X rays.

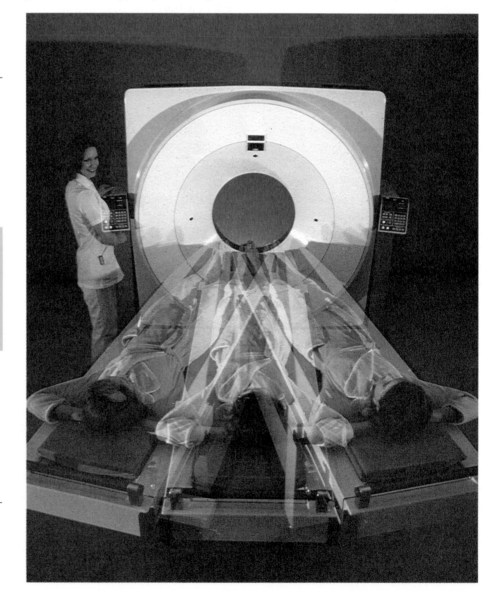

▶ *The patient lies on a couch that moves automatically into the scanner tunnel and is positioned where required beneath the X-ray emitter.*

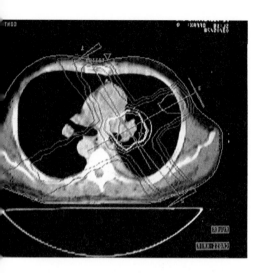

▲ *This scan of a body slice across the chest clearly shows the spine and the rib cage.*

growth of unhealthy tissue in the body.

Scientists use X rays to study the underlying structure of substances. In industry, X rays are used to inspect materials and products, such as metals, plastics, and rubber insulation, in order to discover defects in them before they are put into production. Museums use X rays to examine paintings to identify the artist or period. Sometimes a second painting is discovered underneath the first. X rays can be used in almost any situation where someone wants to see inside something that cannot be penetrated by light.

X rays were discovered in 1895 by the German physicist, Wilhelm Conrad Roentgen. Roentgen was working with cathode rays (electrons) and noticed that when the rays hit the sides of the tube, a nearby fluorescent screen began to glow. The glowing continued, even when a sheet of heavy black paper was placed between the tube and the screen. He could not explain the mysterious rays, so he called them X rays.

ALSO READ: ATOM, CANCER, ELECTRICITY, LIGHT, MEDICINE, RADIATION, RADIOACTIVITY, WAVE.

XYLOPHONE A member of the percussion group of musical intruments, the xylophone has wooden or metal bars that the player strikes with small mallets or hammers. The bars differ in length to sound the notes of several octaves. Metal tubes below the bars are *resonators* that help make a larger, fuller tone.

A *marimba* is a kind of xylophone that uses hollowed gourds as resonators for the wooden bars. This instrument is found in Africa and in Central America. It is especially popular in Guatemala, where some instruments are so large that several persons play on one marimba at the same time. The *vibraphone*, which has metal bars, resembles the marimba.

The xylophone and the *glockenspiel*, a similar instrument, are used in orchestras and concert bands. The glockenspiel has metal bars tuned to the chromatic scale. It is small enough to be carried in marching bands. Simple forms of the xylophone were played in Africa and Asia in ancient times. The instrument is still used in Asian and African folk music. The French composer, Camille Saint-Saëns, used the xylophone in his *Danse Macabre* to suggest the rattling bones of dancing skeletons.

ALSO READ: MUSIC, MUSICAL INSTRUMENTS, ORCHESTRAS AND BANDS, PERCUSSION INSTRUMENTS.

A large xylophone with a resonator, or echo chamber, is called a marimba. This was originally of African origin. A modern version of this, often used by jazz musicians, is the vibraphone, or vibes as it is more familiarly known.

▼ *The xylophone has wooden or metal bars and is played with small mallets or hammers. The sound is reinforced by resonators hanging beneath the bars.*

▼ *The powerful current of the Yangtze River is clearly evident here, beneath the impressive slopes of the Yangtze Gorges.*

YANGTZE RIVER The Yangtze is the longest river in China. It flows about 3,400 miles (5,472 km), from the snow-covered Himalaya Mountains of Tibet (now a region of China) to the East China Sea near Shanghai. (See the map with the article on CHINA.) The Yangtze, or *Ch'ang Ji-ang* ("long river") as the Chinese call it, is the major river of central China.

Near its start, the Yangtze flows southward through deep gorges cut into the high mountains. The river then turns northeastward and flows past Chungking. The Chinese Nationalists made this city their capital while they fought to control China during the 1940's. Beyond Chungking, the Yangtze rushes through the spectacular Yangtze Gorges, which are perilous to shipping. The river then winds through a lowland agricultural region to the sea.

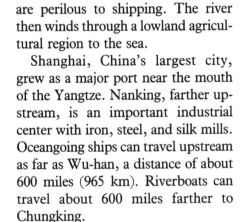

Shanghai, China's largest city, grew as a major port near the mouth of the Yangtze. Nanking, farther upstream, is an important industrial center with iron, steel, and silk mills. Oceangoing ships can travel upstream as far as Wu-han, a distance of about 600 miles (965 km). Riverboats can travel about 600 miles farther to Chungking.

During spring floods, the amount of water in the Yangtze sometimes doubles. The river often overflows, flooding cropland and destroying lives and property.

ALSO READ: CHINA, RIVER.

YEAST A yeast is a plant. The whole plant is made up of one cell, so small that you need a microscope to see it. A yeast is a *fungus*, a plant that cannot make its own food. Yeasts live on sugar. Yeast cells excrete *enzymes*, which change sugar to alcohol and carbon dioxide gas.

New yeast plants are formed by "budding." Part of the plant pushes outward. This part later breaks off and becomes a separate yeast plant.

Great numbers of yeast cells, in the form of a paste, are mixed into bread dough. The yeast enzymes change the sugar in the bread dough to alcohol and carbon dioxide. The carbon dioxide forms thousands of bubbles in the dough. The bubbles make the dough rise—make it light and fluffy. The many holes you see in a slice of bread are the remains of the bubbles. The alcohol evaporates in the heat of the baking oven. Another kind of yeast is used to make beer and ale.

■ LEARN BY DOING

Buy a package of yeast or a yeast cake at the supermarket. Dissolve a spoonful of sugar in a glass of warm water. Drop into the water a small amount of yeast. Place the glass in sunlight. In a few minutes, you will see bubbles of carbon dioxide rising from the yeast. ■

ALSO READ: BAKING AND BAKERIES, ENZYME, FERMENTATION, FUNGUS.

YELLOW RIVER The Yellow River is the main waterway of northern China. It flows for more than 3,000 miles (4,800 km) and is the second longest river in China, after the Yangtze (See the map with the article on CHINA). The Chinese call this important river *Hwang Ho*, Chinese for "yellow river."

The Yellow River rises in the Himalaya Mountains of Tibet (now a region of China). Leaving the moun-

tains, the river flows in a great bend to the north and east, skirting the Ordos Desert. For its last 400 miles (644 km), the river flows across a broad plain to empty into the Yellow Sea. It gets its name from the yellowish soil carried downstream.

The mouth of the Yellow River has actually changed location. A century ago, this river emptied into the East China Sea, south of the Shantung Peninsula. About 1853, natural causes shifted the flow to the north of the Shangtung Peninsula, where the river mouth lies today.

The sediment carried by the Yellow River builds up sandbars and makes navigation difficult. No large port city stands at the mouth of the river. The Yellow River is called "China's Sorrow" because of the many times it has overflowed, ruining crops and homes. For hundreds of years, the Chinese have tried to control the floods by building dikes, or high banks, alongside the river.

ALSO READ: CHINA, RIVER.

YELLOWSTONE PARK Yellowstone Park is the largest national park in the United States. It covers more than two million acres (800,000 hectares), mostly in Wyoming, but extending into Montana and Idaho as well.

▲ *Soil erosion is much in evidence along the banks of the Yellow River. This is caused by terrible seasonal flooding.*

Yeasts contain many vitamins. They are particularly rich in vitamins of the B group.

▲ *The famous geyser "Old Faithful" is one of many geysers and hot springs in Yellowstone National Park. The geyser spouts steam, which is produced by water that seeps down through the rock and is heated by volcanic activity underground.*

More than 200 active geysers can be found in the park. The most famous geyser is called Old Faithful. It erupts on the average every 65 minutes, shooting a column of hot water and a cloud of water vapor 120 to 170 feet (36 to 52 m) into the air. Giant Geyser sends hot water 250 feet (76 m) into the air but is not as predictable as Old Faithful.

About 3,000 hot springs cover the geyser basins of the park. The minerals contained in those hot waters form brightly colored cones and other formations on surrounding land. Mud volcanoes bubble like hot fudge on a stove in some areas.

The Yellowstone River cuts the park in two. It descends into yellowstone's Grand Canyon in two spectacular waterfalls. In the canyon, steep walls display the yellow color that gives the river and park its name. The river also passes through Yellowstone Lake, one of the highest bodies of water of its size in North America.

Yellowstone is an important wildlife refuge. Wapiti (North American elk), moose, coyotes, pronghorn antelope, porcupines, skunks, bighorn sheep, mink, otter, badgers, grizzly bears, and weasels thrive there. Hunting is forbidden in the park, but camping, hiking, and horseback riding are permitted.

Yellowstone was discovered in 1807 by an American trapper named John Colter. No one believed his descriptions of Yellowstone's amazing phenomena until 1870, when a government expedition reported that the stories were true. Yellowstone became the country's first national park in 1872.

ALSO READ: GEYSER, NATIONAL PARK.

YEMEN see ARABIA.

YIDDISH LANGUAGE Few languages match Yiddish in colorfulness and adaptability. It originated in the A.D. 900's, when Jewish immigrants in Germany learned to speak German but used the Hebrew alphabet to write it. They added Hebrew words to their speech which they "Germanized." Although frowned upon by Jewish religious leaders as slang, this dialect gradually took shape as a language separate from German. Years later when Jewish colonies in Germany moved to Poland and Russia, Yiddish survived and grew, adopting many words from Polish and Russian. America has also played an important role in the development of Yiddish. Large numbers of Jews came from Europe around 1882, bringing with them their Yiddish language. Here their language was further enriched with English words, especially the names of things unfamiliar to the immigrants, such as *ice cream*, *subway*, and *baseball*. English has also been enriched by colorful Yiddish expressions, such as *bagel*, *schlemiel*, and *kibitzer*.

Yiddish may be a vanishing language for several reasons. Several million Yiddish-speaking Jews were killed in Europe during the 1930's and during World War II. Hebrew, not Yiddish, is the official language of Israel. In North and South America, the number of new Jewish immigrants is small, and new generations tend to drop the language.

ALSO READ: GERMAN LANGUAGE, JEWISH HISTORY, LANGUAGES.

YOGA To many people, yoga means a form of meditation, or deep thought, practiced in association with certain physical exercises. Yoga is an Eastern philosophy, developed by the Hindus of India. The person wishing to practice Yoga must train both body and mind and pass through certain stages until he or she reaches a state of release from the everyday world.

Yoga is a very ancient philosophy.

▲ *Indians practice their Yoga in Varanasi (Benares), a famous Hindu city on the Ganges River.*

It involves high levels of mental concentration and considerable practice. One way in which people may free themselves from the "distractions" of the world is by exercises in posture and breathing. These exercises, developed by the school of Hatha Yoga, are also practiced by those people who merely seek to relax and to improve their physical condition. This form of Yoga is practiced in many parts of the world besides India. Practicing Yoga makes the body more flexible and tones up the muscles. However, it is unwise for a beginner to attempt Yoga without instruction from an expert.

ALSO READ: HINDUISM.

YOM KIPPUR Yom Kippur is the most solemn holy day of the Jewish faith. It is also called the Day of Atonement. It comes at the end of the Ten Penitential Days, which begin with Rosh Hashanah, the Jewish New Year. Yom Kippur falls in September or early October, on the tenth day of Tishri, the first month of the Hebrew calendar. It actually begins at sundown of the ninth day.

Many Jewish people *fast* (do not have anything to eat or drink, even water) until sundown of the next day. During that time they pray and attend services. The services begin with a beautiful hymn called the *Kol Nidre*. Jewish people pray that they may be forgiven for their sins, both by God and by anyone whom they may have hurt during the year. At the end of the day, a trumpet called the *shofar*, made from a ram's horn, is blown. It makes a long, mournful sound and tells the people that Yom Kippur is over.

ALSO READ: JUDAISM.

YORK, HOUSE OF see ENGLISH HISTORY, WARS OF THE ROSES.

YOSEMITE VALLEY The Yosemite Valley is a narrow gorge in central California, about 200 miles (320 km) east of San Francisco. This spectacular valley in the Sierra Nevada mountain range is only about 7 miles (11 km) long and 1 mile (1.6 km) wide.

Yosemite Valley was made a California state park in 1864. California gave the land to the Federal Government in 1906, and it became part of Yosemite National Park. The park now covers about 760,000 acres (307,000 hectares). It has spectacular waterfalls, unusual rock formations, and high, rugged mountains.

The park has other attractions in addition to the Yosemite Valley, but the valley is the most scenic area. Steep granite walls surround the valley, which is carpeted with evergreen trees. El Capitán, a massive granite mountain, rises 3,604 feet (1,098 m) from the valley floor. Several waterfalls, including Ribbon Fall (1,612 feet / 491 m) and Bridalveil Fall (620 feet / 189 m) pour into the valley. The highest waterfall is Yosemite Falls (2,425 feet / 739 m). It consists of the

▲ *The shofar, a ram's horn, is blown to signify the end of Yom Kippur, the Day of Atonement. Moses, the great leader of the Jews, set Yom Kippur as the most sacred day almost 3,000 years ago.*

The Indians who settled in the valley were of the Miwok tribe. They were called Yosemite, which is Miwok for "grizzly bear," after their clan totem.

YOUNG, ANDREW

▲ *Yosemite National Park is a region of clear sparkling lakes and jagged mountain peaks.*

▲ *Andrew Young, diplomat and political figure.*

▲ *Brigham Young, Mormon leader.*

from a district in Atlanta, Georgia.

Young was an effective Congressman, and in 1977, he was appointed by President Carter to be U.S. ambassador to the United Nations. His support for Third World nations aroused controversy, and in 1979, he resigned after charges that he had had a secret meeting at the U.N. with the Palestine Liberation Organization. In 1981, Young was elected mayor of Atlanta.

ALSO READ: KING, MARTIN LUTHER, JR.

Upper Yosemite Fall (1,430 feet / 436 m), and Lower Yosemite Fall (320 feet / 98 m), with a series of cascades, which cover 675 feet (206 m), in between. The best time to see the falls is in May or June. By the end of the summer, they may dry up from lack of melting snow and rain.

Yosemite includes three groves of giant sequoia trees. The largest tree has a diameter of about 35 feet (11 m) at its base and a height of 209 feet (64 m). It is estimated to be about 3,800 years old. Black bears and mule deer roam the park. So do marmots, ground squirrels, and porcupines. More than 700 miles (1,125 km) of hiking and horsebackriding trails wind through Yosemite. A park museum provides exhibits of plant and animal life and of the history of the local Indians.

ALSO READ: CALIFORNIA, NATIONAL PARK, SIERRA NEVADA.

YOUNG, ANDREW (born 1932) Andrew Young has been a civil rights leader, U.S. Congressman, and U.S. ambassador to the United Nations. He was born in New Orleans, Louisiana, and studied at Howard University, in Washington, D.C. He then turned to the church and became an aide to Martin Luther King, Jr. In 1972, Young was the first black elected to Congress

YOUNG, BRIGHAM (1801–1877) Brigham Young was a leader of the Morman church, officially called the Church of Jesus Christ of the Latter-day Saints. He helped settle what is now the state of Utah.

Young was born in Whitingham, Vermont. As a young man, he worked as a carpenter and a painter in western New York. Young was raised a Methodist but was converted to Mormonism in 1832. Three years later, he became a member of the Quorum of the Twelve Apostles, the ruling body of the Mormon Church. For several years afterward, Young traveled through parts of the United States and Britain, serving as a missionary. When Joseph Smith, the founder of Mormonism, was murdered in 1844, Young became the head of the church.

Young planned and supervised a westward migration of 5,000 Mormons in 1846. He chose their settlement place at the site of what is now Salt Lake City, Utah. Under Young's leadership, the community prospered. In 1850, when the region became the Territory of Utah, Young was made governor. However, he was removed from office in 1857 after he publicly endorsed polygamy (having more than one husband or wife).

ALSO READ: LATTER-DAY SAINTS; SMITH, JOSEPH; UTAH.

YOUNG, WHITNEY MOORE, JR. (1921–1971)

Whitney Young was an American civil rights leader who devoted most of his life to helping other black people in the United States.

Young was born in Lincoln Ridge, Kentucky. He studied at Kentucky State College and the University of Minnesota. In 1947, he joined the National Urban League, an organization that works to give black people in the United States the same opportunities as white people in housing, jobs, and education. Young served as industrial relations director for the branch of the Urban League in Saint Paul, Minnesota, until 1950. He then became executive secretary of the Omaha branch in Nebraska.

In 1954, Young was appointed dean of the School of Social Work at Atlanta University. He left that position in 1961 to become executive director of the National Urban League at its headquarters in New York City. Young set up many programs to encourage young people to train for the careers of their choice. He served on several Presidential commissions investigating social problems in the United States. Young wrote the books *To Be Equal* and *Beyond Racism*. In 1969, he was awarded the Medal of Freedom, the highest civilian award in the United States.

ALSO READ: CIVIL RIGHTS MOVEMENT.

YOUNG PEOPLE'S ASSOCIATIONS

Many young people enjoy belonging to an association, club, or movement that provides recreational activities, outdoor adventure, and the chance to learn new skills and games and make new friends. For example, in 1980 there were over a million American boys who belonged to Boys' Clubs. The national organization of the Boys' Clubs of America was started in 1906.

Camp Fire Girls   This organization was founded in 1910. Its symbol is a flame and crossed logs. Camp Fire Girls are organized in four age groups: Blue Birds (7 and 8), Camp Fire Girls (9 through 11), Junior Hi Camp Girls (12 and 13), and Horizon Club (14 and over). Members are guided by leaders in programs of service to the community and country, and learn skills in homemaking and outdoor life.

Four-H Club   Have you ever wished you knew how to repair a bicycle, raise chickens, preserve foods, or make clothes? Members of a Four-H, or 4-H, Club learn all these skills and more. Anyone between the ages of 9 and 19 can join 4-H, which began in the American farmlands in the early 1900's. Today, only about a fourth of all 4-H members in the United States live on farms. More than 80 countries around the world have 4-H organizations. The United States Department of Agriculture in Washington, D.C., has information on 4-H Clubs throughout the country.

Scouts   The international Scout movement began with the founding of the Boy Scouts by a British army officer, Robert Baden-Powell. In 1907, he organized a boys' camp, and in 1908 he wrote a handbook of activities called *Scouting for Boys*. William D. Boyce and Daniel Beard founded

▲ *Whitney M. Young, Jr., civil rights leader.*

▼ *These young people are crossing the fast-flowing waters of the Wind River in Wyoming. Expeditions for young persons, such as this one, are well supervised by adults.*

▲ *These Boy Scouts in Philadelphia are dressed in their uniforms. They have worked hard to earn their badges.*

the Boy Scout movement in the United States. Boy Scouts are aged 11 to 17 and meet in patrols, several of which form a troop. Boys aged 8 to 10 are *Cub Scouts*.

Girl Scouts are called Girl Guides in some countries. The first U.S. troop was organized by Juliette Gordon Low in Savannah, Georgia. Girl Scouts are organized in four age groups. *Brownies* are 6 through 8. *Junior Girl Scouts* are 9 through 11. *Cadettes* are 12 through 14, and *Senior Girl Scouts* are 15 through 17.

Boy and Girl Scouts all over the world make a pledge, or promise. They share the motto "Be Prepared" and the slogan "Do a Good Turn Daily." The Scout movement promotes international friendship and community service. Camping and conservation are favorite activities. Scouts are awarded badges for achievement in various skills.

YMCA and YWCA The Young Men's Christian Association (YMCA or simply the "Y") was founded in England by George Williams in 1844, mainly for Bible study and prayer. Today, anyone, of whatever religious belief, can join, though most "Y" members are boys and men under 25. Teenagers can join Hi-Y Clubs.

Most YMCA buildings display the "Y" symbol, a red triangle. They often have cafeterias, residence halls, and sports facilities. The YMCA also sponsors educational classes, craft workshops, and hobby centers.

The Young Women's Christian Association (YWCA) was founded in England in 1855. The first U.S. YWCA was founded in New York City in 1858. Girls can join Y-Teen Clubs aged 12 through 18. Men and boys can become associate members.

YUGOSLAVIA The Socialist Federal Republic of Yugoslavia lies along the Adriatic Sea in southeastern Europe. This country is composed of six republics—Serbia (which includes the autonomous provinces of Kosovo and Vojvodina), Croatia, Bosnia-Hercegovina, Slovenia, Macedonia, and Montenegro. Yugoslavia is the largest country of the Balkan Peninsula. (See the map with the article on EUROPE.) The name Yugoslavia means "Land of the Southern Slavs." Ancestors of the Yugoslav people were *Slavs*, tribes that came from the north a thousand years ago.

Mountains and highlands cover most of Yugoslavia. The Dinaric Alps along the coast are the chief mountain range. Dalmatia, the Adriatic coastal plain, is a beautiful place with a warm climate and many islands lying off the coastline. Dubrovnik and Split are old medieval cities, popular with vacationers. The Danube River waters a fertile plain that supports farms and orchards. On a hill overlooking the Danube lies Belgrade, the capital.

The Yugoslav peoples, although closely related, differ from each other

YUGOSLAVIA

Capital City: Belgrade (1,470,000 people).
Area: 98,774 square miles (255,804 sq. km).
Population: 23,100,000.
Government: Federal republic.
Natural Resources: Coal, iron, copper, lead, chrome.
Export Products: Machinery, electrical goods, transport equipment, chemicals.
Unit of Money: Dinar.
Official Languages: Serbo-Croat, Slovene, Macedonian.

in religion and language. The main groups of people are Serbs, Croats, Slovenes, Macedonians, and the Montenegrins of the isolated mountain regions. There are three major languages—Serbo-Croat, Slovene, and Macedonian.

Yugoslavia is rich in minerals, such as coal, and copper, and also in forests that supply lumber. All industry is owned by the state. Textiles, chemicals, and electrical equipment are manufactured. Zagreb is a leading industrial city.

Many farmers work their own little plots. Others work on big, modern farms owned by the state. The main crops are corn, wheat, barley, and rye. Grapes, oranges, and lemons grow along the coast, where tourism is important.

Yugoslavia became a nation in 1918. It was ruled by a king. Before World War I, Serbia and Montenegro were independent countries, and the rest of the country was part of the Austro-Hungarian Empire. During World War II, German troops occupied the country, and Yugoslav partisans (resistance fighters) fought against them.

After the war, a Communist partisan leader, Josip Broz, or Marshal Tito as he was called, was in control. Yugoslavia was declared to be a Communist people's republic. After Tito's death in 1980, a collective presidency, rotating among the presidents of Yugoslavia's republics and provinces, went into effect.

ALSO READ: ADRIATIC SEA, DANUBE RIVER, TITO.

YUKON TERRITORY

The Yukon Territory is a wild, rugged region of Canada in the far northwest corner of the country. The state of Alaska lies along its western border. The Yukon Territory is about twice the size of Colorado, but the Yukon has less than one-hundredth the number of people of that state.

The Yukon lies on a high plateau, stretching south from the Arctic Ocean. More than 20 peaks in the territory rise higher than 10,000 feet (3,000 m). At 19,850 feet (6,050 m), Mount Logan is the highest mountain in Canada. The Yukon River, one of North America's longest rivers, runs across the southern part of the territory. Winters in the Yukon are long and very cold. The land is covered with deep snow for much of the year. During the short summers, some hardy grains and vegetables are grown in some southern regions of the Yukon.

Most of the people work in mining, logging, tourism, or government activities. The territory has deposits of silver, copper, lead, nickel, asbestos, zinc, oil, and natural gas. There are valuable forests of white spruce and pine. Some of the local Indians are fur traders. Muskrat, beaver, and other fur-bearing animals live in the Yukon. The chief cities are Faro, Watson Lake, Dawson, and Whitehorse, the capital.

A British expedition led by Sir John Franklin explored the Yukon's Arctic coast in the 1820's. Fur-trading posts were later set up by the Hudson's Bay Company, which sold its rights to the territory to the Canadian government in 1870.

In 1896, gold was discovered around the Klondike River in central Yukon. Prospectors and miners from all over North America flocked to the Klondike region and the rest of the territory to seek their fortunes. By 1910, most of the gold had been exhausted and many people had left. In the 1940's, thousands of workers went there when part of the Alaska Highway was built in the Yukon. The Canadian government has since encouraged the development of permanent industries in Yukon Territory.

ALSO READ: CANADA, GOLD RUSH, HUDSON'S BAY COMPANY.

▲ *Dubrovnik is a medieval city and port on Yugoslavia's Adriatic coast. It is a popular tourist resort.*

The Yugoslavian seaport of Split is an ancient Roman town. Here, the vast palace of the Emperor Diocletian is one of the most impressive ruins in the ancient world. Its walls are 7 feet (2 m) thick and 72 feet (22 m) high on the seaward side.

At the peak of the gold rush to the Yukon's Klondike, more than 30,000 people moved into the territory. In the year 1900, gold worth $22 million was found in the area.

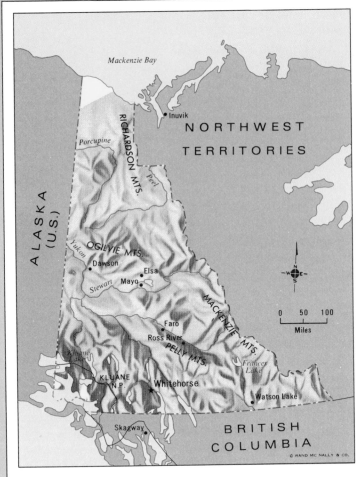

▲ *Dawson is one of the chief cities of the Yukon, but its population, like those of other Yukon cities, is small. The Yukon Territory's total population is only 23,000.*

▲ *The Yukon River runs across the south of the Yukon Territory in Canada. It is one of North America's longest rivers.*

YUKON TERRITORY

Capital and largest city
Whitehorse (17,600 people)

Area
184,931 square miles (478,934 sq. km)

Population
23,000 people

Yukon Territory created
1898

Principal river
Yukon

Highest point
Mt. Logan; 19,850 feet (6,050 m)

PROVINCIAL FLOWER

Fireweed

▲ *Several settlements border the Klondike River.*

ZAIRE The big African country of Zaire was once known as Congo Free State—a colony of Belgium. The country received its independence from Belgium in 1960 and took the name Zaire in 1971.

Zaire is the third largest country in Africa—a quarter the size of the United States. Its western neighbor is Congo (Brazzaville). The Central African Republic and the Sudan lie to the north. Uganda, Rwanda, Burundi, and Tanzania are on the east. Zambia and Angola are its southern neighbors. A small stretch of land forms the Atlantic coastline in the southwest. (See the map with the article on AFRICA.)

Much of the country lies in the basin of the Zaire, or Congo River. This region is surrounded by highlands on the west and south. Mountains lie east of the basin. Zaire's climate is a moist, tropical one because of its location on the equator. Rain falls all year in the river area. The rest of the country has a dry season and a rainy season.

The country is rich in minerals. It

ZAIRE

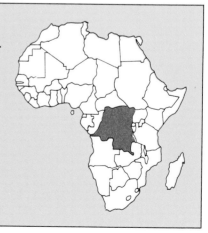

Capital City: Kinshasa (1,855,000 people).
Area: 905,633 square miles (2,345,409 sq. km).
Population: 33,100,000.
Government: Republic.
Natural Resources: Copper, zinc, cobalt, diamonds, timber.
Export Products: Copper, coffee, diamonds, cobalt.
Unit of Money: Zaire.
Official Language: French.

▲ *The Lake Kivu district lies to the far east of Zaire, on the border with Rwanda.*

The Zaire River separates the world's two closest capital cities. People can take a ferry across the river from Kinshasa, the capital of Zaire, to Brazzaville, the capital of the Congo.

is the world's largest producer of industrial diamonds and cobalt, and one of the leading exporters of copper. Coal, manganese, tin, zinc, and gold are also mined. Most of these resources are located in the southeastern section of the country.

Over half the population belongs to various tribal groups speaking Bantu languages. The remainder are members of tribal groups that speak Sudanese or Nilotic languages.

Belgium control over Zaire began in the 1880's. King Leopold II of Belgium claimed the area after hearing about it from the explorer Henry M. Stanley. It was turned over to Belgium in 1908.

The Belgians trained many Zairians in mining and technical jobs before independence. The Belgians, however, took much from the land and educated few people for government jobs and professions. The period following independence was filled with bloodshed. Moise Tshombe, Patrice Lumumba, and Joseph Kasavubu all tried unsuccessfully to lead the country. Joseph Désiré Mobutu finally seized power in 1965.

As part of a plan to go back to older and more authentic (real) names, the name of the country was changed by Mobutu from the Congo to Zaire in late 1971. Zaire was what Portuguese explorers in the 1500's had called the Congo River. The city of Stanleyville

is now Kisangani, and Leopoldville is Kinshasa. President Mobutu took the name of Mobutu Sese Seko.

ALSO READ: AFRICA.

ZAIRE RIVER The Zaire, or Congo, River stretches about 2,900 miles (4,700 km) through central Africa. It flows in a giant semicircle through the lowlands of Zaire and empties into the Atlantic Ocean. The Zaire is the second longest river in Africa—only the Nile is longer—and one of the longest rivers in the world. (See the map with the article on AFRICA.)

The Zaire flows through thick forest, open grasslands called savannas, and marshes near the Atlantic coast. The heavy rainfall of the tropical forest adds water to the river. In fact, the Zaire carries more water to the ocean than any other river does, except the Amazon of South America.

The Zaire is an important means of communication for the people of central Africa. Barges and large ships carry many different cargoes between the inland areas and the coast. The river is divided into three natural parts. The Upper Zaire is shallow, with rapids and waterfalls. The Middle Zaire includes Stanley Pool, a lake formed where the river widens. Livingstone Falls form the mouth of the lake. The two largest cities on the

▼ *A view of the Zaire (Congo) River, the river that drains west-central Africa.*

ZAMBIA

Capital City: Lusaka (538,000 people).
Area: 290,607 square miles (752,614 sq. km).
Population: 7,700,000.
Government: Republic.
Natural Resources: Copper, zinc, lead, coal, cobalt, hydroelectric power.
Export Products: Copper.
Unit of Money: Kwacha.
Official Language: English.

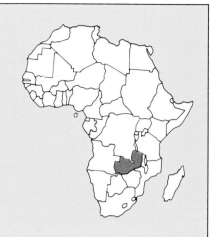

river—Kinshasa and Brazzaville, each the capital of a country—lie near Livingstone Falls. The Lower Zaire stretches from these falls to the Atlantic Ocean. The port of Matadi lies on the Lower Zaire.

European explorers first named the river "Zaire," meaning "river." In the 1600's the name "Congo" was adopted, from the name of a local African kingdom.

ALSO READ: CONGO; LIVINGSTONE, DAVID; RIVER; STANLEY, HENRY MORTON; ZAIRE.

ZAMBIA The Republic of Zambia, formerly the British protectorate of Northern Rhodesia, is a landlocked country located in south-central Africa. It is about twice the size of Montana. Zambia is surrounded by Zaire, Tanzania, Malawi, Mozambique, Zimbabwe, Botswana, Namibia, and Angola. (See the map with the article on AFRICA.) The Zambezi River forms Zambia's border with Zimbabwe. The Kariba Dam project provides hydroelectric power, shared with Zimbabwe. Victoria Falls on the river is wider than Niagara and more than twice its height.

Most of Zambia lies on a fairly high plateau covered with thin forest and grass, making it suitable for both farming and grazing. It is rich in minerals and is one of the world's largest producers of copper. Other minerals mined there are zinc, cobalt, lead, and manganese.

Many Zambians still make their living as farmers. They grow corn, peanuts, and tobacco. They follow their traditional religions, although many of them are Christian. The capital city is Lusaka (Livingstone was the capital until 1935). Lusaka is a modern, busy city and has an international airport. Other cities are Kitwe and Ndola.

Before Europeans came to Zambia, people had migrated for several hundred years from the Congo River basin toward the south of Africa. These Bantu-speaking people took over the area formerly occupied by Bushmen and other groups. The first non-

▼ *Lake Kariba (visible in the distance) forms the border between Zambia and Zimbabwe. The lake was formed by the construction of the Kariba Dam, which supplies power to Zambia and Zimbabwe.*

Africans to go there were Portuguese explorers and Arab traders.

During the 1850's and 1860's, the British missionary David Livingstone explored the territory. Later the British South Africa Company acquired mineral rights from Lewanika, ruler of the Lozi people, in what is now Zambia and Zimbabwe. Cecil Rhodes handled this operation on behalf of Britain. Northern Rhodesia became a British protectorate in 1924 and became fully independent on October 24, 1964. Zambia was Britain's first dependency to become a republic immediately upon independence. It took the name of Zambia from the Zambezi River. Kenneth Kaunda has been president since 1964.

ALSO READ: AFRICA; RHODES, CECIL; ZIMBABWE.

ZEBRA Zebras are members of the horse family. They range over much of eastern and southern Africa. There are three different types of zebra, distinguished mainly by the arrangement and color of their stripes. One of the most common types, Burchell's zebra, has a light yellow coat with bold black stripes over its whole body. Fainter markings, called shadow stripes, sometime show up between the black stripes. The zebra's stripes, a form of camouflage, make the animal very difficult to see in the shadowy tall grass of an African plain. All zebras have a tufted tail and a short mane that stands erect.

Zebras roam in herds, or groups, grazing on grass and leaves. Each herd is led by a stallion, or male zebra. Female zebras usually have one offspring, or foal, every two or three years. Zebras will kick and bite savagely if attacked. Their main natural enemy is the lion, which hunts them for food. A zebra herd will gallop off at great speed when a lion charges. If a foal cannot run fast enough, its mother will stay behind and defend it to the death. Some kinds of zebras have become almost extinct because of hunters who slaughtered them for their hides. An example of this was the quagga, a zebra which had stripes only on its head and neck.

ZIMBABWE The Republic of Zimbabwe, formerly called Rhodesia, is a landlocked country in south-central Africa. It is slightly smaller in size than California. Harare (formerly Salisbury), the capital, and Bulawayo are the largest cities in Zimbabwe.

Most of Zimbabwe is a high, rolling plateau. The land is largely *veld*, or grassland, with shrub trees. The Zambezi River flows between Zambia and Zimbabwe in the north, and the Limpopo River forms Zimbabwe's

▼ *Zebras drinking at a waterhole in Africa. The zebra's stripes are distinctive, yet they provide good camouflage on the grasslands that are home to these fleet-footed relatives of the horse.*

▼ *A tobacco farm in Zimbabwe. Growing tobacco is one of the country's leading industries.*

ZIMBABWE

Capital City: Harare (656,000 people).

Area: 150,815 square miles (390,580 sq. km).

Population: 10,000,000.

Government: Republic.

Natural Resources: Asbestos, gold, chrome, nickel, coal.

Export Products: Tobacco, minerals, cotton lint, sugar.

Unit of Money: Zimbabwe dollar.

Official Language: English.

southern border with South Africa.

Zimbabwe has rich farmland, on which tobacco (the country's main crop), sugarcane, cotton, and corn are grown. Beef cattle are raised on the veld. The country has rich mineral resources, including gold, copper, coal, chrome, nickel, and asbestos.

As is shown by the massive stone ruins of Great Zimbabwe, people have settled in this part of Africa since ancient times. In 1889, the Bantu-speaking people of the region gave the British South Africa Company, operated by Cecil Rhodes, permission to begin mining operations and colonization there. The region became the British colony of Southern Rhodesia in 1923. After a short federation with Northern Rhodesia (now Zambia) and Nyasaland (now Malawi), Southern Rhodesia declared its independence from Britain in 1965. It became the nation of Rhodesia, with a white-minority government. Britain called this declaration of independence illegal, and the United Nations imposed economic sanctions. Guerrilla warfare between black nationalists and the whites disrupted the country until late 1979. Then a new constitution, guaranteeing blacks rights, was agreed upon. In 1980, Rhodesia was officially renamed Zimbabwe, with Prime Minister Robert Mugabe as head of a black majority government.

ALSO READ: AFRICA; RHODES, CECIL; SANCTIONS.

ZODIAC   see ASTROLOGY, CONSTELLATION.

ZOO   The word "zoo" is short for zoological garden. Both terms mean places where live animals are kept on display. People visit zoos just for fun or to learn about different kinds of animals. Modern zoos also make a big contribution to science. *Zoologists* (scientists who study animals) learn by studying animals in zoos, although scientists learn most about animal behavior from observing animals in their natural environment.

There are more than 500 zoos throughout the world. Some large cities, such as New York City, have more than one zoo. But not all zoos are in big cities. Some are in the country, where the animals can have more room. Some are "breeding zoos." Here, groups of wild animals are kept for breeding to raise new populations. Some animals might become extinct if breeding zoos did not help produce new generations. The largest zoo collection is at the San Diego Zoo in California. The National Zoological Park in Washington, D.C., has more than three million visitors a year.

Many modern zoos do not keep all their animals in cages with bars. They have out-of-doors fields, or enclosures. The enclosures are surrounded by *moats*, or wide ditches. Other zoos

▲ *Much time and care are needed to provide the birds in a well-run zoo with a natural, healthy diet.*

The oldest existing zoo is London Zoo in England, owned by the Zoological Society of London. It is also one of the world's largest, housing about 10,000 animals.

▲ *Penguins gather around their keeper, eager to receive a fish. Many zoo animals grow so used to humans that they lose their fear of being approached or even handled.*

▼ *These children are watching an experienced zookeeper handling a python.*

find ways to let people go in with the animals. Enormous flight cages for birds, known as *aviaries*, have pathways, ponds, trees, and bushes. In Jungleworld at the Bronx Zoo, New York, visitors walk through an artificial rain forest. In some country zoos, visitors wander among herds of tame llamas, deer, and other animals. Many zoos include special children's zoos, with animals that can be petted, fed, or even ridden.

Zoos existed in ancient times. A powerful Egyptian queen named Hatshepsut had a zoo in 1400 B.C. The Roman emperors kept animals brought back from all parts of the Roman Empire and beyond. The oldest zoo in the United States is the Philadelphia Zoo, which opened in 1874.

Keeping Animals Healthy   Zoo animals usually live longer than their cousins in the wild. They do not starve or go without water, as wild animals sometimes do. *Veterinarians* care for the health of zoo animals. They give inoculations against diseases and help to plan healthful diets. They trim hoofs or claws and care for skin and teeth. They even perform surgery on sick animals.

SPECIAL NEEDS.   Animal behavior experts know that zoo animals—just like people—need activities to keep them alert and happy. Experiments in one zoo proved that monkeys became

unhappy when the zoo put in special kinds of one-way glass that kept the monkeys from seeing people. But there are limits to the activities a zoo can supply. A lion might feel happier if it could kill a wild zebra, but a zoo could not allow this. Behavior experts have discovered interesting substitutes for the activities that satisfy wild animals; for example, by giving chimpanzees games to play.

Old-fashioned zoos had small cages in which the animals could not get enough exercise to stay well and alert. Modern zoos try to allow each animal the amount of space it likes. Some zoo animals would actually be unhappy in a very large cage or in a big field. In zoos, where food and water are provided, they may feel secure in a small space. Animals that need cool climates live in air-conditioned cages. Animals that need trees are kept in areas containing trees. Aquariums, tanks containing fish and other marine life, are often part of a zoo.

Feeding the Animals   Every animal must have its own diet. Certain snakes will eat only live food, such as mice. Koalas from Australia will eat only fresh eucalyptus leaves.

Zoos plan substitute foods with care. For big cats, such as leopards and tigers, the zoo buys slabs of fro-

▼ *A children's zoo includes animals that children may safely feed.*

▲ *Elephants are always a big attraction in any zoo.*

zen horsemeat. Truckloads of hay arrive for grazing and browsing animals. Fruits and vegetables, as well as insects, mealworms, or other worms are needed for many small mammals and birds. Big zoos have *commissaries*, or food centers. The commissary staff manufacture special diet cakes and pellets, which are convenient for feeding many animals. These cakes are mixtures of nourishing foods that supply protein, carbohydrates, fats, minerals, and vitamins.

Obtaining Animals for a Zoo   Some zoo animals are purchased from professional *animal dealers*. The dealers often buy the animals from hunters or trappers, who specialize in capturing wild animals. Many countries now prohibit the trade in wild animals, especially of endangered species.

Many zoo animals are born in captivity. An important part of a zoo's work is to find ways to breed animals that are scarce. New populations, born in zoos, could save some rare animals from becoming extinct. Zoo directors from different countries have organized the Wild Animal Propagation Trust. It works to get zoos to cooperate in building populations of rare animals.

Zoos obtain animals in other ways, too. Sometimes people, or governments, give animals as gifts. Zoos also trade animals with each other. Zoos all around the world keep in close touch and exchange their knowledge.

■ **LEARN BY DOING**

You can learn a great deal by visiting a zoo, and you'll have fun while you are learning. But make sure that you obey the zoo rules, because they were made to protect you and the animals. When zoo officials put up signs that tell you not to feed a certain animal, it is because the food you might have with you would be bad for it. ■

ALSO READ: ANIMAL, ZOOLOGY.

ZOOLOGY   Zoology is the study of animals. Zoologists collect facts on how different animals are structured, how they function, and how they grow. Some zoologists work in laboratories doing careful experiments. Others work out-of-doors, studying animals in their natural surroundings. Modern zoology is such a large subject that most zoologists study just one special branch, or separate science, in the field. For instance, a zoologist might be an expert in *ecology*, the study of how animals relate to their surroundings and to each other. Some zoologists concentrate on particular functions or body parts found in all animals. Other zoologists study particular animals or groups of animals.

Anatomy is the study of the body parts and structure of animals. *Physiology* is the study of life processes, such as digestion and reproduction. *Cytology* is the study of cells—the "building blocks" of which all animal bodies are made. The science of *genetics* shows how characteristics of parents are passed along to their young. *Taxonomy* is the science or technique of placing, or *classifying*, animals into

▲ *Zoology, the study of animals, helps us understand the delicate balances of nature and how to protect endangered species such as the panda. Through zoology we know that pandas rely mainly on bamboo shoots for their food. So preservation of bamboo forests is essential.*

▲ *It was through studies of the rhesus monkey that zoologists discovered much about human blood systems and disorders. Some people have what is called the Rhesus factor, and their blood is said to be Rhesus positive or negative—or Rh+ or Rh–.*

groups according to their relationships with each other.

A *vertebrate zoologist* specializes in animals with backbones, such as human beings, cats, dogs, or fishes. The *invertebrate zoologist* explores the world of animals without backbones, such as insects, mollusks, and worms. *Ornithologists* study birds, *herpetologists* study snakes, *icthyologists* study fish, and *entomologists* study insects. Zoology overlaps many other sciences. Together with *botany*, the study of plants, it forms *biology*, the study of all living things. Zoologists use *chemistry* to study the chemical properties of animals, and *physics* to study the effects of different forces on animals.

Zoology is important to people in many ways. Understanding the way animals function helps scientists to learn how human beings function. For example, new understanding of the way heartbeats are controlled came from studies of horseshoe crabs. Zoological science is applied in the conservation of wildlife resources, as well as in agriculture. Without zoology, it would be impossible to save many endangered wild animals.

History of Zoology Early people had to know a lot about animals. Wild animals were hunted for food, so hunters studied animals and their habits. Later, animals like cows, sheep, and dogs were kept as domestic animals. Farmers learned what they could about their animals to keep them healthy.

In the 300's B.C., the Greek philosopher Aristotle made careful studies of animal life. He dissected many animals and made careful notes on what he saw. Aristotle's work, with its mistakes, was considered the basis of zoological knowledge for the next 1500 years. There were few advances in zoology during this time. Then from the 1200's onward, people began to travel to distant places and discovered many strange, new ani-

mals, then unknown. Advances in anatomy began to be made in the 1300's.

In the 1500's, the Flemish surgeon Andreas Vesalius dissected human cadavers and corrected mistakes made by Aristotle. In 1660, the Italian anatomist Marcello Malpighi used a microscope and discovered capillaries, the tiny blood vessels that connect arteries and veins.

The microscope was an important tool in the growth of zoology. Using it, Anton van Leeuwenhoek discovered bacteria and protozoans, and Robert Hooke studied and described the cell.

Until the 1750's, animals and plants were known only by their popular names and descriptions. This caused great confusion. Then the Swedish botanist Carolus Linnaeus developed a system in which each separate kind of plant and animal was given a two-word Latin name. For example, *Panthera leo* is the scientific name for lion. Linnaeus's system made zoological study more effective and still serves as the basis for classifying living things.

In the 1800's, more zoologists began to study the strange animal life in exotic lands. This led to one of the most important ideas in science, Charles Darwin's theory of the origin of the species. According to Darwin's

▼ *Charles Darwin, whose ideas did much to shape the modern science of zoology.*

theory, different species (kinds) arise as a result of the "survival of the fittest." Animals that are better suited to their surroundings are more likely to survive. Individual variations that make an animal more fit are also those most likely to be passed on to future generations.

In this century, great advances have been made in zoology. Much has been learned about the chemistry of life and how characteristics are passed from parents to offspring. The behavior of animals is being studied. Ecology has achieved a new importance as people have realized that the resources for life on Earth are limited.

Zoology as a Career Zoology can be a fascinating career for someone who is interested in animals. If you should decide to become a zoologist, you will eventually study zoology in college. In the meantime, you should learn all you can about animals.

■ LEARN BY DOING

Observe how animals live. Why are birds quick and lively, while turtles are slow? Why do dogs eat meat, while rabbits eat plants? You can see many different animals at a zoo, but you can also find many animals just by turning over a rock or digging in the ground. Worms and insects can be as informative as larger animals. ■

ALSO READ: AGASSIZ, LOUIS; AGRICULTURE; AMPHIBIAN; ANATOMY; ANIMAL; ANIMAL KINGDOM; ARISTOTLE; BACTERIA; BIOCHEMISTRY; BIOLOGY; BIRD; BOTANY; COELENTERATE; CONSERVATION; CRUSTACEAN; DARWIN, CHARLES; ECHINODERM; ECOLOGY; EVOLUTION; FISH; FOOD WEB; GENETICS; INSECT; LIFE; LINNAEUS, CAROLUS; MAMMAL; MARINE LIFE; MEDICINE; MICROSCOPE; MOLLUSK; NATURE STUDY; PROTIST; RARE ANIMAL; REPTILE; RODENT; SCIENCE; VERTEBRATE; VETERINARY MEDICINE; ZOO.

SOME BRANCHES OF ZOOLOGY

Anatomy   The study of the way living things are made

Botany   The study of plants

Ecology   The study of how living things relate to their environments

Embryology   The study of how animals grow and develop

Entomology   The study of insects

Histology and **Cytology**   The study of the structure of body cells making up organs (histology) and tissues (cytology)

Ornithology   The study of birds

Paleontology   The study of the fossil remains of living things

Pathology   The study of animal diseases

Physiology   The study of how animals' bodies work

Taxonomy   The study of the classification of animals

ZWORYKIN, VLADIMIR KOSMA (1889–1982)

Vladimir Zworykin, who was born in Russia, was a pioneer in the development of early television. He studied in France but, when World War I broke out, he went back to Russia to help his country. However, when the Communists took over Russia in 1917, he left for the United States.

In this country he made most of the inventions that led to television. (The Scottish scientist John Logie Baird made similar inventions, but Baird's systems were primitive and have been abandoned.) Zworykin realized that the *cathode-ray tube* could be used to make pictures on a screen coated with fluorescent substances called *phosphors*. The cathode-ray tube gives off a stream of electrons, and these make the phosphors glow whenever they strike them. By 1924, Zworykin had invented what he called a *kinescope*, a type of cathode-ray tube that could be used to make a television picture.

A few years later he invented the *iconoscope*. This was the first practicable television camera, though modern television cameras work in a different way. During the 1930's, he did much to improve the electron microscope.

ALSO READ: CHEMISTRY, MICROSCOPE, TELEVISION.

▲ *Vladimir Zworykin, pioneer of television.*

INDEX

USING THE INDEX

An index is a key to the contents of a book. The index section of the *Young Students Learning Library* is arranged to help you find information quickly and easily. It lists all the articles by name and all the important subjects and people within each one.

HOW THE ENTRIES ARE ARRANGED This may be the first time you have used *alphabetical order*. Your *Learning Library* is arranged in this way. It is an easy way to put articles about so many subjects in an orderly fashion. The same is also true of the index. You will find it easy to use. You just have to know your alphabet. As you look for a subject in the index, think to yourself, 'What letter comes before the one I see here? What letter comes after it?'

The index entries are in alphabetical order, letter-by-letter, even if the entry has more than one word. For example, in the index you can find entries in the following order:

> West Indies
> Westo Indians
> Westphalia
> West Point

The first four letters are the same in those entries—W-e-s-t. In this example it is the fifth letter that will determine which entry goes first alphabetically. You should pay no attention to the space between West and Indies, Westo and Indians, West and Point. Comparing the letters after West you find that 'I' of Indies comes

first, the 'o' of Westo, and finally 'p' of Westphalia and West Point. The order of the last two is determined by the 'h' in Westphalia and 'o' in West Point.

Now turn to these entries:

> Stone
> Stone Age
> Stonehenge
> Stone, Lucy
> Stone Mountain

The same principle holds true here; the order after the letters S-t-o-n-e are arranged by the next available letter, ignoring spaces and punctuation.

PAGE NUMBERS Page numbers are given in the form of volume number/page number, thus 18/2195 refers to volume 18 page 2195. If the subject spans more than one page then it is shown as a thru-number 7/776–7. This indicates that the subject is in volume 7 and on pages 776 and 777. Page numbers given in **boldface type** (heavy and dark) indicate where the main reference to the subject is to be found. Thus in the entry:

> **Frogs**, 2/130–1, 9/**1013–14**, 10/1183, 13/1570

the main reference with the maximum amount of information will be found in volume 9 pages 1013 to 1014, but there will also be found other references in less detail on the other pages. You should always check the boldface entries first and then the others if you need more information.

Page numbers in *italic type* (slanting) refer to pages on which

will be found illustrations. Thus

Frost fairs, 9/*1015*

refers to an illustration of a frost
fair in volume 9 page 1015. If you
are only looking for pictures of a
subject or a person you can ignore
the page numbers in ordinary type
and just look for those in italic.

Page numbers that have an
asterisk ⋆ attached to them indicate
that the article on this page
contains a *Learn by Doing* project.

MAIN ENTRIES The main
entries are divided into two types.
Those that are in **boldface** type
(dark and heavy) refer to the main
headings of the articles as they
appear in this *Learning Library*.
Entries in ordinary type refer to
the subjects and people which are
found within these main articles.

SUBENTRIES A main heading
may have several subheadings.
There are two main reasons for
these. Firstly they are used to divide
up a large article that covers several
pages into its main topics. So if you
look up the entry for 'Libraries' you
will see that it has been broken
down to 'bookmobiles', 'catalogs',
'classification' and so on.
Secondly, subentries are used to
bring together subjects which are
scattered throughout the book.
Thus under 'Human body' you
will not only find the page
numbers referring to the main
article, but subheadings of all the
other articles throughout the *Young
Students Learning Library* dealing
with aspects of the body. For
example:

Human body, 10/**1224–5**,
10/*1224*
    aging, 1/50
    anatomy, 2/133
    antibodies, 2/177
    biochemistry, 3/*340*
    blood, 3/359–60
    bone, 3/366, 3/*366*
    brain, 4/382–4, 4/*383*
    breathing, 4/387–9, 4/*388*

Aa

Aardvark, 1/11, 1/*11*, 2/172
Aardwolf, 10/1231
Aaron, Hank, 19/2317
Abacus, 1/12–13★, 1/*12*, 2/212, 4/432, 15/1807
 making, 1/12–13, 1/*13*
Abba, 2/194
Abbai, 7/871
Abbies, 13/1585
Abbots, 14/1628
Abbreviation, 1/13–15★
 acronyms, 1/15
 contractions, 1/15
 table of, 1/14
Abdul-Jabbar, Kareem, 3/315, 19/2317
Abdullah, 11/1341
Abel, Rudolf, 19/2320
Abenaki Indians, 12/1485, 15/1751
Abnaki Indians see Anenaki Indians
Abnormal psychology, 17/2020
Abolition of slavery, 1/15–16
 abolitionists, 18/2238
 John Brown, 4/398
 see also Slavery
Abomey, 3/331
Abominable snowman, 1/16, 1/*16*
Aborigine, 1/16–17, 1/*17*, 5/559
 Australian, 3/263–5, 3/268
 boomerangs, 3/369
Abraham, 11/1334, 11/1344, 19/2352
Abrasives, 1/17–18★
Abruzzo, Ben, 8/893
Absolute zero, 6/682, 10/1169, 20/2401
Absorption, 1/18★, 1/*18*
Abstract art, 1/18–20★, 1/*19–20*, 14/1620
Abstract expressionism, 8/897, 14/1621
Abu Dhabi, 2/193
Abu Simbel, 1/20–1, 1/*20*, 7/809
Abyssal plains, 15/1816
Abyssinia see Ethiopia
Acacia, 3/267
Academy Awards, 1/21, 1/*21*, 1/29
 table, 14/1660–1
Acadia, 15/1746
Acapulco, 13/1573, 13/*1575*
Acceleration, 8, 983, 14/1657
Accelerators:
 automobiles, 7/765
 particle, 16/1880, 18/*2173*
Accidents:
 fire fighting, 8/934–6, 8/*934–6*
 fire prevention, 8/936–7
 first aid, 8/938–40, 8/*939–40*
 insurance, 11/1283–4
Accordion, 1/21, 1/*21*
Accountants, 1/22
Accounting, 1/22★
Accounts:
 advertising, 1/38
 bank, 3/301–2
Accra, 9/*1074*
Achatina, 19/2244

Achilles, 20/2465
Achille's tendon, 14/*1677*
Acid rain, 1/22–3
Acids, 1/23–4★
Ackermann, Rosie, 15/*1831*
Acne, 18/2232
Acoma, 15/1758
Aconcagua, Mount, 2/140, 2/211, 19/2268
Acorn barnacles, 6/681
Acoustics, 16/1923, 19/2262–5, 19/*2263–5*
Acquired Immune Deficiency (AIDS), 7/769, 21/2534
Acquired immunity, 10/1244
Acrobatics, 1/24–5, 1/*24–5*
 acrobats, 5/552
 circuses, 1/25
 safety, 1/25
Acronyms, 1/15
Acropolis, 1/26, 1/*26*, 3/253, 9/*1112*, 9/1113
Acrylic paints, 15/1860
Acrylic plastics, 16/1955
Acta Diurna, 15/1761
ACTH, 10/1201
Acting, 1/26–9★, 1/*27–9*
 becoming an actor, 1/29
 history of, 1/26–7
 makeup, 12/*1488–9*
 movies, 1/27–8
 pantomime, 16/1870
 radio, 1/28
 rewards of, 1/29
 styles of, 1/28
 television, 1/28
 theatrical, 1/27
ACTION, 16/1887, 21/2490
Action painting, 14/1621
Action-reaction, 7/848
Actium, 5/573
Actors and actresses:
 Barrymore family, 3/308–9
 Bernhardt, Sarah, 3/333, 3/*333*
 Booth family, 3/370
 Garrick, David, 9/1044
 Hayes, Helen, 10/1161–2
Actor's Studio, New York, 1/29
Acupuncture, 1/29–30, 1/*30*, 13/*1554*
ACV see Air cushion vehicle
A.D., 4/434, 11/1331
Adam, James, 9/1027
Adam, Robert, 9/1027
Adams, Abigail, 21/2582
Adams, Henry, 1/30
Adams, John, 1/30–1, 1/*31*, 1/126, 1/128, 6/652, 6/707, 6/743, 13/1519–20, 21/2523, 21/2582
Adams, John Quincy, 1/31–2, 1/*32*, 11/1317, 14/1639
Adams, Samuel, 1/31, 1/32, 1/*32*, 1/125, 3/373
Adaption, 7/797
Adbomen, 4/419
Addams, Jane, 1/32–3, 1/*33*, 5/562
Addax, 2/174
Addend, 2/213
Adders, 19/2246
Addiction, 1/33–4
 alcoholism, 1/94
 drugs, 7/769–70
 narcotics, 14/1702–3
Adding machines, 4/432–3
Addison County, 21/2518

Addition, 2/213
Additives, food, 8/978
Adélie penguin, 2/*146*, 16/*1965*
Ade, George, 8/901
Adelaide, 3/266, 3/268
Aden, 2/193
Adenauer, Konrad, 1/34, 1/*34*
Adenoids, 4/389
Ader, Clement, 3/281
Ādi Granth, 18/2223
Adirondack Mountains, 2/183, 15/1765, 15/*1765*
Adjectives, 16/1882
Adler, Felix, 5/583
Adler, Larry, 10/1153
Adler Planetarium, Chicago, 16/1937
Admiral's House, 21/2523, 21/*2523*
Admiralty cases, courts, 6/667
Adobe houses, 5/574, 5/*574*, 17/2026, 18/2204
Adolescence, 1/34–5
 changes in feelings, 1/35
 juvenile delinquency, 11/1350
 physical changes, 1/34–5
Adoption, 1/35–6
Adrenal glands, 9/1081, 9/*1081*
Adrenalin, 7/842, 10/1201
Adrenocortical, 10/1201
Adria, 1/36
Adriatic Sea, 1/36, 1/*36*
Adventists, 17/2013
Adventure, 6/653
Adverbs, 16/1882
Advertising, 1/36–8★, 1/*37–8*, 18/2189
 adverts as persuaders, 1/37
 agencies, 1/38
 media, 1/37–8
 newspapers, 15/1760
 origins, 1/38
 propaganda, 17/2009–10
 public relations, 17/2023
Aegean Sea, 1/38–9, 1/*39*
Aeneas, 18/2129
Aeneid, 21/2530
Aeolian harp, 19/2345
Aerialists, 1/25
Aerial photography, 2/*196*, 2/197, 13/1511
Aerial surveying, 19/2361
Aeries, 3/348
Aeronautics, 1/40
Aerosol, 1/39, 1/*39*
Aerospace, 1/40, 1/*40*
Aerospace Defense Command (ADC), 1/62
Aerotrains, 17/*2059*, 20/2453
Aeschylus, 1/40–1, 2/136, 9/1116
Aesclepius, 10/1187
Aesop, 1/41, 1/*41*, 8/900, 8/*901*
Aesthetics, 16/1915
Afars, 6/745
Afghanistan, 1/41–2, 1/*42*
Africa, 1/43–9, 1/*43–9*
 animal life, 1/46
 art, 2/234
 climates, 1/43, 1/*43*
 colonial rule, 1/48–9
 history, 1/48–9
 land, 1/43–6
 languages, 1/47
 map, 1/44
 nations of, 1/45
 people, 1/46–8

 physical statistics, 6/650
 religions, 1/47–8
 see also individual countries e.g. Egypt
African elephants, 2/*147*, 7/831–3, 7/*832*
African geese, 7/772
African giant frog, 9/1013
African killer bees, 3/*323*
African violets, 10/*1216*
African wild cat, 4/*488*
Africa Red Cross, 8/907–8
Afrikaners, 19/2267
Agama, 10/1123
Agar, 1/97
Agassiz, Louis, 1/50, 1/*50*, 14/1717
Age of Mammals, 13/*1498–9*
Agency for International Development (AID), 8/986
Agincourt, battle of, 7/857, 10/1177, 10/1227
Aging, 1/50
Agnew, Spiro, 8/984, 15/1778, 21/2522
Agni, 9/*1089*
Agora, 3/253
Agra, 20/2377
Agricola, Georgius, 9/1056
Agricultural engineers, 7/851
Agriculture, 1/51–6★, 1/*51–6*
 Aztecs, 3/284
 Babylonian, 3/286
 cacoa, 5/542
 Carver, George Washington, 4/479
 coffee, 5/591
 chicken, 17/1991–2, 17/*1991–2*
 conservation and, 6/639
 corn, 6/659–60
 dairy farming, 6/691
 diversified farming, 1/52–3
 dry farming, 14/1643
 early, 5/615–16
 European farming in America, 1/53–4
 famines, 8/907–8, 8/*908*
 farms, 1/54–5
 fertilizer, 8/925
 food processing and, 8/977–8
 fruit, 9/1016–18, 9/*1016–18*
 grain, 9/1096–7, 9/*1097*
 insect pests, 11/1277
 irrigation, 11/1305, 11/*1305*
 kinds of, 1/52–3
 McCormick, Cyrus, 13/1543
 machinery, 8/908–10, 8/*909–10*
 names for agricultural land, 1/54–5
 one-crop farming, 1/52
 origins of, 1/51–2
 pigs, 16/1928–9
 plantations, 1/54
 plant breeding, 16/1942
 plant products, 16/1950
 ranches, 1/54
 ranching, 17/2061–2
 rice, 17/2100–1, 17/*2100–1*
 rotation, 1/55
 selling produce, 18/2188
 soya, 19/2287
 stock farming, 1/52
 technology, 1/55–6
 truck farming, 20/2467–8
 wheat, 21/2580–1, 21/*2580–1*
Agriculture Department, 4/426
Ahasuerus, 22/2628

Ahmes, 1/98
A'H-mose, 13/1533
Ahura Mazdah, 16/1902
Ai, 19/2240, 19/2241
Aircraft carriers, 14/1730
Aid:
 foundations, 8/995–6
 Peace Corps, 16/1887
AIDS, 7/769, 21/2534
Aigeus-Mortes, 5/555
Ailerons, 1/68, 1/69
Air, 1/56–7*
 absorption, 1/18
 atmosphere, 3/257
 circulation, 1/57
 compression, 1/57
 heated, 1/57
 humidity, 10/1225–6
 pressure, 17/1999
 weather, 21/2561
 wind, 21/2592–3
Air conditioning, 1/58*, 1/58
Aircraft see Airplanes
Aircraft carrier, 1/58–60, 1/59–60,
 14/1728, 14/1729
 history, 1/59–60
 today's carriers, 1/60
Air cushion vehicles (ACV), 1/60–1,
 1/61
Air Force, 1/61–4, 1/62–4
Air Force Academy, 5/597, 21/2498
Air Force One Squadron, 1/62
Airline, 1/64–6, 1/64–6
Airmail, 16/1985
Airplanes, 1/40, 1/66–8*, 1/66–71,
 20/2452, 20/2454
 drag, 1/67
 famous, 1/70–1
 gliders, 9/1085–6, 9/1085
 helicopters, 10/1173–4, 10/1173–4
 jet engines, 11/1332
 lift, 1/66–7, 1/67
 parts, 1/68
 radar, 17/2042–3, 17/2042–3
 thrust, 1/67
 types, 1/68
 windtunnels, 21/2594
 Wright brothers, 22/2623
Air pollution, 1/72–5*, 1/72–5,
 6/661, 16/1969, 16/1970
 dust, 7/774–5
Airports, 1/75–7, 1/75–7
Air Pressure, 1/77–81/, 1/77–8
 barometers, 3/306
Airships, 1/78–9, 1/78–9
Air-to-air missiles (AAM), 13/1608
Air-to-surface missiles (ASM),
 13/1608
Air traffic control (ATC), 1/80–1,
 1/80
Aisles, 4/492
Aix-la-Chapelle, 5/512
Ajax, 14/1697
Ajman, 2/193
Akashi-Kaikyo Bridge, 4/392
Akbar, 11/1254
Akkad, 19/2352
Akkadians, 3, 286, 13/1565
Akosombo Dam, 9/1074
Akron, 15/1826
Akron, 1/79
Alabama, 1/81–4, 1/81–4
 employment, 1/84
 history, 1/83–4

 land, 1/81
 map, 1/82
 state emblems, 1/82
Alamance, battle of the, 15/1788
Alamo, 1/84–5, 1/84, 4/378, 6, 675,
 20/2411, 20/2414
Alamogordo, 15/1758
Alaric, 1/85, 1/85
Alaska, 1/85–9, 1/85–9, 3/253,
 11/1261
 employment, 1/88–9
 history, 1/88
 land, 1/85–7
 map, 1/86
 state emblems, 1/86
 US buys, 1/88
Alaska Highway, 1/88
Alaska king crabs, 6/681
Alaska moose, 6/709–10, 6/709
Alaskan bears, 3/320
Alaska Pipeline, 1/88–9, 1/88
Alaska Range, 1/87
Alaska seals, 18/2184
Albania, 1/89–90, 1/89–90
Albany, 15/1766
Albatross, 3/344, 18/2180
Albatross (golf), 9/1092
Albee, Edward, 7/760
Albee, Edward F., 21/2510
Albemarle Sound, 15/1788
Alberta, 1/90–2, 1/90–1, 4/450
 history, 1/90
 industries, 1/90–2
 map, 1/91
 provincial flower, 1/91
Albert Canal, 4/454
Albert the Great, 16/1915
Albert, Lake, 15/1776
Albert, Prince, 21/2524
Albino, 1/92, 1/92
Al Biqa, 12/1409
Albonos, 18/2233
Albumin, 12/1454
Albuquerque, 15/1757, 16/1967
Alchemy, 1/92–3, 1/93, 5/521,
 18/2172
Alcock, John W., 3/255
Alcoholic beverages, 1/93–4, 1/93
 abuse, 1/769
 cirrhosis, 12/1454
 fermentation, 8/922
 prohibition, 17/2007–8, 17/2007
 wine, 21/2594–5
Alcoholics Anonymous (AA), 1/94
Alcoholism, 1/94
Alcott, Louisa May, 1/94, 1/94,
 5/532
Alden, John, 16/1931
Alder, 20/2461
Aldiss, Brian, 18/2175
Aldrin, Edwin (Buzz), 1/94–5, 1/95,
 2/248, 5/597, 14/1644, 14/1646,
 19/2290, 19/2291
Aleppo, 2/202
Aleutian Islands, 1/95, 15/1854
Aleut Indians, 1/87, 1/88, 1/95,
 1/95
Alexander, Cicely, 21/2581, 21/2581
Alexander the Great, 1/42, 1/96,
 1/96, 2/212, 3/287, 3/319, 7/810,
 8/892, 9/1113, 11/1254, 11/1299,
 11/1335, 11/1368, 12, 11474,
 15/1865, 16/1903, 16/1916
Alexander I, Czar, 18/2147–8

Alexander III, Pope, 3/323, 7/805
Alexander VI, Pope, 3/371, 8/893
'Alexander's Ragtime Band', 3/332–3
Alexandra, Empress, 15/1772
Al Fatah, 10/1124
Alfonso XIII, King of Spain,
 19/2302
Alfred, 11/1340
Alfred the Great, 1/96, 1/97, 2/143,
 7/855, 7/858, 21/2527
Algae, 1/97, 1/97, 16/1, 16/1951,
 17/2016, 17/2016
Algarve, 16/1982
Algebra, 1/98–9*, 13/1533, 13/1535
Alger, Horatio Jr, 1/98, 1/99
Algeria, 1/99–100
Algiers, 1/99–100
Algonkian, 1/100, 1/100, 6/671,
 7/867, 17/2038, 21/2518, 21/2596
Algonkian Bible, 3/336
Alhambra Palace, 8/996, 19/2301
Alias, 14/1699
Alice's Adventures in Wonderland,
 4/475–6
Alidade, 19/2360
Aliens, 5/554
Aligators, 17/2090–1
Alimentary canal, 6/729–30
Ali, Muhammad, 4/381
Alkalis, 1/23–4
Alkaloids, 16/1961
Alkyd paints, 15/1858
Allah, 11/1307, 12/1376
Allahabad, 9/1036, 14/1639
Allan, John, 16/1959
Alleghenies, 2/183
Allegheny Plateau, 15/1824, 16/1893
Allen, Ethan, 1/100–1, 1/101
Allen, Fred, 1/28
Allen, Gracie, 21/2510
Allentown, Pennsylvannia, 16/1894
Allergens, 1/101
Allergies, 1/101, 6/738
 sneezing, 19/2246
Alliances, 11/1290
Alligators, 1/102–3, 1/102–3, 17/2064
Alloys, 1/104, 11/1303, 13/1568–9
Almagro, Diego de, 16/1936
Almanac, 1/105*, 1/105, 17/2075
Almonds, 15/1810
Al-Numeiry, Jaafar, 19/2350
Alpaca, 4/440
Alphabet, 1/105–7*, 1/106
 Arabic, 2/194–5, 2/195
 braille, 4/382, 4/382
 hieroglyphics, 10/1184–5, 10/1184
Alpha Canis Major, 6/642
Alpha Centauri, 2/252
Alpha particles. 17/2048, 17/2049
Alpha Piscium, 6/642
Alpine Club, 14/1671
Alpine plants, 14/1669
Alpine skiing, 18/2230, 18/2231
Alps Mountains, 1/107, 1/107,
 20/2366
Al-Razi, 13/1553
Altaic languages, 2/243
Altai Mountains, 14/1633, 19/2282
Altamira, 2/231, 2/231
Alternating current (AC), electricity,
 7/821–2
Alternators, automobiles, 3/276
Althing, 10/1236

Altocumulus clouds, 5/582
Altos, 18/2227
Altostratus clouds, 5/582
Alvarado, Pedro de, 7/838, 10/1124
Alveoli, 4/388
Alvin, 15/1820
Alzette River, 12/1471
Amargosa Range, 6/704
Amati family, 19/2344
Amazon ants, 2/168
Amazon Basin, 19/2268
Amazon River, 1/108, 1/108, 4/386,
 7/801
Amazons, 1/107, 1/107
Amazon sword plant, 2/189
Ambassadors, 11/1291
Amber, 1/108, 1/108
Ambergris, 21/2580
Ambidexterity, 10/1145
Ambrosia, 9/1088
Ambulance, 1/108–9, 1/109
America, 109–10*
American albinos, 10/1203
American allegators, 1/103
American Ballet Theater, 3/297
American Book Awards, 12/1451
American Broadcasting Company
 (ABC), 20/2398
American buffaloes, 3/351, 3/351,
 13/1591
American Civil War see Civil War
American Colonies, 1/110–15,
 1/110–14
 Church, 1/114
 Declaration of Independence,
 6/707
 early settlements, 1/111
 everyday life, 1/112–13
 people, 1/111–12
 recreation, 1/114–15
 school, 1/114
 transportation, 1/113–14
American Colonization Society,
 18/2236–7
American crocodile, 1/102, 1/103
American egret, 21/2551
American elk, 6/710
American English, 7/862
American Falls, 15/1770, 15/1770,
 21/2553
American Federation of Labor
 (AFL), 12/1380, 12/1419
American Fur Company, 9/1024,
 10/1219, 11/1296
American history, 1/115–22
 timetable, 1/119
 see also individual events and
 places
American Library Association, 4/433,
 15/1744
American Motorcycle Association
 (AMA), 14/1667
American Philosophical Society,
 9/1003
American Railroad Union (ARU),
 6/704
American Red Cross (ARC), 8/940,
 17/2074
 Blood bank, 7/763
 Clara Barton, 3/309
 lifesaving, 12/1430
American Relief Administration,
 10/1200

American Revolution, 1/30, 1/32, 1/100–1, 1/**122–8**, 1/*122–8*, 17/2095
    Articles of Confederation, 2/236–7
    blacks and, 3/353
    Boston Massacre, 3/372–3
    Boston Tea Party, 3/373
    Clark, George Rogers, 5/**570–1**
    Continental Congress, 6/651–2
    Declaration of Independence, 6/707
    Hale, Nathan, 10/1140
    Hancock, John, 10/**1143**
    Henry, Patrick, 10/1179
    Independence Day, 11/1249–50
    Independence Hall, 11/1250, 11/*1250*
    John Paul Jones, 11/1340
    Lafayette, Marquis de, 12/1383
    major events, 1/*123*
    map, 1/*123*
    Marion, Francis, 13/1517–18
    Paine, Thomas, 15/1857–8
    Revenue Marine, 5/587
    Revere, Paul, 17/2094
    Revolutionary flags, 1/*123*
    Washington, George, 21/2547–8
    Wayne, Anthony, 21/2558–9
American robin, 9/*1037*
American saddle horse, 10/*1205*, 10/1206
American Samoa, 16/1971
American Turtle, 6/636
American Woman Suffrage Association, 21/2600
America's Cup, 17/2100
Ameslan, 18/2223
Amiens Cathedral, 19/*2323*
Amin, Idi, 20/2483
Amino acids, 1/24, 13/1565, 15/1810, 17/2013
Amish, 10/1140
Amistad Dam, 17/2104
Amman, 11/1340
Ammonia, 15/1777
Amoeba, 2/**129**, 2/*129*, 2/145, 17/2017, 17/*2017*, 17/2018
Amoebic dysentery, 17/2018
Amorphous solids, 19/2261
Ampére, André Marie, 2/**129**, 2/*129*
Amperes, 2/129, 7/821
Amphetamines, 1/33, 7/769, 14/1702–3
Amphibians, 2/**128**, 2/**129–31***, 2/*130–1*, 9/1013
    eggs, 7/806
    hearing, 10/166
    in cities, 5/559
    metamorphosis, 13/1570
    molting, 14/1626
Amphibious warfare, 13/1514
Amphineura, 14/1625
Amphitheaters, 20/2420, 20/*2420*
Amplifiers, 20/2448
    masers, 12/1393
Amplitude modulation (AM radio), 17/2045, 17/2051–2
AM radio, 17/2045, 17/2051–2
Amr ibn al-As, 7/810
Amsterdam, 2/**132**, 2/*132*, 14/1742
Amu Darya, 2/195
Amundsen, Roald, 2/**132–3**, 2/*132*, 2/171, 2/209, 4/423, 6/653, 8/893, 15/1795, 18/2177

Anabolism, 13/1565
Anaconda snake, 2/*145*
Anaerobic bacteria, 3/289
Anagni Cathedral, 18/*2125*
Analog machines, 7/826–7
Analog recordings, 17/2073
Analytical chemistry, 5/519
Analytical psychology, 11/1348
Anasazi Indians, 2/215
Anatomy, 2/**133**, 3/342, 3/343, 10/1224
    skeletons, 18/2229–30, 18/*2229–30*
    skin, 18/2232–3, 18/*2232–3*
Anchovy, 8/950
Ancient civilizations, 2/**133–8***, 2/*133–8*
    archaeology, 2/196–8
    architecture, 2/136–7
    armies, 2/224–5
    art, 2/230–2
    astronomy, 2/249–50
    cave dwellers, 4/500
    democracy, 2/137
    education, 7/802–3
    furniture, 9/1024–5
    law, 2/137
    libraries, 12/1425
    literature, 2/136
    mathematics, 13/1533
    medicine, 2/135–6
    money, 2/137
    mosaics, 14/1651
    navies, 14/1726
    painting, 2/136–7
    pens, 16/1896
    perfumes, 16/1899
    philosophy, 2/136
    portraits, 16/1980–1
    prophets, 17/2010–11
    puppets, 17/2031
    science, 2/135–6
    sculpture, 2/136–7
    trade, 20/2443–4
    writing, 2/133–5
Andaman Islands, 8/*889*
Andersen, Hans Christian, 2/**139–40**, 2/*139*, 5/532, 6/717, 8/901, 8/905
Anderson Air Force Base, 10/1123
Anderson, Marian, 2/**140**, 2/*140*
Anderson, Max, 8/893
Anderson, Robert, 8/991
Andes Mountains, 2/**140–1**, 2/*141*, 2/211, 3/364–5, 5/535, 7/800, 14/1671, 16/1903, 16/1946, 19/2268
Andorra, 2/**141**, 2/*141*
Andorra la Vella, 2/141
Andrew, Prince, Duke of York, 7/837
Andromeda, 2/*142*
Andromeda Galaxy, 2/*142*, 21/2500
Andropov, Yuri, 9/1092, 19/2286
Anemia, 15/1810
Anemometers, 21/2563
Aneroid barometers, 3/306, 3/*306*
Anerometers, 21/2593
Anesthesiologists, 13/1555
Anesthetics, 2/**142–3**, 2/*142*, 7/767, 13/1553, 19/2358
Angel Falls, 19/2268, 21/2515, 21/*2553*, 21/*2553*
Angelfish, 20/*2466*

Angelico, Fra, 13/1551, 17/2085
Angel, Jimmy, 21/2515
Angiosperms, 16/1947, 20/2458
Angkor Wat, 11/1352, 11/*1352*, 19/2280
Angle, 2/**143***, 2/*143*
Angler fish, 6/708, 8/941–2, 8/*944*
Anglers, 7/855, 7/860
Anglesey, 21/2539
Angling, 8/945–7, 8/*946–7*
Anglo-Saxon language, 7/860
Anglo-Saxons, 2/**143**, 7/855
Angola, 2/**144**, 2/*144*
Angora goats, 9/1086
Angstrom units, 13/1546
Anhinga, 21/2551
Animals, 2/**145–7***, 2/*145–7*
    Africa, 1/46, 1/*46*
    albino, 1/92
    Australia, 3/267, 3/268–9
    beasts of burden, 20/2449
    camouflage, 4/443
    carbohydrates, 4/462
    carnivores, 4/469–70
    cave, 4/498–9
    circuses, 5/552–4
    in cities, 5/**558–9**
    classification, 2/154–8
    conservation and, 6/639
    deep-sea life, 6/708
    defenses, 2/**148–9***, 2/*148*
    desert, 6/721
    distribution, 2/**149–51**
    domesticated, 7/752–4, 7/*753–4*
    domestication, 4/500
    ecology, 7/793–8
    eggs, 7/806
    evolution, 8/885–8
    eyes, 8/899
    families, 2/**151–2**
    fats and oils, 8/916–17, 8/*917*
    feet, 10/1145–6, 10/*1145–6*
    feral, 7/753
    fish, 8/940–5, 8/*941–5*
    food web, 8/978–9, 8/*979*
    fossils, 8/992–5, 8/*993–5*
    fur, 9/1022–4, 9/*1022–4*
    genetics, 9/1050–3
    growth, 9/1121–2
    hearing, 10/1166–7
    heart, 10/1167–8, 10/*1167–8*
    hibernation, 10/1182–3, 10/*1183*
    homes, 2/**152–4***, 2/*153–4*
    hoofed, 10/1200
    intelligence, 11/1285
    kingdom, 2/**154–8***, 3/341
    migration, 13/1591–4
    monsters, 2/161–2
    movement, 2/**159–60***, 2/*158–60*
    muscles, 14/1675–7, 14/*1675–7*
    myth and legend, 2/**160–3**, 2/*160–3*
    nature study, 14/1721
    navigation, 14/1725
    nervous system, 14/1739–41, 14/*1740*
    North America, 15/1785
    noses, 15/1799
    origins of farming, 1/51–2
    parasites, 16/1875–6
    pest control, 16/1904–5
    pets, 16/1905–7, 16/*1905–7*
    pond life, 16/1973–4
    protective coloring, 17/2011–13
    rare, 17/2063–5, 17/*2063–5*

    regeneration, 17/2077
    reproduction, 17/2086–9
    reptiles, 17/2089–91
    respiration, 17/2092–3
    rodents, 18/2115
    sight, 18/2219–20, 18/*2219–20*
    skeleton, 18/2229–30, 18/*2229–30*
    skin, 18/2232–3, 18/*2232–3*
    sleep, 19/2240
    smell, 19/2241
    South American, 19/2270–1
    speed, 2/158
    symbiosis, 20/2369–70, 20/*2370*
    teeth, 20/2386–8
    terrariums, 20/2410
    territories, 2/154
    tracks, 2/**163–4***, 2/*163–4*
    training, 11/1285
    unusual, 16/1907
    vertebrates, 21/2520–1, 21/*2521*
    veterinary medicine, 21/2522
    voices, 2/**164–5**
    zoology, 22/2647–9
    zoos, 22/2645–7, 22/*2645–7*
    see also individual animals
Animated cartoons, 4/478, 14/1663
    Disney, Walt, 6/740
Animism, 17/2079
Anjouan, 5/617
Ankaratra Mountains, 12/1477
Annam, 21/2525
Annapolis, 5/523, 13/1524, 13/1525, 21/2498
Annapolis Convention, 10/1142
Anne, Queen of England, 2/**165**, 2/*165*
Anne of Austria, consort of Louis XIII, 12/1462
Anne of Cleves, 10/1177
Annelida, 2/156, 22/2620
Anne, Princess Royal, 7/837
Anniversary, 2/**165–6**
Annobón, 7/864
Annual flowers, 9/1038
Annual plants, 8/963
Anoa, 4/403
Anoraks, 7/868
Anselm, Archbishop, 5/534
Antananarivo, 12/1477
Antarctic, 2/**132**, 2/**168–71**, 2/*169–71*, 4/423
    Amundsen, Roald, 2/132–3
    animal life, 2/149, 2/170
    exploration, 2/171
    land, 2/169–70
    life, 16/1964–5
    major events, 2/171
    map, 2/*169*
    plant life, 2/170
    Scott, Robert, 18/2176–7
    snow, 2/169–70
Antares, 2/**172**
Anteaters, 2/**172–3**, 2/*172*
Antelope, 1/46, 2/**173–4**, 2/*173–4*
Anthems, national, 14/1705, 14/*1705*
Anthers, 8/961, 16/1941
Anthony, Susan B., 19/2326, 21/2600
Anthozoans, 6/658
Anthracite, 5/586
Anthropologists:
    Heyerdahl, Thor, 10/1182
    Leakey family, 12/1405
Anthropology, 2/**174–6**
    cultures, 6/685–6

Antibiotics, 2/176–7, 7/768
Antibodies, 1/101, 2/177, 6/739,
    10/1244
Anticosti, 13/1518
Anticyclones, 21/2562–3
Antidotes, 16/1961
Antietam, battle of, 7/840, 13/1525
Antigen, 2/177
Antigrams, 21/2603
Antigua and Barbuda, 21/2570
Antihistamine, 1/101
Antila, 21/2569
Anti-Lebanon, 12/1409
Antilles, 21/2569
Antimatter, 2/177
Antiochus, King of Syria, 10/1148
Antiparticles, 2/177
Antiques, 2/178–9*, 2/178–9,
    9/1024–7
Anti-Semitism, 11/1336
Antiseptic, 2/179, 12/1445
Anti-slavery movement, 1/15
Antlers, 6/709, 6/710, 10/1202,
    10/1202
Antoinette Perry Award, 1/29
Antonius Pius, 18/2131
Ants, 2/166–8*, 2/166–8
Anus, 6/731
Aorta, 5/550, 10/1168
Apache Indians, 1/20, 2/179–80,
    2/180, 2/215, 2/217, 3/253,
    4/476, 5/588, 9/1072, 11/1263,
    11/1271, 15/1758
Apache War, 1/120
Apartheid, 18/2157, 19/2267
Apartments, 10/1215, 10/1215
Apatosaurus, 6/734, 8/994
Apennine Mountains, 18/2160
Apes, 2/180–2, 2/180–2
Apocrypha, 3/335
Apogee, 15/1838
Apollo, 6/641, 9/1088, 9/1113,
    13/1584, 13/1585, 14/1696,
    14/1696, 14/1697, 17/2011
Apollo space program, 1/94, 2/224,
    4/458, 5/597, 7/783, 8/894,
    9/1057, 14/1646, 17/2110,
    17/2112, 19/2291–2, 19/2292,
    19/2293, 19/2294, 19/2295
Apongeton, 2/189
Apostles, 2/182–3, 2/183, 5/546
Apostrophe, 17/2030
Appalachian Mountains, 2/183–4,
    2/184, 11/1360–2, 13/1522,
    13/1524, 14/1668, 15/1754,
    15/1782, 15/1787, 16/1893,
    18/2217, 19/2274, 20/2403,
    21/2491, 21/2516, 21/2574
Appalachian Trail, 2/183
Apparitions, ghosts, 9/1075
Appeal courts, 6/667
Appeals, trials, 20/2464
Appendix, human body, 6/731
Appert, Nicholas, 8/977
Apples, 9/1018
Appleseed, Johnny, 2/184–5, 2/184,
    8/971, 12/1411
Applied arts, 2/229–30
Applied science, 18/2174
Appomattox, 21/2533
Apprentices, 2/185, 2/185, 4/465,
    7/803, 10/1125
Apra Harbor, 10/1123

April, 2/185–6
    events in, 2/186
April Fool's Day, 2/185–6
Apse, 4/492
Aquaculture, 15/1817
Aqualungs, 6/668, 15/1820, 18/2177
Aquaplaning, 21/2555
Aquariums, 2/186–90*, 2/186–9
    freshwater, 2/188–9
    making, 2/186–8
    marine, 2/190
    tropical fish, 20/2465–6, 20/2466
Aquatic life, ponds, 16/1973–4,
    16/1974
Aquatic plants, 16/1945
Aqueducts, 18/2119, 18/2119,
    21/2556
Aquidneck Island, 17/2097, 17/2097
Aquinas, St Thomas, 2/190,
    16/1914, 16/1915
Aquino, Corazon, 16/1914
Arab horses, 10/1204, 10/1206
Arabia, 2/190–4, 2/190–4
    countries, 2/191, 2/192–3
    geography, 2/190–1
    history, 2/191–2
    life in, 2/193–4
    map, 2/191
Arabian camels, 4/439, 4/440
Arabian Desert, 6/720
Arabian Nights, 2/194
Arabic, 2/194–5, 2/195, 12/1389
Arabic numerals, 2/212, 13/1533,
    15/1807
Arab-Israeli wars, 7/807–8
Arabs:
    African, 1/47, 1/48
    Cairo, 4/430
    Crusades, 6/678–80
    Libya, 12/1428–9
    mathematics, 13/1533
    Middle East, 13/1589
    Palestine, 13/1590
    Saudi Arabia, 18/2166–7
    science, 18/2172
Arachnids, 19/2312, 19/2312
Aragon, 19/2301
Aral Sea, 2/195
Aramaic, 3/336
Aramid rope, 18/2137
Arapaho Indians, 1/100, 5/602,
    11/1271, 14/1732, 18/2229
Ararat, Mount, 20/2476
Araucanian Indians, 5/536, 6/633,
    12/1388
Arawak, 4/468
Arawak Indians, 10/1133, 17/2027,
    21/2570
Arbela, battle of, 3/319
Arboretums, 3/374
Arbor Tree Day, 14/1732
Archaeopteryx, 3/344, 3/349, 3/349
Archaeterium, 13/1499
Archangel, 18/2147
Archbishops, 18/2121
Arch bridges, 4/390, 4/390
Archeologists, 2/137–8, 2/175, 2/196
    Leakey family, 12/1405
Archeology, 2/196–8, 2/1968
    cave dwellers, 4/500
Archery, 2/198–9, 2/199, 18/2214
    bow and arrows, 4/377
Archimedes, 2/135, 2/200, 2/200
Archimedes screw, 2/200

Architecture, 2/200–6*, 2/201–6
    American Indian, 11/1263
    ancient civilizations, 2/136–7
    building materials, 4/405–7,
        4/405–7
    castles, 4/483–4, 4/483–4
    cathedrals, 4/491–3
    construction, 6/645–9
    Empire State Building, 7/842
    Gothic, 9/1093–4, 9/1093–4
    houses, 10/1213–15, 10/1213–15
    materials, 2/202–4
    modern, 2/204–6
    pagodas, 15/1857, 15/1857
    Roman, 18/2119
    Romanesque, 18/2124
    shelters, 18/2203–5
    stained glass, 19/2323, 19/2323
    styles, 2/201, 2/202–4
    temples, 20/2402
    Wright, Frank Lloyd, 22/2622
Arch of Constantine, Rome, 2/201
Arc lights, 7/801
Arctic, 2/207–210*, 2/208–10,
    10/1179–80
    animals, 2/149–50
    Eskimos, 7/867–8, 7/867–8
    life, 16/1964–5
    major events, 2/209
    map, 2/207
    North Pole, 15/1794, 15/1794
    sailors in, 2/209–10
    tundra, 20/2473
Arctic fox, 8/998, 8/998, 16/1965
Arctic sea blubber, 11/1328
Arctic skua, 13/1593
Arctic terns, 10/1129, 13/1592,
    13/1593, 16/1965
Arctic warblers, 13/1593
Ardennias horses, 10/1204
Area, 6/732
    measurement, 13/1545, 13/1546
Arecibo, 17/2050
Ares, 9/1088
Argall, Samuel, 6/712
Argentina, 2/210–11, 2/210–11
    Buenos Aires, 4/402–3
    Falkland Islands, 8/907
    Perón, Juan, 16/1900
Argentite, 18/2225
Argo, 11/1324
Argon, 1/57
Argos, 10/1181
Argrand, Aimé, 12/1435
Arias, 15/1834
Arikara Indians, 19/2277
Arista, Mariano, 13/1572
Aristocracy, 9/1095
Aristophanes, 2/136, 9/1116
Aristotle, 1/96, 2/136, 2/211–12,
    2/211, 2/250, 7/828, 9/1113,
    9/1116, 22/2648
Arithmetic, 2/212–15, 2/213–14
    binary system, 3/340
    calculators, 4/432–3
    decimal numbers, 6/706
    fractions, 9/999
    numbers, 15/1806–8
    percentages, 16/1897
    quipus, 11/1248
    sets, 18/2192–3
Arizona, 2/215–18, 2/215–16
    employment, 2/217–18
    Grand Canyon, 9/1099

history, 2/215–17
    land, 2/215
    map, 2/216
    natural resources, 2/217
    state emblems, 2/216
Ark, 13/1524
Arkansas, 2/218–20, 2/218–20
    climate, 2/218
    employment, 2/220
    history, 2/220
    land, 2/218
    map, 2/219
    natural resources, 2/218–20
    state emblems, 2/219
Arkansas River, 2/218, 2/220
Arkansas River Navigation System,
    15/1828
Arktika, 15/1974
Arkwright, Richard, 19/2313–14,
    19/2313
Arlington, 20/2414
Arlington National Cemetery,
    11/1359, 11/1360, 20/2433
Armada, Spanish, 7/757–8, 7/837,
    7/854, 14/1727, 16/1912
Armadillo, 2/220–1, 2/221
Armagh, 15/1793
Armenia, 19/2282
Armenians, 20/2373
Armies, 2/224–7, 2/225–7
    ancient, 2/224–5
    good soldiers, 2/225–6
    US Army, 2/226–7
Armor, 2/221–3, 2/221–2, 5/580
    animal, 2/148
    coats of arms, 5/587
    knights, 12/1371
    ships, 14/1727–8
    tanks, 20/2377–8, 20/2377
Armored vehicles, 2/223
Armour, Jean, 4/416
Arms and weapons, 21/2559–60,
    21/2559–60
    control, 6/736
    disarmament, 6/736
Arms Control and Disarmament
    Agency, 21/2491
Armstrong, Louis, 2/223, 2/223,
    11/1325, 11/1325
Armstrong, Neil, 1/94, 2/224, 2/224,
    5/597, 8/894, 14/1644, 14/1646,
    19/2290, 19/2292
Armstrong, William, 5/535
Army, see US Army
Army ants, 2/168
Arnold, Benedict, 1/101, 20/2456
Arnold, Ethan, 1/126
Arnold, Henry H. 'Hap', 1/64
Arnolfini, Giovanni, 13/1519
Arras, 20/2380
Arrow poison frogs, 2/131, 9/1014
Arrows, 2/198–9, 4/377, 4/377
Art, 2/227–30
    abstract, 1/18–20, 1/19–20
    American Indian, 11/1258–60,
        11/1258–60
    ancient, 2/230–2
    applied, 2/229–30
    Baroque, 3/307
    commercial, 5/608–9
    Dadaism, 6/690–1
    drawing, 7/760–2, 7/761–2

(continued)

Dutch, 7/775–6
enamelling, 7/842–3, 7/*842*
engraving, 7/870, 7/870–1, 7/*870*
etching, 7/869–70, 7/*869–70*
fine, 2/229–30
Flemish, 7/776
folk, 8/968–9, 8/*968–9*
galleries, 2/**238★**, 19/2241–2
graphic, 9/1102–3, 9/*1102–3*
history, 2/**230–4**
Impressionism, 10/1245–6,
    10/*1245–6*
Louvre, 12/1468, 12/*1468*
medieval, 13/1588–9
modern, 14/1620–1, 14/*1260–1*
museums, 2/**238★**, 14/1679
oriental, 15/1845–7, 15/*1845–7*
painting, 15/1859–63, 15/*1859–63*
photography, 16/1917–20,
    16/*1917–20*
portraits, 16/1980–1, 16/*1981*
Realism, 17/2068
Renaissance, 17/2083–5
Rococo, 17/2113–14, 17/*2113–14*
Roman, 18/2119–20, 18/*2119–20*
Romanesque, 18/2124–5,
    18/*2124–5*
Romanticism, 18/2127–8
sculpture, 18/2178–80, 18/*2178–90*
stained glass, 19/2323, 19/*2323*
surrealism, 19/2359–60, 19/*2359–60*
symbolism, 20/2370–1, 20/*2370–1*
symmetry, 20/2371
Artemis, 6/641, 14/1697
    temple of, 18/2193, 18/*2193*
Arteries, 3/359, 3/*359*, 5/550–1
Arterioles, 5/551
Artesian wells, 21/2567, 21/*2567*
Arthropods, 2/156, 5/504, 6/680
Arthur, Chester, 2/**235–6**, 2/*235*,
    9/1043
Arthur, King, 2/**236**, 2/*236*, 11/1368,
    12/1411, 21/2539
Articles of Confederation, 1/116,
    2/**236–7**, 6/652, 10/1142, 21/2487
Articulators, 19/2307–8
Artifacts, 2/196
Artificial fibres, 5/521, 5/*521*
Artificial respiration, 2/**237**, 2/*237*
Artigas, José Gervasio, 21/2502
Aruba, 20/*2462*, 21/2569
Arum, 16/*1963*
Aryans, 11/1253–4
Asam family, 17/2113
Asbestos, 13/1598
Asgard, 14/1696
Asheville, 15/1788
Ashford, Evelyn, 3/*356*
Ashley River, 19/2274
Ashton-on-Clun, 6/696
Ash tree, 20/*2461*
Ashurbanipal, King, 2/246
Asia, 2/**238–45**, 2/*239–45*
    ancient, 2/244
    animals, 2/239–42
    climate, 2/239
    land, 2/238–9
    languages, 2/242–3
    map, 2/*240*
    modern, 2/244–5
    nations, 2/241
    natural resources, 2/243–4
    people, 2/242
    physical statistics, 6/650

religions, 2/243
    Southeast, 19/2280–1, 19/*2280*
Asian Elephants, 7/831–3, 7/*831*
Asian red sheep, 18/2201
Asiatic buffalo, 4/403
Asiatic jackel, 11/1315
Asoka, 11/1254
Asorbic acid, 1/24
Assassination, 2/**245**
    Gandhi, Indira, 9/1035
    Gandhi, Mahatma, 9/1035–6
    Kennedy, John Fitzgerald, 11/1359
    Kennedy, Robert Fitzgerald,
        11/1360
    Lincoln, Abraham, 12/1441
    McKinley, William, 13/1544
Assateague Island, 10/1207
Assembly lines, 3/273–6, 13/1507,
    13/*1507*
Assiniboin Indians, 13/1503,
    18/2164
Assisi, 9/1002
Associated Press (AP), 11/1342–3
Associate's degrees, 5/596
Assur, 2/246
Assyria, 2/134, 2/**246**, 2/*246*
    art, 2/246
Astaire, Fred, 6/696, 14/1663
Asteroids, 2/**246–7**, 2/*246*, 19/2260
Astigmatism, 8/899
Astoria, 15/1842
Astor, John Jacob, 9/1024, 10/1219,
    15/1842, 15/1844
Astrakhan, 4/481
Astrolabes, 14/*1724*
Astrology, 2/**247★**, 2/*247*
    fortune-telling, 8/992
Astronautics, 1/40
Astronauts, 2/224, 2/**248**, 2/*248*
    see also individuals eg Armstrong,
    Neil
Astronomers:
    Bowditch, Nathaniel, 4/377–8
    Brahe, Tycho, 4/381
    Copernicus, Nicolaus, 6/657
    Galileo Galilei, 9/1031–2
    Halley, Edmond, 10/1140
    Herschel Family, 10/1181–2
    Hubble, Edwin, 10/1217
    Kepler, Johannes, 11/1364
Astronomy, 2/**248–52★**, 2/*249–52*,
    13/1570–1
    ancient, 2/249–50
    asteroids, 2/246–7
    black holes, 3/356–7
    comets, 5/607–8
    constellations, 6/641–2
    eclipses, 7/792–3, 7/*792–3*
    major events, 2/251
    Milky Way, 13/1594
    modern, 2/250–1
    moon, 14/1644–8, 14/*1645–8*
    North Star, 15/1795
    observatories, 15/1812–14,
        15/*1813–14*
    orbits, 15/1837–8
    planetariums, 16/1936–7, 16/*1937*
    radio, 17/2050–1, 17/*2050–1*
    satellites, 18/2164–5
    solar system, 19/2256–61,
        19/*2256–60*
    space, 19/2287
    stars, 19/2326–7, 19/*2326–7*
    Sun, 19/2353, 19/*2353*

telescopes, 20/2393–5, 20/*2393–5*
    universe, 2/251–2, 21/2499–2501
Astrophysics, 15/1813
Asunción, 16/1874, 16/*1875*, 19/2273
Aswan High Dam, 1/21, 7/807,
    15/1776
Atacama, 6/720, 19/2268
Atacama Desert, 5/535, 5/*536*
Atahualpa, 11/1248, 16/1936
Atakoras Mountains, 3/330
Atatürk, 15/1850, 15/*1850*, 20/2476
Athabscan, 3/**253**
Athena, 9/1088, 20/2465
Athene, 14/1697
Athens, 3/**253–4**, 3/*253*, 9/1110,
    9/1112–13
    Acropolis, 1/26, 1/*26*
Athletics:
    dashes, 20/2440
    distance runs, 20/2441
    hurdling, 20/2441, 20/*2442*
    middle distances, 20/2440–1
    Olympic Games, 15/1830–1
    Owens, Jesse, 15/1851
    relay races, 20/2441
    Thorpe, Jim, 20/2423
    track and field events, 20/2439–43,
        20/*2439–43*
    walking races, 20/2441
Atlantic Charter, 20/2485
Atlantic City, 15/1756
Atlantic Coastal Plain, 13/1522,
    13/1524, 15/1787, 16/1893,
    19/2274, 21/2530
Atlantic Missile Range, 4/458
Atlantic Ocean, 3/**254–5**, 3/*254–5*
Atlantis, 3/**255**, 3/*255*, 4/454, 21/2535
Atlas, 9/1075
Atlases, 3/**256**, 3/*256*
    gazeteers, 9/1047
Atlas Mountains, 1/43, 14/1648,
    20/2473
Atlas rockets, 17/2111
Atmosphere, 3/**257**, 3/*257*, 7/781,
    7/784
    acid rain, 1/22–3
    aerosols, 1/39
    air pressure, 1/77–8
    barometers, 3/306
    climate, 5/575
    clouds, 5/*581–3*
    fog, 8/967–8
    greenhouse effect, 1/73–4, 1/*74*
    humidity, 10/1225–6
    oxygen, 15/1852–3
    planets, 19/2257
    pollution, 1/72–5, 1/*72–5*, 16/1969,
        16/*1970*
    pressure, 17/1999, 17/*1999*
    rainbows, 17/2060, 17/*2060*
    sky, 18/2234
Atmospheric engines, 7/848
Atolls, 11/1308, 15/1854, 16/1972,
    18/*2183*
Atomic bombs, 20/2471
    test sites, 15/ 1743, 15/1758
Atomic clocks, 5/578
Atomic energy, 15/1803–5
Atomic fuel, 9/1019, 9/*1020*
Atomic numbers, 7/829
Atomic physics, 16/1923
Atomic radiation, geiger counters,
    9/1049, 9/*1049*
Atomic weights, 7/829–30

Atoms, 3/**258–60**, 3/*258–60*, 13/1536
    antimatter, 2/177
    chemistry, 5/519–20, 5/521
    particle accelerators, 16/1880
    radioactivity, 17/2048–9, 17/*2048–9*
Aton, 7/809
Atrophine, drugs, 7/768
Atropos, 8/915
Attar of roses, 18/2138
Attica Correctional Facility, 17/2007
Attila the Hun, 3/**260**, 3/*260*
Attorney General, 4/425
    Kennedy, Robert Fitzgerald,
        11/1359
Attornies, 12/1401
Attucks, Crispus, 1/124, 3/353, 3/372–3
Aubrey, John, 19/2336
Aubusson carpets, 4/474
Auckland, 15/1768, 15/1769
Audiometer, 3/329
Audio signals, 7/825–6
Auditorium, 20/2420
Audits, 1/22
Audubon, John James, 3/**260–1**,
    3/*261*, 16/1929
Audubon Society, 6/640
Augean stables, 10/1181
Augite, 13/1597
Augsburg, 10/*1125*
    Peace of, 9/1065
Augurs, 17/2011
August, 3/**261–2**
    special events in, 3/261
Augustan Age, 2/165
Augustine, Saint, 14/1629
Augustus, Emperor, 3/261, 4/477,
    15/1802, 18/*2120*
Auks, 18/2181
Aurochs, 4/493, 13/1501
Aurora, 3/**262**, 3/*262*
Aurora australis, 3/257, 3/262
Aurora borealis, 3/257, 3/262
Austen, Jane, 3/**262–3**, 3/*263*,
    15/1801
Austin, Stephen F., 20/2412
Austin, Texas, 20/2412
Austin, Tracy, 19/2317
Australia, 3/**263–8**, 3/*263–8*, 6/653
    aborigines, 1/16–17, 1/*17*, 3/265
    Commonwealth, 5/610
    Coral sea, 6/659
    culture, 3/267–8
    early history, 3/265–6
    economy, 3/266–7
    education, 3/267
    Great Barrier Reef, 9/1106–7,
        9/*1107*
    kangaroos, 11/1352–3, 11/*1353*
    koalas, 12/1374–5, 12/*1375*
    land, 3/263–5
    mammals, 3/267, 3/268–9
    map, 3/*264*
    Murray-Darling Rivers, 14/1675
    physical statistics, 6/650
    sport, 3/267–8
    Sydney, 20/2369, 20/*2369*
    wildlife, 3/267, 3/268–9
Australian ballot, 7/815
Austral Islands, 16/1971
Australoids, 1/16
Australopithecus, 2/176, 10/1220–1,
    10/*1220*, 10/1222, 12/1405
Austria, 3/**269–70**

Austrian composers
Haydn, Franz Joseph, 10/1161
Mahler, Gustav, 12/1484
Mendel, Gregor, 13/1561–2
Mozart, Wolfgang Amadeus, 14/1673
Schubert, Franz, 18/2170–1
Strauss, Johann, 19/2340
Austrian Imperial crown, 6/677
Austro-Hungarian Empire, 3/279, 6/689
Authorized Version of the Bible, 3/336
Authors *see* Writers
Autobiography, 3/270*
Autographs, 3/270–1, 3/271, 5/594
Automatic pilot, 1/68
Automatic pistols, 10/1132
Automatic transmission, automobiles, 7/765
Automation, 3/271–2, 3/271
manufacturing, 13/1507
robots, 17/2107–8, 17/2107
Automatons, 14/1693
Automobiles, 3/272–7*, 3/272–7, 20/2451
development, 3/272–6
diesel engines, 6/728–9
driving, 7/764–6, 7/764–6
Duryea, Charles and Frank, 7/774
Ford, Henry, 8/985
future, 20/2453–4
gasoline, 9/10466
hydraulic systems, 10/1230
important events, 3/274
insurance, 11/1284
modern, 3/277
operation, 3/276–7
parts of, 7/765–6
tires, 20/2428–9
traffic planning, 20/2445–6
Autonomic nervous system, 14/1741
Auto racing, 3/278, 3/278
Auto-rack cars, 17/2054
Autumn, 3/279*, 3/279
Autumnal equinox, 18/2186
Avalanche, 3/279–80, 3/279
Avenues, 19/2341
Average, statistics, 19/2331
Avery, Oswald T., 9/1052
Aviation, 3/280–2, 3/280–3
aircraft speeds, 3/282
balloons, 3/280, 3/280, 3/297–9
history, 3/280–2
Lindbergh, Charles Augustus, 12/1441–2
modern, 3/282
Avicenna, 13/1553, 13/1553
Avignon, 4/390, 18/2121
Avoirdupois measurement, 13/1546
Avril, Jane, 20/2436, 20/2436
AWACS, 17/2043
Awards, 12/1451–2
medals and decorations, 13/1550–1, 13/1550–1
Nobel Prizes, 15/1778–9, 15/1778–9
orders, 13/1550
Axial flow pumps, 17/2029
Axioms, 13/1533
Axles, 12/1475
Axolotl, 2/131, 18/2155
Axons, 14/1739
Axum (Aksum), 7/871

Ayacucho, 3/364
Ayers Rock, 1/17, 3/263–5, 3/268
Aymara Indians, 3/365, 14/1681, 16/1904
Ayrshire cows, 4/394
Azaleas, 18/2217
Azerbaijan, 19/2282
Azov, 16/1907
Aztec Indians, 3/284, 3/284, 3/295, 6/637, 6/662, 8/951, 11/1267, 13/1575
calendars, 4/434
myths, 14/1697
Azurite, 13/1597

Bb

B-52 Stratofortress, 1/62
Babbage, Charles, 3/285–6, 3/285, 5/622
Babe, Bunyon's ox, 2/163
Babies, incubators, 11/1249, 11/1249
Baboons, 14/1636, 14/1637
Babur, 11/1254
Babylon, Hanging Gardens, 18/2193, 18/2193
Babylonia, 3/286–7, 3/286, 11/1335
education, 7/802
kings, 11/1368
law, 2/137
science, 18/2171
Babylonians, 2/134, 13/1565
Baccalaureus, 13/1588
Bach, Anna, 3/287
Bachelor's degrees, 5/596
Bach family, 3/287
Bach, Hans, 3/287
Bach, Johann Ambrosius, 3/287
Bach, Johann Christian, 3/287, 16/1925
Bach, Johann Sebastian, 3/287, 3/287, 5/544, 17/2114
Bach, Karl Philipp Emanuel, 3/287
Bach, Maria, 3/287
Bach, Veit, 3/287
Bacilli, 3/288
Bacillus subtilis, 3/289
Backbone Mountain, 13/1524
Backbones, vertebrates, 21/2520–1
Backstitch, 18/2194
Backstroke, 20/2365, 20/2365
Backswimmer bug, 4/405
Back to the Future, 1/27
Bacon, Francis, 3/287–8, 3/287, 5/589, 9/1040, 18/2173
Bacon, Francis T., 9/1020
Bacon, Roger, 3/288, 3/288, 8/896
Bacon's Castle, Virginia, 1/113
Bacteria, 3/288–9, 3/288–9, 5/501
antibodies, 2/176–7
antiseptics, 2/179
bioluminescence, 3/343
canned foods, 8/977
diseases, 6/737, 6/737
fermentation, 8/922
fever, 8/926
plant diseases, 16/1943
stains, 7/811
Bacteriologists, 3/288
Fleming, Sir Alexander, 8/953
Pasteur, Louis, 16/1883–4
Bacteriology, 3/343

Bactrian camels, 4/439, 4/440
Bader, Walton, 6/673
Badgers, 10/1183, 21/2560, 21/2561
tracks, 2/164
Badlands, 3/290, 3/290
North Dakota, 15/1790
South Dakota, 9/1056
Badminton, 3/290–1, 3/290
Baekeland, Leo Hendrik, 16/1954
Baez, Joan, 8/973
Baffin, William, 2/209
Baga, 10/1125
Baganda, 20/2483
Bagpipes, 3/291, 3/291
Bahamas, 21/2569, 21/2570
Bahatu, 4/417
Bahia, 6/724
Baikal, Lake, 9/1107, 12/1385, 19/2282
Bailey, James A., 3/305, 5/553
Baird, John Logie, 3/291–2, 3/291–2, 20/2395, 20/2398, 20/2398
Baja California, 13/1573
Bakelite, 16/1954
Baker Island, 16/1971
Baker, Janet, 15/1835
Baker Street Irregulars, 7/756
Baking and bakeries, 3/292–4*, 3/292, 6/655
commercial bakeries, 3/293
flour making, 8/960
yeast, 22/2633
Bakongo, 6/628
Bakonja, 20/2483
Baku, 4/481, 19/2284
Balaguer, Joaquín, 21/2571
Balakirev, Mili, 17/2103
Balaklava, battle of, 6/674–5
Balalaika, 19/2344
Balance, gyroscopes, 10/1134–5, 10/1135
Balance of payments, 11/1292
Balance of power, 11/1290
Balances, 18/2167, 21/2565
Balance wheel, clocks, 5/578
Balanchine, George, 3/297
Balante, 10/1126
Balboa, 16/1868
Balboa, Vasco Núñez de, 3/294*, 3/294, 6/637, 8/893, 15/1857, 16/1935
Balchen, Bernt, 4/423
Bald cypress, 6/633
Bald eagles, 3/347, 3/347, 3/348, 6/639, 17/2063
Balder, 14/1695
Baldness, 10/1138
Baldpates, 3/347
Baldwin, James, 3/294–5, 3/294
Balearic Islands, 19/2298
Baleen whales, 21/2578
Balers, 8/909
Balfour Declaration, 15/1865
Bali, 11/1272, 14/1695
Balkan Mountains, 4/409
Ballads, 8/972, 16/1960
Ballast tanks, 4/412
Ballet, 3/295–7, 3/295–7, 6/696
Fonteyn, Dame Margot, 8/973
history, 3/296
learning the steps, 3/295–6
modern, 3/296–7
Nijinsky, Vaslav, 15/1775
Pavlova, Anna, 16/1886

Ballet Folklorico de Mexico, 3/297, 8/970
Ballet Russe, 3/296–7
Ballet West, 3/297
Ballistic missiles, 13/1608–9
Ball lightning, 12/1437
Balloons, 1/78, 3/280, 3/280, 3/297–9, 3/297–9
Ballot boxes, 7/814
Ballot papers, 7/814
Ballpoint pens, 16/1896, 16/1896
Ballroom dancing, 6/697, 6/697
Balls, 3/295
elasticity, 7/813, 7/813
Balsam fir, 6/632
Baltazar Carlos, Prince, 21/2513
Baltic Sea, 3/299, 3/299
Baltic-White Sea Canal, 4/454
Baltimore, 5/523, 13/1522, 13/1524, 13/1525
Baltimore and Ohio Railroad, 17/2055, 17/2056
Baluchitherium, 2/174, 13/1499
Baluhya, 11/1363
Bamako, 12/1493
Bamba, 20/2483
Bambara, 12/1493
Bamboo, 9/1103, 9/1104, 9/1122, 16/1937, 16/1939
Bambuti, 17/2033
Bamian, 1/42
Bamiléké, 4/442
Bamoun, 4/442
Bananas, 9/1017, 9/1018
Band Aid, 8/908
Bands (musical), 15/1838–40
Sousa, John Philip, 19/2266
Banff National Park, 1/90, 1/92, 12/1385, 14/1713
Bangdung Conference (1959), 5/545
Bangkok, 20/2402, 20/2417, 20/2417
Bangladesh, 3/299–300, 3/299–300, 11/1255, 15/1864
Bangui, 5/505
Banjos, 19/2344
Banjul, 9/1033
Bank of North America, 3/301
Bank of San Giorgio, Genoa, 3/301
Banks and Banking, 3/300–2, 3/300–2
borrowing, 3/301
history, 3/300–1
paying, 3/301
saving, 3/301, 18/2167
Banneker, Benjamin, 3/302
Bannister, Roger, 20/2440–1
Bannockburn, battle of, 4/399, 7/804
Bannock Indians, 10/1239
Banteng, 4/496
Banting, Sir Frederick, 3/302–3
Bantu languages, 3/376
Bantus, 1/47, 1/47, 2/144, 19/2362
Banyan tree, 20/2460
Baptism, 17/2081
Baptist Church, 17/2013
Baraboo, Wisconsin, 5/553
Barbados, 21/2569, 21/2570, 21/2571
Barbarossa, 16/1934
Barbary apes, 14/1635, 14/1636, 14/1637
Barbary Coast, 3/303, 3/303
Barbecuing, 6/655
Barbells, 21/2565
Barbers, 1/38

Barbiturates, 7/768, 7/769, 14/1703
Barbuda, 21/2571
Barca, Hamilcar, 10/1147–8
Bar code, 3/303, 3*303*
Bardeen, John, 3/304, 3/*304*, 20/*2447*
Bare-back bronc riding, 18/2116
Bar examinations, 12/1401
Baritones, 18/2227
Bark, 3/304–5*, 3/*304–5*, 16/1940, 20/2462
Barkers, 4/469
Barkerville Historical Park, 4/394
Barley, 6/659, 9/1097
Bar mitzvah, 11/1345, 11/*1345*
Barnacles, 6/681–2, 6/*681*
Barnard, Christian, 10/1168
Barn owls, 15/1852, 15/*1852*
Barnstormers, 3/281
Barnum and Bailey Circus, 3/305, 5/553
Barnum, Phineas T., 3/305–6, 3/*305*, 5/553
Barometers, 1/77, 3/306*, 3/*306*, 17/*1999*, 21/2563
Barons, 15/1780
Baroque period, 3/307–8
  architecture, 2/201
  music, 3/287
Barre, 21/2516
Barrel cactus, 4/428, 6/*720*
Barrel organs, 14/1693
Barrett, Peter J., 2/171, 16/1964
Barrie, James M., 3/308, 3/*308*
Barrier bars, 18/2183
Barrier beaches, 18/2183
Barrie, Sir James, 5/533
Barringer meteorite crater, 13/*1571*
Barrymore Family, 1/27, 2/228, 3/308–9, 3/*309*
Barter, 5/592, 14/1630, 19/2337, 20/2444
Bartholdi, Frédéric Auguste, 19/2332
Bartholomew Fair, 8/902
Bartók, Béla, 10/1228
Bartolommeo, Fra, 17/2085
Barton, Clara, 3/309, 3/*309*, 17/2074
Basa, 4/442
Basal metabolism, 13/1566
Bascule bridges, 4/389–90, 4/*390*
Baseball, 3/310–13, 3/*310–12*, 19/*2317*
  Babe, Ruth, 18/2150
  Gehrig, Lou, 9/1049
  history, 3/310
  how to play, 3/310–12
  Little League, 12/1453, 12/*1453*
  records, 3/312
  Robinson, Jackie, 17/2106
  terms in, 3/311
  winning, 3/312–13
Bases, 1/23–4
Basic English, 21/2499
Basilicas, 4/491–2
  Roman, 18/2119, 18/2124
Basilisk, 2/162
Basil, St, 18/*2121*
Basketball, 3/313–15, 3/*313–14*, 18/2223, 19/2316
  common terms, 3/315
  playing on court, 3/313–14
  practice and fun, 3/314–215
  records, 3/315
  scoring, 3/314

Basketry, American Indian, 11/1258
Basking sharks, 18/2199
Basotho, 12/1418
Basque, 19/2298
Bassa, 12/1422
Basses, 18/2227
Basse-Terre, 21/2572
Bassoons, 21/2603
Bass viol, 19/2343–4
Bast, 3/305
Bastet, 7/*809*
Bastille, 9/1009, 9/1011, 17/*2007*
Basting stitch, 18/2194
Basuto, 12/1418
Basutoland *see* Lesotho
Bateke, 6/626
Baths, Roman, 18/2119, 18/2132
Bathyscapes, 8/893, 15/1820
Bathyspheres, 15/1820
Batista, Fulgencio, 4/484–5, 6/684
Bats, 3/316–17, 3/*316–17*, 13/1497
Batteries, 3/317, 3/*317–18*
Battering rams, 4/484
Battery hens, 17/*1991*
Battle of Britain, 22/2613, 22/*2614*
Battlefield parks, 14/1709
Battlements, 4/483
Battles, 3/318
  see also individual places eg Lexicon, Battle of
Battleships, 14/1728, 14/1729, 14/*1730*
Battle y Ordóñez, José, 21/2502
Batu Khan, 18/2145
Batwa, 4/417
Bauhaus, 2/205, 2/*205*
Baum, Frank L., 3/318, 3/*318*
Bauxite, 13/1567
Bay Area Rapid Transit (BART), 19/2349
Bayeux Tapestry, 14/1735, 20/*2380*
Bayonets, 20/2368
Bayous, 12/1464
Bay of Pigs, 6/684
Bayreuth, 21/2538
Bays, 18/2183
Bazaars, 4/430
B.C., 4/434, 11/1331
Beaches, 18/2182–3
  sandy, 18/2158
Beaded lizards, 12/1456
Beads, American Indian, 11/1260
Beagle, H.M.S., 6/699, 18/2173
Beam bridges, 4/390, 4/*390*
Beamon, Robert, 20/2440
Beanes, William, 19/2328
Beards, 10/1139–40
Beard, Thomas, 18/2213
Bear River, 17/2105
Bears, 3/320–1, 3/*321–2*, 10/1183
Beast of Baluchistan, 13/1499
Beasts of burden, 20/2449
Beatles, The, 16/1978
Beatrix, Queen of the Netherlands, 14/1742
Beaufort, Duke of, 3/291
Beaufort, Sir Francis, 21/2593
Beaumont, 20/2414
Beauregard, Pierre, 5/567, 8/991
Beaver hats, 9/1024
Beaver Indians, 3/253
Beavers, 2/152, 3/321–2, 3/*321–2*
  lodges, 3/322, 3/*322*
Bebop, 11/1325

Bechuanaland *see* Botswana
Becket, Thomas á, 3/322–3, 3/*322*, 10/1176
Becknell, William, 18/2161
Beckwourth, James P., 5/604
Becquerel, Antoine Henri, 6/686
Bedbugs, 4/404, 11/*1279*
Bedloe's Island, 19/2332
Bedouins, 1/47, 2/*194*, 14/1649, 15/1781, 20/2373, 20/*2408*, 20/*2474*
Beds, 9/*1026*
Beebread, 3/324
Beech, 20/*2461*
Beecher, Henry Ward, 19/2339
Beecher, Lyman, 19/2339
Beechnuts, 15/1810
Beef, 13/1547
Beef cattle, 4/494–5
Bee flies, 8/966
Bee-killer wasps, 11/*1280*
Beer, 1/93
Bees, 3/323–5, 3/*323–4*
  bumblebees, 3/324
  honeybees, 3/323–4
  nests, 2/153
  solitary bees, 3/325
  stingless bees, 3/324–5
Beeswax, 21/2558
Beethoven, Ludwig van, 3/269, 3/325, 3/*325*, 5/544, 10/*1161*, 16/1924
Beetles 3/325–7*, 3/*325–7*
Beets, 9/*1040*
Begin, Menachem, 15/1779
Behavioral psychologists, 17/2020
Behavior psychology, 17/2018–19
Beijerinck, Martinus, 21/2533
Beijing (Peking), 3/*540*, 16/1890, 16/*1890*
Beira, 12/1489, 14/1672
Beirut, 12/1409
Belasco, David, 7/760
Belau, 13/1582
Belfana, La, 5/547
Belfast, 15/1793, 20/*2411*
Belgae, 3/327
Belgian, Zaire, 22/2642
Belgian horses, 10/1207
Belgium, 3/327–8, 3/*327–8*, 12/1468–9
  Rubens, Peter Paul, 18/2141–2
Belin, Jolly, 12/1398
Belize, 3/328–9, 3/*328*, 5/505–7
Bella Coola, 4/392
Bell, Alexander Graham, 3/329, 3/*329*, 5/611, 11/1370, 15/1832, 20/2390, 20/2391
Bellingrath gardens, 1/*83*
Bellini, Giovanni, 15/1861, 15/1862, 15/*1863*, 15/1863
Bellona, 9/1089
Bellow, Saul, 3/330, 3/*330*, 12/1451
Bells, 3/329*, 3/*329*
Bell X-1, 3/282, 3/*283*
Belorussia, 19/2282
Belote, Melisssa, 20/2366
Benares, 5/*615*, 9/1036, 11/*1253*
Benchmarks, 19/2361
Benci, Ginevre de, 12/1417
Bends, knots, 12/1374
Benedictines, 18/2122
Benedict, Saint, 14/1628, 14/*1628*, 14/1629

Benguela current, 19/2266
Ben-Gurion, David, 3/330, 3/*330*
Benidorm, 13/*1556*
Benign tumors, 6/738
Benin, 3/330–1, 3/*331*, 15/1774
Benjamin, Judah, 6/626, 6/*626*
Bennett, Floyd, 4/423
Ben Nevis, 4/396, 18/2176
Benny, Jack, 1/28, 21/2510
Benthos, 13/1517
Benton, Thomas Hart, 13/1615
Bent's Fort, 18/2161
Ben-Yehuda, Eliezer, 10/1172
Benz, Carl, 3/272
Benz cars, 3/*274*
Benzene, 5/586
Benz, Otto, 20/*2452*
Beowulf, 3/331
Bequerels, Antoine Henri, 17/2049
Berbers, 1/47, 1/100, 3/303, 10/*1204*, 12/1427, 14/1649, 19/2301, 20/2474
Bergman, Ingman, 19/2360
Bergman, Ingrid, 14/*1661*, 14/*1663*
Beriberi, 17/2102
Bering Island, 3/331
Bering Sea, 3/331
Bering Strait, 3/253, 3/331, 11/1261, 11/*1261*
Bering, Vitus, 2/209, 3/331, 8/893
Berkshire Hills, 13/1527
Berle, Milton, 21/2511
Berlin, 3/332, 3/*332*, 9/1067, 9/1069
Berlin, Irving, 3/332–3, 3/*332*, 14/1687
Berlin Wall, 3/332, 3/*332*, 9/1069
Berlioz, Hector, 5/*619*
Berlioz, Louis-Hector, 8/917
Bermuda, 21/2572
Bermúdez, Juan de, 21/2572
Bernhardt, Sarah, 3/333, 3/*333*, 7/*760*
Bernini, Gianlorenzo, 18/2178, 18/*2179*
Bernini, Giovanni, 2/204, 3/307, 3/*307*
Bernstein, Leonard, 3/333, 14/1688
Berries, 9/*1017*, 18/2188
Berry, William, 12/1439
Bessemer, Sir Henry, 11/1303
Best, Charles, 3/303
Beta particles, 17/2048
Beta Piscium, 6/642
Bethlehem, 11/*1309*
Bethlehem, Pennsylvannia, 16/1894
Bethlehem Asylum, London, 13/*1563*
Bethune, Albertus, 3/334
Bethune, Mary McLeod, 3/333–4, 3/*333*
Beverly, Mass., 13/1530
Beverly Hills, 12/1460
Bhotias, 18/2223
Bhutan, 3/334, 3/*334*, 14/1704
Biafra, 15/1774
Bible, 3/334–7, 3/*335–6*, 3/368, 11/1319
  Books of, 3/335
  Dead Sea Scrolls, 6/703–4
  history of, 3/336–7
  New Testament, 11/1330, 17/2081
Bibliography, 3/337*, 17/2075
Bicameral legislatures, 12/1412
Bicknell, Maria, 6/641
Bicuspids, 20/2386

Bicycles, 3/**337-8**, 3/*337-8*
  motorcycles, 14/*1666-7*
Biennial plants, 8/963
Bifocal glasses, 9/1084, 9/*1084*
Bigamy, 6/673
Big Bang, origin of the universe, 2/252, 3/357, 21/2500-1, 21/*2500*
Big Ben, 3/**338-9**, 3/*339*
Big Bend National Park, 17/*2104*
Big Dipper, 6/641, 6/*641*, 6/642
Bigfoot, 1/16
Big Horn Basin, 22/2625
Bighorn Crags, 10/1239
Big Horn Mountains, 22/2625, 22/2626
Bighorn River, 14/1642
Bighorn sheep, 18/*2202*
Big pin bowling, 4/378-9, 4/*379*
Big Sioux River, 11/1295
Bihar, 11/*1252*
Bijagós Islands, 10/1126
Bikini Island, 13/1582
Bilateral symmetry, 20/2371
Bile, 12/1453, 12/1454
Billiards, 3/**339**, 3/*339*
Billie Creek, Indiana, 11/*1255*
Billiken, 7/750
Bill of Rights, 3/**340**, 5/560, 5/561, 6/644, 6/645, 6/673, 6/716, 10/1179, 12/1479
Bills:
  Congress, 6/630-1
  money, 14/1631
Billy the Kid, 15/1851
Bilma, 15/*1773*, 20/*2444*
Biloxi, 13/1612, 13/1613
Bimini, 16/1973
Binary code, 5/623, 5/*623*
  bar codes, 3/303
Binary system, 3/**340**, 15/1807
Binding knots, 12/1374
Bingham Canyon, 21/2505
Bingham Canyon Copper Mine, 13/*1601*, 17/2035
Binoculars, 14/*1718*, 20/2395
Binocular vision, 18/2220
Biochemistry, 3/**340-1**, 5/519, 10/1224-5
  carbohydrates, 4/462
  enzymes, 7/862-3
  fats and oils, 8/916-17, 8/*917*
Biogeography, 9/1054
Biograph Company, 9/1119
Biography, 3/270, 3/**341***
Bioko, 7/864, 7/865
Biological chemistry, 5/519
Biological clock, 1/50
Biologists:
  Darwin, Charles, 6/699-700
  Huxley, Andrew Fielding, 10/1229
  Huxley, Sir Julian, 10/1229
  Huxley, Thomas Henry, 10/1229
Biology, 3/**341-3**
  anatomy, 2/133
  ecology, 7/793-8, 7/*794-8*
  evolution, 8/885-8
  fats and oils, 8/916-17, 8/*917*
  genetics, 9/1050-3
  see also Botany; Zoology
Bioluminescence, 3/**343**, 3/*343*
Biopsy, 6/738
Biosatellites, 19/2288
Biosociology, 3/343
Biosphere, 7/781

Biplanes, 1/68
Birch, 16/*1942*
Birchard, Sardis, 10/1162
Bird hawks, 3/349
Birdies (golf), 9/1092
Birds, 3/**343-7***, 3/*343-7*
  Antarctic, 2/170
  Australia, 3/267
  in cities, 5/558
  eggs, 3/345-7, 7/806
  feathers, 8/918-9, 8/*918*
  feet, 10/*1146*
  flight, 2/160, 3/343-4, 3/*345*
  flightless, 8/954-5, 8/*954-5*
  from the past, 3/349-50, 3/*349*
  game birds, 9/1033-4
  garden, 9/1036-8, 9/*1037*
  hazards for, 3/347
  hearing, 10/1166
  John James Audubon, 3/260-1, 3/*261*
  migration, 13/1591, 13/1592-4, 14/1720
  molting, 14/1627
  nests, 2/152-3, 2/*154*, 3/345-7
  pet, 16/*1905*, 16/1906
  seabirds, 18/2180-2, 18/*2180-2*
  speed, 2/158
  tracks, 2/163
  vision, 3/349
  water, 21/2550-2
  ways of life, 3/344
  where found, 3/344
  see also individual breeds of birds eg Bitterns
Birds of prey, 3/**347-9**, 3/*347-8*, 4/422-3
  falconry, 8/906
  owls, 15/1851-2, 15/*1852*
Bird watching, 14/1717-20, 14/*1717-19*
Biremes, 18/2206
Birmingham, USS, 1/59
Birth certificate, 3/**350**
Birth control, 18/2159
Birthday cards, 9/1118
Birthdays, 2/165-6
Birthstones, 9/1050, 9/*1050*
Bishops, 18/2121
Bismarck, Otto von, 3/**350-1**, 3/*350*, 9/1065-8
Bison, 3/**351**, 3/*351*, 3/356, 6/639, 10/*1202*, 13/1591, 17/*2064*
Bissell, Mr, 4/473
Bites, first aid, 8/940
Bitterns, 21/2551
Bitterroot Mountains, 10/1237
Bitterroot River, 14/1642
Bittersweet, 18/*2187*
Bituminous coal, 5/585
Bivalves, 5/570, 18/2203
  mollusks, 14/1625, 14/*1625*, 14/1626
Bizet, Georges, 12/1445
Black Americans, 3/**351-6**
  history, 3/351-2
  leaders, 3/354-5
  Reconstruction, 3/354
  slavery, 3/352-4
  today, 3/355-6
Black-backed jackel, 11/1315
Blackbeard, 16/1935, 16/*1935*
Black bears, 3/320, 14/*1712*
Blackbuck, 2/173, 2/*174*

Black buzzard, 4/423
Black caiman, 1/103
Black-capped chickades, 9/1037
Black Death, 7/804, 13/1588
Black duck, 7/771
Blackfoot Indians, 1/90, 1/100, 1/*100*, 3/356, 11/1262, 14/1642
Blackfoot penguin, 16/1892
Black Hawk, 11/1296
Black Hawk War, 10/1242, 11/1296
Black Hills, Dakota, 3/290, 18/2228, 19/2277, 19/2278
Black holes, 3/**356-7**
Black jaguar, 13/*1498*
Black-letter type, 20/2480-1
Black Mountains:
  Arizona, 2/215
  North Carolina, 15/1787
Black mulberry, 18/*2187*
Black Muslims, 3/355, 3/357, 3/*357*, 12/1491
Black panther, 4/*489*
Black people, civil rights, 5/561-4
Blackpine, 6/633
Black Pirate, 14/*1659*
Blackpoll warblers, 13/1591
Black rats, 17/2066, 17/*2066*
Black rhinoceros, 17/*2097*
Black Sea, 3/357, 3/*357*, 18/2126
Black Shirts, 14/1694
Black spruce, 6/633˙
Blackstone River, 17/2099
Blacktail deer, 6/709
Black vultures, 3/349
Black walnuts, 15/1810
Blackwell, Elizabeth, 3/**358**, 3/*358*
Bladderworts, 11/1281-2, 11/*1281*
Blake, Lyman, 13/1530
Blake, William, 4/396
Blanche, Queen of France, 12/1462
Blanc, Mount, 20/*2474*
Blanco, Jorge, 21/2571
Blantyre, 12/1489
Blast furnaces, 11/1303
Blasting caps, 8/895
Bleaching, 3/**358***
Bleda, 3/260
Bleeding, first aid, 8/938-9, 8/*939*
Blenheim, battle of, 3/319, 7/857
Blenkinsop, John, 20/*2449*
Blennies, 13/*1517*
Bligh, Wiliam, 14/1694-5, 14/*1694*
Blimps, 1/78
Blind people:
  braille, 4/382, 4/*382*
  education, 19/2305
  Keller, Helen, 11/1357
Blindfish, 3/**358**
Blitzkrieg, 22/2612
Block, Adriaen, 6/636, 17/2097
Block House, 21/2585
Block Island, 17/2097
Block mountains, 14/1668
Block planes, 4/472
Bloemfontein, 19/2267
Blondin, 1/25
Blood, 3/**359-60**, 13/1565-6
  antibodies, 2/177
  blood types, 3/359-60
  cells, 5/502
  circulatory system, 5/**550-1**
  diseases, 6/739
  heart, 10/1167-8, 10/*1167-8*
  kidneys, 11/1365-6

  liver, 12/1453-4, 12/*1453*
  oxygen supply, 4/388
  preservation, 7/763
  transfusions, 3/359, 3/*359*, 7/763
  types of cells, 3/359
Bloodworms, 22/2620
Bloomer, Amelia, 8/928
Blücher, Gebhard von, 21/2553-4
Blubber, 18/2184, 21/2580
Bluebottles, 8/966
Blue crabs, 6/681
Blue Grotto, Capri, 4/497
Blue Hills, Mass., 13/1528
Bluejays, 3/344
Blue Nile, 7/871, 15/1775, 19/2349
Blueprints, 11/1273
Blue puller fish, 13/*1516*
Blue Ridge Mountains, Georgia, 9/1062
Blue Ridge Mountains, North Carolina, 2/183, 15/1787
Blue Ridge Mountains, Virginia, 2/183, 21/2547
Blue Ridge Parkway, 15/1790
Blue ring angelfish, 13/*1516*
Blues, 11/1324-5
  Handy, W.C., 10/1147
Blue whales, 2/170, 13/1515, 21/2579
Bluff Hills, 13/1610
Blume, Judy, 3/**360**, 12/*1449*
Blurb, 3/368
BMW motorcycles, 14/*1667*
Böttger, Friedrich, 16/1990
Board of directors, 6/661
Boars, 16/1928
Boas, 19/2244, 19/2245
Boats and boating, 3/**360-2**, 3/*360-2*
  cabin cruisers, 3/362
  canoes, 3/361-2
  hydrofoils, 10/1230, 10/*1230*
  rowing, 18/2139-40, 18/*2139*
  sailing, 18/2153-4, 18/*2153-4*
  houseboats, 3/362
  motorboats, 3/362
  new materials for, 3/360-1
  rowboats, 3/362
  safety, 3/362
  shapes, 3/361
  types, 3/361-2
  work boats, 3/362
  see also Ships
Bobbed hair, 10/1139
Bobbers, fishing, 8/946
Bobbin lace, 12/1382
Bobcats, 4/*489*
Bobolinks, 13/*1593*
Bobsled, 19/2239
Bobwhites, 3/345, 9/1034, 13/1591
Boccaccio, Giovanni, 15/1801
Bocce, 4/379
Bock, Jerry, 14/1688
Bodiam Castle, 8/*992*
Body scanners, 3/**363**
Boeing 707, 1/64, 1/65, 1/69
Boeing 747, 3/282, 20/*2454*
Boeing 767, 20/*2453*
Boeing AWACS, 17/*2043*
Boers, 19/2267
Boer War, 3/**363-4**
Bogart, Humphrey, 14/*1661*, 14/*1662*
Bogey (golf), 9/1092
Bogoliubsky, Andrew, 18/2144
Bogotá, 5/597-8, 5/*598*
Bogs, 19/2361

Bohemia, 6/689
Bohr, Niels Henrik David, 3/364
Boiling, 6/655
Bokassa, Jean-Bédel, 5/505
Bolas spiders, 19/2312
Bold face (typesetting), 20/2480–1
Boleyn, Anne, 7/836, 10/1177, 14/1648, 17/2015
Bolívar, Simón, 3/364, 3/364, 3/365, 5/598, 15/1845, 19/2273, 21/2515
Bolivia, 3/364–5, 3/365
   Indian art, 11/1259
Boll weevil, 1/83, 6/665
Bollworms moth, 4/422
Bologna, University of, 5/595
Bolsheviks, 18/2149, 19/2285
Bolshoi Ballet, 3/297
Bombay, 3/365–6, 3/365, 16/1887
Bonaire, 21/2569
Bond, 19/2334–5, 19/2235
Bones, 3/366*, 3/366
   antlers, 10/1202
   fractures, 9/999
   growth, 9/1122
   skeleton, 18/2229–30
Boneset, 13/1552
Boneshakers, 3/337
Bon Homme Richard, 1/126, 1/128, 11/1340
Boniface VIII, Pope, 16/1911–12
Bonin Islands, 13/1582
Bonneville Flats, 21/2502
Bonneville, Lake, 21/2502
Bonney, William H., 15/1851
Bonpland, Aimé, 10/1225
Bonsai, 20/2459
Booby, 3/346, 18/2182
Bookbinding, 3/369
Bookkeeping, 1/22
Book of Kells, 11/1301
Bookmobiles, 12/1425
Books, 3/366–9*, 3/367–9
   bibliography, 3/337, 17/2075
   catalogs, 4/491
   censorship, 5/503–4
   children's, 5/531–5
   communication, 5/611
   copyright, 16/1884–5
   encyclopedias, 7/843–4, 7/843–4
   indexes, 11/1250–1
   libraries, 12/1423–6, 12/1423–6
   paper, 3/367
   printing, 3/367
   producing a book, 3/368–9
   publishing, 3/367–8, 17/2025–6
   reference books, 17/2075–6
   see also, Fiction; Literature; Writers
Boomerangs, 1/17, 1/17, 3/369, 3/369
Boone, Daniel, 2/184, 3/369–70, 3/370, 11/1362, 15/1790, 21/2576, 21/2585, 21/2586, 21/2586
Boonesborough, 11/1362
Booth, Ballington, 18/2157
Booth, Catherine, 18/2157
Booth, Edwin Thomas, 3/370, 3/370
Booth family, 2/228, 3/370
Booth, John Wilkes, 1/120, 3/370, 3/370, 5/569, 12/1441
Booth, Junius Brutus, 3/370
Booth, William, 18/2157, 18/2157
Bop, 11/1325
Bophuthatswana, 19/2266

Boquete, 16/1867
Bora Bora, 11/1307
Bora, Katharine von, 12/1471
Bordars, 8/925
Borgia, Cesare, 3/371, 12/1475
Borgia family, 3/370–1
Borgia, Lucrezia, 3/371, 3/371
Borgia, Rodrigo, 3/371
Borglum, Gutzon, 18/2142–3, 18/2142–3, 19/2337
Boriquén, 16/1973
Borja, Alfonso de, 3/370–1
Borja, Franceso de, 3/371
Borneo, 3/371, 3/371, 11/1271, 13/1526
Bornu, 15/1773
Boroughs, 6/666
Bosch, Juan, 21/2570–1
Bosphorus Strait, 3/357, 20/2475, 20/2476
Bossy, Mike, 19/2317
Bos taurus, 4/494
Boston, 1/111, 3/372, 3/372, 5/557, 13/1528, 13/1530, 13/1530
   American Revolution, 1/124–5
   police, 16/1966, 16/1967
   post offices, 16/1985
   subway, 19/2348
Boston Massacre, 1/124, 3/353, 3/372–3, 3/372
Boston Mountains, 2/218
Boston Tea Party, 1/32, 1/124, 3/373, 3/373, 17/2094
Boswash, 5/557
Boswell, James, 11/1340
Bosworth Field, battle of, 21/2543
Botanical gardens, 3/373–4, 3/373
Botany, 3/342, 3/374–5*, 3/374–5
   cytology, 3/375
   ecology, 3/375
   flowers, 8/961–3, 8/961–3
   genetics, 3/375
   grasses, 9/1103–4
   morphology, 3/375
   nature study, 14/1720–1
   pathology, 3/375
   photosynthesis, 16/1920–1, 16/1921
   physiology, 3/375
   plants, 16/1937–41
   taxonomy, 3/375
   see also Flowers; Plants; Trees
Botha, General, 3/363
Bothwell, Earl of, 13/1522
Botswana, 3/376, 3/376, 17/2100
Botticelli, Sandro, 11/1331, 13/1551, 17/2085
Bottle-nosed dolphins, 7/752
Boudin, Louis, 14/1629
Boulder, 5/602
Boulder Dam, 2/217
Boulevards, 19/2341
Boulton & Watt, 18/2210
Boulton, Matthew, 21/2557
Boundary Waters Canoe Area, 21/2585
Bounty, 14/1694–5, 14/1694
Bourbon, 1/93
Bourbon dynasty, 9/1008
Bourges Cathedral, 2/201
Bourse, 19/2335
Boutu, 7/751
Bovet, Daniel, 1/101
Bow and Arrow, 4/377, 4/377
Bowditch, Nathaniel, 4/377–8, 4/378

Bowed instruments, 19/2343–4
Bowie, David, 18/2228
Bowie, James, 1/84, 4/378, 4/378
Bowie knives, 20/2368
Bowknot, 12/1374
Bowline, 12/1374
Bowling, 4/378–9, 4/379
Bowls, 4/379
Bows, archery, 2/198–9
Box caisson, 4/430–1, 4/431
Boxcars, 17/2054
Boxer Rebellion, 5/538, 5/540
Boxing, 4/379–81, 4/380–1
   weight divisions, 4/381
Box kites, 11/1370
Box turtles, 20/2478
Boxwood, 18/2216, 18/2217
Boyaca, battle of, 3/364
Boyars, 18/2145
Boyle, Robert, 9/1045, 21/2506
Boyle's Law, 9/1045
Boys, adolescence, 1/34–5
Brachiosaurus, 6/733
Bracken, 8/923
Bradawls, 4/472
Bradford, Sarah, 20/2473
Bradford, William, 16/1931, 20/2419
Bradley, Omar, 22/2617
Brady, Mathew, 5/567
Bragi, 14/1695
Brahe, Tycho, 2/250, 4/381, 4/381, 11/1364, 15/1838
Brahman, 10/1187
Brahman cattle, 4/495
Brahmaputra, 11/1252, 11/1253
Brahms, Johannes, 4/381–2, 4/381
Braille, 4/382, 4/382
Braille, Louis, 4/382, 4/382
Brain, 4/382–4*, 4/383
   nervous system, 14/1739–40
Brakes:
   automobiles, 7/765
   hydraulic, 10/1230
Bran, 8/960
Branca, Giovanni, 7/848
Brandenburg Gate, Berlin, 3/332, 9/1067
Brando, Marlon, 14/1660
Brands, cattle, 6/669
Brandywine State Park, 16/1896
Brantford, Ontario, 15/1832
Brantford Reserve, 11/1304
Braque, Georges, 5/509, 14/1620
Brasilia, 19/2273
Brass, 13/1568
Brass bands, Sousa, John Philip, 19/2266
Brass instruments, 4/384–6, 4/385, 14/1689, 15/1839
Brattain, Walter, 20/2447
Brazil, 4/386–7, 4/386–7, 6/725, 19/2268
   Rio de Janeiro, 17/2103–4, 17/2103
   São Paulo, 18/2161, 18/2161
Brazil Current, 3/254
Brazil nuts, 15/1810
Brazzaville, 6/627, 22/2643
Bread:
   baking, 3/292–4
   diet, 15/1811, 15/1811
   flour making, 8/960, 060
   types, 8/975
Breakwaters, 10/1149
Breaststroke, 20/2365, 20/2365

Breathing, 4/387–9, 4/388, 13/1565, 17/2092–3
   hiccups, 10/1183–4
   nose, 15/1799, 15/1799
   see also Respiration
Brecht, Bertold, 7/760
Breton, André, 19/2359
Brett, George, 19/2317
Breuer, Marcel, 6/721
Brewster, William, 16/1930
Brezhnev, Leonid, 19/2286
Brick buildings, 4/407, 4/407
Bricks, building materials, 6/646
Bridalveil Fall, 22/2635
Brides, marriage, 13/1518–19
Bridge of Sighs, Venice, 4/391, 4/392
Bridgeport. Conn., 5/553
Bridger, Jim, 22/2625
Bridges, 4/389–92, 4/376, 4/389–91
   caisons, 4/430–1, 4/431
   construction, 6/647
   famous, 4/390–2
   longest, 4/391
Brindisi, 19/2303
Brindled gnu, 2/174
Brisbane, 3/266, 6/659
Bristlecone, 6/632
British Broadcasting Corporation (BBC), 17/2052, 20/2395, 20/2398
British Cameroons, 4/443
British Colombia, 4/392–4, 4/393, 4/450
   climate, 4/392
   history, 4/392–4
   industry, 4/394
   land, 4/392
   map, 4/392
   provincial flower, 4/392
British Commonwealth, 7/858
British Empire, 4/394–5, 5/610
British Honduras see Belize
British India Company, 11/1254
British Isles, 4/395–6, 4/396
   England, 7/852–3, 7/852–3
   English Channel, 7/853–4
   map, 4/395
   see also United Kingdom
British Library, 12/1426
British South Africa Company, 17/2100
British thermal units (BTUs), 9/1019–20
British Virgin Islands, 21/2572
Brittain, Benjamin, 5/544
Brittain, Walter, 3/304
Brittle star, 7/791–2, 7/792
Broadcasting:
   journalism, 11/1342–3
   radio, 17/2045–7, 17/2045–7, 17/2051–3, 17/2051–2
   see also Television
Broadloom carpets, 4/473
Broadswords, 20/2368
Broadwood, Thomas, 16/1924
Brogue, 11/1301
Broilers, 17/1991
Broiling, 6/655
Broken bones, 9/999
Bronchi, 4/387
Bronchioles, 4/388
Bronco busting, 18/2116, 18/2117, 22/2625
Brontë, Anne, 4/397, 4/397

Brontë, Branwell, 4/397
Brontë, Charlotte, 4/397, 4/*397*
Brontë, Emily Jane, 4/397, 4/*397*
Brontë family, 4/397
Brontë, Patrick, 4/397
Brontosaurus, 6/733, 8/994
Bronze, 1/104, 13/1568
  casting, 18/2179
Brooches, 11/*1333*
Brooke, Edward, 4/397, 4/*397*,
  13/1530
Brooklyn Bridge, 4/392
Brooklyn Dodgers, 17/2106
Brooks, Gwendolyn, 4/397–8
Brordin, Aleksandr, 17/2103
Brotherhood of Sleeping Car Porters,
  5/562
Brown bats, 3/317
Brown bears, 3/320
Brown coal, 5/585
Brown, George, 8/916, 12/1473
Brown hyenas, 10/1231
Brownies, 7/839
Browning, Elizabeth Barrett,
  4/398–9, 4/*399*
Browning, Robert, 4/398–9, 4/*399*
Brown, John, 1/15, 4/398, 4/*398*,
  11/1355, 21/2575
Brown pelicans, 16/1891
Brown rats, 17/2066
Brownsville, Texas, 17/2104
Brown Swiss cows, 4/494
Brown University, 17/2100
Broz, Josip *see* Tito
Bruce, Blanche K., 3/354, 4/*399*,
  5/561
Bruce, Robert, 4/399, 7/804
Bruckner, Anton, 3/269
Bruegel, Pieter the Elder, 7/776
Brulé, Etienne, 15/1832
Brummell, Beau, 8/913
Brunei, 4/399–400, 4/*400*
Brunel, Isambard Kingdom, 18/*2210*,
  20/*2450*
Brunelleschi, Filippo, 2/203, 13/1551,
  17/2083
Brunner, John, 18/2175
Brunswick Cathedral, 18/*2124*,
  18/2125
Brush-tailed opossum, 13/*1520*
Brussels, 8/*882*
Brussels carpets, 4/473
Brussels lace, 12/1382
Bryan, John Neely, 6/693
Bryan, William Jennings, 20/2375
Bryophyta, 14/1655
Bryophytes, 16/1947, 16/*1948*
Bryum capillare, 14/*1655*
Bubbles, soap, 19/*2247*
Buccaneers, 16/1934, 19/2303
Bucchero, 7/872
Bucephalus, 1/96
Buchanan, James, 4/400–1, 4/*400*,
  8/991
Bucharest, 18/2126
Buckaroos, 6/668
Bucket brigades, 8/934
Buckingham Memorial Fountain,
  Chicago, 8/996, 8/997
Buck, John L., 4/401
Buck, Pearl, 4/401, 4/*401*, 12/1451,
  12/*1451*
Bucks, 6/708
  hares, 17/2040

Buckskin, 9/1023
Buda, 10/*1228*
Budapest, 10/1228, 10/*1228*
Budapest slug, 19/*2243*
Buddha, 4/401, 4/*401*
  sculpture, 15/1846, 15/*1846*
Buddhism, 2/243, 4/402, 11/1332,
  12/1377, 17/2079, 17/*2080*
  India, 11/1254
  pagodas, 15/1857, 15/*1857*
  Thailand, 20/2417
  Tibet, 20/2424
Budding, reproduction, 17/2086
Budgerigars, 16/*1879*, 16/1880
Buenos Aires, 4/402–3
Buffalo, 4/403, 4/*403*, 5/573
Buffalo, New York, 4/446, 10/1149,
  15/1766
Buffalo Bill, 4/404, 4/*404*, 15/1812
Buffoons, 5/583
Buggy, 4/475
Bugles, 4/385
Bugs, 4/404–5, 4/*404*
Buhl Planetarium, Pittsburgh,
  16/1837
Buick, David, 3/273
Building materials, 4/405–7*,
  4/*405–7*, 6/646–7
  concrete, 6/625
  granite, 9/1099–1100, 9/*1099*
Buildings:
  carpenters, 4/470–2
  castles, 4/483–4, 4/*483–4*
  cathedrals, 4/491–3
  cleaning, 1/17
  construction, 6/645–9
  Gothic, 9/1093–4, 9/*1093–4*
  houses, 10/1213–15, 10/*1213–15*
  pagodas, 15/1857, 15/*1857*
  see also Architecture
Bujumbura, 4/417
Bulawayo, 22/2644
Bulbils, 4/408
Bulbs (electric), 7/816, 12/1435–6
Bulbs (plants), 4/408–9*, 4/*408*
  garden flowers, 9/1039
Bulfinch, Charles, 4/461
Bulgaria, 4/409–10, 4/*409*
Bulgars, 4/409
Bulk carriers, 13/1564
Bulkheads, 18/2210
Bulldogging, 18/2116
Bullfighting, 4/495, 4/*496*, 19/2298
Bullfrog, 9/1013
Bullion, 8/991
Bull Island, 19/2276
Bull, John, 14/1705
Bull riding, 18/2116, 18/*2116*
Bull Run, 5/567, 5/568
  battle of, 11/1318, 19/2319,
  21/2533
Bulls Island, 21/*2585*
Bulrush, 16/*1974*
Bumblebees, 3/324
Bunche, Ralph, 4/410, 4/*410*,
  15/1779
Bundesrat, 9/1068
Bunker Hill, battle of, 1/*125*, 1/126,
  3/353
Bunsen burners, 4/410, 4/*410*
Bunsen, Robert Wilhelm, 4/410
Bunyan, John, 4/410–11, 4/*411*
Bunyan, Paul, 2/163, 4/411, 8/972,
  9/1076, 12/1412, 13/1606

Buoyancy, 4/411–12*, 4/*412*
Buoys, 5/587
Burbage, James, 1/27
Burbage, Richard, 1/27
Burbank, Luther, 4/412–13,
  4/*412*
Bureau of Customs, 16/1966–7
Bureau of Mines, 6/639
Bureau of Narcotics, 16/1967
Burgesses, 8/*925*
Burgoyne, John, 1/127, 3/319
Burial customs, 4/413–14, 4/*413–14*
Burials, 7/810, 17/2081
Burial sites, archaeology, 2/197
Burin, 7/870
Burke, John, 15/1780
Burkina Faso, 4/414, 4/*414*
Burlington, 21/2518
Burma, 2/243, 4/415, 4/*415*
Burnett, Frances Hodgson,
  4/415–16, 4/*416*, 5/532
Burns, first aid, 8/940
Burns, George, 21/2510
Burns Harbor, 11/1258
Burns, Robert, 4/416, 4/*416*
Burnu, 15/1774
Burr, Aaron, 4/416, 4/*416*, 7/773,
  10/1142, 20/2456
Burro, 7/755
Burroughs, Edgar Rice, 4/417
Burrowa, Abe, 14/1687
Burrowing owl, 15/1852
Burundi, 4/417–18, 4/*417*, 15/1776
Burying beetles, 3/326, 3/*326*
Buschmann, C.F.L., 10/1153
Buschmann, Friedrich, 1/21
Buses, 4/418, 4/*418–19*
Bush cricket, 4/*443*
Bush, George, 4/418–19, 17/2067
Bushmen, 1/46, 1/*46*, 2/144, 3/376,
  14/1699, 19/2267
Bushnell, David, 6/636
Bush rats, 17/2066
Bushtits, 3/345
Bushy-tailed wood rats, 17/2066
Businesses, public relations,
  17/2022–3
Buskins, 18/2213
Butler, Frank, 15/1812
Butresses, 9/1093
Butte, 14/1642
Buttercups, 21/*2587*
Butterflies, 2/145, 4/419–22*,
  4/*419–22*, 10/*183*
  migration, 13/1594
Butterfly stroke, 20/*2365*, 20/2366
Buttermilk, 6/692
Buttons, 4/422
  campaign, 4/422
Button, Thomas, 13/1503
Buttress dams, 6/*695*
Buttresses, 18/2125
Butts, 2/199
Buzzard hawks, 3/348
Buzzards, 4/422–3, 4/*422*
Byelorussia, 18/2147
Byrd, Richard E., 2/*168*, 2/171,
  2/209, 4/423, 4/*423*
Byron, George Gordon, 4/423–4,
  4/*424*, 18/2203
Bytown, 15/1849
Byzantine architecture, 2/201
Byzantine art, mosaics, 14/1651–2
Byzantine Empire, 4/424, 18/2131

Cc

Caballeros, 12/1371
Cabbages, 9/*1040*
Cabin cruisers, 3/362
Cabinet:
  government, 17/1998, 17/2000
  United States, 4/425–6*, 4/*424*
Cable cars, 4/426–7, 4/*426*
Cables, fiber optics, 8/927, 8/*927*
Caboclos, 4/386
Cabomba, 2/*189*
Cabot, John, 4/427, 4/446, 8/893,
  10/1177, 12/1485, 15/1748,
  15/1800
Cabot, Sebastian, 4/427, 4/*427*,
  10/1177, 15/1754
Cabral, Pedro Alvares, 4/387
Cabriolet, 4/475
Cacao beans, 5/542
Cactus, 4/427–9*, 4/*428–9*, 10/*1215*,
  16/1944
Cactus wren, 9/*1037*, 14/*1719*
Caddies, 9/1092
Caddo Indians, 12/1464, 15/1827,
  20/2412
Cadillacs, 3/*275*
Cadillac, Antoine, 4/429, 6/724,
  8/893, 13/1580
Cady, Daniel, 19/2325
Caecilians, 2/130
Caernarfon Castle, 4/*484*
Caesar, Augustus, 18/*2129*, 18/2131
Caesar, Julius, 3/327, 4/429–30,
  4/*429*, 4/434, 4/477, 5/557,
  6/705, 6/726, 7/854, 8/919,
  9/1064, 11/1347, 14/1643,
  14/*1643*, 15/1761, 15/1802,
  15/1821, 18/2130–1
  as leader, 11/1368
Caetano, Marcelo, 16/1983
Cafeterias, 17/2093
Caffeine, 5/591, 7/767
Cagel, John, 7/825
Cahaba, Alabama, 1/83
Cahokia Mounds State Park,
  10/1240–2
Caimans, 1/103
Cairo, 4/430, 4/*430*, 7/807
Cairo, Illinois, 10/1240
Caisson, 4/430–1, 4/*431*
Cajuns, 12/1464, 15/1746
Cakes, baking, 3/293
Calais, 19/2300
Calamites, 16/1952
Calcite, 13/*1598*
Calcium, 4/431–2
Calculating, abacus, 1/13
Calculators, 4/432–3, 4/*432*, 7/826
Calculus, 15/1763
Caldecott Award, 4/433*, 4/*433*
Caldecott, Randolph, 4/433, 5/533
Calder, Alexander, 18/2178
Calendars, 4/433–5, 4/*434*
  April, 2/185–6
  August, 3/260–1
  B.C. and A.D., 11/1331
  days of the week, 6/702
  December, 6/705–6
  early, 4/433–4

(continued)

lions, 12/1443, 12/*1443*
wild cats, 4/488–90
Caro, Anthony, 18/*2180*
Carolina parakeets, 3/350
Caroline Islands, 13/1582
Caroline, Queen, 9/1060
Carols, 4/**470**, 4/*470*, 5/548
Carotene, 18/2233
Carp, 2/188
Carpathian Mountains, 16/1963, 18/2126
Carpeaux, Jean-Baptiste, 18/*2179*
Carpenter bees, 3/325
Carpenter, Malcolm S., 2/248
Carpentry, 4/**470–2★**, 4/*471–2*
buildings, 4/405–6
Carpetbaggers, 17/2070
Carpet beetles, 3/326
Carpets, 4/**472–4**, 4/*473*
history, 4/473–4
making, 4/473
oriental, 15/1846–7, 15/*1847*
Carraccii, Annibale, 18/*2154*
Carriages, 4/**474–5**, 4/*474–5*
Carrier Indians, 3/253
Carrier signals, 17/2045, 17/2046, 17/2047
Carroll, Lewis, 4/**475–6**, 4/*475*, 5/532, 12/*1447*
Cars, 3/272–7, 3/*272–7*
armoured, 2/223
driving, 7/764–6, 7/*764–6*
Carson, Kit, 4/**476**, 4/*476*, 14/1723
Carson River Valley, 15/1743
Carteret, Sir George, 15/1754
Carter, James Earl (Jimmy), 3/355, 4/**476**, 4/477, 8/985, 9/1064, 17/2067
Carthage, 4/**477**, 16/1916, 18/2130, 20/2474
Hannibal, 10/1147–8
Cartier, George, 8/915
Cartier, Jaques, 4/446, 4/448, 4/**477–8**, 4/*477*, 8/893, 14/1644, 15/1746, 17/2002, 17/2038
Cartilaginous fish, 8/941
Cartographers, 9/1054
Cartography, 13/1509–12
Cartooning, 4/**478–9**, 4/*478–9*
motion pictures, 14/1663
Thurber, James, 20/2423–4
Cartridges, 10/1132
film, 4/482
Cartwright, Alexander, 3/310
Caruso, Enrico, 4/**479**, 4/*479*
Carver, George Washington, 1/83, 4/**479–80**, 13/1618
Carver, John, 13/1531, 16/1931
Carving, 4/**480–1**, 4/*471*, 18/2178
Caryatides, 1/26
Casablanca, 14/1648, 14/1649
Casablanca, 14/*1661*
Cascade Range, 15/1743, 15/1841, 15/1842, 21/2544
Casco Bay, 12/1485
Casette players, 17/2071–3, 17/*2072*
Caseworkers, 19/2251–2
Cash on delivery (COD), 19/2339
Cashew nuts, 15/1810
Cashmere goats, 9/1086
Caspian Sea, 4/**481**, 4/*481*, 12/1384, 12/1385, 19/2282
Caspian tigers, 17/*2064*

Cassatt, Mary, 4/**481–2**, 4/*481*, 12/1468, 15/1846
Cassein paint, 15/1860
Cassette, 4/**482**, 4/*482*
Cassidy, Butch, 15/1851
Cassiopeia, 2/142
Cassowary, 3/267, 8/954, 8/*954*
Caste system, 10/1187, 11/1254
Castile, 19/2301
Casting:
bronze, 18/2179
fishing, 8/946
jewelry, 11/1333
moulds, 6/728, 6/*728*
Cast iron, 11/1303
Castle, Irene, 10/1139
Castles, 4/**483–4**, 4/*483–4*, 8/990, 8/*990*
Medieval, 13/1586, 13/*1586–7*
Castro, Fidel, 4/**484–5**, 4/*485*, 6/684, 11/*1364*
Catabolism, 13/1565
Catacombs, 4/**490**, 4/*490*, 18/2128
Catalan, 2/141
Catalog, 4/**491**, 12/1423, 12/*1424*, 12/*1425*
Catalysts, enzymes, 7/862
Catalytic converters, 1/73, 7/849
Catamarans, 3/361
Cataracts, 21/2553
Categories word game, 21/2604
Caterpillars, 4/*419*, 4/420–1, 4/*420*, 13/1569
Caterwauling, 4/487
Catfish, 2/188
Catherine of Aragon, 10/1177, 13/1522, 14/1648
Catherine de Medici, 5/514
Catherine the Great, 4/**493**, 4/*493*, 8/913, 16/1908, 18/2147, 18/*2147*
Catherine of Siena, St, 18/*2155*
Cather, Willa, 14/1734
Cathode-ray tubes, 7/*825*, 7/827, 22/2649
Catholic Church *see* Roman Catholic Church
Catlin, George, 11/*1263*, 18/2127–8
White Cloud, Head Chief, 18/*2128*, 18/*2128*
Catnip, 4/486
Cato, 4/477, 11/1333
Catoctin Mountain, 13/1524
Catoosa, 15/1828
Cats (domestic), 2/161, 4/**485–8**, 4/*485–7*, 7/753, 16/*1905*, 16/1906
and people, 4/487–8
caring for, 4/485–6
characteristics, 4/486–7
choosing, 4/485
falling, 4/*487*
tracks, 2/163
Catskill Mountains, 15/1765
Cats (wild), 4/**488–90**, 4/*488–9*
American, 4/488–9
common features, 4/488
from other lands, 4/489–90
see also Lions; Tigers *and other cats*
Cattail, 16/*1974*
Cattle, 4/**493–6**, 4/*494–6*
beef breeds, 4/494–5
cowboys, 6/668–9, 6/*668*
dairy breeds, 4/494
dairy farming, 6/691

ranching, 17/2061–2
related animals, 4/495–6
rodeos, 18/2116–17, 18/*2116–17*, 21/*2494*
sport, 4/495
terms for, 4/495
Caucasoids, 2/242
Caucasus Mountains, 4/**496**, 19/2282
Caudal fins, 8/943
Caulking, 18/2211, 20/*2474*
Caustic soda, 1/23
Cavaliers, 6/675, 7/857
Cavalry, 2/224
Cave dwellers, 4/**500**, 4/*500*, 18/2203
Cavelier, Robert, *see* La Salla, Sieur de
Cavell, Edith Louisa, 4/**500**
Cavendish, Henry, 7/783
Cave paintings, 2/231, 2/*231*
Caves, 4/**497–9**, 4/*497–9*
inside, 4/498–9
spelunking, 19/2310
stalactites and stalagmites, 4/498, 4/*498*, 4/*499*, 4/500
types, 4/497–8
Caviar, 4/481
Cavill, Richard, 20/2366
Cavour, Camillo, 9/1043, 11/1311
Caxton, William, 1/38
Cayenne, 9/1006
Cayman Islands, 21/2572
Cayuga Indians, 8/950, 11/1270, 11/1304
Cayuse Indians, 21/2544
Cecopia moth, 4/422
Celandine, 4/*408*
Celebations, anniversaries, 2/165–6
Celebes, 11/1271
Celestial navigation, 14/1724
Cellini, Benvenuto, 4/465, 5/**503**, 5/*503*, 7/842
Cell membranes, 5/502
Cellos, 19/2343–4
Cells, 2/145, 5/**501–3**
batteries, 3/317
biochemistry, 3/340–1
blood, 3/359
cancer, 4/455
cytology, 3/342
electric, 7/*819*
fuel, 9/1020
function, 5/502
human, 10/1224
nerve, 14/1739
plants, 16/1939
protists, 17/2016
protozoa, 17/2017
reproduction, 5/502–3
special, 5/502
structure, 5/501–2
Celluloid, 16/1954
Cellulose, 5/502
Celluloosis, 16/1955
Cell walls, 5/502
Celsius, Anders, 20/2401
Celsius temperature scale, 20/2401
Celsus, 13/1556
Celts, 7/855, 21/2539
Cement, 6/625
Cement-mixer trucks, 20/2469
Cemeteries, 4/413
Cenozoic era, 7/785, 7/786, 17/*1996*
Censorship, 5/**503–4**
Census, 16/1979

Centaurs, 2/160, 2/*161*
Centennial Exposition, Philadelphia, 8/903
Centerboards, 18/2153
Center for Disease Control, 6/650
Centigrade temperature scale, 20/2401
Centipedes, 5/**504**, 5/*504*
Central African Rebublic, 5/**504–5**, 5/*505*
Central America, 5/**505–7**
Central American Common Market, 5/506, 5/507
Central banks, 3/302
Central heating, 10/1171, 10/*1172*
Central Intelligence Agency (CIA), 5/**508**, 19/2319, 21/2490, 21/2491
Centralized Traffic Control System (CTC), 17/2054
Central nervous system, 14/1740
Central Pacific Railroad, 17/2058, 21/2578
Central Park, New York, 16/1878
Centrifugal force, 15/1837
Centrifugal pumps, 17/*2028*, 17/2029
Centrifuges, 15/1837
Centripetal force, 15/1837
Cephalocerus senilis, 4/*428*
Cephalopods, 14/1625
Cepheus, 2/142
Ceramics, 16/1987–90, 16/*1988–9*
American Indian, 11/1259, 11/*1260*
Cerargyrite, 18/2225
Ceratophyllum, 2/*189*
Cereals, 9/1089, 9/1096–7, 9/*1097*
corn, 6/659–60
development, 16/1954
diet, 15/1811
harvesting machinery, 8/909
wheat, 21/2580–1, 21/*2580–1*
Cerebellum, 4/384
Cerebrum, 4/384
Ceres (asteroid), 2/246, 2/*246*, 19/2260
Ceres (god), 9/1089
Cerus cactus, 4/428, 4/*428*
Cervantes, Miguel de, 5/**508**, 5/*508*, 15/1801, 16/1913
Cessna, 3/*283*
Cetaceans, 7/751–2
Ceuta, 19/2298
Ceylon *see* Sri Lanka
Cézanne, Paul, 1/18, 5/**508–9**, 5/*509*, 14/1620
Chachalaca, 9/1034
Chaco, 16/1875
Chad, 5/**509–10**, 5/*509*
Chaff, 21/2581
Chaffee, Roger, 19/2292
Chagall, Marc, 19/2323
Chagga, 20/2379
Chagres River, 6/694
Chain, Ernest B., 2/176, 8/953
Chain lightning, 12/1437
Chain mail, 2/221, 2/*221*
Chain stores, 19/2338
Chairs, 6/*721*, 9/*1026*
Chalets, 20/2367
Challenger, 8/889, 19/2292
Challenger, HMS, 15/1817–20
Chama River, 15/1758
Chambered nautilus, 14/1625
Chamberlain, Neville, 22/2612
Chamberlain, Wilt, 3/315, 19/2317

Chamber music, 14/1682
Chamber orchestras, 15/1839, 15/*1840*
Chameleons, 12/1455, 17/2011
Chamorros, 10/1123
Champagne, fairs, 8/902
Champlain, Lake, 15/1765, 21/2518, 21/*2519*
Champlain, Samuel de, 4/446, 5/**510**, 5/*510*, 15/1746, 15/1752, 15/1765, 15/1832, 17/2038
Champlain Valley, 21/2518
Champollion, Jean-François, 10/1185, 18/2138
Chance, 5/**510–11**★
Chandeliers, 4/456, 12/*1436*
Chandler, Jennifer, 6/*743*
Chandragupta, 11/1254
Chang, 14/1699–1700
Changelings, 7/839
Changing energy, 7/845–6
Chanters, 3/291
Chao Phraya River, 20/2417
Chapbooks, 5/531
Chapel Hill, 15/1788–90
Chaplin, Charlie, 1/27, 5/**511**, 5/*511*, 9/1119, 14/*1658*, 14/1659, 21/2510
Chapman, John, 2/184
Character dolls, 7/750
Charades, 16/1870
Charbonneau, Toussaint, 12/1420
Charcoal, 9/1019
Charcot, Jean Martin, 9/1012
Charge of the Light Brigade, 6/674–5
Charigot, Aline, 17/2086
Chariots, 4/474, 5/**511–12**, 18/2132, 20/*2448*
Charlemagne, 2/141, 3/269, 3/327, 5/**512**, 5/*512*, 8/880, 9/1001, 9/1007, 9/1065, 9/*1066*, 10/1196, 11/1310, 11/1368–9, 16/1966
Charleroi, 21/2554
Charles I, Holy Roman Emperor, 5/513
Charles I, King of England, 5/**514**, 5/*513*, 6/675–6, 7/858, 7/*858*, 11/1319, 11/*1368*, 13/1524
Charles I, King of France, 5/514
Charles I, King of Spain *see* Charles V, Emperor
Charles II the Fat, Emperor, 9/1065
Charles II, Holy Roman Emperor, 5/513
Charles II, King of England, 5/**514–15**, 6/677, 10/1218–19, 11/1319, 15/1752, 15/1754, 15/1765, 15/1788, 16/1893, 17/2099
Charles II, King of France, 5/514
Charles II, King of Spain, 19/2302
Charles III, Holy Roman Emperor, 5/513
Charles III, King of France, 5/514, 21/2527
Charles IV, Holy Roman Emperor, 5/513
Charles IV, King of France, 9/1008
Charles IV, King of Spain, 19/2302
Charles V, Holy Roman Emperor, 5/513, 5/*512*, 9/1002, 9/1065, 12/1468, 12/1494, 16/1912, 19/2301, 19/*2302*

Charles V, King of France, 5/514, 5/*514*
Charles V, King of Spain, 2/223
Charles VI, Holy Roman Emperor, 5/513
Charles VI, King of France, 5/514
Charles VII, Holy Roman Emperor, 5/513
Charles VII, King of France, 5/514, 9/*1008*, 11/1337
Charles VIII, King of France, 5/514
Charles IX, King of France, 5/514, 10/1178
Charles X, King of France, 5/514
Charles, J.A.C., 3/298
Charles, Jacques, 9/1045
Charles Martel, 5/**515**, 5/*515*, 9/1007
Charles, Prince (Bonnie Prince Charlie), 5/**514**
Charles, Prince of Wales, 5/**514**, 5/*514*, 7/837
Charles River, 13/*1530*
Charles's Law, 9/1045–6
Charleston, 18/2237, 19/2274, 19/*2274*, 19/2276, 21/2575
Charleston (dance), 6/697
Charleston and Hamburg Railroad, 17/2053, 17/2055
Charles Towne, 19/2274–6
Charlotte, North Carolina, 15/1790
Charlotte Amalie, 21/2572
Charlottetown, 4/450, 17/2002
Charms, 19/2354
Charnin, Martin, 14/1688
Charon (Pluto's moon), 19/2257, 19/*2258*
Charter airlines, 1/65
Charts, 14/1724
Chasms, 4/457
Chattanoog, 5/568
Chaucer, Geoffrey, 5/**515**, 5/*515*, 7/*862*, 12/1411, 15/1801, 18/2216
Chauffeur's licence, 20/2469
Checkers, 5/**516**, 5/*515*
Checkerspot butterfly, 4/*420*
Checks, 3/301, 14/1631–2
Cheese, 5/**516–17**, 5/*517*★, 6/692
Chehalis Indians, 5/541
Chekhov, Anton, 5/**517**, 5/*517*, 7/759–60, 18/2216
Chemical energy, 7/845, 16/1923
Chemical engineering, 5/519, 7/851
Chemical industry, 5/521
Chemical Society, 1/22
Chemical weapons, 5/**518**
Chemistry, 5/**518–22**★
alchemy, 1/92–3
atomic number, 7/829
atomic weight, 7/829–30
atoms, 3/258–60, 5/519–20
biochemistry, 3/340–1
branches of, 5/519
bunsen burners, 4/410
compounds, 5/520
crystals, 6/682–3
Curie, Marie and Pierre, 6/686
development, 5/521–2
distillation, 6/740–1
elements, 5/519–20, 7/828–31, 7/*828–31*
fats and oils, 8/916–17, 8/*917*
Lavoisier, Antoine Laurent, 12/1398

liquid crystals, 12/1444
matter, 5/518, 13/1536–7
molecules, 5/520
oxygen, 15/1852–3, 15/*1853*
Pasteur, Louis, 16/1883–4
periodic table, 7/830–1, 7/*830*
physical and chemical changes, 5/520–1
Priestly, Joseph, 17/1999–2000
properties of matter, 5/519
symbols, 7/830–1
Cheng Ho, 5/**522–3**
Chenille carpets, 4/473
Cheops, 17/2033
Chernenko, Konstantin, 9/1092, 19/2286
Chernobyl, 8/907, 9/*1020*, 12/1392, 15/1805, 17/2049
Cherokee Indians, 1/83, 5/**522–3**, 5/*523*, 11/*1264*, 11/1362, 13/1517, 15/1788, 15/1827–8, 18/2192, 19/2274, 20/2403
Cherrapunji, 2/239
The Cherry Orchard, 5/517
Chesapeake and Delaware Canal, 4/454, 6/712, 13/1524
Chesapeake Bay, 5/**523**, 13/1524, 21/2530–2
Chesapeake Bay Bridge-Tunnel, 21/2532
Chesil beach, 18/*2183*
Chess, 5/**524–5**, 5/*524–5*
history, 5/525
movements, 5/524–5
Chester, Pennsylvania, 16/1894
Chestnuts, 15/1809–10
Chevaliers, 12/1371
Chewing, digestion, 6/730
Chewing the cud, 10/1180
Cheyenne Indians, 1/100, 5/602, 6/687, 11/1262, 11/1271, 14/1732, 14/1734, 18/2229, 22/2625
Chiang Kai-shek, 5/**525–6**, 5/*525*, 5/540, 13/1508, 16/1890, 20/2377, 20/2402
Chiaroscuro, 15/1862
Chibcha Indians, 7/814
Chicago, 3/352, 5/**526**, 5/*526*, 10/1240, 10/1242
riots, 5/*573*, 5/574
Chicago Sanitary and Ship Canal, 13/1615
Chichicastenango, 5/*507*
Chickahominy Indians, 16/1959
Chickamuga, 5/568
Chickasaw Indians, 1/83, 13/1612, 15/1827, 20/2404
Chicken, 17/1991–2, 17/*1991–2*
incubators, 11/1249
Chicken pox, 6/649
Chihuahua dogs, 6/747
Chikees, 11/1263
Child psychologists, 17/2019
Children:
adolescence, 1/34–5
adoption, 1/35–6
care, 5/**527–8**
child labor, 5/**529–30**
civil rights, 5/560
diseases, 5/**528–9**★
games, 5/**530–1**
literature, 5/**531–5**
museums, 14/1680

Children's Book Week, 5/534
Children's Crusade, 6/680
Children's literature:
Caldecott Award, 4/433, 4/*433*
Newbery Medal, 15/1744–6, 15/*1746*
see also Writers
Chile, 5/**535–6**, 5/*535–6*
Chimborazo, 7/800, 10/1225
Chimera, 2/162, 2/*162*
Chimes, 3/329
Chimpanzees, 2/145, 2/180, 2/181
China, 5/**536–40**, 5/*536–40*
abacus, 1/13
acupuncture, 1/29–30, 1/*30*
archaeology, 2/198
architecture, 2/201
art, 2/*138*, 2/231, 2/234, 15/*1845*, 15/1846
astronomy, 2/249
Beijing (Peking), 3/540, 16/1890
books, 3/*368*
Chiang Kai-shek, 5/525–6
chopsticks, 5/543
Chou En-lai, 5/545
civil service, 5/564
clocks, 5/578
Communism, 5/614
compass, 5/617, 5/*617*
Confucius, 6/626–7
Great Wall, 9/1109–10, 9/*1109*
gunpowder, 8/895, 8/896
history, 5/538
Hong Kong, 10/1199
Korean War, 12/1378
Macao, 12/1473
Mao Tse-tung, 13/1508
medicine, 2/177
names, 5/536
Peking, 3/*540*, 16/1890
philosophers, 2/136
Polo, Marco, 16/1970–1
population, 16/1979
pottery in, 16/1988, 16/*1989*, 16/1990
printing, 17/2002
propaganda, 17/*2010*
Republic of, *see* Taiwan
rockets, 17/*2109*, 17/2111
Shangai, 18/2198–9
Sun Yat-sen, 19/2354
Taoism, 20/2379
Teng Hsiao-p'ing, 20/2402–3
Tibet, 20/2424
Yangtze River, 22/2632, 22/*2632*
Yellow River, 22/2633, 22/*2633*
China pottery, 16/1987–90★, 16/*1988–90*
Chincoteague ponies, 10/1207
Chinese alligators, 1/103
Chinese alphabet, 1/106
Chinese language, 5/**541**
Chinese Revolution, 17/2095
Chinese water deer, 6/710
Chinook, 1/90, 14/1640–2, 14/1732, 21/2592
Chinook Indians, 5/**541**, 15/1842, 21/2544
Ch'in-shih-Huang, 2/*198*
Chinstrap penguin, 16/*1892*
Chipewyan Indians, 3/253, 18/2164
Chipmunks, 9/1120, 9/1121
Chippendale, Thomas, 9/1026, 9/1027

Chippewa Indians, 11/1270, 15/1826, 21/2559
see also Ojibwa Indians
Chips, computers, 5/621, 5/622
Chiricahua Apache Indians, 5/588
Chiron (asteroid), 2/247
Chiron (centaur), 2/160, 2/161
Chiropractic, 5/542
Chisholm, Shirley, 21/2601
Chissano, Joaquim, 14/1672
Chitin, 6/680, 11/1280, 13/1569, 18/2229
Chiton, 9/1113, 14/1625, 18/2203
Chittagong, 3/300
Chitterlings, 13/1547
Chivalry, 12/1372
Chlorella, 1/97
Chlorine, bleaching, 3/358
Chloroform, 2/143
Chlorophyll, 5/502, 16/1876, 16/1920, 16/1937, 16/1940, 16/1947, 16/1951
protozoa, 17/2017
Chloroplasts, 5/502
Choco Indians, 16/1867
Chocolate, 5/542, 5/542
Choctaw Indians, 1/83, 5/542–3, 5/543, 13/1612, 15/1827
Choirs, 5/544–5
choral music, 5/543–4
Choirs (architecture), 4/492
Cholesterol, 15/1810
Chol Indians, 13/1541
Chopin, Frédéric François, 5/543, 5/543
Chopsticks, 5/543
Choral music, 5/543–4
Chordates, 2/156
Choreography, 6/696–7
Choristers, 5/545
Choroid, 8/898
Chorophyll, 12/1402
Choruses, 5/544–5
opera, 15/1834
Choson, 12/1376
Chou dynasty, 5/538
Chou En-lai, 5/525, 5/545, 5/545
Chowan River, 15/1788
Christian Church, Reformation, 12/1470–1
Christian, Fletcher, 14/1695
Christianity, 5/546–7, 8/880, 17/2079
Apostles, 2/182–3
art and, 2/231
Bible, 3/334–7
carols, 4/470
catacombs, 4/490
cathedrals, 4/491–3
Crusades, 6/678–80
Easter, 7/790
evangelists, 8/883
Jesus Christ, 11/1330–1
Middle Ages, 13/1585–8
missionaries, 13/1610
Orthodox Church, 15/1847–8, 15/1848
prophets, 17/2011
Protestant churches, 17/2013–14, 17/2014
Roman Catholic Church, 16/1976–7, 18/2120–3, 18/2121–3
saints, 18/2154–5, 18/2154–5
Salvation Army, 18/2157

Christian Science, 5/547
Christian Science Monitor, 15/1761
Christina, Queen of Sweden, 6/714
Christmas, 5/547–8, 5/548, 6/706, 21/2595
cards, 5/548, 5/548, 9/1118
carols, 4/470
crib dolls, 7/749
Santa Claus, 15/1772
Christmas Carol (Dickens), 6/725
Christmas Island, 16/1971
Christopher, John, 18/2175
Chrome tanning, 12/1408
Chromosomes, 5/502, 8/888, 9/1051, 9/1052, 17/2087
Chronometers, 20/2427
Chrysalis, 4/421
Chubb Crater, 17/2036
Chukar, 9/1034
Chukkers, 16/1970
Chumash Indians, 4/436
Chungking, 22/2632
Chunkey yard, 6/672
Church:
American Colonies, 1/114
Christianity, 5/546–7
clergy, 5/573
Middle Ages, 13/1585–8
and State, 5/548–9*
see also Christianity; Religion and individual Churches
Church, Ellen, 1/65
Churches:
cathedrals, 4/491–3
Rococo, 17/2113
Romanesque, 18/2124–5
Churchill Falls, 15/1748
Churchill, Lord Randolph, 5/549
Churchill River, 15/1748
Churchill, Sarah, 2/165
Churchill, Sir Winston, 5/549, 5/549, 7/859, 9/1095, 17/2000, 18/2134, 18/2135, 20/2485
hobbies, 10/1192
World War II, 22/2612, 22/2613, 22/2616, 22/2619
Church of the Latter-Day Saints, 21/2504–5
Smith, Joseph, 19/2241
Young, Brigham, 22/2636
Chusan palms, 15/1866
CIA see Central Intelligence Agency
Cibola, 6/637, 6/660, 7/869, 15/1758
Seven Cities of, 5/549
Cicadas, 11/1277, 13/1570
Cid, El, 5/550, 5/550
Cigarette smoking, 19/2242–3
Cigars, 20/2431, 20/2431
Cilia, comb jellies, 5/607
Cimabue, Giovanni, 9/1077
Cinch bug, 4/404
Cincinnati, 15/1824, 15/1826
Cinema see Motion pictures
Cinemascope, 14/1663
Cinerama, 14/1663, 14/1664
Cinnabar, 13/1599
Cinnabar moth, 17/2012
Cinnamon, 19/2311
Cintra, Piedro da, 18/2217
Cipango, 4/427
Ciphers, 5/589*
Circuit breakers, 7/817
Circulatory system, 5/550–1, 5/550–1, 10/1224

diseases, 6/739
heart, 10/1167–8, 10/1167–8
Circus, 5/500, 5/552–4, 5/552–3
acrobats, 1/25
calliope, 4/439
clowns, 5/583–4
history, 5/553
people, 5/553
Phineas T. Barnum, 3/305–6
towns, 5/553
Circus Maximus, Rome, 18/2131, 18/2132
Cire-perdu casting, 18/2179
Cirrhosis, 12/1454
Cirrocumulus clouds, 5/582
Cirrostratus clouds, 5/582
Cirrus clouds, 5/582, 5/583
Ciskei, 19/2266
Cities, 5/555–8, 5/555–8, 19/2347
of the future, 5/558
government, 12/1457
growth, 5/555–7
life in, 5/557–8
streets, 19/2340–3
traffic, 5/557, 20/2445–6
wildlife in, 5/558–9*
Citizens, 6/715
Citizens Band (CB), 17/2048, 17/2048
Citizenship, 5/554
Citlaltépetl, 13/1573
Citric acid, 1/24
Citrus fruit, 5/555, 5/555, 9/1017, 9/1018
Civil cases, court sytem, 6/666–7
Civil engineers, 7/851
Civilian Corporations Corps, 6/639
Civilization, 5/559–60
ancient, 2/133–8, 2/133–8
history, 10/1189–90
Civil law, 12/139
Civil Rights, 5/560
children, 5/560
Harris, Patricia Roberts, 10/1154
King, Martin Luther, 11/1366–7
Marshall, Thurgood, 13/1520
NAACP, 14/1705–6
Thoreau, Henry David, 20/2423
Young, Whitney Moore, 22/2637
Civil Rights Movement, 5/561–4
Civil service, 5/564
Civil War, 1/117–20, 5/564–9, 13/1525
blacks in, 3/353–4
Confederate States, 6/625–6
Davis, Jefferson, 6/701
Farragut, David, 8/910
Fort Sumpter, 8/991
Gettysburg Address, 9/1072–3
Grant, Ulysses Simpson, 9/1100–1
Indiana, 11/1256
Jackson, Thomas Jonathan ('Stonewall'), 11/1318
Lee, Robert E., 12/1410
Mason-Dixon Line, 13/1527
Monitor and *Merrimack* battle, 14/1634
navy, 14/1728
Reconstruction, 17/2068–71, 17/2069–70
spying, 19/2319
Civil War (English), 6/675–6, 7/857–8
Civil War (Spanish), 9/1002–3
Clams, 5/570, 5/570, 14/1626
Clam worms, 22/2620

Clans, 18/2176
Clare, Saint, 9/1002
Clarinets, 21/2603
Clarke, Arthur C., 18/2175
Clark, George Rogers, 1/128, 5/570–1, 10/1242, 11/1256, 21/2576
Clark, Joe, 14/1674
Clark, Kenneth, 14/1664
Clark, William, 1/116, 5/571, 5/605, 10/1239, 12/1420–1, 15/1842, 15/1844
Classical music, 14/1686
Classification:
libraries, 12/1423–4
plants and animals, 12/1442
Classification yards, railroads, 17/2053
Claudius, Emperor, 14/1739
Clavichords, 16/1925
Claws, 5/571, 5/571
cats, 4/488
Clay building materials, 6/646
Clay, Cassius, 4/381
Clay, Henry, 5/571–2, 5/571, 20/2479, 21/2541
Clay modelling, 5/572, 5/572*, 18/2180
Clay pigeon shooting, 18/2214
Cleaner fish, 20/2369
Cleaning, soaps and detergents, 19/2247–8
Cleanliness, 10/1164
Clearwater Mountains, 10/1237–9
Cleary, Beverly, 12/1449
Cleft lip, 19/2308
Cleft palate, 19/2308
Clemenceau, Georges, 21/2609, 21/2610
Clemens, Samuel Langhorne see Twain, Mark
Clement IV, Pope, 3/288
Clement VII, Pope, 9/1049, 13/1552, 14/1648, 17/2015
Clement VIII, Pope, 10/1177
Cleopatra, 4/429, 5/572–3, 6/663, 7/810, 18/2131
Clepsydra, 5/577
Clerestory, 4/492
Clerestory windows, 18/2125
Clergy, 5/573
Clermont, 9/1020, 20/2452
Cleveland, Ohio, 15/1823, 15/1826
Cleveland, Grover, 5/573–4, 10/1155, 12/1438, 19/2332
Click beetles, 3/326, 3/327
Click languages, 14/1700
Cliff dwellers, 5/574–5
Cliffs, sea, 18/2182
Climate, 5/575–7*
changing, 5/577
clouds, 5/581–3
droughts, 7/767
Equator, 7/864
fog, 8/967–8
frosts, 9/1015, 9/1015
hail, 10/1137, 10/1137
humidity, 10/1225–6
hurricanes, 10/1228–9, 10/1228
lightning, 12/1437
monsoon, 14/1639–40, 14/1639–40
plants and, 16/1944–5

(continued)

rain, 17/2059–60, 17/*2060*
snow, 17/2059–60
thunder, 12/1437
weather, 21/2561–4, 21/*2561–3*
Climatologists, 5/575
Climbing, mountain, 14/1671–2, 14/*1671*
Clinch, Nicholas, 2/171
Clinics, 10/1209
Clio, 14/1677
Clippers, 13/1530, 18/*2206*, 18/*2207–8*
Clipperton Island, 16/1971
Clive, Robert (Clive of India), 11/1254
Clocks, 5/**577–8**, 5/*577–8★*, 20/2427
Big Ben, 3/338–9
pendulums, 16/1891–2
Cloisonné, 7/842
Cloisters, 4/491, 14/1628
Closed court, 20/2464
Cloth, 5/579, 20/2415–16, 20/*2415–16*
fibres, 8/926–7
spinning and weaving, 19/2313–14
Clothes moth, 4/422
Clothing, 5/**578–81**, 5/*579–81*
buttons, 4/422
cleaning, 12/1397–8
design, 6/722, 6/*722*
fashion, 8/912–15, 8/*912–15*
fibres, 8/926
fur, 9/1023, 9/*1023*
hats, 10/1156–7, 10/*1156–7*
lace, 12/1381–2, 12/*1382*
racing silks, 10/1209
riding habits, 10/1208
shoes, 18/2212–14, 18/*2213–14*
Clotho, 8/915
Cloudbursts, 8/955
Clouded leopard, 4/490
Cloud forests, 11/1350
Clouds, 5/**581–3**, 5/*581–3*
thunder and lightning, 12/1437
Clove, 19/2311, 19/*2311*
Clove hitch, 12/*1374*
Clover, 15/1777
Clovis, 9/1007
Clowns, 5/**583–4**, 5/*583–4*
rodeos, 18/2116
Club moss, 5/**584**, 5/*584*, 16/1939, 16/1947, 16/*1953*
Clubs, 5/**584–5★**
Cluster flies, 8/*966*
Clutch, automobiles, 3/276, 7/766
Clyde River, 18/2176
Clydesdale horses, 10/1207
CN Tower, 2/205
Coaches, carriages, 4/474
Coal, 5/**585–6**, 5/*585–6*, 9/1018
mining, 5/585–6, 5/586, 13/*1600*, 13/*1602*
types, 5/585–6
Coalbrookdale iron bridge, 4/*391*
Coalbrookdale Ironworks, 11/*1304*
Coal forests, 16/1952, 16/*1952*
Coal miners, Lewis, John L., 12/1419
Coal oil, 11/1364
Coal tar, 5/586
Coast guard, 5/**586–7**, 5/*587*, 13/1564, 16/1967, 18/2211
Coast Guard Academy, 5/597, 21/2498
Coast Mountains, British Columbia, 15/*1786*

Coast Range, Oregon, 15/1841
Coasts, 18/2182–3, 18/*2182–3*
Coat of arms, 5/**587–8**, 5/*588★*
Coats, fur, 9/1023, 9/*1023*
Cobblers, 18/2214
Cobblestones, 19/2342
Cobras, 19/2246
Cobs, 7/772
Cocaine, 1/33, 7/769, 14/1703
Cocci, 3/288
Cochin China, 21/2525
Cochise, 2/180, 2/217, 5/**588**, 5/*589*, 11/1271
Cockatiels, 16/1880
Cockatoos, 16/1880
Cockcroft, Sir John, 16/*1881*
Cocklebur, 16/1962
Cockpits, aircraft, 1/68
Cocoa powder, 5/542
Coconino Plateau, 9/1099
Coconut palms, 15/1866
Coconuts, 15/1810
Cod, 8/*949*
Codes, 5/**589★**
Cody, William Frederick (Buffalo Bill), 4/404, 4/*404*, 10/1184, 14/1734, 16/1975
Co-education, 5/596, 7/803
Coelenterates, 2/156, 5/**589–91**, 5/*589–90*, 11/1328
Coeur d'Arlene Indians, 10/1239
Coeur d'Arlene Lake, 10/1237
Coffee, 5/**591**, 5/*591*, 5/598
Cogs, ships, 18/*2207*
Cohan, George M., 5/**591**, 5/*591*, 14/1687, 14/1688
Coimbra, 16/1982
Coins, 5/**592**, 5/*592★*, 14/1631
dies for, 6/728, 6/*728*
silver, 18/2225
Coke, 5/586, 11/1303
Colbert, Claudette, 1/21
Colbert, Edwin H., 16/1965
Cold, 10/1168–70, 10/*1169–70*
cryogenics, 6/682
insulation, 11/1282–3
Cold fronts, 21/2562
Colds, 5/**609**, 6/*649*
sneezes, 19/2246
Cold type, 20/2480–1
Cold War, 8/881, 11/1359, 11/1365
Coleridge, Samuel Taylor, 21/2604
Cole, Thomas, 18/2128
The Notch of the White Mountains, 18/2128, 18/*2128*
Collage, 6/722
photographic, 6/691
Collared anteater, 2/172
Collecting, 5/**593–5**, 5/*593–4*, 10/119102
museums, 14/1678–80
Collective bargaining, 12/1381
Collectivization, 19/2324
Colleges, 5/**595–7**, 7/804
physical education, 16/1921–2
Collies, 6/*745*
Collins, Michael, 5/**597**, 5/*597*, 9/1106
Collins, Wilkie, 15/1802
Collip, James, 3/303
Collodi, James, 5/534
Colloid chemistry, 5/519
Coloane, 12/1472

Colombia, 5/507, 5/**597–8**
Colonial National Historical park, 11/1320
Colonies, 2/244, 5/**598–9**
Africa, 1/48–9
British Empire, 4/394–5
Colons, punctuation, 17/2030
Color, 5/**599–601**, 5/*599–600★*
below sea, 15/1817
interior decorating, 11/1287
metal, 13/1566
minerals, 13/1597
protective, 17/2011–13, 17/*2012*
spectrum, 19/2305–7, 19/*2305–6*
television, 20/2396–7
Coloradas, Mangus, 2/217
Colorado, 5/**601–4**, 5/*601–2*, 16/1930
climate, 5/602
history, 5/602–3
industries, 5/603
land, 5/601–3
state emblems, 5/*603*
Colorado beetle, 8/*326*
Colorado City, 5/602
Colorado Desert, 9/*1056*
Colorado Plateau, 15/1757, 21/2504
Colorado River, 5/602, 12/1385
Colorado Springs, 21/2498
Color blindness, 5/**604–5**, 5/*604*
Color engraving, 17/2005
Color printing, 17/2003, 17/*2004*
Color vision, 8/899, 18/2220
Colosseum, Rome, 18/2119, 18/2128, 18/2132, 20/*2420*
COLOSSUS, 5/622
Colossus of Rhodes, 18/*2193*, 18/2194
Colter, John, 22/2626, 22/2634
Colt Navy revolvers, 10/*1131*
Colts, 10/1203
Colugos, 8/967
Columbia, Mount, 1/90
Columbia Broadcasting System (CBS), 20/2398
Columbia Plateau, 21/2544
Columbia River, 5/541, 5/**605**
Columbia Space Shuttle, 8/889, 19/2294, 19/*2296*
Columbia University, 5/595
Columbine, 16/1870
Columbus, Bartholomew, 21/2570
Columbus, Christopher, 3/255, 3/352, 4/468, 5/555, 5/**605–6★**, 5/*605*, 6/663, 6/684, 8/*891*, 8/892–3, 8/*892*, 8/893, 9/1006, 10/1133, 10/1179, 10/1188, 10/1189, 10/1199, 11/1261, 11/1306, 11/*1306*, 11/1335, 15/1771, 15/1822, 18/2207, 19/2301
Columbus Day, 15/1822
Columns, architectural types, 2/202
Comanche Indians, 5/602, 5/**606**, 5/*606*, 11/1271
Combat, karate, 11/1356, 11/*1356*
Combination locks, 12/1457, 12/1458
Combine harvesters, 8/909, 13/1543
Comb jelly, 5/**607**
Combustion, 8/932
Comedies, 7/759
Comenius, John Amos, 5/531
Comets, 5/**607–8**, 5/*607–8*, 19/2260
Halley, Edmond, 10/1140
Comet West, 5/*608*
Comic books, 5/532–3

Comics, 5/**608**, 5/*608*
cartooning, 4/478–9
Comino, 12/1494
Cominotto, 12/1494
Commas, 17/2030
Commedia dell'arte, 16/1870
Commensalism, 7/795, 20/2369
Commerce Department, 4/426
Commercial art, 5/**608–9**, 5/*609*
Commercial banks, 3/302
Commercials, 1/38
Commercial treaties, 20/2458
Commodity money, 14/1631
Commodus, 18/2131
Common cold, 5/**609**
Common-law marriage, 13/1519
Common oryx, 2/173
Commonwealth, 4/395
Commonwealth of Nations, 5/**610**, 7/858
Communication, 5/**610–12**, 5/*611–12*
books, 3/366–9
dolphins and porpoises, 7/752
drawing, 7/760–2
fiber optics, 8/927, 8/*927*
journalism, 11/1342–3
language arts, 12/1386–8
languages, 12/1388–91
letter writing, 12/1418–19
libraries, 12/1423–6, 12/*1423–6*
literature, 12/1446–52
magazines, 12/1479–80
modern devices, 5/611–12
Morse Code, 14/1651
Morse, Samuel F.B., 14/1650
newspapers, 15/1760–2, 15/*1760–2*
postal services 19/1983–6
printing, 17/2002–6, 17/*2002–5*
propaganda, 17/2009–10, 17/*2010*
public relations, 17/2022–3
public speaking, 17/2023–4
publishing, 17/2025–6
railroads, 17/2053–9
satellites, 5/**612–14**, 5/*613–14*, 18/2165–6
signals, 18/2220–2, 18/*2221–2*
sign language, 18/2222–3, 18/*2222–3*
speech, 19/2307–9
spelling, 19/2309
teaching, 20/2385–6, 20/*2385*
telecommunications, 20/2388, 20/*2388*
telegraph, 20/2388–90, 20/*2389*
telephone, 20/2390–3, 20/*2390–2*
television, 20/2395–8, 20/*2395–7*
transport, 20/2448–54, 20/*2448–54*
uses, 5/612
written language, 5/611, 22/2624–5, 22/*2624*
Communism, 5/**614**, 19/2249
Bulgarian, 4/410
capitalism and, 4/459–60
China, 5/537, 5/540
Lenin, Vladimir Ilich, 12/1414
Mao Tse-tung, 13/1508
Soviet Union, 19/2285–6
Marx, Karl, 13/1521
Communism, Mount, 19/2282
Communist governments, 9/1095
Communities, ecology, 7/794
Community, 5/**615**
Community colleges, 5/596
Community hospitals, 10/1209

Commutative Laws, 2/213
Commuter airlines, 1/65
Commuters, 19/2347, 20/2445, 20/2446
Commuter trains, 17/2054–5
Comnsumer Product Safety Commission, 21/2490
Como, Lake, 12/1384
Comoro Islands, 5/616–17
Compact cameras, 4/441
Compact discs, 5/617, 5/617, 17/2073
Comparative anatomy, 2/133
Compass, 5/617–18, 5/617–18
  geometry, 9/1059
  gyroscopes, 10/1135, 10/1135
  sun, 4/423
Competition:
  ecology, 7/795
  economics, 7/799
Complementary colors, 5/601
Composers, 5/618–20*
  see also Music
Composite flowers, 8/965
Composition, 5/620–1
Composition, typesetting, 20/2480–1
Compound eyes, 18/2219
Compounds, chemical, 5/520, 7/829
Computers, 5/621–4, 5/621–4, 7/826, 13/1560
  Babbage, Charles, 3/285
  bar codes, 3/303
  calculators, 4/432–3
  communications, 5/612
  data protection, 6/700
  early, 5/622
  hardware, 5/623–4
  how it works, 5/623
  languages, 12/1391
  learning and, 12/1406, 12/1407
  robots, 17/2107–8
  software, 5/624
Comstock, Henry, 15/1743
Comte, Auguste, 19/2253
Conakry, 10/1125
Concave lens, 12/1415
Concentration, card game, 4/464
Concepción, 5/535
Concepcion Mission, battle of, 4/378
Concert bands, 15/1840
Concertina, 1/21
Conchs, 14/1625
Concord, 15/1751
Concorde, 3/282, 3/282, 3/283
Concord and Lexicon, Battle of, 1/116, 1/125, 3/318, 13/1530
Concrete, 6/625, 6/625
  building materials, 4/407, 6/646
Condamine, La, 14/1627
Condensation, 5/582, 5/582, 21/2552–3
Condensed milk, 6/692
Condiments, 19/2310
Conditioned behaviour, 16/1886
Condominiums, 10/1215
Conduction, 10/1170
Conduction wires, electric motors, 7/816
Conductivity, 13/1567
Conductors, 18/2189
  electricity, 7/820
  orchestral, 15/1839
Conestoga wagons, 21/2577
Confederate Army, 5/564, 5/566–9

Confederate States of America, 1/83, 1/120, 5/566–9, 6/625–6, 6/626
  Davis, Jefferson, 6/701
  Lee, Robert E., 12/1410
Confederation of Senegambia, 9/1033
Confiance, 21/2542
Confucianism, 2/243, 12/137, 17/2079
Confucius, 2/136, 5/539, 6/626–7, 6/627, 16/1915
Congenital diseases, 6/738
Congo, 6/627–8, 6/626
Congo Free State, 22/2641
Congo-Ocean railroad, 6/628
Congo River, 6/627, 6/628
  see also Zaire River
Congress (US), 6/628–31, 6/628–30, 6/642
  Capitol, 4/4602
  House of Representatives, 6/628–30
  law making, 6/630–1
  Senate, 6/630
Congress of Industrial Organizations (CIO), 12/1380–1, 12/1419
Congressional districts, 6/629
Congressional Medal of Honor, 13/1550, 13/1551
Coniferous forests, 16/1945
  animals, 2/150
Conifers, 6/624, 6/631–4*, 6/631–3, 8/884, 16/1953
  pines, 6/632–3
Conjugation, 16/1882, 17/2089
Conjunctions, 16/1882
Conjurors, magic, 12/1481–3
Conkling, Roscoe, 2/235
Connecticut, 6/634–7, 6/634–6
  climate, 6/636
  history, 6/636
  industry, 6/636–7
  land, 6/634–6
  map, 6/635
  state emblem, 6/635
Connecticut River, 6/636, 13/1528
Connecticut Valley, 15/1751, 15/1752
Conners, Jimmy, 19/2317
Conquistadors, 6/637–8, 6/637–8
  farming, 1/53
  Pizarro, Francisco, 16/1935–6
Conrad, Emperor, 6/679
Conrad, Joseph, 6/638, 6/638
Conrail, 17/2059
Conscription, 2/224–5
Conservation, 6/638–40, 6/639–40
  energy, 7/846–7
  forests, 12/1470
  minerals, 13/1602
  national forests, 14/1706–7
  national parks, 14/1709–13
  wilderness areas, 21/2585
Conservative Jews, 11/1345
Conservators, 2/238, 14/1678
Conshelf I, II, III, 15/1820–1
Constable, John, 2/232, 6/640–1, 6/640
Constantine, Emperor, 5/546, 9/1080, 11/1329, 15/1847, 18/2131, 18/2131
Constantinople, 3/260, 4/424, 18/2121, 18/2131
  trade, 20/2444
Constellations, 6/641–2*, 6/641–3
Constitution (US), 1/116, 5/560,

5/561, 6/642–5 6/644, 21/2488, 21/2541
  amendments, 6/644–5
  Article 1, 6/629
  changing, 6/644–5
  Madison, James, 12/1478–9
  making, 6/644
  presidency, 17/1997–8
Constitution, USS, 15/1782
Constitutional Convention, 21/2488
Constitutional law, 12/1400
Constitutional monarchies, 9/1095
Constitutions, Magna Carta, 12/1483
Constrictor snakes, 19/2245–6
Construction, 6/645–9, 6/645–8
  houses, 6/648–9
  materials, 6/646–7
  skyscrapers, 6/647–8
Consuls, 18/2129
Consumer protection, 18/2189
Contact lenses, 9/1084
Contagious diseases, 6/649–50, 6/649–50, 6/737
Containerization, 20/2452
Container ships, 13/1564
Contemplation, 14/1628
Continental Army, 2/226
Continental Association, 1/125
Continental climate, 5/576
Continental Congress, 6/651–2, 6/651
  see also First, Second and Third Continental Congress
Continental divide, 5/602, 6/650, 6/652, 17/2113
Continental drift, 6/652, 7/782
Continental Navy, 14/1728
Continental shelf, 6/650–1, 15/1815, 15/1816
Continental slope, 6/651, 15/1816, 15/1816
Continents, 6/650–1, 6/650–2
  formation, 7/785
Contour maps, 13/1511
Contra Costa Laundry, 12/1397
Contras, 15/1771
Control, automation, 3/271–2
Conundrums, 17/2102
Convection, 10/1170
Convents, 14/1628
Convex lenses, 12/1415
Conveyor belts, 13/1507
Cook, Captain James, 2/171, 3/265, 4/392, 4/395, 6/652–3, 6/653, 8/893, 10/1158, 16/1972, 19/2356
Cooke, Hope, 18/2224
Cook, Frederick, 16/1889
Cooking, 6/653–5, 6/653–4
  diet, 15/1811
  Gingerbread faces, 6/655
  Hamburgers, 6/654
  Potato Salad, 6/654–5
  spices and herbs, 19/2310–11
  terms used, 6/655
  see also Food
Cook Islands, 16/1971
Cooksonia, 16/1952
Coolidge, Calvin, 6/656, 6/656, 10/1152
Cooper, Gary, 1/28
Cooper, James Fenimore, 6/656–7, 6/656
Cooper, Leon, 3/304

Cooper, Leroy G., 2/248
Cooper River, 19/2274
Cooperstown, 3/310
Coot, 6/671
Copacabana beach, 17/2103
Cope, Edward Drinker, 6/733
Copenhagen, 2/140, 6/717, 6/717
Copepods, 6/682, 13/1516
Copernicus, Nicolaus, 2/250, 6/657, 6/657, 9/1031, 11/1364, 15/1838, 18/2173, 21/2499
Copiers, photocopiers, 16/1916
Copland, Aaron, 6/657–8, 6/657
Copper, 13/1567
Copy editors, 17/2025
Copyright, 16/1884–5, 20/2458
Copywriter, 5/609
Coracles, 3/360
Coral, 5/590, 5/590, 6/658–9, 6/658–9, 9/1050
Coral islands, 15/1854
Corallite, 6/658
Coral reefs, Great Barrier Reef, 9/1106–7, 9/1107
Coral Sea, 6/659
Coral Sea, USS, 6/659
Coral snakes, 19/2245, 19/2246
Corcovado, 17/2103
Cordage, 18/2136
Cordaites, 16/1952
Corday, Charlotte, 9/10011
Core Mantle, 7/784
Coriolis effect, 21/2561, 21/2563
Cork (bark), 3/304, 3/304
Cormorants, 21/2551, 21/2552
Corms, 4/408
  garden flowers, 9/1039
Corn, 6/659–60, 6/659–60, 9/1097, 9/1097, 9/1103
  flour making, 8/960
Corn belt, 6/660
Corn borers, 4/422
Corncob, 6/659
Cornea, 8/898
Cornell, Katherine, 1/27
Cornet, 4/385
Corn oil, 6/660
Corn picker, 8/909
Cornsilk, 6/659
Cornstarch, 6/660
Corn syrup, 6/660
Cornwallis, Lord, 1/128
Coronado, Francisco, 2/217, 5/549, 6/637, 6/660, 7/869, 8/893, 11/1355, 15/1758
Coronations, 11/1368
Corporations, 6/661
Correggio, 17/2085
Corrosion, 6/661, 6/661
Corsairs, 16/1934
Corsets, 8/914
Cortés, Hernando, 3/284, 6/637, 6/661–2, 6/662, 13/1573, 13/1575, 13/1576, 14/1697
Cortex, 4/384
Cortisone, 10/1201
Corydon, 11/1256, 11/1258
Cos, 10/1187
Cosmetics, 6/662–3, 6/662–3
  makeup, 12/1488–9
  perfume, 16/1899, 16/1899
Cosmologists, 17/1996
Cosmonauts, 2/248
Cossacks, 18/2146

Costa Rica, 5/505–7, 6/*663–4*, 6/*663–4*
Costume jewelry, 11/1334
Côte d'Ivoire, 11/1313–14
Coteries, 17/*1995*
Cotopaxi, 7/800
Cottage cheese, 5/517
Cottingham, Robert, 14/*1621*
Cotton, 5/581, 6/**664–5**, 6/*664–5*
growing, 1/83
spinning and weaving, 19/2313–14
Cotton gin, 21/2583
Cotton mouse, 17/2067
Cottontail rabbits, 17/2040
Cotton-tuft rugs, 4/473
Cotylosaurs, 17/2089–90
Coubertin, Pierre de, 15/1830, 15/*1830*
Cougar, 4/488
Counselors, 12/1401
Counterespionage, 19/2319
Counterfeiting, 6/**665**, 6/*665*, 6/673
Counter Reformation, 3/307,
17/2015–16, 18/2121
Counterrevolutions, 17/2095
Countertenors, 18/2227
Countesses, 15/1780
Counties, 6/**666**★, 6/*666*
Counting, 15/1806
abacus, 1/12–13
systems, 15/1807
Countries:
national anthems, 14/1705
nations, 14/1704
see also individual countries
Counts, 15/1780
County agents, 1/55
County Boards, 12/1457
County government, 12/1457
Coups d'état, 17/2095
Courantyne River, 10/1133
Courbet, Gustave, 15/1860, 15/*1861*,
17/2068
Beach in Normandy, 17/2068,
17/*2068*
Court of appeals, 6/667
Court of Claims, 6/667
Court of Customs and Patent Appeals, 6/667
Court jesters, 5/583
Court-martial, 6/667
Court of Military Appeals, 6/667
Court systems, 6/**666–8**, 6/*667*
lawyers and judges, 12/1401–2
Supreme Court, 19/2355–6
Cousteau, Jacques-Yves, 6/**668**,
8/*893*, 14/1627, 15/1820–1,
18/2177
Covens, 21/2599
Coventry Cathedral, 20/2379
Coves, 18/2183
Cowbirds, 3/345
Cowboy boots, 18/2214
Cowboys, 6/**668–9**, 6/*668*, 15/*1841*,
17/2061–2
rodeos, 18/2116–17, 18/*2116–17*,
21/*2494*, 22/*2625*
Cowcatchers, 17/2058
Cow-keeping ants, 2/168
Cowpox, 11/1328–9
Cows, dairy farming, 4/494, 6/691–2
Coxswains, 18/2139
Coydogs, 6/670
Coyotes, 4/*469*, 6/**669–70**, 6/*669*,
21/2599

Crabeater seals, 16/*1965*
Crab Nebula, 19/*2326*, 19/2327
Crabs, 6/681
Cracking, petroleum, 9/10466
Cradles, 2/*178*
Crafts:
enamelling, 7/842–3, 7/*842*
folk art, 8/968–9, 8/*968–9*
Craftsmen:
apprentices, 2/185
carpenters, 4/471–2
guilds, 10/1124–5
Craft unions, 12/1380
Crakow shoes, 18/2213
Cramp, 14/1677
swimming, 12/1432
Crampons, 14/1671, 14/*1671*
Cram, Steve, 20/2441
Crane and Alexander, 21/*2511*
Cranes, 3/*346*, 6/**670–1**, 6/*670*,
21/2551
Crane, Stephen, 6/**671**, 6/*671*
Cranium, 4/383
Crankshafts, 3/276, 7/849
Crassus, Marcus Licinius, 4/429,
18/2130, 19/2303
Cratere du Nouveau-Quebec, 17/2036
Crater Lake, 12/1385, 15/1842
Crawl, swimming, 20/2365, 20/*2365*
Crayfish, 6/681
Crazy Horse, Chief, 6/687, 11/1271,
18/2143, 18/2228
Crécy, battle of, 10/1227, 16/1912
Cream, 6/692
Credit cards, 14/1631–2, 19/2338–9
Creditors, 1/22
Cree Indians, 1/100, 6/**671**, 6/*671*,
13/1503, 18/2164
Creek Indians, 1/83, 6/**672**, 6/675,
9/1062, 11/1270, 15/1827,
18/21189, 20/2404
Creoles, 12/1463
Crested dog's-tail grass, 9/*1104*
Crested porcupine, 16/*1980*
Crete, 9/1110, 9/1111, 13/1543,
21/2535
Minoan art, 9/1114–15
Minoans, 9/1111
Crew cuts, 10/1139
Crib dolls, 7/749
Cricetidae, 17/2065
Cricket, 6/**672–3**, 6/*672*
Crick, Francis H.C., 9/1052, 9/*1052*
Crime, 6/**673–4**, 6/*673–4*
juvenile delinquency, 11/1350
murder, 14/1675
outlaws, 15/1851
police, 16/1966–7, 16/*1966–7*
prisons, 17/2006–7, 17/*2006–7*
reasons for, 6/674
spies, 19/2319–20
terrorism, 20/2411
treason, 20/2456–7, 20/*2456*
trials, 20/2463–5
Crimean War, 6/**674–5**, 6/*675*
Nightingale, Florence, 15/1775
Crime fiction, 12/1450
Criminal cases, court sytem, 6/666
Criminal law, 12/1399
Crimson rosellas, 16/*1880*
Crinolines, 8/*913*
Crippen, Robert, 19/*2296*
Cristóbal, 16/1868
Cristofori, Bartolommeo, 16/1925

Croats, 22/2639
Crockett, Davy, 1/84, 6/**675**, 6/*675*,
12/1412
Crocodiles, 1/**102–3**, 1/*102*,
17/2090–1, 17/*2090*
Crocodilians, 17/2090–1
Crocus, 4/408
Croix de Guerre, 13/1550, 13/*1551*
Croker, Thomas Crofton, 8/905
Cro-Magnon man, 10/*1220*,
10/1222–3
Crompton, Samuel, 19/*2313*, 19/2314
Cromwell, Oliver, 6/**675–6**, 6/*676*,
6/677, 7/858, 17/2032–3
Cromwell, Richard, 6/676, 7/858
Crook, George, 2/217
Crops, agricultural machinery,
8/908–10
Crossbows, 4/377, 4/*377*, 21/2559
Crossbreeding, 4/412
Cross-examination, 20/2464
Cross, John Walter, 7/836
Cross-pollination, 8/961, 16/1942
Cross-stitch, 14/1736, 14/*1736*
Crossties, 17/2055
Crossword puzzles, 6/**676**, 6/*676*,
21/2603
Croton, 17/2034
Crow Indians, 11/1262, 14/1642,
18/2229, 22/2625
Crowned cranes, 6/*670*
Crowned pigeons, 3/*346*, 16/1929
Crown jewels, 6/**676–7**, 6/*677*
Crown-of-thorns starfish, 9/1106–7
Crows, 6/**678**, 6/*678*
Crucifixes, 17/*1995*
Cruikshank, George, 5/533
Cruisers, 14/1728
Crusades, 4/424, 4/430, 6/663,
6/**678–80**, 6/*679–80*, 8/880,
12/1372, 12/*1372*, 12/1462,
13/1588, 13/1590, 17/2101
Children's, 6/680
Eighth, 6/680
Fifth, 6/680
First, 6/678
Fourth, 6/679
furniture and, 9/1025
Second, 6/678–9
Seventh, 6/680
Sixth, 6/680
Third, 6/679
Crust, Earth's, 7/782
Crustaceans, 6/**680–2**★, 6/*680–2*
barnacles, 6/681–2
ten-legged, 6/681
tiny, 6/682
Cryogenic engineering, 7/852
refrigeration, 17/2076
Cryogenic probes, 19/2358
Cryogenics, 6/**682**, 10/1170, 16/1923
Crystalline solids, 19/2261
Crystal Palace, 8/903
Crystals, 6/**682–3**★, 6/*682–3*
minerals, 13/1596
piezo-electric, 17/2071
solutions and, 6/683
unit crystals, 6/682–3
Ctenophora, 5/607
Cuauhtemoc, 3/284
Cuba, 6/662, 6/**684–5**, 6/*684*,
11/1359, 21/2569, 21/2570
Castro, Fidel, 4/484–5
CIA and, 5/508

Missile Crisis, 11/1359, 11/1365
Revolution, 17/2095
Spanish-American War, 19/2299
Cuban bee hummingbird, 10/1226
Cubism, 2/234, 5/509, 14/1620–1
Cuckoo bees, 3/325
Cuckoos, 3/*346*, 13/*1593*
Cud, 2/173
Cuernavaca, 13/1573
Cugnot, Nicolas, 3/272, 3/*272*
Cui, César, 17/2103
Cullet, 9/1082
Cultivator, 8/909
Cultural anthropologists, 2/175
Cultural Revolution, 13/1508
Cultures, 6/**685–6**, 6/*685*
customs, 6/687–8
geography, 9/1055
Cumans, 18/2144
Cumberland, Duke of, 11/1362
Cumberland Gap, 11/1362, 21/2576
Cumberland Mountains, 2/183
Cumberland Plateau, 11/1360,
20/2403
Cumulonimbus clouds, 5/*582*
Cumulus clouds, 5/582, 5/*582*
Cuna Indians, 16/1867
Cuneiform, 7/802, 19/2352, 19/*2352*
writing, 2/135
Cupronickel, 13/1568
Curaçao, 19/2345, 21/2569
Curators, 2/238, 14/1678
Cured foods, 8/976
Curie, Eve, 6/686
Curie family, 6/**686**, 6/*686*
Curie, Frédéric, 6/686
Curie, Marie, 6/686, 6/*686*, 17/2049
Curie, Piere, 6/686, 6/*686*, 17/2049
Curlews, 21/2552
Curling, 6/**686–7**, 6/*686*
Currency, money, 14/1630–3
Current, electricity, 7/819
Currents, ocean, 15/1815, 15/*1815*
Cursive scripts, 10/1146
Curtain walls, 6/648
Curtiz, Michael, 14/*1661*
Cusabo Indians, 19/2274
Cuser, George, 18/2229
Cuspids, 20/2386
Custer Battlefield, 14/1708
Custer, George, 6/**687**, 6/*687*,
11/1271, 14/1642, 18/2228
Custis, Martha, 21/2547
Customs, 6/**687–8**, 6/*687*
burial, 4/**413–14**, 4/*413–14*
cultures, 6/685–6
folklore, 8/971
Customs Court, 6/667
Customs duties, 20/2382
Cuticles, 2/146, 14/1626
Cutlasses, 20/2368
Cuts, first aid, 8/939, 8/*939*
Cutters, dies, 6/728, 6/*728*
Cutting, sewing, 18/2195
Cuttings, plant breeding, 16/1942
Cuttlefish, 14/1625
Cutworms moth, 4/422
Cuvilliers Theater, Munich, 20/*2421*
Cuzco, 16/*1904*, 16/1936
Cycads, 16/1953
Cycling, 3/337–8
Cyclones, 10/1228, 21/2562–3
Cyclopes, 9/1076
Cygnets, 7/772, 7/*772*

Cylinder presses, 17/2004
Cypress family, 6/633
Cypress Gardens, 21/2555, 21/2555
Cyprus, 6/**688–9,** 6/688, 13/1589
Cyril, Bishop, 18/2143
Cyrillic alphabet, 1/106, 18/2143
Cyrus the Great, 11/1299, 16/1902
Cytology, 2/133, 3/342, 3/343
    plant, 3/375
Cytoplasm, 5/502
Czar 18/2146
Czechoslovakia, 6/**689,** 6/689
Czechs, 6/689
Czolgosz, Leon F., 13/1544

Dd

Dacia, 18/2126
Dacron, 20/2372
Dadaism, 6/**690–1,** 6/690
Daedalus, 3/280, 6/**691,** 13/1543
Daffodils, 4/408, 4/408
Da Gama, Vasco, 8/892
Daggers, 20/2368
Daguere, Louis, 16/1920
Daguerreotypes, 16/1920
Dahlia anemone, 5/590
Dahomey see Benin
Daily Food Plan, 15/1811
Daimler, Gottlieb, 14/1666
Daimler motorcycles, 14/1666
Dairy cattle, 4/494
Dairy farming, 6/**691–2,** 6/691–2
Dairy products, 6/**692–3,** 6/692–3
Daisies, 21/2586
Dakar, 18/2190, 18/2190
Dakota Indians, 18/2228, 21/2596
Dalai lama, 20/2424
D'Alembert, Jean, 7/843
Dallas, 6/**693,** 6/693, 20/2414,
    20/2414
Dallas, George Mifflin, 6/693
Dalmatia, 22/2638
Dalmatian dogs, 6/747
Dalton, John, 3/258, 5/604, 7/829
Damage, insurance, 11/1283–4
Damages, 6/673
Damascus, 14/1654, 20/2372, 20/2373
Damietta River, 15/1776
Damocles, 6/**695**
Dams, 6/**693–5,** 6/694–5
    floods, 8/955–6, 8/955–6
    gateways, 6/695
    highest, 6/695
    largest, 6/695
    spillways, 6/695
    types, 6/694–5
Damsel flies, 7/757
Danaë, 16/1902
Dance, 6/**695–8,** 6/696–8
    ballet, 3/295–7, 6/696
    ballroom, 6/697, 6/697
    choreography, 6/696–7
    Duncan, Isadore, 7/774
    folk, 6/697, 8/969–70, 8/970
    modern dance, 6/696
    national, 8/970
    Pavlova, Anna, 16/1886
    rock 'n' roll, 6/697
    square dancing, 19/2320–1
Dance Theater of Harlem, 3/297
Dandelions, 18/2188

Dandyhorse, 3/337
Danish, 18/2168
Dante Alighieri, 6/**698,** 8/956
Dante, Nicholas, 14/1688
Danton, Georges, 9/10011
Danube River, 4/409, 6/**698–9,**
    6/698–9, 10/1227–8, 18/2126,
    22/2638
Danubians, 5/616
Dardanelles, 3/357, 20/2475
Dar es Salaam, 20/2379
Dare, Virginia, 15/1788
Darien, 16/1867
Darion, Joe, 14/1688
Darius I, King, 3/318, 11/1367,
    16/1903
Darius III, King, 3/319
Darjeeling, 20/2384
Darkrooms, photography, 16/1919
Darling River, 14/1675
Darnley, Lord, 13/1522
Darrow, Clarence, 5/562
Dartmoor pony, 10/1205
Dartmouth College, Hanover,
    18/2169
Darts, 6/**699,** 6/699
Darwin, Charles, 6/**699–700,** 6/700,
    8/886, 8/887, 9/1030, 18/2173,
    19/2254, 21/2539–40, 22/2648,
    22/2648
Dash, punctuation, 17/2030
Dashes, track event, 20/2440
Data protection, 6/**700**
Daughters of the Confederacy,
    19/2337
Dauphine, La, 12/1485
David, King of the Jews, 11/1329,
    11/1335
Davies, Jim, 5/608
Davis, Benjamin Oliver, 6/**700,**
    6/700
Davis, Benjamin Oliver Jr., 6/**700–1,**
    6/701
Davis, Bette, 14/1663
Davis Cup, 20/2407
Davis, Jefferson, 1/120, 6/625–6,
    6/**701,** 6/701, 9/1062, 12/1410,
    13/1613, 18/2180, 19/2337,
    19/2337
Davis, Sammy Jr., 21/2511
Davy, Sir Humphrey, 8/908, 10/1169
Dawes, William, 1/125, 17/2094
Dawn redwood, 6/633
Dawson, Yukon, 22/2640
Dayan, Moshe, 13/1591
Day and night, 6/**701–2★,** 6/702
Day at the Races, 1/28
Day, Stephen, 17/2025
Days of the week, 6/**702**
Dayton, Ohio, 15/1826
D-Day, 22/2614, 22/2617
DDT, 11/1277, 16/1904, 17/2065
Dead-letter office, 16/1985
Dead reckoning, 14/1724
Dead Sea, 6/**702–3★,** 6/703, 12/1385
Dead Sea Scrolls, 3/336, 6/**703–4,**
    6/703
Deaf and dumb language, 18/2222–3
Deafness, 10/1165–5
    education, 19/2303–4
    Keller, Helen, 11/1357
    speech and, 19/2308
Dearborne, 13/1581
Death, life after, 7/810

Death penalty, 6/674
Death Valley, 4/436, 6/**704,** 6/704,
    14/1622, 14/1709, 15/1784,
    21/2494
DeBeers Consolidated Mines Com-
    pany, 17/2100
Debs, Eugene, 6/**704,** 6/704
Debtors, 1/22
Debussy, Claude, 5/543, 6/**704–5,**
    15/1775
Decaffeinated coffee, 5/591
Decapods, 6/681
Decathlon, 20/2443
Decatur, 10/1242
Decatur, Stephen, 3/303
Deccan Plateau, 11/1252
December, 6/**705–6,** 6/705–6
    special events, 6/705
Decibels, 19/2265
Deciduous forests, 16/1945
Deciduous trees, 20/2458
Decimal numbers, 2/214, 6/**706,**
    6/706, 13/1571, 15/1807
    fractions, 9/999
Decks, 18/2210
Declaration of Independence, 1/30,
    1/32, 1/115, 1/122, 1/123, 1/126,
    6/652, 6/**707,** 6/707, 10/1143
    Articles of Confederation, 2/236–7
    Independence Day, 11/1249–50
    Independence Hall, 11/1250,
    11/1250
    Jefferson, Thomas, 11/1326–7
    Liberty Bell, 12/1422
Declaration of Rights, 6/651
Declaration of the Rights of the
    Child, 5/560
Declension, 16/1882
Decomposition, 7/797, 8/922
Decorah, 11/1298
Decoration:
    carving, 4/480
    interior, 11/1286–7, 11/1286–7
Decoration Day, 13/1559–60
Decoration Militaire, 13/1550
Decorations, awards, 13/1550–1
Decorative arts, folk art, 8/968–9,
    8/968–9
Decuma, 8/915
Deep-sea life, 6/**708,** 6/708
Deer, 6/**708–10,** 6/708–10
    antlers, 10/1202, 10/1202
Deere, John, 17/1994
Deerskin, 9/10023
Defecation, 6/731
Defendants, 6/674
    court sytem, 6/667
    trials, 12/1401
Defense:
    animal, 2/148–9, 2/148
    space weapons, 19/2297
    see also Arms and Armor; Weapons
Defense Intelligence Agency (DIA),
    19/2319
Deficiency diseases, 6/738
Definitions, dictionaries, 6/727
Defoe, Daniel, 6/**710–11,** 6/711,
    12/1446, 12/1480, 15/1801
De Forest, Lee, 17/2051
Degas, Edgar, 4/482, 6/**711,** 6/711,
    10/1245, 15/1846
De Gaulle, Charles, 6/**711–12,**
    6/712, 9/1001, 9/1010, 9/1010
Degeneration diseases, 6/739

Dehydrated foods, 8/976
Dekaawida, 8/950
De la Mare, Walter, 5/533
DeLarge, Robert, 17/2069
Delaware, 6/**712–15,** 6/712–14
    employment, 6/714–15
    history, 6/714
    land, 6/712–14
    map, 6/713
    state emblems, 6/713
Delaware Indians, 1/100, 11/1270,
    15/1824, 16/1894, 21/2574
Delaware River, 16/1893, 16/1910
De La Warr, Lord, 6/712,
    11/1319–20
Del Cano, Juan Sebastián, 12/1481
Delft, 16/1989, 16/1990
Delftware, 16/1990
Delmarva Peninsula, 5/523, 13/1524,
    21/2532
Delphi, 9/1113, 17/201
Delta-wing aircraft, 1/68
Demand, economics, 7/798
Demavend, Mount, 13/1590
Demerara River, 10/1133
Demerol, 14/1703
Demeter, 9/1088, 9/1089
Demian, Cyril, 1/21
Demigods, 14/1695
De Milles, Agnes, 3/297
Democracy, 6/**715–16,** 6/715, 9/1094,
    9/1113
    ancient civilizations, 2/137
    elections, 7/814–16, 7/815
    Magna Carta, 12/1483
Democratic Party, 16/1968, 21/2489
Democritus, 3/258, 7/828, 7/829
Demography, 16/1979–80
Dempsey, Jack, 4/381
Dendrites, 14/1739
Denmark, 6/**716–17,** 6/716–17
    Anderson, Hans Christian,
    2/139–40
    Bohr, Niels Henrik David, 3/364
    Bering, Vitus, 3/331
    Greenland, 9/1117–18, 9/1117–18
    King Canute, 4/457, 4/457
    Vikings, 21/2527
    Brahe, Tycho, 4/381
Dennis, Patrick, 14/1688
Denominators, 2/214, 9/999
Dens, coyotes, 6/669
Density, 13/1537
    bouyancy, 4/411–12
Dental care, 20/2387–8
Dental hygienist, 6/717
Dentistry, 6/**717–18,** 6/718
Dentures, 6/718
Denver, 5/602, 5/604, 15/1781
Denver, John, 8/973
Deoxyribonucleic acid (DNA),
    9/1052–3, 9/1052
Department stores, 19/2338
Depreciation, 1/22
Depressants, 1/33, 1/94
Depression, 1/119, 1/120, 1/121,
    6/**718–19,** 6/718–19, 10/1200,
    10/1201
Depressions (weather), 21/2563
Depth perception, 18/2220
Derham, James, 13/1554
Dermatologists, 13/1555
Dermis, 10/1224, 18/2232
Desalinization, 21/2556

Descartes, René, 13/*1532*, 13/1534, 16/1882, 16/1915
Descent of Man, 6/700
Desert fox, 8/998, 8/*998*
Deserts, 6/719–21, 6/*719–21*, 16/1945, 18/2158, 18/*2158*
  African, 1/43
  animal life, 2/150
  Australia, 3/263, 3/*265*
  cactus, 4/427–8
  climate, 5/576
  cold deserts, 6/720
  Death Valley, 6/704
  famous, 6/719
  Gobi, 9/1087, 9/*1087*
  Mohave, 14/1622, 14/*1622*
  Sahara, 18/2152–3, 18/*2153*
  soils, 19/*2255*
  wildflowers, 21/2587
Design, 6/721–2*, 6/*721–2*
  industrial, 11/1273
Designers, publishing, 17/2025, 17/*2025*, 17/*2026*
Des Moines, 11/1298
Des Moines River, 11/1295
Desmologos, 14/1727
DeSoto bend, 21/*2555*
De Soto, Hernando, 2/220, 6/**723**, 6/*723*, 8/893, 12/1464, 13/1614, 20/2404
Dessalines, Jean-Jacques, 21/2570
Destroyers, 14/1728
Destructive distillation, 6/741
Destroying angel, 16/1963
Detectives, 6/723
  Federal Bureau of Investigation, 8/920
  fingerprints, 8/930–1
  forensic science, 8/986
  Holmes, Sherlock, 7/756
Detention homes, 17/2007
Detergents, 19/2247–8, 19/*2248*
Detonators, 8/895
Detroit, 6/**723–4**, 6/*723*, 9/1023, 13/1580, 13/1581, 16/1975
Detroit Automobile Company, 3/273
Dettingen, battle of, 9/1060
Deuterium, 21/2550
Developing photographs, 16/*1918*, 16/1919
Devil Canyon, Montana, 14/*1643*
Devil's Den State Park, 2/218
Devil's Island, 9/1006, 17/2006
Devils Postpile, 14/1708
Devils Tower, 14/1708, 22/2625, 22/2626
De Vries, Hugo, 9/1051–2
Dewey Decimal System, 4/491, 12/1423–4
Dewey, George, 19/2299
Dewey, Thomas E., 20/2472
Dew point, 21/2562
Dextrose, 19/2351
Dhahran, 2/193
Diabetes, 3/302–3
  drugs, 7/768
Diablo Plateau, 20/2412
Diaghilev, Sergei, 3/296–7, 15/1775, 16/1886, 19/2340
Dial locks, 12/1458
Dialysis machines, 11/*1365*, 11/1366
Diamonds, 6/**724**, 6/*724*
  abrasives, 1/17, 1/18

baseball, 3/310
  gems, 9/1049–50
  mines, 13/1601, 13/*1602*
Diana, 14/1697
Diana, Princess of Wales, 5/514, 5/*514*
Diaphram, 4/388
Diaries, 6/724–5*
Dias, Bartolomeu, 6/**725**, 6/*725*, 8/892, 9/1032, 14/1700, 16/1982
Dias, Diego, 12/1478
Diaspora, 11/1335
Diatoms, 1/97, 13/1515, 13/*1517*, 17/2109
Díaz, Porfirio, 21/2529
Dickens, Charles, 5/530, 5/533, 6/**725–6**, 6/*725*, 12/*1449*, 15/1801, 15/1802, 15/*1802*
Dickinson, Charles, 7/773
Dickinson, Emily, 2/228, 6/**726**, 6/*726*, 11/1317
Dicotyledons, 3/374, 8/964, 16/1947, 16/*1949*
Dictators, 11/1368
Dictators, 6/**726**, 6/*726*, 9/1095
  fascism, 8/910–11
  Franco, Francisco, 9/1002–3
  Hitler, Adolf, 10/1190–1
  Mussolini, Benito, 14/1693–4
Dictionaries, 6/**726–8**, 6/*727*, 17/2075
  Webster, Noah, 21/2564–5
Diderot, Denis, 7/843, 17/*2075*
Didin014, 17/2017
Dido, 4/477, 21/2530
Dien Bien Phu, battle of, 3/319, 21/2526
Diesel-electric locomotives, 17/2055
Diesel engines, 6/**728–9**, 6/*729*, 7/849
Diesel locomotives, 17/2055
Diesel, Rudolf, 6/728
Dies and molds, 6/**728**, 6/*728*
Diet, 8/974–6, 8/*974–6*
  acids in, 1/24
  Daily Food Plan, 15/1811
  meat, 13/1547
  minerals, 21/2534–5
  nutrition, 15/1811
  nutritional diseases, 6/738
  vegetarian, 21/2512–13
  viatmins, 21/2534–5
  see also Food
Diffraction patterns, 5/500
Digestion, 6/**729–31**, 6/*730–1*, 8/922, 10/1224
  alimentary canal, 6/729–30
  mouth, 6/730
  stomach, 6/730–1
Digger wasps, 21/2549
Digitalis, 13/1552
  drugs, 7/768
Digital machines, 7/826–7
Digital recording, 17/2073, 17/*2073*
Digital watches, 5/*578*
Digue, La, 18/2197
Dikes, 8/955
Dill, Sir John, 22/2616
Dimensions, 6/**732**, 6/*732*
Dinaris Alps, 22/2638
Dingo, 3/267
Dinkas, 1/47
Dinoflagellates, 13/1515

Dinosaurs, 6/**732–3**, 6/*733–5*, 8/885, 8/888
  fossils, 8/992, 8/*993*
Dinwiddie, Robert, 21/2547
Diocese, 4/491, 18/2121
Diocletian, 18/2131
Diodes, 7/827
Diof, Abdou, 18/2190
Dionysius the Elder, 6/695
Dionysus, 9/1088, 13/1584, 14/*1652*, 14/1697
Diphtheria, 5/528, 6/650
Diplodocus, 6/733
Diplomats:
  Hammarskjöld, Dag, 10/1142–3
  Harris, Patricia Roberts, 10/1154
  see also Politicians and Statesmen
Dipper, 3/344
Direct current (DC), electricity, 7/821
Direct Distance Dialing (DDD), 20/2392
Direct mail advertising, 1/38
Dirigibles, 1/78, 20/2454
Disarmament, **6/736**
Disasters, military aid, 2/227
Disc cameras, 4/441
Disciple of Christ, 17/2013
Discipline, soldiers, 2/226
Discovery, 6/653, 10/1218, 11/1319
Disc players, 17/2071–3
Discrimination, 6/**736**, 6/*736*
Discus, 7/802, 20/2442
Discus Thrower, 9/*1114*, 9/1115
Diseases, 6/**736–40**, 6/*737–9*
  allergies, 6/738
  antibiotics, 2/176–7
  antibodies, 2/177
  antiseptics, 2/179
  bacteria, 3/288–9, 6/737, 6/*737*
  body scanners, 3/363
  cancer, 4/455
  childhood, 5/**528–9**
  circulatory, 6/738
  congenital, 6/738
  contagious, 6/649–50
  degeneration, 6/739
  diabetes, 3/302–3
  drugs, 7/767–9, 7/*767–9*
  environmental, 6/738
  fever, 8/926, 8/*926*
  heart, 10/1168
  hereditary, 6/738
  homeopathic medicine, 10/1196–7
  hormonal, 6/738
  hospitals, 10/1209–11, 10/*1209–11*
  immunity, 10/1244
  infections, 6/737
  kinds, 6/737
  medicine, 13/1552–6
  mental, 6/739
  mental health, 13/1562–3
  metabolic, 6/739
  Middle Ages, 13/1553
  mosquitoes, 14/1655
  neoplasm, 6/737–8
  noncontagious, 6/649
  nutrition and, 8/974
  nutritional, 6/738
  parasites, 16/1875–6
  Pasteur, Louis, 16/1883–4
  plant, 16/1942–3, 16/*1943*
  plant pathology, 3/375
  prevention, 6/739

  rabies, 17/2040–1
  respiratory, 4/388–9
  treatment, 6/739
  viruses, 6/737, 21/2533–4, 21/*2533*
  see also individual diseases
Dismal Swamp, 19/2362, 21/2530
Disneyland, 6/740, 12/*1460*
Disney, Walt, 1/**28**, 4/478, 6/**740**, 6/*740*, 8/901, 14/1663
Disney World, 8/959, 8/*959*
Dispatchers, 19/2348
  railroads, 17/2053
Displacement, bouyancy, 4/412
Displacement hulls, 3/361
Displacement pumps, 17/2028, 17/*2028*
Displays, liquid crystals, 12/1444
Disraeli, Benjamin, 21/2524
Distaff, 19/2313
Distance, measurement, 13/1545, 13/1546
Distance runs, 20/2441
Distillation, 6/**740–1***, 6/*740*, 9/1046, 21/2556
Distribution, economics, 7/798
Distributors, automobiles, 3/276
District of Columbia, 6/**741–3**, 6/*741–3*
  map, 6/742
  state emblems, 6/742
Divers, 15/1814, 15/1820
  Cousteau, Jacques-Yves, 6/668
Diversified farming, 1/52–3
Dividends, mathematics, 2/214
Divi-divi trees, 20/*2462*
Divine Comedy, 6/698
Diving, 6/**743–4**, 6/*743–4*
  scuba, 18/2177–8
  skin, 18/2178
Diving beetles, 3/326
Diving ducks, 7/771
Division, 2/214
Divisors, mathematics, 2/214
Divorce, 13/1519
Dix, Dorothea, 6/**744**, 6/*744*
Dixie Highway, 21/2586
Dixon, Jeremiah, 13/1527
Djajapura, 13/1558
Djerma-Songhai, 15/1772
Djibouti, 6/**745**, 6/*745*
Dmitri, 18/2146
DNA, 3/341, 8/888, 9/1052–3, 9/*1052*
Dnieper River, 21/2528
Dobby weaves, 20/2415
Doctors:
  hospitals, 10/1209–11
  specialist, 13/1555
  training, 13/1554–5
  see also Medicine
Doctor's degrees, 5/596
Documentary movies, 14/1663
Dodder, 7/795, 16/1876, 16/1877
Dodge City, 11/1353, 11/*1353*
Dodge Dart, 3/274
Dodge, Horace, 6/723
Dodge, John, 6/723
Dodge, Mary Mapes, 5/534, 12/1480
Dodgson, Charles Lutwidge *see* Carroll, Lewis
Dodoma, 20/2379
Dodos, 3/350, 13/1539, 17/2065
Does, 6/709
  hares, 17/2040
Doges, 11/1311

Dogfish, 18/*2199*, 18/2200
Doggerbank, 15/1795
Dogrib Indians, 3/253
Dogs, 6/**745–8**, 6/*745–8*, 7/753, 10/*1145*
  anatomy, 6/*746*
  breeds, 6/746
  care, 6/747–8
  coyotes, 6/669–70
  dreams, 7/762
  pet, 16/1906, 16/*1906*
  rabies, 17/2040–1
  selection, 6/747
  sporting, 6/746
  toy, 6/747
  tracks, 2/163
  training, 6/748
  types, 6/745–7
  working, 6/746–7
Doldrums, 21/2562
Dole, Sandford, 10/1160
Dolls, 7/**749–51★**, 7/*749–50*
  American, 7/749–50
  ancient, 7/749
  character, 7/750
  children's, 7/749
  collections, 7/750
  crib dolls, 7/749
  fashion dolls, 7/749
  paper, 7/750
  rag, 7/749
Dolomites, 14/*1671*
Dolphins and porpoises, 7/**751–2**, 7/*751–2*, 9/1022, 13/1495
  intelligence, 11/1285
Dome mountains, 14/1669
Domesday Book, 21/2589
Domesticated animals, 1/51–2, 7/**752–4**, 7/*753–4*
Dominant characteristics, 9/1051
Dominica, 21/2570, 21/*2570*, 21/2571
Dominican Republic, 21/2570
Dominicans, 18/2122
Dominion of Canada, 550
Dominis, John, 12/1438
Dominoes, 7/**754–5**
Donatello, 13/1551
  David, 17/2083, 17/*2083*
Donkeys, 7/**755**, 7/*755*
Donner Pass, 18/2218
Don Quixote, 5/508
Donskoi, Dmitri, 18/2145
Doomsday Book, 7/*861*
Doré, Gustave, 12/*1446*
Dori, Angelo, 17/*2085*
Dorians, 9/1111
Dories, 8/948–9
Dormice, 10/*1183*, 18/*2116*
Dorsal fins, 8/943–4
Dorsey, Jimmy, 11/1325
Dorsey, Tommy, 11/1325
Douala, 4/442
Douay Bible, 3/336
Double-agents, 19/2319
Double bass, 19/2344
Doubleday, Abner, 3/310
Double eagle, 9/1092
Double stars, 10/1182
Dough, baking, 3/292, 3/293–4
Douglas fir, 6/632
Douglass, Frederick, 1/15, 7/**756**, 7/*756*, 13/1525, 13/1530
Douglas, Stephen A., 7/**755–6**, 7/*756*, 12/1440

Dounreay, 15/*1805*
Douro River, 16/1982
Dove, 13/1524
Dovekies, 16/*1965*, 18/2181
Dover, White Cliffs, 4/431
Dover, New Hampshire, 15/1752
Doves, 16/1929
Down, feathers, 7/770
Doyle, Sir Arthur Conan, 7/**756**, 7/*756*, 15/1802
D'Oyly Carte Opera Company, 9/1077
D'Oyly Carte, Richard, 9/1077
Draft, armies, 2/224–5
Drafting, 13/1549
Drag, aerodynamics, 1/67
Dragonflies, 7/**756–7**, 7/*757*
Dragons, 2/161–2
Drag racing, 3/278
Drainage basins, 17/2105
Draisine, 3/*337*
Drake, Edwin L., 16/1909
Drakensberg Mountains, 1/43, 12/1417
Drakes, 7/770
Drake, Sir Francis, 4/436, 7/**757–8**, 7/*757*, 7/836–7, 8/893, 16/1935, 17/2061
  Spanish Armada, 19/2300
Drama, 7/**758–60★**, 7/*758–60*
  development, 7/759
  famous dramatists, 7/758
  modern, 7/759–60
  stage makeup, 12/1488–9
  theater, 20/2419–22, 20/*2420–1*
Dramatists:
  Barrie, James M., 3/308
  Chekhov, Anton, 5/517
  Eliot, T.S., 7/836
  famous, 7/758
  Ibsen, Henrik, 10/1232–3
  Shakespeare, William, 18/2197–8
  Wilder, Thornton, 21/2584–5
  Williams, Tennessee, 21/2590
Draught horses, 10/1207
Dravidians, 11/1253–4
Drawbridges, 4/389, 4/484
Drawing, 7/**760–2★**, 7/*761–2*
  cartooning, 4/478–9
  freehand, 7/761
  importance of, 7/761
  mechanical, 13/1549–50, 13/*1549*
  origins, 7/760–1
  pencils, 16/1896–7
Dreadnought, HMS, 14/*1729*
Dreaming, 19/2240
Dreams, 7/**762–3**, 7/*763*
  interpretation, 7/763
Dredging, 10/1149
Dred Scott Decision, 18/2237
Dreiser, Theodore, 11/1255
Dress, fashion, 8/912–15, 8/*912–15*
Dressage, equestrianism, 7/865
Dressmakers, 5/580
Drew, Charles, 7/**763**, 7/*763*
Drew, Georgina, 3/308
Drew, John, 3/308
Dried foods, 8/976
Dried fruit, 9/*1018*
Drilling rigs, 7/**763–4**, 7/*764*
drills, 4/472, 4/*472*
Drinks:
  coffee, 5/*591*
  tea, 20/2384–5, 20/*2385*
  wine, 21/2594–5

Driskill Mountains, 12/1464
Driver ants, 2/168
Driveshafts, automobiles, 3/276
Driving, 7/**764–6**, 7/*764–6*
  road signs, 7/766, 7/*766*
Dromedary, 2/150, 4/440
Drone pipes, 3/291
Drosophila, 7/**766–7**, 7/*766*, 8/966
Drought, 7/**767**, 7/*767*
  famines, 8/907–8
Drowning, lifesaving, 12/1430–2, 12/*1431*
Drugs, 7/**767–9**, 7/*767–9*
  abuse, 1/33–4, 7/**769–70**, 14/1702
  antibiotics, 2/176–7
  insulin, 3/303
  medicinal plants, 13/1552
  narcotics, 14/1702–3
  side effects, 7/768–9
  sources, 7/768
Drugstores, 19/2338
Druids, 10/1141
Drumheller Valley, 1/90
Drum majors, 15/1840
Drupes, 9/*1017*, 18/2188
Dry cell batteries, 3/*318*
Dry cleaners, 12/1397–8
Dry farming, 15/1841
Dryopithecus, 10/*1220*
Dry subtropical climate, 5/576
Duarte, José Napoleon, 7/838
Dubai, 2/193
Dubbing, motion pictures, 14/1662
Dublin, 21/2528
Du Bois, W.E.B., 3/354–5, 5/562
Dubrovnik, 22/2638, 22/*2639*
Dubuque, Julien, 11/1296
Duchamp, Marcel, 1/20, 1/*20*
Duck-billed platypus, 3/267, 3/269, 16/1957
Duck hawks, 3/348
Duckpin bowling, 4/379
Ducks and geese, 3/344, 7/**770–2**, 7/*770–2*, 10/*1146*, 21/25502–1
  poultry, 17/1992
Duckweed, 2/*189*
Ductibility, metal, 13/1567
Dudley, Lord Guildford, 9/1119
Duels, 7/**773**, 7/*773*, 8/921–2, 8/*912–2*
Dugongs, 13/1501–2, 13/1564
Dugout canoes, 18/*2206*
Duiker, 2/174
Dukes and duchesses, 15/1779
Dulcimer, 19/2344
Dulles International Airport, 1/76
Duluth, 13/1604
Duma, 18/2149
Dumas, Alexandre the Elder, 7/**773–4**, 7/*773*
Dumas, Alexandre the Younger, 7/**773–4**
Dumbarton Oaks, 20/2485
Dumbbells, 21/2565–6
Dump trucks, 20/2469, 20/2470
Dunant, Jean Henri, 17/2073, 17/*2073*
Duncan, Isadora, 6/696, 7/**774**, 7/*774*
Dunes, 6/719
Dungeons, castles, 4/484
Dunlop, Joey, 14/*1667*
Dunmore, Lord, 11/1270
Duodecimal system, 15/1807

Du Pont de Nemours, Eleuthère Irénée, 6/714
Duralumin, 13/1568
Duran, Carolus, 18/2162
Duration, music, 14/1682
Durban, 19/2267
Dürer, Albrecht, 7/870–1, 7/*870*
Durham, North Carolina, 15/1790
Durham Cathedral, 18/2125, 18/*2125*
Durum wheat, 21/2581
Duryea, Charles, 7/**774**, 7/*774*
Duryea, Frank, 7/**774**
Duryea Motor Wagon Company, 7/774
DuSable, Jean, 3/352
Duse, Eleanora, 1/27
Dust, 7/**774–5**
Dust Bowl, 7/767, 9/*1108*
Dutch art, 7/**775–6**, 7/*775–6*
  Hals, Frans, 10/1141–2
Dutch Guiana *see* Suriname
Dutch people, 14/1741–2
Duvalier, François ('Papa Doc'), 6/726, 21/2570
Duvalier, Jean-Claude ('Baby Doc'), 6/726, 21/2570
Dwarf anteaters, 2/*172*, 2/173
Dwarf caiman, 1/103
Dwarfs, 7/839
Dyak, 3/371
Dyes, 7/**776–7**, 7/*777*
  synthetic, 20/2372
Dylan, Bob, 7/**777**, 7/*777*, 8/973
Dynamics, 16/1923
Dynamite, 8/895
Dyslexia, 18/2168
Dzongs, 3/334

Ee

Eagle, 1/94, 2/224
Eagle owl, 15/*1852*
Eagles, 3/348
Eagles (golf), 9/1092
Eakins, Thomas, 16/1981
Eardrum, 10/1165
Earhart, Amelia, 7/**780**, 7/*780*
Earless seals, 18/2184, 18/2185
Earls, 15/1780
Early Bird, 18/2166
Earp, Wyatt, 7/**780**, 7/*780*
Ears, 7/**778–9**, 7/*779*
  first aid, 8/939–40
  hearing, 10/1165–7, 10/*1165–7*
  wax, 7/778
Earth, 7/**780–4★**, 7/*781–3*, 19/2257
  atmosphere, 7/781, 7/784
  continental formation, 7/785
  creation, 7/784–8
  day and night, 6/701–2
  Equator, 7/864
  facts, 7/782
  from space, 18/2165, 19/*2287*, 19/2289
  geology, 9/1055–7
  geysers, 9/1073–4, 9/*1074*
  gravity, 9/1105–6
  history, 7/**784–8**, 7/*784–7*
  internal features, 7/782–3
  islands, 11/1307–8, 11/*1307–8*

(continued)

jungles, 11/1348–50, 11/*1349–50*
lakes, 12/1384–5, 12/*1384–5*
latitude and longitude, 12/1395–6, 12/*1395–6*
measuring, 7/783
molten, 7/784
mountains, 14/1668–71
ocean formation, 7/785
plate tectonics, 16/1956
radiation belts, 17/2044–5, 17/*2045*
recent history, 7/786
rivers, 17/2104–6, 17/*2104–6*
rock, 17/2108–9, 17/*2108–9*
seacoasts, 18/2182–3, 18/*2182–3*
soil, 19/2254–5, 19/*2255*
surface features, 7/781–2
tropics, 20/2466–7, 20/*2467*
volcanoes, 21/2535–6, 21/*2534–6*
Earthenware, 16/1987–8
Earth-fill dams, 6/694
Earthquakes, 7/788–9*, 7/*788–9*
California, 4/438
Central America, 5/507
Los Angeles, 12/1461
Earthworms, 7/789–90*, 7/*790*
Easel painting, 15/1859
Easter, 7/**790**, 7/*791*
Easter eggs, 7/790
Easter Island, 10/1182, 16/1971, 16/1972, 16/*1972*
Eastern European Mutual Assistance Treaty, 21/2542
Eastern Ghats, 11/1252
Eastern Orthodox Church, 5/546–7, 15/1847–8, 18/2121
East Germany, 9/1064
formation, 9/1069
geography, 9/1070–1
see also Germany (before 1945)
Eastman, George, 16/1920, 16/1954
Easton, Pennsylvannia, 16/1894
East Pakistan, 15/1864
see also Bangladesh
Ebb, Fred, 14/1688
Ebb tides, 20/2425
Eboracum, 7/855
Ecdysone, 14/1626
Echidna, 2/172, 3/269, 19/2315
Echinoderms, 2/156, 7/**791–2**, 7/*791–2*
Echinodorus, 2/*189*
Echoes, 19/2264, 19/*2264*
Echo spacecraft, 3/298, 14/1697, 19/2288
Eclipse, 7/**792–3***, 7/*792–3*, 14/1644
Ecology, 3/342, 3/343, 7/**793–8***, 7/*794–8*
conservation, 6/638–40
food web, 8/978–9
marine, 13/1517
plant, 3/375
wilderness areas, 21/2585
Economic geography, 9/1054
Economic geology, 9/1055
Economics, 7/**798–800**, 7/*798–800*
capitalism, 4/459–60
communism, 7/799–800
definition, 7/798–9
depressions, 6/718–19
international affairs, 11/1290
Marx, Karl, 13/1521
savings, 18/2167
socialism, 7/799–800, 19/2249–50
supply and demand, 19/2355
taxes, 20/2381–2

Economic sanctions, 18/2157
Ecosystems, 7/794, 11/1348
Ecuador, 7/**800–1**, 7/*800*, 9/1030
Ecumenical movements, 5/547
Eddas, 14/1696
Eddy, Mary Baker, 5/547, 5/*547*
Eden, Sir Anthony, 17/*2000*
Ederle, Gertrude, 20/*2366*
Edict of Milan, 5/546
Edict of Nantes, 9/1008
Edinburgh, 18/2176
Edison, Edward Alva, 5/612, 7/750, 7/**801–2**, 7/*801*, 11/*1293*, 12/1435–6, 14/1659, 16/1884, 16/*1884*, 16/1954, 17/2071
Editorials, 11/1343, 15/1760
Editors, publishing, 17/2025
Edmonton, 1/90
Edo, 20/2432
Education, 7/**802–4**, 7/*802–4*
American Colonies, 1/114
ancient civilizations, 7/802–3
apprentices, 2/185
Australia, 3/267
colleges, 5/**595–7**
deaf people, 10/1165–5
free public schools, 7/803
industrial arts, 11/1272–4, 11/*1273*
learning, 12/1406–8
Mann, Horace, 13/1505
Mary McLeod Bethune, 3/333–4
medieval, 13/1588
Middle Ages, 7/803
modern American, 7/803–4
Reformation, 7/803
Renaissance, 7/803
schools, 18/2168–70
Soviet Union, 19/2284
special, 19/2303–5, 19/*2304–4*
teaching, 20/2385–6, 20/*2385*
universities, 5/**595–7**
Webster, Noah, 21/2564–5
Willard, Emma, 21/2588
Educational psychology, 17/2019
Education Department, 4/426
Edward, Prince, 7/837
Edward I, King of England, 7/**804**, 7/*804*, 8/990, 9/*1095*, 10/1176, 21/2539
Edward II, King of England, 5/514, 6/677, 7/**804**
Edward III, King of England, 7/**804**, 7/*857*, 10/1227, 13/1550, 16/1912
Edward IV, King of England, 7/**805**, 17/2102, 21/2543
Edward V, King of England, 7/**805**, 21/2543
Edward VI, King of England, 7/**805**, 9/1119
Edward VII, King of England, 7/**805**, 7/*805*, 13/1522
Edward VIII, King of England, 7/**805**, 7/*805*
Edward the Confessor, 7/**805–6**, 7/*805*, 21/2572, 21/2588
Edward the Elder, King of England, 7/804
Edward the Martyr, King of England, 7/804
Edwards Plateau, 20/2412
Eels, 2/*145*
Effigy Mounds National Park, 11/1296
Efik, 15/1774

Eggs, 7/**806***, 7/*806*
birds, 3/345–7
chicken, 17/1991
Easter, 7/790
embryos, 7/840–1, 7/*840*
incubators, 11/1249
reproduction, 17/2087, 17/2088
fish, 8/945
Egg tempera, 15/1860
Ego, 9/1012
Egrets, 8/*883*, 21/2551, 21/*2585*
Egypt, 7/**807–8**, 7/*807*, 13/1589
abacus, 1/13
Cairo, 4/430, 4/*430*
Illinois, 10/1240
irrigation, 11/*1305*
Israel and, 7/807–8, 11/1310
Nasser, Gamal Abdel, 14/1703–4
Nile River, 15/1775–6
pottery, 16/*1988*, 16/1989
pyramids, 18/2193, 18/*2193*
Sudan, 19/2350
Suez Canal, 19/2350–1, 19/*2350–1*
Egypt, Ancient, 1/48, 2/*136–7*, 7/**808–11**
Abu Simbel, 1/20–1, 1/*20*
accomplishments, 7/810
advertising, 1/38
architecture, 2/201
art, 2/136, 2/231
burials, 4/413, 4/*413*, 7/810
calendars, 4/434
cats, 2/161, 4/*485*
Cleopatra, 5/*572–3*
clothing, 5/580
cosmetics, 6/662, 6/663
dolls, 7/750
drawing, 7/761
education, 7/802
fashion, 8/912
geometry, 9/1057
hairstyles, 10/1139
hieroglyphics, 5/611, 5/*611*, 10/1184–5, 22/*2624*
Israel and, 11/1335
jewelry, 11/1333
lighthouses, 12/1434
mathematics, 2/213, 13/1532, 13/1533
Middle Kingdom, 7/808–9
myths, 14/1697
New Kingdom, 7/809–10
Old Kingdom, 7/808, 7/809
payment, 2/137
pharoahs, 11/1368
pyramids, 17/2033
roads, 19/2341
Rosetta Stone, 18/2138, 18/*2138*
summary, 2/134
writing, 2/135
Egyptian vultures, 3/349
Ehrenburg, Ilya, 19/2284
Ehrlich, Paul, 7/**811**, 7/*811*
Eiffel, Gustave, 2/204, 8/903, 16/*1877*, 19/2332
Eiffel Tower, 2/204, 2/*204*, 8/903, 9/*1000*, 16/1877, 16/*1877*
Eighteenth Amendment, 17/2008
Eighth Amendment, 3/340
Eilean Donan Castle, 18/*2176*
Einstein, Albert, 7/**812**, 7/*812*, 8/875, 9/1106, 13/1533, 16/*192*, 18/2172, 18/2174, 20/2428
relativity, 17/2078

Einstein spacecraft, 19/2288
Eire *see* Ireland
Eisenhower, Dwight David, 3/319, 7/**812–13**, 7/*812*, 19/*2330*, 21/2526
hobbies, 10/1192
World War II, 22/*2613*, 22/2617
Eisenstein, Sergei, 14/1662, 19/2284
Eisteddfod, 21/2539
Eland, 2/173, 2/174
Elasticity, 7/**813**, 7/*813*
Elba, 14/1702
El Baru, 16/1867
Elbert, Mount, 17/2113
El Caney, 19/2299
El Capitán, 22/2635
El Dorado, 6/638, 7/**814**
Eleanor of Aquitaine, 7/**814**, 7/*814*, 10/1176, 12/1462
Election register, 7/815
Elections, 5/554, 7/**814–16**, 7/*815*
democracy, 6/715–16
Electrical energy, 7/844
Electrical engineers, 7/851
Electric appliances, 7/**816–18***, 7/*816–18*
Electric cars, 3/273, 3/277
Electric cells, 7/819
Electric eel, 7/818, 7/*818*, 8/*944*
Electric energy, 16/1923
Electric eyes, 16/1916–17
Electric fishes, 7/**818**, 7/*818*
Electric furnaces, 11/1303
Electric guitars, 7/*824*
Electricity, 1/108, 7/**818–21***, 7/*819–20*, 16/1923
amperes, 7/821
Ampère, André Marie, 2/129
batteries, 3/317
Bell, Alexander Graham, 3/329
current, 7/819, 220
dams, 6/694
Faraday, Michael, 8/908
Franklin, Benjamin, 9/1003–4
fuel cells, 9/1020
Galvani, Luigi, 9/1032
generating, 7/822–3
hydroelectricity, 10/1230, 10/*1230*
insulation, 11/1282
lightning, 12/1437
measuring, 7/820–1
ohms, 7/821
solar energy, 19/2256
static, 7/819
volts, 7/820–1
watts, 7/821
Electric lights, 7/816
bulbs, 7/801
Electric locomotives, 17/2055, 17/*2059*
Electric motors, 7/816–17, 7/*817*, 14/1664–6
linear motors, 12/1442, 12/*1442*
Electric organs, 15/1845
Electric power, 7/**821–3**, 7/*821–2*
nuclear energy, 15/1803–5
Electrochemistry, 5/519
Electrodialysis, 21/2556
Electrolysis, 7/**823**, 7/*823*
metal ores, 13/1568
Electromagnetic radiation, 13/1584, 17/2043–4
Electromagnetic spectrum, 19/2306–7
Electromagnetic waves, 21/2557–8

Electromagnets, 7/823–4, 7/824, 12/1484
  motors, 14/1664–5, 14/1665
Electronic engineers, 7/851
Electronic music, 7/824–5, 7/824
Electronics, 7/825–8, 7/825–7
  semi-conductors, 18/2189
Electron microscopes, 8/986, 13/1583–4
Electrons, 3/258–9, 7/819, 7/825
  batteries, 3/317
Electroplating, 7/823
Electrum, 14/1630
Elementary schools, 18/2169–70
Elements, 3/258, 7/828–31*, 7/828–31
  atomic numbers, 7/829
  atomic weights, 7/829–30
  atoms, 3/258–60
  chemical symbols, 7/830–1
  chemistry, 5/519–20
  definition, 7/828
  Earth's composition, 7/783
  periodic table, 7/830–1, 7/830
Elephant Butte Reservoir, 15/1757
Elephants, 2/147, 7/831–3, 7/831–2, 10/1145
Elephant seals, 18/2184, 18/2185
Elevated trains, 19/2348
Elevators, 7/833–4, 7/833
  aircraft, 1/68
Elf owl, 15/1852
Elgar, Edward William, 7/834, 7/834
El Greco, 7/834–5, 7/835, 16/1913, 17/2085
Eliot, George, 7/835–6, 7/835, 12/1449
Eliot, John, 13/1610, 13/1610
Eliot, T.S., 7/836, 7/836, 16/1959
Elizabeth, New Jersey, 15/1754
Elizabeth, the Queen Mother, 18/2134
Elizabeth I, Queen of England, 6/663, 7/805, 7/836–7, 7/836, 7/857, 8/912, 10/1177, 11/1319, 13/1522, 14/1693, 17/2061
  Spanish Armada, 19/2300
Elizabeth II, Queen of England, 6/677, 7/837, 7/837, 11/1369, 11/1369, 17/2022
  Commonwealth, 5/610
Elk, 6/710
Elk Island, 14/1713
Elk Mountain, 14/1669
Ellesmere Island, 15/1796
Ellice Islands, 13/1582
Ellicott, George, 3/302
Ellington, Duke, 11/1325, 11/1325
Elliot, Robert Brown, 17/2069
Elliott, Obadiah, 4/475
Ellipses, 15/1838
Ellis Island, 10/1243, 19/2333
El Morro, 17/2027
Elodea, 2/189
El Paso, 17/2104, 20/2414
El Salvador, 5/505–7, 7/837–8, 7/838
Eluard, Paul, 19/2359
Elves and fairies, 7/839, 7/839
Ely, Eugene, 1/59
El Yunque, 17/2027
Emancipation proclamation, 5/568, 7/840, 7/840, 12/1440, 18/2238
Embezzlement, 6/673
Emblems, flags, 8/951–3, 8/951–3

Embouchure, 4/385
Embroidery, 14/1735–6, 14/1735–6
Embryology, 3/343
Embryos, 7/840–1, 7/840, 17/2088–9
Emden geese, 7/772
Emerald Isle see Ireland
Emergencies:
  fire fighting, 8/934–6, 8/934–6
  fire prevention, 8/936–7
  first aid, 8/938–40, 8/939–40
  National Guard, 14/1707–8
Emerson, Ralph Waldo, 7/841, 7/841, 10/1161, 12/1449
Emetics, 16/1962
Emigration, 5/554, 10/1243
Emmett, Daniel, 16/1977
Emotions, 7/841–2
Emperor Bell, Moscow, 3/329, 3/329
Emperor penguins, 2/171, 16/1892, 16/1892, 16/1965
Empire State Building, 2/201, 7/842
Empire style, 8/914
Emus, 8/954, 8/954
Enameling, 7/842–3, 7/842
Encaustic painting, 15/1861
Encyclopedias, 7/843–4*, 7/843–4, 17/2075
Endangered animals, 17/2063–5, 17/2063–5
Endeavour, 6/653
Enderbury Island, 16/1971
Endocarp, 9/1016
Endocrine glands, 9/1080, 10/1201
Endoskeleton, 18/2229
Endosperm, 18/2186
Energy, 7/844–7, 7/844–7
  changing, 7/845–6
  chemical, 7/845
  conservation, 7/846–7
  electrical, 7/844
  fire, 8/932–3
  fuel, 9/1018–20, 9/119–20
  heat, 7/845, 10/168–70
  hydroelectricity, 10/1230, 10/1230
  kinetic, 7/844
  light, 7/845
  measuring, 7/845–6
  microwaves, 13/1584
  motion, 14/1656–7
  nuclear, 7/845, 15/1803–5, 15/1804–5
  physics, 16/1922–3
  potential, 7/844
  quantums, 17/2035
  radiant energy, 7/845
  solar, 19/2256, 19/2256
  sound, 7/845
  waves, 21/2557
Energy Department, 4/426
Engagements, 13/1518
Engdahl, Sylvia Louise, 18/2175
Engels, Friedrich, 5/614, 13/1521
Engineering, 7/850–2, 7/850–2
  roads, 19/2342–3
  stress, 19/2343
Engineers:
  Fulton, Robert, 9/1020
  Stephenson, George, 19/2333–4
  Watt, James, 21/2556–7
Engines, 7/847–50, 7/847–50
  diesel, 6/728–9, 6/729
  Duryea brothers, 7/774
  electric motors, 14/1664–6

  gas turbines, 7/849
  internal combustion engines, 7/849–50, 7/849
  jet propulsion, 7/849–50, 11/1332, 11/1332
  linear motor, 12/1442, 12/1442
  rocket, 7/849–50, 17/2109–12
  rotary engines, 7/850
  steam engines, 7/847–9, 7/847–8
England, 7/852–3, 7/852–3
  British Commonwealth, 7/856
  early government, 7/855
  early inhabitants, 7/854–5
  Empire, 7/856
  Great Council, 7/857
  history, 7/854–9, 7/854–9
  kings and queens, 7/856
  Magna Carta, 7/855–6
  Normans, 7/855
  Romans, 7/855
  Unification, 7/858
  see also British Isles; United Kingdom
English Channel, 4/395, 7/853–4, 20/2366
English common law, 12/1399
English horns, 21/2603
English language, 7/859–62, 7/860–2, 12/1389
  American English, 7/862
  early history, 7/860
  forms of, 7/860–2
  Middle English, 7/860–1
  Modern English, 7/861–2
  Old English, 7/860
  spelling, 19/2309
English saddle, 10/1208
English Separatist Church, 16/1930
English yew, 6/633
Engraving, 7/869, 7/870–1, 7/870
ENIAC, 5/621, 5/622
Eniwetok, 13/1582
Enterpris, Alabama, 1/83
Enterprise, USS, 1/59, 14/1729
Entertainment:
  juggling, 11/1345–6
  motion picture, 14/1658–64
  musical comedy, 14/1687–8
  opera, 15/1834–5
  operetta, 15/1835
  pantomime, 16/1870, 16/1870
  popular music, 16/1977–8
  puppets, 17/2030–2, 17/2030–1
  radio, 17/2051
  theater, 20/2419–22
  vaudeville, 21/2510–11, 21/2510–11
  video, 21/2524–5
Entomologists, Fabre, J. Henri, 8/901
Entomology, 11/1276–81
Entrechat (ballet), 3/296
Environment, ecology, 7/794
Environmental diseases, 6/738
Environmental Protection Agency, 21/2490
Enzymes, 3/341, 3/343, 7/862–3, 7/863, 14/1676
  digestion, 6/730, 6/731
  fermentation, 8/922
Eocene Epoch, 7/786
  mammals, 13/1499
Eohippus, 10/1204
Epée, 8/921
Ephesus, Temple of Artemis, 18/2193, 18/2193

Epicenters, earthquakes, 7/788
Epic poetry, 16/1960
Epidemics, 6/649
Epidermis, 10/1137, 10/1224, 18/2232
Epiglottis, 6/730
Epimetheus, 16/1870
Epiphany, 11/1321
Episcopal Church, 17/2013, 17/2016
Epistemology, 16/1915
Epoxies, 16/1955
Epstein, Sir Jacob, 7/863–4, 7/863
Equal Employment Opportunity Commission, 21/2490
Equal Rights Amendment (ERA), 21/2601
Equator, 7/864, 7/864
  crossing, 19/2355
Equatorial Guinea, 7/864–5, 7/865
Equestrianism, 7/865–6, 7/865
Equidae, 10/1203
Equus caballus, 10/1204
Erasmus, 10/1193
Erato, 14/1678
Eratosthenes, 7/783, 13/1546
Erebus, Mount, 2/169
Erechtheum, 1/26, 1/26
Eric the Red, 2/209, 15/1786, 21/2527, 21/2528
Ericsson, John, 14/1635
Erie Canal, 4/454
Erie, Lake, 9/1107–8, 16/1902, 21/2541
Eriksson, Leif, 15/1786, 15/1800, 21/2528
Eritrea, 7/872
Ermine, 21/2560
Ernst, Max, 19/2360
Eros, 9/1088
Erosion, 6/639, 7/782, 7/866–7*, 7/866
Er Rif, 14/1648
Esbats, 21/2599
Escalators, 7/833, 7/834
Escape velocity, 19/2290
Escapement, 5/578
Escapology, 12/1482
  Houdini, Harry, 10/1212–13
Escargots, 19/2244
Escoril, 19/2301
Eskimo curlew, 3/350
Eskimos, 1/85, 1/87, 1/88, 5/577, 7/867–8, 7/867–8, 15/1749
  Canada, 4/451
  clothing, 5/578–9
  Innuit, 7/867
Esophagus, 6/730
Esperanto, 21/2498–9
Espionage, 19/2319–20
Esprit de corps, 2/226
ESP see Extrasensory perception
Esquivel, Adolfo Pérez, 15/1779
Essenes, 6/703
Essential oils, 16/1899
Estancias, 2/211
Esterházy, Prince, 10/1161
Estevanico, 2/217, 3/352, 7/868–9, 8/893
Estivate, 10/1183
Estonia, 7/869, 7/869, 19/2282
Estoril, 16/1982
Estrogen, 10/1201
Estuaries, 18/2183
Estuarine crocodiles, 1/103

Etching and engraving, 7/**869–71**, 7/*869–70*
Ether, 2/142
Ethics, 16/1915
Ethiopia, 1/49, 7/**871–2**, 7/*871*
  coffee, 5/591
  Somalia and, 19/2262
Ethnic dances, 6/697
Ethnic groups, 10/1224
Ethnologists, 2/175
  Heyerdahl, Thor, 10/1182
Etiquette, 13/1505–6
Etruscans, 7/**872**, 7/*872*, 11/1310, 18/2129
Etymology, 6/727
Eucalyptus, 3/267
Eucharist, 18/2123
Euclid, 2/135, 8/**875**, 8/*875*, 9/1058, 9/1059
Euler, Leonhard, 13/1533, 13/*1533*
Euphrates River, 20/2426–7, 20/*2427*
Eurasia, 8/875
Euripides, 2/136, 9/1116
Europa, 8/879
Europe, 8/**875–82**, 8/*875–81*
  animal life, 8/878–9
  climate, 8/878
  employment, 8/879–80
  history, 8/880–1
  land, 8/877–8
  nations, 8/877
  people, 8/879
  physical statistics, 6/650
European Atomic Energy Community (Euratom), 8/882
European Coal and Steel Community (ECSC), 8/882
European Economic Community (EEC), 3/*328*, 6/712, 8/881, 8/**882–3**, 8/*882*, 11/*1291*, 20/2445
European Parliament, 8/883
European Recovery Plan, 20/2471
European wild cat, 4/*488*
Euryale, 9/1092
Eurystheus, 10/1181
Euterpe, 14/1678
Evangelists, 8/**883**, 8/*883*
  Wesley, John and Charles, 21/2568
Evans, Edgar, 18/2177
Evansville, 11/1258
Evaporation, 21/2553–3
Evening primroses, 6/*720*
Even numbers, 15/1808
Everest, Mount, 1/*16*, 2/239, 7/780, 8/892, 8/893, 10/1185, 10/*1185*, 14/1669, 14/1672, 18/2183
Everett, Edward, 9/1073
Everglade kites, 3/348
Everglades, 8/**883–4**, 8/*883–4*, 8/957, 18/21189, 19/2361–2, 21/*2492*
Evergreen trees, 8/**884–5**, 8/*884*, 20/2458
Evers, Charles, 13/1613
Evers, Medgar Wiley, 13/1613
Evil eye, 19/2354
Evolution, 3/342, 3/343, 8/**885–8**, 8/*885–7*, 18/2173
  Darwin, Charles, 6/699–700
  mammals, 13/1495–6, 13/1498–501
  man, 10/1220–4, 10/*1220–3*
  Wallace, Alfred Russel, 21/2539–40
Ewe people, 20/2432
Excalibur, 2/236
Exchange, economics, 7/798

Excise taxes, 20/2382
Exclamation point, 17/2030
Excommunication, 3/323
Exercise, 8/**888**, 8/*888*, 10/1163
  gymnastics, 10/1133–4, 10/*1134*
  health, 10/1163, 10/*1164*
  physical education, 16/1921–2
  weight lifting, 21/2565–6, 21/*2566*
  yoga, 22/2634–5
Exeter Cathedral, 9/1093
Exeter, Hew Hampshire, 15/1752
Exocarp, 9/1016
Exocrine glands, 9/1080
EXOSAT, 18/*2166*
Exoskeleton, 18/2229
Exosphere, 3/257
Experimental psychologists, 17/2019
Experiments, scientific, 18/2173
Exploration, 8/**888–94**, 8/*889–93*
  early, 8/889–92
  famous explorers, 8/890
  great age of, 8/892–3
  Henry the Navigator, 10/1179
  Lewis and Clark expedition, 12/1420–1
  Middle Ages, 8/892
  modern, 8/893–4
  space, 8/894
Explorers, 8/890
  Amundsen, Roald, 2/132–3
  Balboa, Vasco Núñez de, 3/294
  Bering, Vitus, 3/331
  Boone, Daniel, 3/369–70
  Byrd, Richard E., 4/423
  Cabot, John, 4/427
  Cabot, Sebastian, 4/427
  Cartier, Jacques, 4/477–8
  Cheng Ho, 5/522
  Columbus, Christopher, 5/*605–6*
  Cook, Captain James, 6/653
  Coronado, Francisco, 6/660
  Cortés, Hernando, 6/662
  De Soto, Hernando, 6/723
  Dias, Bartholmeu, 6/725
  Drake, Sir Francis, 7/757–8
  Estevanico, 7/868
  Gamo, Vasco da, 9/1032–3
  Henson, Matthew, 10/1179–80
  Heyerdahl, Thor, 10/1182
  Hillary, Sir Edmund, 10/1185
  Hudson, Henry, 10/1218–19
  Humboldt, Alexander von, 10/1225
  Ibn Battuta, 10/1232
  Joliet, Louis, 13/1518
  La Salle, Sieur de, 12/1392–3
  Livingstone, David, 12/1454
  Mackenzie, Sir Alexander, 12/1476
  Magellan, Ferdinand, 12/1481
  Marquette, Jacques, 13/1518
  Peary, Robert, 16/1889
  Pike, Zebulon, 16/1930
  Polo, Marco, 16/1970–1
  Ponce de León, Juan, 16/1973
  Raleigh, Sir Walter, 17/2060–1
  Scott, Robert, 18/2176–7
  Stanley, Sir Henry Morton, 19/2325
  Verrazano, Giovanni da, 21/2520
  Vespucci, Amerigo, 21/2521
Explorer satellites, 18/2165, 19/2288, 19/2289
Explosives, 8/**895–6**, 8/*895–6*
  fireworks, 8/937–8
Expo 67, 8/903, 8/*903*

Expo 70, 8/903
Expo 86, 8/903
Export-Import Bank of the United States, 21/2490, 21/2491
Exports, 11/1291–2
Expositions, 8/902–3, 8/*903*
Expressionism, 8/**896–7**, 8/*896*, 14/1620, 21/2509
Expressways, 19/2341
Extensors, 14/1676
External combustion engines, 7/848
Extinct birds, 3/349–50, 3/*349*
Extinct mammals, 13/1498–501
Extrasensory perception, 8/**897–8**★, 8/*897*
Extroverts, 11/1348
Extruded plastics, 16/1955
Extrusion, 6/728
Eyas, 8/906
Eyebrows, 10/1138
Eyes, 8/**898–9**★, 8/*898–9*
  first aid, 8/939–40
  glasses, 9/1084
  insect, 11/1278
  lens, 12/1415
  sight, 18/2219–20, 18/*2219*
Eyre, Lake, 3/263

Ff

F-111 bomber, 1/*63*
F-14A Tomcat, 3/*282*
Fabian Society, 18/2200
Fables, 8/**900–1**★, 8/*900–1*, 8/971
  Aesop, 1/41
  La Fontaine, Jean de, 12/1384
Fabre, J. Henri, 8/**901**
Fabrics, 20/2415–16, 20/*2415–16*
  dyes, 7/776–7
  fibres, 8/926–7
  sewing, 18/2195
  silk, 18/2224–5, 18/*2224*
  spinning and weaving, 19/2313–14
Faces, masks, 13/1526
Facsimiles, 8/**901–2**, 8/*901*
Factories:
  automation, 3/272, 13/1507
  Industrial Revolution, 11/1274–6
  manufacturing, 13/1506–8, 13/*1506–8*
Fado, 16/1982
Faduz, 12/1428
Faeroe Islands, 6/716
Fahrenheit, Gabriel Daniel, 20/2401
Fahrenheit scale, 20/2400–1
Faïence, 16/1990
Fainting, first aid, 8/938
Fairbanks, Douglas, 9/1119
Fairbanks, Richard, 16/1985–6
Fair Deal, 20/2472
Fairfax, Lord, 21/2547
Fairies, 7/839, 7/*839*
Fairmount Park, 16/1911
Fairs, 8/**902–3**, 8/*902–3*
  in the US, 8/902
  world fairs, 8/902–3
Fairways, 9/1091
Fairy armadillo, 2/221
Fairy rings, 7/839
Fairy tales, 8/**904–5**★, 8/*904–5*
  Andersen, Hans Christian, 2/139–40

  Grimm Brothers, 9/1120
  Perrault, Charles, 16/1901
Falcon Dam, 17/2104
Falconry, 8/**906**, 8/*906*
Falcons, 3/348
Falkland Islands, 2/211, 8/**906–7**, 8/*907*
Falkland, Viscount, 8/907
Fall, 3/279, 3/*279*
Fall, Albert B., 10/1152
Fallen Timbers, battle of, 11/1270, 15/1824, 21/2559
Fall Line, 19/2274
Fallout, 8/**907**
False Face Society, 11/1304–5
False teeth, 6/717, 6/718, 20/2387
Families, animal, 2/151–2
Family practitioners, 13/1555
Famines, 8/**907–8**, 8/*907–8*
Fanatics, 2/245
Fangs, snake, 19/2245
Fantail pigeons, 16/1929
Fantasy fiction, 12/1450
Fanworms, 22/*2620*
Faraday, Michael, 8/**908**, 8/*908*, 14/1664–5
Faraday's Laws, 8/908
Farads, 8/908
Farad, Wali, 3/357
Farmer, James, 14/*1706*
Farming *see* Agriculture
Farm machinery, 8/**908–10**, 8/*909–10*
Farnese, Ranuccio, 20/2429
Farouk, King of Egypt, 7/807, 14/1703
Farragut, David, 8/**910**, 8/*910*
Farsighted, 8/899, 8/*899*
Farthingales, 8/912
Far West, 21/2577
Fascism, 8/**910–11**, 8/*911*
  Franco, Francisco, 9/1003
  Mussolini, Benito, 14/1693–4
Fashion, 8/**912–15**, 8/*912–15*
  cosmetics, 6/662–3
  customs, 6/688
  design, 6/722, 6/*722*
  hairstyles, 10/1138–40, 10/*1139–40*
  hats, 10/1156–7, 10/*1156–7*
Fashion dolls, 7/749
Fate, 17/2010
Fates, 8/**915**, 9/1089
Fathers of Confederation, 8/**915–16**
Fatimids, 4/430
Fats and oils, 8/**916–17**, 8/*917*
  diet, 8/975
Faulkner, Roy, 19/2337
Faulkner, William, 12/1451, 12/*1451*, 13/1613
Faults, geological, 14/1668
Faust, Johann, 8/**917**, 8/*917*
Fauves, Les, 14/1620
  Matisse, Henri, 13/1535–6
Fawkes, Guy, 8/**917–18**, 8/*918*
Fawns, 6/709
Fax machines, 8/901–2, 8/*901*, 16/1916
Fay, Frank, 21/2510
Fazendas, 4/386
FBI *see* Federal Bureau of Investigation
Fear, 7/841–2
Feathers, 8/**918–19**, 8/*918*, 11/*1282*
  molting, 14/1627
Feature articles, 11/1343

Feature stories, 15/1760
February, 8/**919–20**, 8/*920*
  table of events, 8/919
**Federal Bureau of Investigation
  (FBI)**, 8/**920**, 8/*920*, 16/1966,
  21/*2489*
  finger prints, 8/930–1
Federal Communications Commission
  (FCC), 17/2047, 17/2051,
  20/2398, 21/2490, 21/2491
Federal Court system, 6/667
Federal Deposit Insurance Corpora-
  tion, 21/2490
Federal Election Commission, 21/2490
Federal government, 21/2487
Federal Holidays, 10/1193
Federalists, 1/30
Federal Maritime Board, 13/1564,
  18/2211
Federal Maritime Commision, 21/2490
Federal penitentiaries, 17/2007
Federal Reserve Board, 21/2591
Federal Reserve System, 3/302,
  17/1998, 21/2490
Federal Trade Commission, 21/2490,
  21/2491
Feeling, touch, 20/2435
Feet, 10/1144–6, 10/*1145–6*
  shoes, 18/2212–14, 18/*2213–14*
Feline enteritis, 4/486
Fellahin, 7/807
Felonies, 6/673
Fels Planetarium, Philadelphia,
  16/1937
Felted textiles, 20/2416
Felt-tip marker pens, 16/1896
Feluccas, 15/1776, 18/*2154*
Feminist movement, 21/2600–1
Femur, 18/2230
Fencing, 8/**921–2**, 8/*921–2*
Fennec, 8/**998**, 8/*998*
Feral animals, 7/753
Ferdinand, Archduke, 21/2605
Ferdinand V, King of Spain, 8/893,
  11/1306, 11/*1306*, 19/2301
Fermentation, 1/93, 8/**922**, 8/*922*
  yeast, 22/2633
Fermi, Enrico, 8/**922–3**, 8/*923*,
  15/1804
Fernando Po, 7/864
Ferns, 8/**923–4★**, 8/*923–4*, 16/1939,
  16/1944, 16/1947
  seed, 16/1953
Ferrets, 21/2560
Ferry boats, 3/362
Fertile Crescent, 13/1565, 20/2426–7
Fertilization, reproduction, 17/2088
Fertilizers, 8/**925**
Fessenden, Reginald, 17/2045
Festivals:
  carnivals, 4/469
  Easter, 7/790
  Halloween, 10/1140–1, 10/*1141*
  Hanukkah, 10/1148–9, 10/*1149*
  New Years Day, 15/1763
  Passover, 16/1883
  spring, 19/2319
  summer, 19/2352, 19/2353
  Thanksgiving, 20/2418–19, 20/*2419*
  Valentine's Day, 21/2507
Fetus, 7/841
Feudalism, 7/855, 8/880, 8/**925–6**,
  8/*925*, 13/1585
Fever, 8/**926**, 8/*926*

Fez, 14/1648
Fiat money, 14/1631
Fiber, diet, 15/1811, 15/*1811*
Fiberglass, 9/1083
Fiber optics, 8/**927**, 8/*927*
Fibers, 8/**926–7**, 8/*926*
  artificial, 5/521, 5/*521*, 20/*2371*,
    20/*2372*
  plant, 16/1950–1
  rope, 18/2137
  see also Textiles
Fiber-tip marker pens, 16/1896
Fibrinogen, 12/1454
Fibrous roots, 16/1939
Fiction, 15/1801–2, 15/*1801–2*
  definition, 5/534
  Gothic novel, 18/2127
  literature, 12/1446–7
  science fiction, 18/2175
  short stories, 18/2215–16
  see also Children's Literature; Lit-
    erature; Writers
Fiddleheads, 8/924
Fief, 8/925
Field, Cyrus, 20/2389
Field events, 20/2439–43, 20/*2439–43*
  discus throw, 20/2442
  hammer throw, 20/2442–3
  high jump, 20/2441–2
  long jump, 20/2441
  pole vault, 20/2442
  shot put, 20/*2441*, 20/2442
  triple jump, 20/2441
Field hockey, 8/**927–8**, 8/*927–8*
Field maple, 20/*2461*
Field mice, 5/559, 17/2067
Field of vision, 18/2220
Fields, Dorothy, 14/1687
Fields, Herbert, 14/1687
Fields, W.C., 14/1662
Fifteenth Amendment, 17/2069
Fifth Amendment, 3/340
Fighter aircraft, 3/*281*, 20/*2451*
  World War II, 22/*2612*
Fighting, karate, 11/1356, 11/*1356*
Fights, duels, 7/773
Figure skating, 10/1237, 19/*2317*
Fiji, 13/1557, 13/1558, 15/1854
Filaments, electric bulbs, 7/816
Filberts, 15/1810
Filfla, 12/1494
Fillies, 10/1203
Fillings, dentistry, 6/718
Fillmore, Millard, 8/**928–9**, 8/*928*,
  20/2382
Film cartridges, 4/482
Film, photographic, 16/1918
Films, 14/1658–64, 14/*1658–64*
  Academy Awards, 1/21
  acting, 1/27–8
  censorship, 5/504
  science fiction, 18/2175
  surrealism, 19/2360
  see also Motion pictures
Filters, 8/**929**, 8/*929*
Finance:
  accounting and bookkeeping, 1/22
  banking, 3/300–2
  insurance, 11/1283–4
  interest, 11/1285–6
  savings, 18/2167
  taxes, 20/2381–2
Finches, 10/*1146*
Fine arts, 2/229–30

Finger painting, 15/1860
Fingerprints, 8/**930–1★**, 8/*930*
Finger puppets, 17/2031
Fink, Mike, 12/1412
Finland, 8/**931–2**, 8/*931*
  Sibelius, Jean, 18/2217
Finnish language, 18/2168
Finn MacCool, 15/*1793*
Fins, fish, 8/943–4
Fiords, 8/877, 10/1236, 15/1798,
  15/*1798*, 18/2168, 18/*2168*,
  18/2183
Fir club moss, 5/*584*
Fire, 8/**932–3**, 8/*932*
  bunsen burners, 4/410
  forest fires, 8/986–7, 8/*986–7*
  matches, 13/1531–2, 13/*1531*
  plants and, 16/1946
Fire ants, 2/168
Fireballs, 13/1570
Fireboats, 3/362
Firecrackers, 8/938
Firearms, 10/1129–32, 10/*1129–31*
Fire extinguishers, 8/**933★**, 8/*933*
Fire fighting, 8/**934–6**, 8/*934–6*
Fireflies, 3/326, 3/*343*
Fire hydrants, 8/935
Fireplaces, 10/1171, 10/1214
Fire prevention, 8/**936–7★**
Fire Prevention Week, 8/936
Fireproof substances, 8/937
Fire salamander, 2/*131*, 18/*2155*
Fireworks, 8/**937–8**, 8/*937*, 17/*2109*
First aid, 8/**938–40**, 8/*939–40*
  artificial respiration, 2/237, 2/*237*
  fractures, 9/999
  hiccups, 10/1183
  lifesaving, 12/1430–2, 12/*1431*
  poisons, 16/1961–2
First Amendment, 3/340
First Bank of the United States,
  3/301
First Continental Congress, 1/126,
  6/651
Firths, 8/877, 18/2176
Fischer, Bobby, 5/525
Fish, 8/**940–5**, 8/*941–5*
  air bladders, 8/943
  Antarctic, 2/170
  aquarium, 2/186–90
  blindfish, 3/358
  bodies of, 8/*941–5*
  bony, 8/941
  cartilaginous, 8/941
  deep-sea life, 6/708
  electric, 7/818, 7/*818*
  fins, 8/943–4
  flying, 8/944
  food web, 8/979
  gills, 8/942–3
  jawless, 8/941, 8/*943*
  marine life, 13/1516–17, 13/*1516*
  migration, 13/1594
  pet, 16/*1905*, 16/1906
  rays, 18/2199–2200
  reproduction, 8/945
  scales, 8/942
  seahorses, 18/2183–4, 18/*2184*
  senses, 8/944
  sharks, 18/2199–2200
  swimming, 8/*942*, 8/943–4
  tropical, 20/2465–6, 20/*2466*
  see also Dolphins, Porpoises,
    Whales *and individual fish*

Fish hawks, 3/349
Fishing, 8/**945–7**, 8/*946–7*
  sea, 8/878
Fishingboats, 3/362
Fishing cat, 4/490
Fishing industry, 8/**947–50**, 8/*948–50*
  North Sea, 15/1794–5
Fish ladders, 6/695
Fissures, 17/2108
  earthquakes, 7/788
Fitness, exercises, 8/888
Fitzgerald, Ella, 11/*1325*
Five Civilized Tribes, 15/1827
Five Nations, 8/**950–1**, 8/*951*,
  11/1304
Flagella, 3/288
Flagellates, 17/2017
Flageolet, 21/2602
Flagg, James Montgomery, 20/*2483*
Flags, 8/**951–3**, 8/*951–3*
  components, 8/951, 8/*951*
  displaying, 8/952–3
  signal, 8/953
  Stars and Stripes, 8/952, 8/*952*
  as symbols, 8/951
  Union Jack, 8/951, 8/*953*
Flaherty, Robert, 14/1663
Flamenco guitar, 19/2344
Flamingoes, 2/145, 3/345, 21/2552
Flammable substances, 8/937
Flanders, Rubens, Peter Paul,
  18/2141–2
Flaps, aircraft, 1/68, 1/*69*
Flash floods, 8/955
Flat, music, 14/1684
Flatbed trucks, 20/2470
Flatcars, 17/2054
Flatfish, 2/*148*, 8/941
Flathead Indians, 14/1642
Flatworms, 2/156, 22/2620
Flax, 5/579
Fleas, 11/*1279*
Flemings, 3/327
Fleming, Sir Alexander, 2/176,
  7/768, 8/**953**, 8/*953*, 13/1554
Flemish art, 7/776
Flemish people, 3/327
Flesh eaters, 4/469–70
Fletcher, John, 18/2198
Fleury, Cardinal, 12/1463
Flexors, 14/1676
Flies, 8/**965–7**, 8/*966*
Flight:
  birds, 3/343–4, 3/*345*
  helicopters, 10/1173–4, 10/*1173–4*
  parachutes, 16/1873–4, 16/*1874*
  see also Aircraft; Balloons
Flight controls, aircraft, 1/68
Flightless birds, 8/**954–5**, 8/*954–5*
Flint, 13/1581
Flintlocks, 10/1130, 10/*1131*
Flip-books, 4/478–9
Flippers, 18/2184
  mammals, 13/1497
Floodplains, 17/2106
Floods, 8/**955–6**, 8/*955–6*
Flood tides, 20/2425
Floor Leaders, 6/629
Flora (goddess), 13/1540
Florence, 4/390, 5/503, 8/**956**, 8/*956*,
  12/1474–5
  Cathedral, 2/*201*
  Medici family, 13/1551–2
  Renaissance, 17/2083–4

Florey, Howard, 2/176, 8/953
Florida, 8/**956–60**, 8/*957–9*, 16/1973
  employment, 8/959–60
  Everglades, 8/883–4, 8/957
  history, 8/957
  land, 8/956–7
  map, 8/*958*
  state emblems, 8/*958*
Florida Keys, 8/957, 8/*957*
Flotation, bouyancy, 4/411–12
Flour:
  baking, 3/292
  making, 8/**960**, 8/*960*
Flower bug, common, 4/*404*
Flowers, 8/**961–3**, 8/*961–3*
  American, 8/964
  botany, 3/374–5
  bulbs, 4/408–9, 4/*408*
  families, 8/**964–5***, 8/*965*
  fertilization, 8/963
  garden, 9/1038–9, 9/*1038–9*, 9/1040
  insect-eating, 11/1281–2, 11/*1281*
  orchids, 15/1840
  parts of, 8/961
  pressing, 8/*963*
  reproduction, 8/961–3
  roses, 18/2137–8, 18/*2137*
  seeds and fruit, 8/963, 18/2186–8,
    18/*2187*
  wildflowers, 21/2586–8, 21/*2586–8*
  see also Plants
Fluid mechanics, 16/1923
Fluids, 8/**965***
  buoyancy, 4/411–12
  gas, 9/1044–6, 9/*145–6*
  liquids, 12/1444
Flukes, 21/2578
Fluorescence, 8/**965**
Fluorescent lighting, 12/1336
Fluorescent paints, 15/1858
Fluoroscopes, 22/2629
Flutes, 14/*1692*, 21/2602
Fly amanita, 16/1963
Fly casting, fishing, 8/946, 8/*947*
Flyers:
  Byrd, Richard E., 4/423
  Earhart, Amelia, 7/780
  Lindbergh, Charles August,
    12/1441–2
  Wright bothers, 22/2623
Flying:
  aviation, 3/280–2, 3/*280–3*
  hang gliding, 10/1147, 10/*1147*
Flying buttresses, 9/1093
Flying fish, 8/944
Flying fox, 3/*316*, 3/317
Flying lemurs, 8/967
Flying mammals, 8/**967**, 8/*967*
Flying saucer sleds, 19/2239
Flying squirrels, 8/967, 8/*967*
Flyways, duck and geese, 7/772
FM radio, 17/2045, 17/2051–2
Foals, 10/1203
Foam fire extinguishers, 8/933
Focal length, lenses, 12/1415
Foch, Ferdinand, 21/2609, 21/*2610*
Foehn, 21/2592
Fog, 1/39, 8/**967–8**, 8/*967*
Foils, fencing, 8/921–2, 8/*912–2*
Fokine, Michael, 7/774, 16/1886
Fold mountains, 14/1668, 14/*1668*
Foliage:
  leaves, 12/1402–4, 12/*1402–3*
  houseplants, 10/1215

Folk art, 8/**968–9**, 8/*968–9*
Folk dancing, 6/697, 6/698,
  8/**969–70**, 8/*970*
Folklore, 8/**970–2**, 8/*971–2*
  elves and fairies, 7/839
  fairytales, 8/904–5
  Paul Bunyan, 4/411
Folk museums, 14/1680
Folk singers, 18/2227
  Dylan, Bob, 7/777
Folk songs, 8/**972–3**, 8/*972–3*
Folk tales, 5/534, 8/970–1
  Arabian Nights, 2/194
Folsom culture, 8/**973**
Folsom, Frances, 5/574
Fontana Reservoir, 15/1788
Fonteyn, Dame Margot, 3/297,
  8/**973**, 8/*973*
Fonts, 20/2480–1
Food, 8/**974–6**, 8/*974–6*
  acids in, 1/24
  additives, 8/978
  baking, 3/292–4
  candy, 4/456
  canning, 8/977
  carnivores, 4/469–70
  cooking, 6/653–6
  digestion, 6/729–31, 6/*730–1*
  dried, 8/977
  ecological chains, 7/795–7, 7/*796*
  famines, 8/907–8, 8/*907–8*
  fats and oils, 8/916–17, 8/*917*
  fish, 8/947–50
  flour making, 8/960, 8/*960*
  freezing, 8/977
  fruit, 9/1016–18
  for garden birds, 9/1037
  growth and, 9/1122
  health, 10/1163
  hospitals, 10/1210
  ice cream, 10/1234
  jam, 11/1320–1, 11/*1320*
  jellies, 11/1320–1, 11/*1320*
  malnutrition, 8/975
  mammals, 13/1496–7
  meat, 13/1547–9
  metabolism, 13/1565–6
  minerals, 21/2534
  nutrition, 15/1810–11, 15/*1811*
  nuts, 15/1809–10
  pickling, 8/976
  processing, 8/**976–8**, 8/*976–8*,
    15/1810
  protein, 17/2013
  refrigeration, 17/2076
  restaurants, 17/2093–4,
    17/*2093–4*
  rice, 17/2100–1
  salt, 18/2156, 18/2157
  slating, 8/976
  smoking, 8/976
  snails, 19/2244
  soya, 19/2287
  spices and herbs, 19/2310–11
  sugar, 19/2351
  taste, 20/2381
  vacuum packed, 21/2506
  vegetables, 21/2511–12,
    21/*2511–12*
  vitamins, 21/2534–5
Food and Agriculture Organization
  (FAO), 8/875

Food and Drug Administration
  (FDA), 7/768, 18/2160, 18/2189
  standards, 8/978
Food web, 8/**978–9**, 8/*979*
Fools, 5/583
Football, 8/**979–83**, 8/*980–2*, 19/2317
  Canadian, 8/979
  common terms, 8/982
  records, 8/982
  Rockne, Kurt, 17/2112
  scoring, 8/983
  soccer, 19/2248–9, 19/*2248–9*
Forbes, Esther, 15/1746
Force, 8/**983–4**, 8/*984*
  power, 17/1992–3
Ford, Gerald Rudolph, 2/245, 4/476,
  8/**984–5**, 8/*984*, 21/2522, 21/2523
Ford, Henry, 1/*117*, 3/273–6, 6/723,
  6/724, 8/**985**, 8/*985*, 10/1190,
  13/1581, 20/*2451*
  philanthropy, 8/995
Ford Mercury Cougars, 3/275
Ford Motor Company, 3/273, 8/985
Forecastles, 18/2206
Foreign Claims Settlement Commis-
  sion, 21/2491
Foreign service, 8/**985–6**
Forensic science, 6/723, 8/**986**,
  8/*986*
Foresight, 8/897
Forest buffalo, 4/403
Forest fires, 8/**986–7***, 8/*986–7*
Forest rangers, 14/1707
Forestry, 8/**987–8**, 8/*987–8*
Forests, 20/2459–60
  animal life, 2/150
  coal, 16/1952, 16/*1952*
  fires, 16/1946
  jungles, 11/1348–50, 11/*1349–50*
  lumbering, 12/1469–70, 12/*1469–70*
  national, 14/1706–7
  Petrified Forest, 16/1908, 16/*1908*
Forgery, 6/673, 10/1146
Forget-me-nots, 8/*962*, 9/*1039*,
  21/*2587*
Forked lightning, 12/1437
Formosa *see* Taiwan
Formula One cars, 3/278
Forsythia, 18/2217
Fort Chippewyan, 12/1476
Fort Christina, 6/714
Fort Cook, 5/571
Fort Crèvecoeur, 12/1392
Fort Dearborn, 5/526, 8/990
Fort-de-France, 21/2572
Fort Dummer, 21/2518
Fort Duquesne, 8/990, 9/1005,
  9/1006, 16/1894
Fort Frontenac, 9/1006
Fort Garry, 10/*1218*
Fort Henry William, 9/1006
Forth railroad bridge, 4/392, 18/2176
Fortifications, 8/**989–91**, 8/*989–91*
  castles, 4/483–4, 4/*483–4*
  Great Wall of China, 9/1109–10,
    9/*1109*
  underground, 8/990–1
  walled, 8/889–90
Fort Knox, 8/**991**, 8/*991*
Fort Laramie, 22/2626
Fort McHenry, 13/1522, 13/1525,
  19/2328, 19/*2329*
Fort Mandan, 12/1420
Fort Meigs, 21/2541

Fort Niagara, 9/1006
Fort Orange, 15/1765, 15/1766
Fort Oswego, 9/1006
Fort Pierre, 19/2277, 19/2278
Fort Pitt, 16/1894
Fort Pontchartrain, 13/1580
Fort Pont-chartrain d'Etroit, 6/724
Fort St Anthony, 13/1604
Fort Stephenson, 21/2541
Fort Sumner, 14/1723
Fort Sumter, 1/120, 5/566, 8/**991**
Fort Ticonderoga, 1/101, 1/126,
  9/1006, 15/*1765*, 21/2519
Fortune-telling, 8/**992**, 8/*992*
Fort Vincennes, 5/571
Fort Wayne, 11/1258
Fort Worth, 8/990, 20/2414
Forty-Niners, 1/117, 9/1090
Forum, Roman, 18/2128, 18/*2132*
Fossil Butte, 14/1708
Fossils, 4/457, 8/**992–5**, 8/*993–5*,
  9/1056
  in amber, 8/993, 8/994
  Antarctica, 16/1965
  birds, 3/349–50
  formation, 8/994
  frozen, 8/994
  mammals, 13/1498
  paleontology, 15/1865
  sand-buried, 8/994
  in stone, 8/993
  in tar, 8/*993–4*
Foster homes, 11/1350
Foster, Stephen, 5/620, 8/**995**,
  8/*995*, 16/1977
Foucault, Jean Bernard Léon,
  16/1891
Foucault pendulum, 16/1891,
  16/*1892*
Foulbé, 4/442
Foundations:
  bridges, 4/430–1, 4/*431*, 6/647
  skyscrapers, 6/647
Foundations, philanthropic, 8/**995–6**
Foundries, 6/728
Foundry type, 20/2480–1
Fountain of Youth, 8/**997**
Fountain pen, 16/1896
Fountains, 8/**996**, 8/*996–7*
Fourdrinier brothers, 16/1871
Four freedoms, 8/**997**
Four-H Club, 22/2637
Fourier, François, 19/2249
Fourteenth Amendment, 17/2069,
  18/2238
Fourth Amendment, 3/340
Fourth of July, 11/1249, 11/1346–7
Fowler, Gene, 3/309
Foxes, 5/559, 8/**997–8**, 8/*997–8*
  tracks, 2/*164*
Fox, George, 19/2252
Fox Indians, 11/1296, 13/1616,
  21/2596
Foxtail grass, common, 9/*1104*
Foxtrot, 6/697
Foy, Eddie, 21/2510
Fractional distillation, 6/741, 16/1909
Fractions, 2/214, 9/**999**, 9/*999*,
  15/1808
  decimal numbers, 6/706
Fractures, 999, *999*
Fram, 2/132
France, 9/**1000–1**, 9/*1000–1*
  and Algeria, 1/100

American colonies, 1/110, 1/115, 2/220, 11/1256, 11/1296, 13/1616, 14/1642
American Revolution, 1/127, 1/128
Cadillac, Antoine, 4/429
and Canada, 4/446–7, 14/1644, 15/1746
Cartier, Jacques, 4/477–8
and Chad, 5/510
Charlemagne, 5/512
climate, 9/1000
colonies, 1/48–9
Comoro Islands, 5/617
Cousteau, Jacques, 6/668
Debussy, Claude, 6/704–5
Degas, Edgar, 6/711
De Gaulle, Charles, 6/711–12
Djibouti, 6/745
Dumas, Alexandre, 7/773–4
Dumas, Alexandre the Younger, 7/773–4
French and Indian Wars, 9/1005–6, 9/*1005*
French Guiana, 9/1006–7
French Revolution, 9/1010–12, 9/*1011*
furniture, 9/126
Gauguin, Paul, 9/1046–7
Guinea, 10/1126
history, 9/**1007–10**, 9/*1007–10*
Hugo, Victor Marie, 10/1219
Hundred Years War, 10/1227
Impressionists, 10/1245–6, 10/*145–6*
Indochina, 21/2525–6
introduction of farming to America, 1/54
Ivory Coast, 11/1314
Joan of Arc, 11/1336–7
Lafayette, Marquis de, 12/1383
La Fontaine, Jean de, 12/1384
La Salle, Sieur de, 12/1392–3
Lavoisier, Antoine Laurent, 12/1398
Lebanon, 12/1410
Louisiana, 12/1464, 12/1467
Madagascar, 12/1478
Manet, Edouard, 13/1502
Marie Antoinette, 13/1514
Marquette, Jacques, 13/1518
Martel, Charles, 5/515
Mauritania, 13/1538
Mexico, 11/1344
Monet, Claude, 14/1629–30
Ohio, 15/1824
Paris, 16/1877, 16/*1877*
Pascal, Blaise, 16/1882–3
Pasteur, Louis, 16/1883–4
Perrault, Charles, 16/1901
Renoir, Pierre Auguste, 17/2085–6
Rodin, Auguste, 18/2117–18
rulers, 9/1009
Seychelles, 18/2197
Toulouse-Lautrec, Henri de, 20/2436
Verne, Jules, 21/2519
Versailles, 21/2520, 21/*2520*
War of 1812, 21/2541
World War II, 22/2611–18
see also French Revolution, *and individual kings*
Franciscan monks, 9/1002
Francis I, Emperor, 13/1514
Francis I, King of France, 2/230,

5/503, 9/**1002**, 9/*1002*, 10/1177, 21/2520
Francis II, Emperor, 10/1196
Francis II, King of France, 9/**1002**, 10/1178, 13/1521–2
Francis of Assisi, 9/**1002**, 9/*1002*, 14/1629
Franco, Francisco, 6/726, 8/911, 9/**1002–3**, 9/*1003*, 14/1694, 19/2299, 19/2302, 22/2611
Franconia Notch, 15/1751
Franco-Prussian War, 9/1068
Frank, Anne, 6/725
Franklin, Benjamin, 1/30, 1/105, 3/367, 6/642, 6/644, 6/652, 6/707, 9/**1003–4**, 9/*1003–4*, 12/1480, 17/1999
American Revolution, 1/126, 1/127, 1/128
bifocal glasses, 9/1084, 9/*1084*
Franklin, James, 9/1003
Franklin, Northwest Territories, 15/1796
Franklin, Sir John, 15/1795, 22/2639
Franklin (state), 20/2404
Franks, 9/1064–5, 11/1310, 12/1468
Franz Ferdinand, Archduke, 9/1068
Franz Josef II, Prince of Liechtenstein, 12/1429
Fraser River, 4/392
Fraser, Simon, 4/394
Frazier, Joe, 4/381
Frémont, John Charles, 4/476, 15/1844
Freckles, 18/2233
Frederick I, King of Prussia, 9/**1004**, 9/*1005*, 9/1065
Frederick I Barbarossa, Emperor, 6/679
Frederick II, Emperor, 6/680
Frederick II the Great, King of Prussia, 9/**1004–5**, 9/*1005*, 9/1065, 9/*1066*, 17/2114
Frederick III, King of Prussia, 9/**1005**
Frederick Louis, Prince of Wales, 9/1060
Frederick William, Elector of Brandenburg, 9/1065
Fredericton, 15/*1748*
Freebooters, 16/1934
Freedmen's Bureau, 17/2070, 17/*2070*
Freedom, four freedoms, 8/997
Freedom of information, 504
Free fall parachuting, 16/1874
Free French Army, 6/712
Freehand drawing, 7/761
Free-range chicken, 17/*1991*
Freetown, Sierra Leone, 18/2218
Free verse, 16/1960
Freeways, 19/2341
Freezer trawlers, 8/950
Freezing, cryogenics, 6/682
Freight cars, 17/2054
Freighters, 13/1564, 18/2206
Frelimo, 14/1672
French and Indian War, 1/115, 9/**1005–6**, 9/*1005*, 16/1975
French Cameroun, 4/443
French-Canadians, 4/451, 4/452
French Equatorial Africa, 5/505, 5/510, 9/1029
French Foreign Legion, 2/225, 2/*226*
French Guiana, 9/**1006–7**, 9/*1006–7*

French Guinea *see* Guinea
French horn, 4/4/385, 4/*385*
French Indochina, 12/1392, 21/2525
French language, 18/2123
French Revolution, 1/30, 9/1009, 9/**1010–12**, 9/*1011*, 12/1463, 13/1514, 13/1571, 17/*2007*, 17/2095
Lafayette, Marquis de, 12/1383
months, 14/1644
French Somaliland, 6/745
Frequency, sound, 19/2265
Frequency modulation (FM radio), 17/2045, 17/2051–2
Frescos, 15/1859
Freshwater aquarium, 2/188–9
Freud, Sigmund, 7/763, 9/**1012**, 9/*1012*, 11/1348, 13/1554, 13/1562, 13/1563, 13/*1563*, 17/2021
Frey, 14/1695
Freya, 14/1695
Fria, 10/1126
Friction, 9/**1012–13**, 9/*1012–13*, 14/1657, 16/1901
Friday, 6/702
Friedan, Betty, 21/2601
Friedrich, Caspar David, 2/232, 2/*233*, 18/2127, 18/2128
Two Men Gazing at the Moon, 18/2127, 18/*2127*
Friendship 7, 9/1084
Frigate birds, 18/2181
Frigates, 14/1728, 14/*1730*, 14/*1731*
Frigg, 14/1695, 14/1696
Frigga, 6/702
Friml, Rudolf, 14/1687
Fritillary butterfly, 4/*420*
Frobisher, Sir Martin, 15/1795, 15/*1795*
Frogs and toads, 2/*128*, 2/130–1, 2/*130–1*, 9/**1013–14**, 9/*1013–14*, 10/*1183*, 13/1570
spawn, 7/*806*
Froissart, Jean, 12/*1446*
Froncha, 11/1318
Fronds, 8/923
Frontier, 16/1931–2
Frontiersmen:
Westward Movement, 21/2575–8
Wilderness Road, 21/2585–6, 21/*2586*
Frost, 9/**1015★**, 9/*1015*
Frost Fairs, 9/*1015*
Frost, Robert, 9/**1015–16**, 9/*1016*, 12/1451, 16/*1961*
Frozen foods, 8/977
Fruit, 9/**1016–18**, 9/*1016–18*, 18/2186–8, 18/*2187*
development, 16/1954
diet, 15/1811, 15/*1811*
nuts, 15/1809–10
seedless, 15/1017
Fruit bats, 3/*316*
Fruit flies, 7/766–7, 7/*766*, 8/966
Frying, 6/655
Fuchsias, 9/*1039*
Fuchs, Sir Vivian, 2/171
Fuel, 9/**1018–20**, 9/*1019–20*
atomic, 9/1019
charcoal, 9/1019
coal, 5/585–6, 9/1018
coke, 9/1019
fire, 8/932–3

heating, 10/1171–2
heat measurement, 9/1019–20
lignite, 9/1019
liquid oxygen, 9/*1019*
natural gas, 9/1019, 9/*1019*, 14/1713–14
nuclear, 9/1019
oil, 9/1019, 9/*1019*
peat, 9/1019
petroleum, 9/1019
plant based, 16/1951
producer gas, 9/1019
wood, 9/1018
Fuel cells, 9/**1020**
Fuerteventura, 4/454
Fugitive Slave Law, 4/400–1, 8/928, 18/2237
Fujairah, 2/193
Fuji, Mount, 14/*1670*
Fujiyama, 11/1322
Fulani, 4/442, 10/1125, 10/1126, 12/1493, 15/1774
Fulcrum, 12/1475
Fulgurites, 9/1083
Full moon, 14/1648
Fulmars, 18/2180–1
Fulton, 16/1902
Fulton, Robert, 9/**1020**, 9/*1020*, 14/1727, 18/2206, 18/2208, 18/*2210*
Fundamentalists, 17/2013
Fundy, Bay of, 4/446, 15/1746
Fundy National Park, 14/1713, 15/1746
Funerals, 4/413–14, 4/*413–14*
Fungal diseases, 6/737
Fungus, 9/**1020–2★**, 9/*1021–2*, 16/1939, 16/1943, 16/1947, 16/1951
bioluminescence, 3/343
mushrooms, 14/1680–1, 14/*1681*
parasites, 16/1876
poisonous, 16/1961, 16/1963
Fur, 9/**1022–4**, 9/*1022–4*
coats, 9/1023
hair, 10/1137–8, 10/*1137–8*
mammals, 13/1495
trading, 9/1023–4
Furnaces:
blast, 11/1303
electric, 11/1303
Furnishings, interior decoration, 11/1286–7, 11/*1286–7*
Furniture, 9/**1024–7**, 9/*1024–7*
ancient, 9/1024–5
English, 9/1026
interior decorating, 11/1287
Middle Ages, 9/1025
modern, 9/1027
North American, 9/1026–7
Shaker, 2/228, 2/*228*
Fur seals, 18/2184
Fuses, electrical appliances, 7/817
Futuna Island, 16/1971
Fyodor II, Czar, 18/2146

Gg

Gable, Clark, 1/21, 1/27, 14/*1660*
Gabon, 9/**1028–9**, 9/*1028*
Gabor, Dennis, 10/1195

Gadsden Purchase, 2/217, 15/1758, 16/1927
Gadwall, 7/*770*, 7/771
Gaelic, 11/1301, 18/2176
Gagarin, Yuri, 2/*248*, 9/**1029**, 9/*1029*, 15/1837, 19/2291
Gage, Thomas, 1/124, 1/125
Gagnan, Emile, 18/2177
Gaillard Cut, 16/1868, 16/*1868*
Gainsborough, Thomas, 2/232, 9/**1029–30**, 9/*1029*
Galápagos Islands, 7/801, 9/**1030**, 9/*1030*, 18/2173
Galápagos Rift, 15/1817, 15/1820
Galaxies, 2/252, 10/1217, 14/1657, 21/*2499*–2500
  Milky Way, 13/1594
  movement, 21/2500–1
Galen, 2/133, 9/1116, 13/1553
Galena, 10/1243, 13/*1567*, 13/1597
Galilean telescope, 20/2394
Galilee, Sea of, 9/**1030–1**, 9/*1031*, 12/1385
Galileo Galilei, 2/250, 3/262, 9/**1031–2**, 9/*1031*, 9/1105, 15/1813, 16/1891, 17/2016, 18/2172
Gallaudet, Thomas Hopkins, 10/1165
Gall bladder, 12/1453
Galleons, 14/1727, 14/*1727*, 18/*2206*, 18/2207, 18/*2208*
Galleries:
  art, 2/238
    Louvre, 12/1468, 12/*1468*
    Smithsonian Institution, 19/2241–2
Galleys (boats), 18/2139, 18/*2206*
Galleys (publishing), 17/2025
Gallinules, common, 6/671
Gallup, George, 15/*1836*
Galton, Sir Francis, 8/930
Galvani, Lucie, 9/1032
Galvani, Luigi, 9/**1032**, 9/*1032*
Galvanizing, 7/823
Galvanometer, 2/129, 7/820, 9/1032
Galway Bay, 11/*1302*
Gama, Vasco da, 9/**1032–3**, 9/*1032*, 10/1179, 11/1254, 14/1672, 16/1982
Gambia, 9/**1033**, 9/*1033*
Gambia River, 9/1033
Gambier Islands, 16/1971
Game birds, 9/**1033–4**, 9/*1034*
Game preserves, 11/1363
Games, 9/**1035**, 9/*1035*
  billiards, 3/339
  bowling, 4/378–9
  cards, 4/464
  children's, 5/**530–1**
  curling, 6/686–7, 6/*686*
  darts, 6/699
  dominoes, 7/754–5
  field hockey, 8/927–8, 8/*927–8*
  football, 8/979–83, 8/*980–2*
  golf, 9/1091–2, 9/*1091–2*
  gymnastics, 10/1133–4, 10/*1134*
  handball, 10/1143–4, 10/*1143*
  ice hockey, 10/1235, 10/*1235*
  jai alai, 11/1318, 11/*1318*
  lacrosse, 12/1382–3, 12/*1383*
  Little League baseball, 12/1453, 12/*1453*
  marathon races, 13/1512, 13/*1512*
  Olympic Games, 15/1830–1, 15/*1830–1*

physical education, 16/1921–2, 16/*1922*
  polo, 16/1970
  pool, 3/339
  racquetball, 17/2042, 17/*2042*
  snooker, 3/339
  soccer, 19/2248–9, 19/*2248–9*
  sport, 19/2316–18, 19/*2316–18*
  squash, 19/2321
  table tennis, 20/2374–5, 20/*2375*
  tennis, 20/2406–7, 20/*2406–7*
  volleyball, 21/2536–7, 21/*2537*
  word games, 21/2603–4
  see also Sport
Gamma rays, 17/2048, 17/*2049*
Gampers, Samuel, 12/*1380*
Gandak River, 14/1738
Ganders, 7/772
Gandhi, Feroze, 9/1035
Gandhi, Indira Priyadarshini, 9/**1035**, 9/*1035*, 11/1255
Gandhi, Mahatma, 9/**1035–6**, 9/*1035*, 11/1255, 14/1737
Gandhi, Rajiv, 9/1035, 11/1255, 14/1737
Ganges River, 9/**1036**, 9/*1036*, 11/1252, 11/1253, 11/1254, 17/*2081*
Ganglia, 11/1280
  mollusks, 14/1624–5
Gangtok, 18/2224
Gannets, 3/*346*, 18/2181, 18/*2181*
Gannett, Deborah, 3/353
Ganymede, 18/2165
Gao, 19/2262
Gapon, Father, 18/2148
Garbage, 18/2159–60
Garden birds, 9/**10368**, 9/*1037*
Garden flowers, 9/**1038–9**, 9/*1038–9*, 9/1040
  bulbs, 4/408–9, 4/*408*
  roses, 18/2137–8, 18/*2137*
  wildflowers as, 21/2587–8
Gardening, 9/**1040–2**, 9/*1041–2*
  Burbank, Luther, 4/412–13
  greenhouses, 9/1116–17, 9/*1117*
  houseplants, 10/1215–17, 10/*1215–17*
  fertilizer, 8/925
Garden snail 19/2244
Garfield, James A., 2/235, 2/245, 4/399, 9/**1042–3**, 9/*1043*
Gargantua, 9/1076
Gargoyles, 9/*1094*
Garibaldi, Giuseppe, 9/**1043**, 9/*1043*, 11/1311
Garnerin, André Jacques, 16/1873
Garnets, 9/1050
Garrett, Thomas, 20/2484
Garrick, David, 1/27, 9/**1044**, 9/*1044*
Garrison Dam, 15/1790
Garrison, William Lloyd, 1/15, 18/2238, 21/2583
Garth, 14/1628
Garvey, Marcus, 3/355, 5/562, 12/1491
Gary, 11/1258
Gas, 9/**1044–6**, 9/*1045–6*, 13/1537, 17/1999–2000
  Boyle's Law, 9/1045
  bunsen burners, 4/410
  Charles' Law, 9/1045–6
  hydrogen, 10/1231, 10/*1231*
  nitrogen, 15/1776–8, 15/*1777*

oxygen, 15/1852–3, 15/*1853*
  natural, 9/1019, 9/*1019*, 14/1713–14, 14/*1714*
  producer, 9/1019
  see also air
Gas lights, 12/1435
Gas masks, 13/1527
Gasoline, 9/**1046**, 9/*1046*
Gasoline piston engines, 7/849
Gaspé Peninsula, 17/2038
Gas pipelines, 16/1933–4
Gastric juices, 6/731
Gastroenterologists, 13/1555
Gastropods, 14/1625, 19/2243
Gas turbines, 7/849
Gates, dams, 6/695
Gates, General, 3/319
Gatling guns, 10/*1130*
Gatun Lake, 6/694, 16/1868
Gatun Locks, 16/1868
Gauchos, 2/211, 6/668, 17/*2061*, 19/2272
Gauguin, Paul, 9/**1046–7**, 9/*1047*, 14/1620, 20/2370, 21/2509
  Tahitian Woman, 20/2370, 20/*2371*
Gaullist movement, 6/712
Gauls, 9/1007
Gaur, 4/496
Gauss, Karl F., 13/1533
Gautreau, Madame, 18/2162
Gavials, 1/103
Gayal, 4/496
Gazelles, 2/174
Gazetteers, 3/256, 3/*256*, 9/**1047**
Gears, 9/**1047–8**, 9/*1048*
  automobiles, 7/766
Geb, 21/*2499*
Geba River, 10/1126
Gecko, 12/1455, 12/1456
Geese, 3/344, 7/770, 7/771, 7/772
  poultry, 17/1992
Gehrig, Lou, 9/**1049**, 9/*1049*
Geidel, Paul, 17/2006
Geiger counters, 9/**1049**, 9/*1049*
Geiger, Hans, 9/1049
Geldings, 10/1203
Geldof, Bob, 8/908, 16/*1978*
Gemini spacecraft, 1/95, 2/224, 5/597, 19/2291, 19/*2291*, 19/2292, 19/2294
Gems, 9/**1049–50**
  diamonds, 6/724
General Accounting Office, 21/2490
General anesthetic, 2/142
General Services Administration, 21/2490
Generators, 7/820
  electricity, 7/821–3, 7/*821*
  hydroelectricity, 10/1230
Genes, 3/341, 5/502, 8/888, 9/1052
Genetic engineering, 7/852, 9/1051, 9/1053
Genetics, 3/342, 3/343, 5/503, 9/**1050–3**, 9/*1051–3*
  Mendel, Gregor, 13/1561–2
  plant, 3/375
Geneva, 20/2368
Geneva Convention, 17/2074
Geneva, Lake, Wisconsin, 18/*2186*
Genghis Khan, 1/42, 9/**1053–4**, 9/*1053*, 14/1634
Gennesaret, Lake of, 9/1031
Genoa, 20/2444
Gentoo penguin, 16/*1892*

Genus, animals, 2/154
Geodetic surveying, 19/2361
Geography, 9/**1054–5**, 9/*1054*
  gazetteers, 9/1047
  latitude and longitude, 12/1395–6, 12/*1395–6*
  maps, 13/1509–12, 13/*1509–11*
  mountains, 14/1668–71
  social studies, 19/2250–1
Geologic time, 7/788
Geologists, 13/1599
  Agassiz, Louis, 1/50
Geology, 9/**1055–7**, 9/*1055–7*
  caves, 4/497–9
  earthquakes, 7/788–9, 7/*788–9*
  erosion, 7/866, 7/*866*
  fossils, 8/992–5, 8/*993–5*
  glaciers, 9/1079–80, 9/*1079–80*
  Grand Canyon, 9/1099
  granite, 9/1099–1100, 9/*1099*
  mountains, 14/1668–71
  origin of the Earth, 7/784–8
  plate tectonics, 16/1956
  rocks, 17/2109
  sand, 18/2158
  seacoasts, 18/2182–3
  volcanoes, 21/2535–6, 21/*2534–6*
Geometry, 9/**1057–60★**, 9/*1058–9*, 13/1533, 13/1534–5
  Euclid, 8/875
  figures, 9/1059
  history, 9/1057–8
  objects of, 9/1058–9
  pyramids, 17/2033
  Pythagoras, 17/2034
  uses of, 9/1060
Geomorphology, 9/1055
Geophysics, 9/1055, 9/1056
George I, King of England, 9/**1060**, 10/1144, 17/2000
George II, King of England, 9/**1060**, 9/*1060*
George III, King of England, 1/115, 9/**1060**, 9/*1060*
George IV, King of England, 9/**1060**
George V, King of England, 9/**1061**, 9/*1061*
George VI, King of England, 7/837, 9/**1061**, 18/2134
George Leygues-type frigates, 14/*1730*
George, St, 2/162
Georgetown, 6/743, 6/*743*, 10/1133
Georgia, 9/**1061–4**, 9/*1061–4*, 19/2282
  climate, 9/1062
  employment, 9/1064
  history, 9/1062–4
  land, 9/1061–2
  map, 9/*1063*
  state emblems, 9/*1063*
Georgian architecture, 2/201
Ger, 20/*2408*
Gerbils, 10/1126–7, 10/*1127*
Germani, 9/1064
Germanic languages, 12/1390
German language, 9/**1070**
German measles, 5/528, 6/738
Germany, 9/**1070–1**, 9/*1070–1*
  American colonies, 1/112
  Bismarck, Otto von, 3/350–1, 9/1065–8
  colonies, 1/49
  Grimm brothers, 9/1120

Gutenberg, Johannes, 10/1132
Handel, George Frederick, 10/1144
history, 9/**1064–9**, 9/*1064–9*
Hitler, Adolf, 10/1190–1
Holy Roman Empire, 9/1064–5
Humboldt, Alexander von, 10/1225
land, 9/1070
Luther, Martin, 12/1470–1
main events, 9/1066
Mendelssohn, Felix, 13/1562
Planck, Max, 16/1936
Prussia, 9/1065
Reformation, 9/1065
Rhine River, 17/2096
Rococo art, 17/2113
Schubert, Franz, 18/2170–1
Schweitzer, Albert, 18/2171
Von Braun, Wernher, 21/2537
Wagner, Richard, 21/2538
World War I, 21/2604–10
World War II, 22/2611–20,
22/*2611–20*
see also East Germany; West
Germany
Germs, 6/737
Gernsback, Hugo, 18/2175
Geronimo, 2/180, 2/217, 9/**1072**,
9/*1072*, 11/1271
Gershwin, George, 8/972, 9/**1072**,
9/*1072*, 14/1688
Gershwin, Ira, 9/**1072**, 9/*1072*,
14/1688
Gessler, 20/2400
Gestalt psychologists, 17/2020
Gestation period, 13/1496
Gethsemany, Bardstown, 14/1629
Gettysburg, 5/568, 5/*569*
battle of, 3/319
Gettysburg Address, 9/**1072–3**,
12/1441
Geysers, 9/**1073–4**, 9/*1074*, 21/2567,
21/*2567*
Gezira Plain, 15/1776
Ghana, 3/252, 9/**1074–5**, 9/*1074–5*
Ghats, 9/1036
Ghenghis Khan, 14/1633
Ghent, 10/1125
treaty of, 21/2542
Ghettos, 11/1336
Ghiberti, 13/1551
Ghirlandaio, Domenico, 17/2084
Ghost Dance cult, 18/2228, 18/2229
Ghosts, 9/**1075**, 9/*1075*
Ghoutra, 2/194
Giant anteaters, 2/172, 2/*172*
Giant armadillo, 2/221
Giant eland, 2/174
Giant flying squirrels, 8/967
Giant ground sloth, 13/1500
Giant hummingbird, 10/1226
Giantism, 9/1076
Giant kelp, 16/1947
Giant land turtle, 13/1539
Giant pandas, 13/*1495*, 16/1869,
16/*1869*
Giants, 9/**1075–6**, 9/*1076*
Giant's Causeway, 15/*1793*
Giant sequoia, 6/633
Giant squid, 14/1625
Gibbons, 2/182, 2/*182*
Gibraltar, 9/**1076**, 9/*1076*
monkeys, 14/1635, 14/1637
Gibson, Althea, 9/**1076–7**, 9/*1077*
Gibson, Kenneth A., 15/1756

Gide, André, 16/1959
Giffard, Henri, 1/78
Gigantism, 9/1076
Gila monster, 12/*1455*, 12/1456
Gila River, 2/215
Gilbert Islands, 13/1582
Gilbert, Sir Humphrey, 4/448,
17/2061
Gilbert and Sullivan, 9/**1077**, 9/*1077*,
14/1687
Gilbert, William, 9/1077
Gill net, 8/949–50, 8/*949*
Gills, 8/942–3, 8/*942*
Gin, 1/93
Ginger, 19/2310
Gingerbread faces, 6/655
Ginkgoes, 16/1954
Giorgione, 17/2085
Giotto di Bondone, 2/231–2, 2/*232*,
8/956, 9/**1077–8**, 9/*1078*
Giotto space probe, 5/607, 19/2288
Giraffes, 9/**1078–9**, 9/*1079*
Girls, adolescence, 1/34–5
Giscard d'Estaing, Valéry, 9/1010
Gist, 18/2192
Given names, 14/1698
Giza, 17/2033–4, 17/*2034*
Glacier Bay, 14/1709
Glacier National Park, 14/1640
Glaciers, 4/396, 9/**1079–80**,
9/*1079–80*, 12/1384, 12/1384,
14/1640
avalanches, 3/279–80
erosion, 7/866
ice ages, 10/1233
icebergs, 10/1233–4
Gladiators, 9/**1080**, 18/2132, 19/2303
Gladioli, 4/408, 4/*408*
Gladstone, William, 17/2000
Glands, 9/**1080–1**, 9/*1081*
hormone, 10/1201–2
Glasgow, 18/2176
Glass, 9/**1081–4**, 9/*1081–4*
stained, 19/2323, 19/*2323*
Glassblowers, 9/1082, 9/*1082*
Glasses, 9/**1084**, 9/*1084*, 12/1415
Glass snakes, 12/1455
Glazes, 16/1988
Glee clubs, 5/545
Glen Canyon Dam, 12/1385
Glendower, Owen, 21/2539
Glenn, John, 2/248, 9/**1084–5**,
9/*1085*, 19/2291
Glens, 18/2176
Gliders, 3/280–1, 3/*283*, 9/**1085–6**,
9/*1085*
hang gliding, 10/1147, 10/*1147*
Globe and Mail, 8/916
Globes, maps, 13/1511, 13/*1511*
Globe Theatre, 18/2197
Glockenspiel, 3/329, 22/2631
Gloire, 14/1727, 14/*1729*
Glomar Challenger, 15/1820
Glossary, 6/727
Gloss paints, 15/1858
Glucose, 4/462, 12/1402, 12/1453–4,
13/1565, 19/2351
Glycerides, 8/916
Glycogen, 4/462, 12/1453
Glyptodonts, 13/1500
Gnomes, 7/839
Gnu, 2/174
Gómez, Juan Vincente, 21/2515
Goat Island, 15/1770

Goats, 9/**1086**, 9/*1086*
Gobelin tapestries, 20/2380, 20/*2380*
Gobi Desert, 2/239, 6/720, 9/**1087**,
9/*1087*, 14/1633
'God Bless America', 3/332
Goddard, Robert H., 9/**1087**, 9/*1087*
Goddard Space Flight Center, 9/1087
Gods and goddesses, 9/**1087–9**,
9/*1088–9*
Fates, 8/915
mythology, 14/1695–7
Norse, 14/1695, 14/1696–7
see also Religion
Godspeed, 11/1319
Godunov, Boris, 18/2146
Godwin, Earl, 7/805
Godwin Austen, Mount, 10/1186
Godwin, William, 18/2203
Godwits, 21/2552
Goering, Hermann, 22/2613
Goethals, George, 16/1869
Goethe, Wolfgang von, 8/917
Gogol, Nikolai, 18/2216
Gold, 9/**1089–90**, 9/*1089–90*,
13/1567
alloys, 1/104
Colorado, 5/602
Fort Knox, 8/991
Gold Coast *see* Ghana
Gold coins, 5/592, 5/*592*
Golden cat, 4/490
Golden Eagle, 2/*148*, 3/344, 3/348,
3/*348*
Goldeneye, 7/771
Golden Fleece, 11/1324
Golden Gate suspension bridge,
4/*391*, 4/392, 18/2159
Golden Hind, 7/757
Golden Horsehoe Revue, 20/2421
Golden jackal, 11/1315
Golden plovers, 13/*1593*
Goldenrod, 8/965
Goldfish, 16/*1905*
Gold leaf, 9/1090
Gold mining, 3/267, 13/1600,
13/*1600*, 19/2266
Gold rushes, 9/**1090–1**, 9/*1091*,
16/*1969*, 19/2278, 21/2577,
22/2639
California, 4/438
Montana, 14/1642
Gold standard, 9/1090
Golf, 9/**1091–2**, 9/*1091–2*
Goliath, 9/1075
Goliath beetles, 3/326, 11/*1279*
Gomera, 4/454
Gondolas, 3/362, 21/2515
Gone With the Wind, 14/*1660*,
14/1663
Goodell, Brian, 20/2366
Good Friday, 7/790
Goodman, Benny, 11/1325
Good Neighbor Policy, 14/1639
Goods, selling, 18/2188–9
Goodyear airship, 1/79
Goodyear, Charles, 11/1293–4,
18/2141, 20/2428
Gooseneck barnacles, 6/681
Goose pimples, 18/*2233*
Gophers, 9/1120
Gopher turtles, 20/2478
Gorbachev, Mikhail Sergeyevich,
9/**1092**, 9/*1092*, 17/2068, 19/2286
Gordon, Charles, 19/2350

Gorgas, William Crawford, 1/83,
16/1869, 17/2075
Gorges, 4/457
Gorgon, 9/**1092–3**, 9/*1093*
Gorilla, 21/2535
Gorillas, 2/*180*, 2/181
Gorky, 21/2535
Goshawks, 3/*347*, 3/349
Goslings, 7/772
Gospel singers:
Jackson, Mahalia, 11/1317–18
Gothic architecture, 2/201, 2/203,
9/**1093–4**, 9/*1093–4*
Gothic armor, 2/222
Gothic novel, 18/2127
Goths, 1/85, 9/1064
Gouache, 15/1860
Gounod, Charles François, 8/917
Goura, 16/1929
Govenor Thomas E. Dewey Thru-
way, 15/1766
Government, 9/**1094–6**, 9/*1095–6*
Cabinet, 4/425–6, 17/1998, 17/2000
censorship, 5/503
democracy, 6/715–26
dictators, 6/726
forms of, 9/1094
legislature, 12/1412–13
local, 12/1456–7, 12/*1456*
parliament, 16/1878–9
presidency, 17/1996–9
prime ministers, 17/2000
revolutions, 17/2094–5, 17/*2095*
Soviet Union, 19/2284–5
United States, 21/2487–9,
21/*2487–9*
White House, 21/2582, 21/*2582*
see also Congress
Government agencies, 21/2489–91,
21/*2490–1*
Government Printing Office, 21/2490
Goya, Francisco, 7/*869*, 7/870,
13/1502
Goyathlay, 9/1072
Gozo, 12/1494
Grace, 18/2123
Grace, Princess, 14/1627
Graduation, 7/*804*
Grafting, plant breeding, 16/1942,
16/*1942*
Graf Zepplin, 1/78–9
Graham, Alexander, 11/1293
Graham, Billy, 8/883
Grahame, Kenneth, 5/532, 9/**1096**,
9/*1096*
Graham, Martha, 6/658
Grain, 9/**1096–7**, 9/*1097*
corn, 6/659–60
flour making, 8/960
harvesting machinery, 8/909
Grammar, 9/**1097–8**★
capitalization, 4/460
parts of speech, 16/1881
punctuation, 17/2029–30
Gran Chaco, 2/211
Grand Banks, 8/948–9
Grand Canal, China, 4/454
Grand Canary, 4/454
Grand Canyon, 2/127, 4/457, 4/*457*,
4/458, 9/1056, 9/1057, 9/**1099**,
9/*1099*, 17/2105, 17/*2109*
Grand Canyon National Park, 9/1099
Grand Comoro, 5/616
Grande-Terre, 21/2572
Grandfather clocks, 5/578, 5/*578*

Grand jeté, 3/296
Grand opera, 15/1835
Grand Prix auto racing, 3/278
Grand Union flag, 8/952
Granite, 9/**1099–1100**, 9/*1099*,
  17/*2108*
Granite Falls, Minnesota, 7/785
Grant, Alabama, 4/*498*
Grant, Ulysses Simpson, 1/120,
  2/235, 5/567, 5/568, 5/569,
  9/**1100–1**, 9/*1101*, 10/1162,
  10/1243, 11/1342, 12/1410,
  14/1709, 19/2319, 20/*2389*,
  21/2533
Grapefruit, 5/555
Grapes, wine, 21/2594–5
Graphic arts, 9/**1102–3★**, 9/*1102–3*,
  11/1273
  mechanical drawing, 13/1549–50
Graphite Peak, 16/1964
Graphology, 10/1146
Graphosoma italicum, 4/*404*
Graphs, 9/**1101–2★**, 9/*1101–2*
Grass, 9/**1103–4**, 9/*1104*
  development, 16/1954
  herbivores, 10/1180, 10/*1180*
Grasshopper Creek, 14/1642
Grasshopper mouse, 17/2067
Grasshoppers, 9/**1104–5**, 9/*1104–5*
Grassland, 16/1945
Grass snakes, 17/*2091*, 19/*2245*
Graubünden, 20/2367
Gravity and gravitation, 9/**1105–6★**,
  9/*1105–6*, 15/1763
  black holes, 3/356–7
  escape velocity, 19/2290
  moon, 14/1647
  orbits, 15/1837
  tides, 20/2425
  weight, 21/2565
Gravity dams, 6/694
Gravity meter, 13/1600
Gravure printing, 17/2003, 17/*2003*
Gray, Elisha, 11/1293
Gray fox, 8/998
Gray heron, 18/*2180*
Gray partridge, 9/1034
Gray, Robert, 5/605, 15/1842,
  21/2544
Gray seal, 18/*2184*
Gray shark, 18/*2199*
Grayson Highlands State Park, 2/184
Gray squirrel, 19/*2322*
Gray whales, 13/*1592*, 13/*1593*
Great auk, 3/350
Great Barrier Reef, 3/263, 3/*265*,
  3/*267*, 6/659, 9/**1106–7**, 9/*1107*,
  11/*1308*
Great Basin, 15/1743
Great Bear, 6/641, 6/*641*, 6/642
Great Bear Lake, 15/1796
Great Bed of Ware, 9/*1026*
Great black slug, 19/*2243*
Great Britain *see* United Kingdom
Great-crested grebe, 21/*2551*
Great Depression, 6/719, 6/*719*,
  18/2134
  black people, 5/562
Great Divide, 5/602, 5/604
Great Dividing Range, 14/1675
Great Eastern, 20/*2450*
Greater flamingos, 21/*2551*
Great European Plain, 8/877
Great Exhibition (1851), 8/903

Great Fire of London, 12/1459
Great gray shrike, 3/*346*
Great gray slug, 19/*2243*
Great horned owl, 15/1852
Great Lakes, 9/**1107–8**, 9/*1108*
Great Lakes megalopolis, 5/557
Great Lakes Plain, 15/1824
Great Plains, 9/**1108–9**, 14/1640,
  14/1732, 15/1757, 15/1790,
  15/1827, 20/2412, 22/2625
  ranching, 17/2061–2
Great pond snail, 19/*2244*
Great ram's horn, 19/*2244*
Great Rift, 17/2074
Great Rift Valley, 11/1363
Great Salt Lake, 9/**1109★**, 9/*1109*
Great Salt Lake City, 21/2505
Great Salt Lake Desert, 21/2502
Great Salt Pond, 17/2097
Great shearwaters, 13/*1593*
Great Slave Lake, 12/1476, 15/1796,
  15/*1796*
Great Smokey Mountains, 2/183,
  15/1787, 20/2403–4
Great Sphinx, 2/*136*
Great spotted cuckoo, 3/*346*
Great spotted woodpecker, 9/*1037*
Great Swamp Wilderness Area,
  21/2585
Great Wall of China, 5/*538*, 8/989,
  8/990, 9/**1109–10**, 9/*1109*
Great Wallendas, 1/25
Great Western, 18/*2210*
Great white sharks, 18/2200
Greaves, 2/221
Grebes, 21/2551
Greece, 9/**1110–11**, 9/*1110*
  Aegean Sea, 1/39
  Cyprus, 6/688–9
Greece, Ancient, 8/880, 9/**1111–13**,
  9/*1111–13*
  abacus, 1/13
  Acropolis, 1/26, 1/*26*
  advertising, 1/38
  Aeschylus, 1/40–41
  Aesop, 1/41
  alchemy, 1/92
  Alexander the Great, 1/96
  alphabets, 1/105–6, 1/*106*
  Amazons, 1/107
  Archimedes, 2/200
  architecture, 2/201, 2/*202*
  Aristotle, 2/211–12
  armies, 2/224
  art, 2/137, 2/*138*, 2/*178*, 2/231,
    9/**1114–15**, 9/*1114–15*
  astronomy, 6/641, 2/249–50
  Athens, 3/253–4
  battles, 3/318
  beginning, 9/1111
  burials, 4/413
  cities, 5/556
  clothing, 5/580
  coins, 5/592
  Daedalus, 6/691
  drama, 7/758, 7/759
  education, 7/802
  electricity, 7/818
  elements, 7/828
  Euclid, 8/875
  exploration, 8/892
  fashion, 8/912
  Fates, 8/915
  furniture, 9/1024–5

games, 9/113
geometry, 9/1058, 13/1532–3
giants, 9/1075–6
gods, 9/1087–9, 9/1113
growth, 9/1111–12
helmets, 5/580
Hercules, 10/1181, 10/*1181*
Homer, 10/1197
jewelry, 11/1333
laws, 2/137
legends, 12/1411
literature, 9/**1115–16**, 9/*1116*
marathons, 13/1512, 13/*1512*
masks, 13/1526, 13/*1526*
mathematics, 2/212
muses, 14/1677–8
mythology, 9/142, 11/1324,
  13/1584, 14/1695–6, 14/*1695*,
  14/1697, 16/1870, 16/1902,
  17/2008–9, 17/2102
Olympic Games, 15/1830
philosophers, 16/1914
philosophy, 2/136
Plato, 16/1956–7
Plutarch, 16/1958
pottery, 16/*1988*, 16/1989
Pythagoras, 17/2034
republic, 17/2091
science, 3/258, 18/2171–2
sculpture, 9/1115, 9/*1115*
ships, 18/2206
slavery, 18/2235
Socrates, 19/2254
summary, 2/134
temples, 20/2402
theater, 1/26, 20/2420
trade, 20/2444
Trojan War, 20/2465, 20/*2465*
war, 9/1111–12
Xerxes I, 22/262
Greek language, 9/**1114**
Greek Orthodox Church, 17/*2079*
  clergy, 5/573
Greeley, Horace, 9/**1116**, 9/*1116*,
  15/1761
Green, David (Ben-Gurion), 3/330
Greenaway, Kate, 5/*531*, 5/*532*, 5/533
Greenbacked turtles, 20/*2478*
Greenbacks, 14/1632
Greenbottle, 8/966
Green caspid, common, 4/*404*
Greene, Nathaniel, 17/2099
Greenfield Village, 13/1581
Greenhouse effect, 1/73–4, 1/*74*,
  9/1117
Greenhouses, 9/**1116–17**, 9/*1117*
  orchids, 15/1840
Greenhow, Rose, 19/2319
Greenland, 6/716, 9/**1117–18**,
  9/*1117–18*, 16/1889
  icebergs, 10/1234
Greenland sharks, 18/2200
Green Mountain Boys, 1/101, 1/126,
  21/2519
Green Mountains, 2/183, 21/2516–18
Greenpeace, 6/*640*, 17/2065
Greensboro, 15/1790
Greenwich, England, 11/1288
Greenwich Mean Time, 20/2428
Greenwich meridian, 12/1395
Greer, Germaine, 21/2601
Greeting cards, 9/**1118**, 9/*1118*
Gregg, John Robert, 18/2215

Gregg Shorthand, 18/2215, 18/*2215*
Gregorian calendar, 4/433
Gregorian chant, 5/544
Gregory, 18/*2121*
Gregory IX, Pope, 9/1002
Gregory XIII, Pope, 4/433, 16/1976
Grenada, 21/2571
Grendel, 3/331
Greyhound buses, 4/418
Grey, Lady Jane, 9/**1119**, 9/*1119*
Greysolon, Daniel, 13/1604
Grieg, Edvard, 9/**1119**, 9/*1119*
Grierson, John, 14/1663
Griffins, 2/*161*
Griffith, D.W., 9/**1119–20**, 9/*1119*,
  14/1659
Griffith Planetarium, Los Angeles,
  16/1937
Griffon, 12/1392
Grimaldi family, 14/1628
Grimaldi, Joseph, 5/583
Grimm brothers, 5/532, 8/*904*,
  8/905, 9/**1120**, 9/*1120*
Grimthorpe, Lord, 3/339
Grindstones, 8/960
Grissom, Virgil I., 2/248, 19/2292
Grist mills, 8/960
Grizzly bears, 3/320
Groin vaults, 18/2124
Grooms, marriage, 13/1518–19
Grootfontein, 13/1571
Gropius, Walter, 2/205
Groseilliers, Medard des, 10/1218
Gross anatomy, 2/133
Grotius, Hugo, 11/1289
Groton, 6/634
Groundhogs, 8/920, 9/**1120**, 9/*1120*,
  10/1182, 10/1183
Ground pine, 5/584
Ground squirrels, 9/**1120–1**, 9/*1121*,
  17/1994–5, 17/*1995*
Groups, communities, 5/615
Grouse, 9/1033, 9/1034
Grouse Mountain, 4/394
Growth, 9/**1121–2**
  regeneration, 17/2077
Growth hormones, 10/1201
Guadaljara, 13/1573
Guadalquivir, 19/2298
Guadalupe Hidalgo, Treaty of,
  13/1572, 20/2458
Guadalupe Mountains, 20/*2412*
Guadeloupe, 21/2572
Guam, 10/**1123**, 13/1544, 13/1582,
  19/2299
Guanaco, 2/*155*, 4/440
Guarneri family, 19/2344
Guatemala, 10/**1123–4**, 10/*1123–4*,
  15/*1786*
Guatemaltecos, 10/1123
Guayaquil, 7/800
Guericke, Otto von, 21/*2506*
Guernsey cows, 4/394
Guerriére, 21/2541
Guerrilla warfare, 10/**1124**, 10/*1124*
Guest bees, 3/325
Guiana, 17/2061
Guiana Highlands, 19/2268, 21/2514
Guided missiles, 13/1608–9
Guilds, 10/**1124–5**, 10/*1125*, 12/1380,
  13/1588
Guilford Courthouse, battle of,
  15/1788
Guillemot, 18/*2181*

Guillotine, 6/674
Guinea, 10/**1125–6**, 10/*1125*
Guinea-Bissau, 10/**1126**, 10/*1126*
Guinea fowl, poultry, 17/1992
Guinea pigs, hamsters and gerbils, 10/**1126–7**, 10/*1126–7*
Guinevere, 2/236
Guise, Duke of, 10/1178
Guitars, 19/2344
Gulf of Mexico, 10/**1127–8**, 10/*1128*
Gulfs, 18/2183
Gulf Stream, 3/254, 0/*1128*, 10/*1128*
Gulliver's Travels, 9/1076, 20/2364
Gulls and terns, 10/**1129**, 10/*1129*, 18/2182, 18/*2182*
Gulpers, 6/708
GUM (store), 19/**2286**
Gum diseases, 6/718
Gums, plant, 16/1951
Gunpowder, 5/538, 8/895, 8/896, 21/2559
Gunpowder Plot, 8/917–18
Gunsmiths, 10/1131
Guns and rifles, 10/**1129–32**, 10/*1129–31*
Gunston Hall, 21/*2532*
Guppies, 2/188
Gurkhali, 18/2223
Gustavus Adolphus, King of Sweden, 11/*1369*
Gustav V, King of Sweden, 12/*1451*
Gutenberg Bible, 3/336, 10/*1132*
Gutenberg, Johannes, 3/336, 5/611, 5/*611*, 9/1102, 10/**1132**, 10/*1132*, 17/*2002*, 17/2003
Guthrie, Woody, 7/777, 8/973
Guthrum, King, 1/96
Guyana, 10/**1132–3**, 10/*1133*
Guy Fawkes Day, 8/917
Guyots, 15/1855
Guzmán, Antonio, 21/2571
Gymnastics, 7/802, 10/**1133–4★**, 10/*1134*
Gymnosperms, 6/632, 16/1947, 16/*1949*, 20/2458
Gypsies, 10/**1134**
Gypsy moths, 8/967
Gyrfalcons, 3/348
Gyrocompass, 5/618
Gyroscopes, 10/**1134–5★**, 10/*1135*
Gyroscopic inertia, 10/1135

Hh

Habitats, 7/793
Habits, 10/**1136–7★**, 10/*1136*
 customs, 6/687–8
Hackers, 6/700
Hackney horses, 10/1206
Hades, 9/1088
Hadj, 11/1307
Hadrian, 18/*2130*, 18/2131, 19/2301
Hadrian's Wall, 7/*854*, 7/855, 8/*989*
Hadrosaurus, 6/*734*
Haeckel, Ernst, 17/2016–17
Haflinger horses, 10/*1205*
Hagfish, 8/941
Haggia Sophia, Istanbul, 4/424
Hahnemann, Christian, 10/1196
Haida Indians, 1/88, 3/253
Haifa, 11/1309, 11/*1310*
Haiku, 16/1961

Hail, 10/**1137★**, 10/*1137*
Haile Selassie, Emperor, 7/872, 11/1369, 22/2611
Hair, 10/**1137–8**, 10/*1137–8*
 fur, 9/1022–4, 9/*1022–4*
 mammals, 13/1495
 molting, 14/1627
Hair follicles, 18/2232
Hair seals, 18/2185
Hairstyles, 10/**1138–40**, 10/*1139–40*
Haiti, 21/2570, 21/2571
Haleakala, 10/1158
Hale, Nathan, 10/**1140**, 10/*1140*, 19/2320
Hale Telescope, 2/*250*
Haley, Alex, 3/356, 18/2238
Half hitch, 12/1374, 12/*1374*
Half-life, radioactivity, 17/2048–9
Half Moon, 6/714, 10/1218
Halftone engraving, 17/2005
Halicarnassus, mausoleum, 18/2193, 18/*2193*
Halifax, Nova Scotia, 15/1800
Halifax Resolves, 15/1788
Hallam, Arthur Henry, 20/2407
Halley, Edmond, 5/607–8, 10/**1140**
Halley's Comet, 5/607–8, 5/*607*, 10/1140, 15/1838
Hallidie, Andrew S., 4/426
Halloween, 8/971, 8/*971*, 10/**1140–1**, 10/*1141*
Hallucinations, drugs, 7/769
Hallucinogens, 1/33
Hals, Frans, 2/232, 7/775, 7/*775*, 10/**1141–2★**, 10/*1141*, 13/1502
Haltares, 8/966
Hamburgers, 6/654
Hamilton, 15/1832
Hamilton, Alexander, 1/30, 4/416, 4/425, 6/642, 6/652, 7/773, 10/**1142**, 10/*1142*, 15/1756, 21/2488
Hamilton, Andrew, 16/1986
Hamilton, Bermuda, 21/2572
Hamlet, 6/716
Hammarskjöld, Dag, 10/**1142–3**, 10/*1142*
Hammerfest, 10/*1149*
Hammerstein, Oscar, 14/1687
Hammer throwing, 20/2442–3
Hammond, Laurens, 15/1845
Hammurabi the Great, King, 2/137, 2/*138*, 3/286, 13/*1565*
 Code of, 12/*1399*
Hampton, 15/1752
Hampton Court, 13/1543
Hams, amateur radio, 17/2047–8
Hamsters, 10/1126–7
Hancock, John, 1/125, 10/**1143**, 10/*1143*
Hancock, Walter, 18/2180, 19/2337
Handball, 10/**1143–4**, 10/*1143*
Hand bells, 3/329
Handel, George Frederick, 3/307, 5/544, 5/*620*, 10/**1144**, 10/*1144*, 17/2114
Handguns, 10/1131–2
Handicapped people, education, 19/2303–5
Hand lotions, 6/662
Hands, 10/**1144–6★**, 10/*1144–5*, 13/1497
 reading palms, 8/992, 8/*992*
Handwriting, 10/**1146★**

Han dynasty, 5/538
Handy, W.C., 10/**1147**, 10/*1147*
Hangars, 1/75
Hang gliding, 10/**1147**, 10/*1147*, 20/*2451*
Hanging Gardens of Babylon, 3/286, 18/2193, 18/*2193*
Hanging valleys, 21/2553
Han Kuang-wu, Emperor of China, 5/*539*
Hannibal, 4/477, 10/**1147–8**, 10/*1148*
Hannu, 8/889
Hanseatic League, 10/1125
Hansom cab, 4/475
Hansom, J.A., 4/475
Hanukkah, 6/706, 10/**1148–9**, 10/*1149*
Hapsburgs, 3/269–70
Haran, 10/*1214*
Harare, 22/2644
Harbor seals, 18/2185
Harbors and ports, 10/**1149–51**, 10/*1149–51*
Harburg, E.Y., 14/1688
Hard coal, 5/586
Hard hats, 2/223
Harding, Warren G., 2/245, 6/656, 10/**1151–2**, 10/*1152*
Hardness, minerals, 13/1597, 13/*1598*
Hardwar, 9/1036
Hardware, 5/623, 5/623–4
Hard water, 21/2550
Hardwood, 12/1469–70, 21/2601–2
Hardy, Thomas, 10/**1152–3**, 10/*1152*
Hare, George, 17/2095, 17/*2095*
Hare Indians, 3/253
Hares, 17/2039–40, 17/*2039*
Hargreaves, James, 19/2313, 19/*2313*
Harlem Globetrotters, 3/313
Harlequin, 16/1870
Harlequin bug, 4/404
Harmonicas, 10/**1153**
Harmonics, 19/2265
Harmony, music, 14/1683
Harness horses, 10/1206
Harness racing, 10/1208
Harnick, Sheldon, 14/1688
Harold the Fairhaired, King of Norway, 15/1798
Harold, King of England, 2/143, 3/319, 7/805–6, 7/855, 21/2588
Harpers Ferry, 1/15, 14/1709, 21/2575
Harpies, 11/1324
Harps, 10/**1153**, 10/*1153*, 19/2344
Harpsichords, 16/1925
Harrier hawks, 3/349
Harriers, 3/*343*
Harris, Benjamin, 15/1761
Harris, Joel Chandler, 5/*534*, 10/**1153–4**, 10/*1153*
Harrison, Benjamin, 4/399, 10/**1154–5**, 10/*1154*, 11/1255, 15/1793, 19/2278
Harrison, George, 16/1978
Harrison, John Scott, 10/1154, 10/1155
Harrison, William Henry, 2/245, 10/**1155–6**, 10/*1155*, 11/1255, 11/1256, 20/2386, 21/2508, 21/2541
Harris, Patricia Roberts, 3/355, 10/**1154**, 10/*1154*
Harrod, James, 11/1362

Harrodsburg, 11/1362
Harrows, 8/909
Harrow School, 19/2321
Harte, Bret, 9/1091
Hartford, Connecticut, 6/*634*, 6/636, 11/1284
Hart, Lorenz, 14/1688
Harts, 6/709
Hartsfield International, 1/77
Hart's tongue fern, 8/*923*
Harvard University, 5/595, 13/1530
Harvard University Library, 12/1426
Harvester ants, 2/167
Harvest mice, 2/*153*
Harvests, reapers, 13/1543
Harvey, William, 13/1553
Hasidim, 10/1139
Haslam, Pony Bob, 16/1975
Hassan II, King of Morocco, 11/1369
Hastings, battle of, 3/319, 7/806, 7/855
Hatchet fish, 8/*944*
Hathaway, Anne, 18/2197
Hats, 10/**1156–7**, 10/*1156–7*
Hatshepsut, 11/1368
Hausa, 15/1772, 15/1774
Haustoria, 16/1876–7
Havanna, 6/684, 6/*684*
Hawaii, 6/653, 10/**1157–60**, 10/*1157–60*, 11/1351, 13/1544, 15/*1855*
 employment, 10/1160
 history, 10/1158–6
 land, 10/1157–8
 Liliuokalani, Lydia Kamekeha, 12/1438
 map, 10/*1159*
 people, 10/1160
 state emblems, 10/*1159*
Hawkins, Gerald, 19/2336
Hawks, 3/344, 3/348
 falconry, 8/906
Hawthorne, Nathaniel, 5/532, 10/**1161**, 15/1751, 15/1802, 16/1927, 18/2127
Hayden Planetarium, New York, 16/1937
Haydn, Franz Joseph, 3/325, 10/**1161**, 10/*1161*, 14/1693, 14/1705
Haydon, Benjamin, 11/*1357*
Hayes, Helen, 10/**1161–2**, 10/*1162*
Hayes, Rutherford B., 2/235, 10/**1162–3**, 10/*1162*, 17/2071
Hay fever, 1/101, 6/649
Hayne, Robert Y., 21/2564
Haywain, 6/6401
Hazel, 20/*2461*
Hazelnuts, 15/1810
Headlands, 18/2183
Heads, hats, 10/1156–7, 10/*1156–7*
Health, 10/**1163–5**, 10/*1163–4*
 cleanliness, 10/1164
 dentistry, 6/717–18
 exercise, 8/888, 10/1163, 10/*1164*
 first aid, 8/938–40, 8/*939–40*
 food, 10/1163
 hospitals, 10/1209–11, 10/*1209–11*
 physical education, 16/1921–2
 sleep, 10/1163
 smoking, 19/2242–3
Health and Human Services Department, 4/426

Healy, Ted, 21/2510
Hearing, 10/**1165–7**, 10/*1165–7*
    ears, 7/778–9, 7/*779*
    education for the deaf, 19/2303–4
Hearing aids, 10/1165
Hearne, Samuel, 15/1796
Hearst, William Randolph, 15/1761
Heart, 10/**1167–8**, 10/*1167–8*
    circulatory system, 5/550–1, 5/*550*
    transplants, 10/1168
Heat, 10/**1168–70***, 10/*1169–70*
    absorption, 1/*18*
    energy, 7/845, 16/1923
    fire, 8/932–3, 8/*932*
    insulation, 11/1282–3
    measuring, 10/1170
    temperature scales, 20/2400–1
    transfer, 10/1170
Heathcote, John, 9/1029–30, 9/*1029*,
    12/1382
Heath, Edward, 20/2419
Heathfield, Lord, 17/*2096*
Heathrow airport, 1/77
Heating, 10/**1171–2**, 10/*1171–2*
Heat lightning, 12/1437
Heavy water, 21/2550
Hebrew calendar, 4/434
Hebrew language, 1/106, 10/**1172**,
    10/*1172*
Hebrews, 2/134
Hebrides, 18/2176
Hector, 14/1697, 20/2465
Hedge bindweed, 8/*962*
Hedgehogs, 14/1623–4, 14/*1623*
Heem, Jan de, 7/776, 7/*776*
Hegira, 4/434, 11/1307, 14/1673
Heidi, 19/2320
Heimdall, 14/1695
Heinlein, Robert, 18/2175
Heisenberg, Werner, 18/2172
Hel, 14/1695
Helen of Troy, 14/1697, 20/2465
Helicopters, 10/**1173–4**, 10/*1173–4*,
    19/*2286*
Helium, 6/682
Helium balloons, 3/298
Hellas, 9/1112
Hellbender, 18/2155
Hellenes, 9/1112
Hells Canyon, 10/1237
Helmets, 5/580
Helmholtz, Hermann von, 3/286
Helsinki, 8/931
Hemicyclaspis, 8/*941*
Hemingway, Ernest, 10/**1175**,
    10/*1175*, 12/1451
Hemlocks, 6/632
Hemming stitch, 18/2194
Hemoglobin, 21/2535
Hemophilia, 6/738
Hemp, 18/2136
Hendrick, 8/*951*
Henequen, 18/2137
Henges, 19/2336, 19/*2336*
Hennepin, Louis, 13/1604
Henrietta Maria, Queen, 13/1524
Henry I the Fowler, Emperor,
    10/**1175**
Henry I, King of England, 10/**1176**
Henry I, King of France, 10/**1177**
Henry II, Emperor, 10/**1175**
Henry II, King of England, 3/322–3,
    7/814, 10/**1176**, 11/1337,
    16/1911, 19/2333

Henry II, King of France,
    10/**1177–8**, 10/*1177*
Henry III, Emperor, 10/**1175**
Henry III, King of England,
    10/**1176**, 11/1337, 12/1462
Henry III, King of France, 10/**1178**,
    10/*1178*
Henry IV, Emperor, 10/**1175**,
    10/*1175*
Henry IV, King of England,
    10/**1176**, 10/*1176*, 17/2102
Henry IV, King of France, 5/510,
    9/1008, 10/**1178**, 10/*1178*
Henry V, Emperor, 10/**1175**
Henry V, King of England, 6/677,
    10/**1176–7**, 10/*1227*
Henry VI, Emperor, 10/**1175**
Henry VI, King of England,
    10/**1177**, 10/*1176*, 21/2543,
    21/*2543*
Henry VII, Emperor, 10/**1175**
Henry VII, King of England, 7/857,
    9/1119, 10/**1177**, 10/*1176*,
    17/2102, 21/2539, 21/2543,
    21/*2543*
Henry VIII, King of England, 7/836,
    7/857, 8/921, 9/1002, 10/**1177**,
    10/*1177*, 10/1193, 13/1522,
    14/1648, 17/2015
Henry the Navigator, 10/**1179**,
    10/*1179*, 16/1982
Henry, O., 10/**1178**, 10/*1178*
Henry, Patrick, 1/32, 1/*122*, 10/**1179**,
    20/*2459*
Henry of Portugal, 8/892
Henry, Sir Edward Richard, 8/930
Henson, Matthew, 10/**1179–80**,
    10/*1179*, 16/1889
Hephaestus, 9/1088
Hepplewhite, George, 9/1027
Hepworth, Barbara, 18/2179
Hera, 10/1181, 20/2465
Heracles, 10/1181, 14/1697
Heraldry, 5/**587–8**
Herbaceous flowers, 9/1038
Herbalists, 3/374
Herbals, 3/374
Herbert, Frank, 18/2175
Herbert, Victor, 14/1687, 15/1835
Herbivores, 4/470, 7/794, 10/**1180**,
    10/*1180*, 10/1203, 13/1496
    digestive tracts, 6/731
Herb Robert, 8/*962*
Herbs, 19/2310–11*, 19/*2310*
Herculaneum, 2/198, 16/1973
Hercules, 1/107, 10/**1181**, 10/*1181*,
    14/1697, 17/2009
Herders, nomads, 15/1780–1
Hereditary diseases, 6/738
Heredity, 9/1050
Hereford cattle, 4/495, 4/*496*
Heresy, 18/2122
Herman, Jerry, 14/1687
Hermes, 2/231, 2/*232*, 9/1088
Hermitage, Leningrad, 2/228
Hermit crabs, 6/681
Hernandez, Amalia, 3/*297*
Hero, 7/847, 7/*847*, 7/848, 11/1332,
    20/2438
Herod, King, 20/2402
Herodotus, 9/1116, 16/1984
Heroin, 1/33, 7/769, 14/1703
Heron Island, 3/263
Herons, 21/2551, 21/*2585*

Herrick, Margaret, 1/21
Herring gull, 10/1129
Herrings, 8/*949*, 8/950
Herron, Helen, 20/2375
Herschel, Caroline, 10/**1182**
Herschel, John, 10/**1182**, 10/*1181*
Herschel, William, 21/*2499*
Hertz, Heinrich, 17/2051
Herculaneum, 21/2535
Herzl, Theodor, 11/1336
Hesiod, 9/1115, 14/1696
Hesperornis regalis, 3/349, 3/*349*
Hestia, 9/1088
Heteroptera, 4/404
Heyerdahl, Thor, 8/*889*, 10/**1182**,
    10/*1182*
Hiawatha, 8/950, 12/1460, 13/1580
Hibernation, 8/916, 10/**1182–3**,
    10/*1183*
    frogs and toads, 9/1014
    groundhogs, 9/1120
    rodents, 18/2115
Hiccups, 10/**1183–4**
Hickok, Wild Bill, 10/**1184**, 10/*1184*,
    16/1975
Hickory nuts, 15/1810
Hidalgo y Costilla, Miguel, 10/**1184**,
    13/1575
Hide, leather, 12/1408–9
Hides, birdwatching, 14/*1718*
Hieroglyphics, 5/611, 5/*611*, 7/810,
    10/**1184–5**, 10/*1184*, 22/*2624*
    alphabets, 1/105
    Rosetta Stone, 18/2138, 18/*2138*
    writing, 2/135
Hierro, 4/454
High explosives, 8/895
High jump, 20/2441–2
Highland fling, 8/969
High-relief sculpture, 18/2178
High schools, 18/2170
    social studies, 19/2250–1
High Sierra, 18/2218
Highways, 5/557, 5/*557*, 19/2340,
    19/2341
    traffic planning, 20/2445–6
High-wire artists, 1/25
Hijacking, 16/1935
Hillary, Sir Edmund, 1/16, 8/*892*,
    8/893, 10/**1185**, 10/*1185*, 14/1672
Hilo, 10/1158
Hilts, 20/2368
Himalaya Mountains, 2/239, 3/334,
    10/**1185–6**, 10/*1185*, 11/1252,
    14/*1669*, 14/1671, 18/2223
    Abominable snowman, 1/16, 1/*16*
    Nepal, 14/1738, 14/*1738*
    Tibet, 20/2424
Himmler, Heinrich, 22/2612
Hinayana Buddhists, 4/402
Hindenburg, 1/791/79
Hinds, 6/709
Hinduism, 2/243, 10/**1186–7**,
    10/*1186*, 17/2079
    dance, 6/696, 6/*696*
    Ganges River, 9/1036
    India, 11/1254
    yoga, 22/2634–5
Hindu Kush, 1/42, 2/239
Hindus, 17/*2081*
Hindustani language, 12/1390
Hinny, 7/755
Hippocrates, 2/135, 9/1113, 10/**1187**,
    10/*1187*, 13/1552, 19/2358

Hippocratic Oath, 13/1552–3
Hippolyta, 1/107
Hippopotamuses, 10/**1188**, 10/*1188*
Hirohito, Emperor, 11/1324, 22/2619
Hiroshige, Ando, 15/1846
Hiroshima, 8/*895*, 20/2471, 22/2619
Hispanic Americans, 10/**1188–9**,
    10/*1189*
Hispaniola, 21/2569
Hiss, Alger, 15/1778
Histology, 2/133
Historical geology, 9/1055
History, 10/**1189–90**, 10/*1190*
    archaeology, 2/196–8
    fossils, 8/992–5, 8/*993–5*
    museums, 14/1678–80
    social studies, 19/2250
Hitches, knots, 12/1374
Hitler, Adolf, 6/689, 6/719, 6/726,
    6/*726*, 8/897, 8/911, 8/*911*,
    9/1068–9, 9/1095, 10/**1190–1**,
    10/*1191*, 11/1311, 11/1336,
    15/1831, 15/1851, 19/2324,
    21/2537, 22/2611–18
Hittites, summary, 2/134
Hoarfrosts, 9/1015, 9/*1015*
Hoban, James, 4/461, 21/2582
Hobart, 3/266
Hobbies, 10/**1191–2**, 10/*1191–2*
    amateur radio, 17/2047–8, 17/*2048*
    collecting, 5/593–5, 5/*593–4*
    industrial arts, 11/1274
    needlework, 14/1735–6, 14/*1735–6*
    stamp collecting, 19/2324–5,
        19/*2324*
    terrariums, 20/2410
    see also Games; Pastimes
Hobbyhorse, 20/*2438*
Hobo clown, 5/583
Ho Chi Minh, 21/2526
Ho Chi Minh City, 21/2525
Hockey, 8/927–8, 8/*927–8*, 19/2317
    roller-hockey, 18/2119
Hoder, 14/1695
Hoes, Hannah, 21/2507
Hoffman, Dustin, 1/27
Hogan, 3/253, 14/1723
Hogmanay, 6/706
Hogs, 16/1928
Hohner, Matthias, 10/1153
Hohokam Indians, 2/215
Hokkaido, 11/1322
Holbein, Hans the Younger,
    10/**1192–3**, 10/*1193*
    Sir Thomas More, 16/1981, 16/*1981*
Hole-in-one (golf), 9/1092
Holidays, 10/**1193–4**, 15/1763
    Memorial Day, 13/1559–60
    Passover, 16/1883
    Thanksgiving, 20/2418–19, 20/*2419*
    travel, 20/2454–6
    Valentine's Day, 21/2507
    Veterans Day, 21/2521–2
Holland, John Philip, 19/2346
Holland *see* Netherlands
Holliday, Doc, 7/780
Holly, 8/884–5, 8/*885*, 18/2217
Hollywood, 4/439, 12/1460, 14/1659–62
    Academy Awards, 1/21
    star system, 1/27
    see also Motion pictures
Holmes, Larry, 4/381
Holmes, Oliver Wendell Jr.,
    10/**1195**, 10/*1195*

Holmes, Oliver Wendell Sr., 10/**1195**, 10/*1195*
Holmes, Sherlock, 7/756
Holm oaks, 20/*2461*
Holography, 3/270, 10/**1195–6**, 10/*1195*, 12/1394
Holstein cattle, 4/494, 4/*494*
Holy Land, Crusades, 6/678–80, 13/1588
Holy Roman Empire, 9/1064–5, 10/**1196**, 10/*1196*
emperors, 5/**512–13**
Holy Thursday, 7/790
Holy Week, 7/790
Homeopathic medicine, 10/**1196–7**
Homer, 2/136, 2/221, 9/1075–6, 9/1115, 10/**1197**, 10/*1197*, 12/1411, 14/1696, 14/*1696*, 14/1703, 17/2102
Home runs, 3/312–13
Homer, Winslow, 10/**1197–8***, 10/*1197*, 15/1846, 15/*1862*
Homes:
electrical appliances, 7/816–18, 7/*816–18*
houses, 10/1213–15, 10/*1213–15*
see also Houses
Homespun, 5/580
Homesteads, 21/2578
Homicide, 14/1675
Homing instinct, 13/1593
Homing pigeons, 16/1929
Homo erectus, 10/*1220*, 10/1221–2
Homo habilis, 12/1405
Homo neanderthalensis, 10/*1220*, 10/*1221*, 10/1222
Homo sapiens, 10/1223
Honda knot, 12/1374
Honda motorcycles, 14/*1667*
Honduras, 5/505–7, 10/**1198–9**, 10/*1198*
Honey, 19/2351
Honey ants, 2/168
Honeybees, 3/323–4, 11/1279
Honeycomb, 2/153, 3/323, 3/*324*
Honeydew, 2/167–8
Hong Kong, 10/**1199**, 10/*1199*
Honiara, 13/1558
Honolulu, 10/1158
Honshu, 11/1322
Hooch, 3/253
Hood, Mount, 15/1842, 15/*1842*, 15/*1844*
Hood, Robin, see Robin Hood
Hoofed animals, 10/**1200**, 10/*1200*
antelopes, 2/173–4
bison, 3/351
buffalo, 4/403
camels, 4/439–40, 4/*440*
cattle, 4/493–6
deer, 6/708–10
donkeys, 7/755
hippopotamus, 10/1118, 10/*1188*
horses, 10/1203–7, 10/*1203–6*
rhinoceroses, 17/2096–7, 17/*297*
sheep, 18/2201–2, 18/*2201–2*
tapirs, 20/2380
zebras, 22/2644, 22/*2644*
Hoofs, 10/1202, 13/1497
Hooked rugs, 4/473
Hooke, Robert, 3/375, 22/2648
cells, 5/501
Hooker, Thomas, 17/2032
Hooks, fishing, 8/946

Hooks, Benjamin L., 14/1706
Hookworms, 22/2620
Hoosiers, 11/1255, 11/1258
Hoosier, Samuel, 11/1255
Hoover, Herbert, 10/1152, 10/**1200–1**, 10/*1201*, 14/1639, 19/2328
Hoover, J. Edgar, 8/920, 8/*920*, 21/*2489*
Hope, Bob, 21/2510
Hopi Indians, 2/215, 5/575, 11/1258, 15/1757, 19/2246
Hopkins, Elizabeth, 16/1930
Hopkins, Oceanus, 16/1930
Hopkins, Stephen, 16/1930
Hoppers, 17/2054
Horace, 2/136, 18/2132
Horizon, 18/2183, 18/2234
Hormonal diseases, 6/738
Hormones, 3/341, 9/1080–1, 10/**1201–2**
drugs, 7/768
Hornbeam, 20/*2461*
Hornbooks, 5/531, 5/*531*
Hornets, 21/2548–9
Horns and antlers, 10/**1202**
Hornwort, 2/189
Horoscopes, 2/247
Horror fantasy fiction, 12/1450
Horse chestnuts, 15/1809, 15/*1809*, 18/*2187*, 20/*2461*
Horseflies, 8/966, 18/2220
Horse latitudes, 21/2562
Horses, 10/*1145*, 10/**1203–7***, 10/*1203–6*, 16/*1906*
agriculture, 1/55
carriages, 4/474–5, 4/*474–5*
Comanche Indians and, 5/606
equestrianism, 7/865–6, 7/*865*
evolution, 8/887
racing, 10/**1208–9**, 10/*1208*
riding, 10/**1207–8**, 10/*1207–8*
horsemanship, 10/1207–8
rodeos, 18/2116–17, 18/*2116–17*
see also Donkeys
Horseshoe Bend, battle of, 11/*1271*
Horseshoe crabs, 6/681
Horseshoe Falls, 15/1770, 15/*1770*, 21/2553
Horsetail, 10/**1209**, 10/*1209*, 16/1939, 16/1947, 16/1952
Horticulture:
garden flowers, 9/1038–9, 9/*1038–9*
gardening, 9/1040–2, 9/*1041–2*
greenhouses, 9/1116–17, 9/*1117*
Hospitals, 10/**1209–11**, 10/*1209–11*
ambulances, 1/108–9
departments, 10/1210–11
food service, 10/1210
history, 10/1211
laboratory, 10/1210
medical records, 10/1210
medical service, 10/1210
Nightingale, Florence, 15/1774–5
nurses, 15/1808
pharmacy, 10/1210
rehabilitation, 10/1211
scanning and X-ray department, 10/1210
surgical service, 10/1210
types, 10/1209
Hot-air balloons, 3/280, 3/297–9
Hot and cold, thermometers, 20/2422, 20/*2422*

Hotels and motels, 10/**1211–12**, 10/*1211–12*
Hot Springs National Park, Arkansas, 2/*219*, 2/220
Hottentots, 1/46, 14/1700, 19/2267
Houdini, Harry, 10/**1212–13**, 10/*1213*, 12/1482
Hounds, 6/746–7
Houseboats, 3/*361*, 3/362
House of Commons, 16/1878–9
House of Lords, 16/1878–9
House Majority Leader, 6/629
House mice, 17/*2065*, 17/2066–7, 17/*2066*
House Minority Leader, 6/629
Houseplants, 10/**1215–17***, 10/*1215–17*
House of Representatives, 6/628–30, 6/*628*
Houses, 10/**1213–15**, 10/*1213–15*
building, 6/648–9
electrical appliances, 7/816–18, 7/*816–18*
frontier, 16/1932, 16/*1932*
heating, 10/1171–2
history, 10/1213–14
insulation, 11/1282
insurance, 11/1283–4
interior decoration, 11/1286
lake dwellers, 12/1386, 12/*1386*
lighting, 12/1435–6, 12/*1435–7*
modern, 10/1214–15
plumbing, 16/1957–8, 16/*1958*
shelters, 18/2203–5
Houses of Parliament, Big Ben, 3/338–9, 3/*339*
Housing and Urban Development Department, 4/426
Houston, 10/1217, 20/2414
Houston, Samuel, 1/85, 4/378, 10/**1217**, 10/*1217*, 20/2414
Houston Ship Canal, 4/453, 4/454, 10/1128
Hovercraft, 1/60–1, 1/*61*, 20/2453
Hoverflies, 8/966, 17/*2021*
Howard, Catherine, 10/1177
Howdah, 7/833
Howe, Elias, 13/1530, 18/2196
Howe, General, 10/1140
Howe, Julia Ward, 21/2600
Howell, Varina, 6/701
Howe, Sir William, 1/127
Howland Island, 16/1971
Howling monkeys, 14/1635, 14/1636
Hoxha, Enver, 1/89, 1/90
Hoyland, John, 2/233
Hubble, Edwin, 10/**1217**, 10/*1217*, 21/2500
Hubble's Constant, 10/1217, 21/2500
Hub City, 3/372
Hudson Bay, 4/444, 10/**1218**, 15/1832
Hudson, Henry, 2/209, 4/447, 6/714, 8/893, 10/**1217–18**, 10/*1218*, 15/1754, 15/1765, 15/1795, 15/1832
Hudson River, 4/458, 10/1217–18, 15/1765, 15/1766
Hudson River School, 18/2128
Hudson's Bay Company, 1/90, 4/447, 4/450, 9/1023, 10/**1218–19**, 10/*1218*, 12/1474, 15/1796, 18/2164
Hughes, Charles, 10/1152

Hughes Hercules flyingboat, 1/67
Hughes, James Langston, 10/**1219**, 10/*1219*
Hugo, Victor Marie, 10/**1219**, 10/*1219*
Huguenots, 1/112, 9/1008, 10/1178, 17/2016, 17/2061
Hula dancers, 6/697, 8/970, 10/1157
Hull, Ottawa, 15/1848
Hull, Bobby, 19/2317
Hull House, Chicago, 1/33, 1/*33*
Hulls:
displacement, 3/361
materials, 3/360–2
planing, 3/361
shapes, 3/361
Human beings, 10/**1220–4**, 10/*1220–3*, 13/1500
Cro-magnon man, 10/122–3
ethnic groups, 10/1224
first, 10/1221–2
Leakey family research, 12/1405
modern man, 10/1223
Neanderthal man, 10/1222
origins, 10/1220–1
pygmies, 17/*2033*, 17/*2033*
races, 10/1223–4
Human body, 10/**1224–5**, 10/*1224*
ageing, 1/50
anatomy, 2/133
antibodies, 2/177
biochemistry, 3/*340*
blood, 3/359–60
bone, 3/366, 3/*366*
brain, 4/382–4, 4/*383*
breathing, 4/387–9, 4/*388*
calcium, 4/431–2
cells, 10/1224
digestion, 6/729–31, 6/*730–1*
disease, 6/736–40
embryos, 7/840–1, 7/*840*
enzymes, 7/862–3
eyes, 8/898–9, 8/*898–9*
feet, 10/145
fingerprints, 8/930–1, 8/*930*
food, 8/974–6, 8/*974–6*
glands, 9/1080–1, 9/*1081*
growth, 9/1121–2
hair, 10/1137–8, 10/*1137–8*
hands, 10/1144–5, 10/*1144–5*
health, 10/1163–5
hearing, 7/778–9, 7/*779*, 10/1165–6
heart, 10/1167–8, 10/*1167–8*
hormones, 10/1201–2
kidneys, 11/1365–6, 11/*1365*
liver, 12/1453–4, 12/*1453*
metabolism, 13/1565–6
muscles, 14/1675–7, 14/*1675–7*
nervous system, 14/1739–41, 14/*1740*
noses, 15/1799
nutrition, 15/1810–11
organs, 10/1224
posture, 16/1986
proteins, 17/2013
respiration, 17/2092–3
sight, 18/2219–20, 18/*2219*
skeleton, 18/2229–30
skin, 10/1224
sleep, 19/2239–40
sneezes, 19/2246
teeth, 20/2386–8, 20/*2386–7*
Human flea, 11/*1279*
Human geography, 9/1054

Human louse, 11/*1279*
Human rights, Roosevelt, Eleanor, 18/2133
  see also Civil rights
Humason, Milton, 21/2500
Humber Bridge, 4/392
Humboldt, Alexander von, 10/**1225**, 10/*1225*
Humboldt River, 15/1743
Humidity, 1/58, 10/**1225–6★**
  plants and, 16/1944
  water vapour, 5/582
Hummingbird hawkmoth, 4/*421*
Hummingbirds, 3/343, 3/344, 3/*346*, 10/**1226–7**
Humorists:
  Rogers, Will, 18/2118
  Thurber, James, 20/*2423–4*
Humors, eyes, 8/*898*
Humphrey, Hubert, 15/1778
Humus, 19/2254
Hundred Years' War, 7/857, 9/1008, 10/1176, 10/**1227**, 10/*1227*, 12/1462
Hungary, 10/**1227–8**, 10/*1228*
  Liszt, Franz, 12/1445
  Revolution, 17/2095
Hung juries, 20/2464
Huns, 3/260
Hunt, E.B., 11/1317
Hunters, 10/*1205*
Hunting:
  falconry, 8/906, 8/*906*
  game birds, 9/1033–4
Hunt, Irene, 5/535
Hunt, Leigh, 11/1357
Huntsville, Alabama, 1/*82*, 1/83, 1/84
Hunt, Walter, 18/2196
Hurdling, 20/2441
Huron Indians, 5/510, 15/1832, 21/2518
Huron Lake, 9/1107–8
Hurricanes, 4/468, 8/955, 10/**1228–9**, 10/*1228*
Hurt, John, 7/*760*
Hussein, King of Jordan, 11/1341
Huss, John, 17/2014
Hutchinson, Anne, 20/*2463*
Huton, James, 9/1056
Hutu, 4/417, 4/418
Huxley, Aldous, 10/**1229**, 10/*1229*, 18/2175
Huxley, Andrew Fielding, 10/**1229**
Huxley, Sir Julian, 10/**1229**
Huxley, Thomas Henry, 10/**1229**, 10/*1129*
Huygens, Christiaan, 16/*1891*, 16/*1922*
Hwang-Ho River, 8/*956*, 22/2263
Hyatt, John Wesley, 16/1954
Hybrids, 16/1942
Hybrid tea roses, 18/2137
Hydrangeas, 1/*23*
Hydrants, 8/935
Hydras, 5/589, 10/1181, 10/**1229–30**, 10/*1229*
Hydraulic engineering, 7/851
Hydraulics, 10/**1230**
Hydraulus, 14/1692
Hydrocarbons, 4/463, 9/1046, 10/1231
Hydrochloric acid, 1/23, 1/24, 6/731
Hydroelectric engineering, 7/851

Hydroelectricity, 6/694, 7/822, 10/**1230**, 10/*1230*
  Niagara Falls, 15/1770
Hydrofoils, 10/**1230–1**, 10/*1230*, 20/2453
Hydrogen, 10/**1231**, 10/*1231*
Hydrogen balloons, 3/298
Hydrogen peroxide, bleaching, 3/358
Hydrographic surveys, 19/2361
Hydrophobia, 17/2040–1
Hydroplanes, 3/362, 19/2345
Hydrothermal vents, 15/1817
Hyenas, 10/**1231**, 10/*1231*
Hygiene:
  public health, 17/2021–2
  sanitation, 18/2159–60
Hygrometers, 10/1226, 21/2563
Hygrophila, 2/*189*
Hyksos, 7/808–9
Hyperactivity, 19/2303
Hyperbola, 15/1838
Hyphae, 9/*1021*
Hyphens, 17/2029
Hypothesis, 18/2173
Hyracotherium, 8/*887*
Hyrax, 13/*1496*

Ii

Iban, 3/371
Iberian Peninsula, 16/1982, 19/2297
  see also Portugal, Spain
Ibex, 10/*1200*
Ibibio, 15/1774
Ibn Battuta, 10/**1232**
Ibn Majid, 9/1032
Ibo, 15/1774
Ibsen, Henrik, 7/759, 7/839, 10/**1232–3**, 10/*1232*
Icarus, 3/280, 6/691
Ice:
  avalanches, 3/279–80
  curling, 6/686–7, 6/*686*
  erosion, 7/866
  glaciers, 9/1079–80, 9/*1079–80*
  hail, 10/1137, 10/*1137*
Ice Ages, 5/577, 10/**1233**, 10/*1233*
Icebergs, 10/**1233–4**, 10/*1234*
Icebreakers, 5/587
Ice cream, 6/693, 10/**1234–5★**
Ice hockey, 10/**1235**, 10/*1235*
Iceland, 10/**1235–6**, 10/*1235–6*, 21/2528
Icelandic language, 18/2168
Iceland moss, 12/1428
Ice sheets, 9/1080
Ice shows, clowns, 5/583–4
Ice skating, 10/**1236–7**, 10/*1236–7*
  dancing, 6/698
Ichthyologists, 8/941
Ichthyology, 1/50
Ichthyomis victor, 3/*349*
Iconoscope, 22/2649
Icons, 15/1848
Id, 9/1012
Idaho, 10/**1237–40**, 10/*1237–40*
  climate, 10/1239
  employment, 10/1240
  history, 10/1239
  land, 10/1237–9
  map, 10/*1238*
  state emblems, 10/*1238*

Ides, calendars, 4/434
Idiom neutral, 21/2499
Ido, 21/2499
Idris, King of Libya, 12/1428
Idun, 14/1695
Ife, 15/1774
Igloos, 7/867, 7/868, 18/2204
Ignatius of Loyola, St, 17/*2082*
Igneous rocks, 17/2108
Ignition systems, 3/276
Ignition temperatures, fire, 8/933
Iguanas, 12/1456
Iguanodon, 6/*734*
Ijaw, 15/1774
Ijsselmeer, 14/1742
Ikhnaton, 7/809
Iliad, 9/1115, 10/1197
Illinois, 10/**1240–3**, 10/*1241–2*
  climate, 10/1240
  employment, 10/1242–3
  history, 10/1240–2
  land, 10/1240
  map, 10/*1241*
  state emblems, 10/*1241*
Illinois Indians, 1/100
Illinois River, 13/1615
Illinois Seaway, 9/1108
Illinois Waterway, 10/1240
Illiteracy, 18/2168
Illness *see* Disease; Medicine
Illumination, painting, 13/1602, 15/1861
Illustration, graphic arts, 9/1102–3, 9/*1102–3*
Illyria, 12/1474
Imagos, 4/421, 11/1281, 13/1569
Imams, 11/1307
Immigrants, refugees, 17/2077
Immigration, 10/**1243–4**, 10/*1243*
Immune system, 21/2534
Immunity, 5/528, 10/**1244**, 10/*1244*, 11/1328–9
  antibodies, 2/177
Impala, 2/173
Impasto, 15/1860
Impeachment, 6/630, 10/**1244–5**, 11/1337–8
  Nixon, Richard Milhous, 15/1778
Imperial Valley, California, 4/436
Imports, 11/1291–2
  tariffs, 5/574
Impressionism, 2/228, 2/234, 4/482, 5/508, 10/**1245–6★**, 10/*1245–6*
  Degas, Edgar, 6/711
  Manet, Edouard, 13/1502
  Monet, Claude, 14/1629–30
  music style, 6/705
  Renoir, Pierre Auguste, 17/2085–6
Imprisonment, 17/2006–7
Improvisation, 11/1326
Impulse turbines, 7/848
Incandescent bulbs, 7/801
Incas, 2/141, 2/*141*, 3/361, 5/536, 6/637, 11/**1247–9**, 11/*1247–8*, 11/1268, 16/1903, 16/*1904*, 16/1935–6, 19/2272–3
  buildings, 4/407
  civilization, 11/1247
  engineering, 11/1247
  fall of, 11/1248–9
  government, 11/1248
  language, 12/1389
  life, 11/1247
  scientific achievements, 11/1247
  Spanish conquerors, 6/723

Incisors, 18/2115, 20/2386
Inclined planes, 12/1475
Income tax, 20/2381–2
Incorporated (Inc.), 6/661
Incubators, 11/**1249**, 11/*1249*
  chicken rearing, 17/1991
Indentured servants, 1/112, 3/352–3
Independence Day, 11/**1249–50**, 11/*1249*, 11/1346–7
Independence Hall, 11/**1250**, 11/*1250*
  Liberty Bell, 12/1422, 12/*1422*
Independence National Historical Park, 11/1250
Indexes, 11/**1250–1★**, 11/*1250*
India, 11/**1251–5**, 11/*1251–4*
  Bombay, 3/365–6
  burials, 4/413
  caste system, 11/1254
  climate, 11/*1251*, 11/1252
  Gandhi, Indira Priyadarshini, 9/1035
  Gandhi, Mahatma, 9/1035–6
  Ganges River, 9/1036, 9/*1036*
  geography, 11/1252
  Hinduism, 10/1186–7
  history, 11/1253–4
  modern, 11/1254–5
  natural resources, 11/1252
  Nehru, Jawaharlal, 14/1737
  Pakistan and, 11/1255
  people, 11/1253
  Taj Mahal, 20/2377
  wildlife, 11/1252–3
Indiana, 11/**1255–8**, 11/*1255–8*
  climate, 11/1255
  employment, 11/1258
  history, 11/1256
  land, 11/1255
  map, 11/*1257*
  state emblem, 11/*1257*
Indiana Dunes State Park, 11/1258
Indianapolis, 11/1255
Indianapolis 500 race, 3/278
Indian cobra, 19/*2245*
Indian elephants, 7/831–3, 7/*831*
Indian motorcycles, 14/*1666*
Indian Ocean, 11/**1260–1**, 11/*1260*
Indian rope trick, 12/*1482*
Indians:
  American, 11/**1261–70**, 11/*1261–70*
  art, 2/231, 11/**1258–60**, 11/*1258–60*
  burials, 4/413
  Central American, 11/1267
  clothing, 11/*1264*, 11/1266–7
  conquistadors and, 6/637–8
  European settlers and, 1/111, 1/115
  food, 11/1263–6
  French and Indian Wars, 9/1005–6
  fur trading, 9/1023
  Geronimo, 9/1072, 9/*1072*
  houses, 11/1263
  languages, 1/100
  life-style, 11/1262–7
  modern, 11/1269
  myths, 2/162–3
  sign language, 18/2222
  smoking, 19/2242, 19/*2242*
  South American, 11/1267–9
  tents, 20/2408
  tipis, 11/1262–3
  totems, 20/2435, 20/*2435*
  US expansion, 1/120
  white people and, 11/1261–2

Indian summer, 3/279
Indian Territory, 5/523, 5/543
Indian Wars, 11/1262, 11/**1270–1**, 11/*1271*
Indirect taxes, 20/2382
Indo-European languages, 12/*1389*, 12/1390
Indonesia, 11/**1271–2**, 11/*1272*
Inductive reasoning, 18/2173
Indulgences, 12/1470
Indus River, 11/1252, 11/1253, 11/1254, 15/1864
Industrial air parks, 1/75
Industrial arts, 11/**1272–4**, 11/*1273*
  designers, 6/721
  drawing, 11/1273
Industrial diamonds, 6/724
Industrial psychologists, 17/2020
Industrial Revolution, 7/853, 8/879, 11/**1274–6**, 11/*1274–5*, 11/1294, 13/1507, 14/1715, 19/2249
  child labor, 5/530
  cities and, 5/556
  communism and, 5/614
Industrial suburbs, 19/2347
Industrial unions, 12/1380
Industry:
  automation, 13/1507
  manufacturing, 13/1506–8, 13/*1506–8*
Inertia, 8/983, 14/1657
Infant care, 5/527
Infantry, 2/224
Infections, 6/737
Inflation, economics, 7/799, 7/*799*
Inflexible, 2/223
Influenza, 18/2156
Information:
  books, 3/366–9
  communication, 5/**610–14**/
  data protection, 6/700
  dictionaries, 6/726–8
  encyclopedias, 7/842–3
  indexes, 11/1250–1
  journalism, 11/1342–3
  learning, 12/1406–8
  libraries, 12/1423–6, 12/*1423–6*
  magazines, 12/1479–81
  microfilm, 13/1581, 13/*1581*
  newspapers, 15/1560–2, 15/*1560–2*
  printing, 17/2002–6, 17/*2002–5*
  propaganda, 17/2009–10, 17/*2010*
  public relations, 17/2022–3
  publishing, 17/2025–6
  reference books, 17/2075–6
Infra Red Astronomical Satellite (IRAS), 18/2165
Infrared rays, 10/1170
Ingalik Indians, 3/253
Inheritance, 8/887
Ink, 11/**1276***, 11/*1276*
Inlets, 18/2183
Inner ear, 7/778–9, 7/*779*
Innocent III, Pope, 6/680
Innocent X, Pope, 21/2513
Innuit (eskimoes), 7/867
Inorganic chemistry, 5/519
Insect-eating plants, 11/**1281–2**, 11/*1281*
Insecticides, 11/1277
Insectivores, 4/470, 14/1622–3
Insects, 11/**1276–81**, 11/*1277–80*
  Fabre, J. Henri, 8/901
  growth, 11/1280–1

harmful, 11/1277
hearing, 10/1167
helpful, 11/1278
metamorphosis, 13/1569–70
migration, 13/1594
molting, 14/1626
pest control, 16/1904–5, 16/*1904*
reproduction, 11/1280–1
respiration, 17/2093
structure of, 11/*1277*, 11/1278
survival of, 11/1276–7
see also individual insects
Instant cameras, 4/441
Instant coffee, 5/591
Instinct, 2/151, 11/1285
Institutions of higher learning, 5/**595–7**
Instruments:
  organs, 15/1844–5, 15/*1844*
  percussion, 16/1897–8, 16/*1897–8*
  piano, 16/1924–5, 16/*1924–5*
  woodwind, 21/2602–3
  see also Stringed Instruments
Insulation, 11/**1282–3***, 11/*1282*
Insulators, 10/1170, 18/2189
  electricity, 7/820
Insulin, 3/303, 7/768, 10/1201
Insurance, 11/**1283–4**
Integers, 2/214
Intelligence, 11/**1284–5**, 11/*1285*
Intelligence agencies, 5/508
Intelligence quotient (IQ), 11/1284
Intelsat I, 18/2166
Intensity, music, 14/1682
Inter-American Conference, 15/1845
Inter-American Highway, 5/506, 7/838
Intercity trains, 17/2054
Intercontinental ballistic missiles (ICBM), 19/2297
Interest, 11/**1285–6**, 18/2167
Interferometers, 15/1813–14, 17/2050
Interior decorating, 11/**1286–7**, 11/*1286–7*
  carpets, 4/474
  design, 6/721–2
Interior Department, 4/426
Interjections, 16/1882
Interlingua, 21/2499
Internal combustion engines, 3/273, 7/849–50, 7/*849–50*
Internal Revenue Service, 16/1966
International airports, 1/76–7
International Communications Agency, 21/2491
International Court of Justice, 11/1289, 20/2486
International Currency Agency, 21/2490
International Date Line, 11/**1288–9**, 11/*1288*
International flag carriers, 1/65
International Labor Organization (ILO), 5/530, 20/2486
International law, 11/**1289**, 12/1400
  treaties, 20/2457–8
International Peace Garden, 9/1041
International Peace Park, 14/1640
International Postal Union, 20/2458
International relations, 11/**1289–91**, 11/*1289–91*
  economics, 11/1290
  history, 11/1290–1
  self-interest, 11/1289–90

International Signal Code, 18/2221, 18/*2221*
International System of Units (SI Units), 13/1571
International trade, 11/**1291–2**, 11/*1291*
  economics, 7/799
International Workingmen's Association, 13/1521
Internists, 13/1555
Interstate Commerce Commission (ICC), 17/1998, 17/2058, 21/2490, 21/2491
Interstate highways, 19/2341
Intertype, 20/2481
Intracoastal Waterway, 10/1128
Introverts, 11/1348
Inventions, 11/**1292–5**, 11/*1292–5*
  history of, 11/1294–5
  patents, 16/1884–5
  process of, 11/1294
  see also individual inventions eg Camera
Inventors:
  Archimedes, 2/200
  Babbage, Charles, 3/285–6
  Baird, John Logie, 3/291–2
  Bell, Alexander Graham, 3/329
  Duryea, Charles, 7/774
  Duryea, Frank, 7/774
  Edison, Thomas Alva, 7/801–2
  Fulton, Robert, 9/1020
  Gutenberg, Johannes, 10/1132
  Leonardo da Vinci, 12/1416–17
  McCormick, Cyrus, 13/1543
  Marconi, Guglielmo, 13/1513–14
  Morse, Samuel F.B., 14/1650
  Stephenson, George, 19/2333–4
  Watt, James, 21/2556–7
  Whitney, Eli, 21/2583
  Zworykin, Vladimir Kosma, 22/2649
Inventory, 1/22
Invertebrates, 2/154, 5/504
Investigators:
  detectives, 6/723
  Federal Bureau of Investigation, 8/920
  forensic science, 8/986
  Holmes, Sherlock, 7/756
Invisible ink, 11/1276
Ionia, 9/1111
Ionosphere, 3/257
Ions, 3/259–60, 3/*260*
  electrolysis, 7/823
Iowa, 11/**1295–8**, 11/*1294–8*
  climate, 11/1295
  employment, 11/1298
  history, 11/1295–8
  land, 11/1295
  map, 11/*1297*
  state emblem, 11/*1297*
Iowa Indians, 11/1295, 11/1296, 21/2596
IQ, 11/1284
Iran, 11/**1298–9**, 11/*1298–9*, 13/1589
  see also Persia
Iraq, 11/**1299–1300**, 11/*1300*, 13/1589
IRAS, 18/2165, 19/2288, 19/2289
Irazu, 6/663
Ireland, 4/396, 8/*878*, 11/**1300–2**, 11/*1301–2*, 15/1793
  names, 14/1699
  St Patrick, 16/1885

Irene, Empress, 10/*1190*
Irian Java, 11/1271
Irian Jaya, 13/1558, 15/1750
Iris, 4/408, 4/*408*
Irish harps, 10/1153
Irish Republican Army (IRA), 15/1794
Irish setters, 6/*748*
Iron, 11/**1302–4**, 11/*1302–4*
  cast, 6/728
  diet, 21/2535
  galvanized, 7/823
  Industrial Revolution, 11/1275
  ore, 13/1567
  rust, 6/661
Ironclads, 14/1727–8, 14/*1729*
Iron Cross, 13/1550, 13/*1550*
Iron Curtain, 9/1070
Irons (golf), 9/1092
Iroquois Confederacy, 11/1305
Iroquois Indians, 1/*111*, 2/162, 5/510, 8/950–1, 11/1263, 11/1266, , 11/**1304–5**, 11/*1304*, 15/1824, 21/2518
Irrigation, 3/286, 11/**1305**, 11/*1305*
  Middle East, 13/1590
Irving, Washington, 4/378, 5/532, 11/**1306**, 11/*1306*
Isaac, 11/1334
Isabella and Ferdinand, 5/606, 8/893, 11/**1306**, 11/*1306*, 19/2301
Isinglass, 8/948
Isis River, 20/2418
Islam, 2/191–2, 11/**1306–7**, 11/*1307*, 16/1903, 17/2079
  India, 11/1254
  Koran, 12/1375–6, 12/*1375*
  mosques, 14/1654, 14/*1654*
  Muhammad, 14/1673–4
  Saudi Arabia, 18/2166–7
Islamabad, 15/1864
Islamic calendars, 4/434
Islands, 11/**1307–8**, 11/*1307–8*
  largest, 11/1308
Islets of Langerhaus, 9/1081
Isometrics, 8/888
Isotopes, 3/259–60, 17/2049
Israel, 11/**1308–10**, 11/*1309–10*, 13/1589, 15/1865
  Arabs, 13/1590
  Ben-Gurion, David, 3/330, 3/*330*
  Egypt and, 7/807–8
  Hebrew, 10/1172, 10/*1172*
  irrigation, 13/1590
  Jordan and, 11/1341
  Meir, Golda, 13/1557
  Syria and, 20/2373
Israelites, 15/1865
Issas, 6/745
Issihak II, 19/2262
Issus, battle of, 11/*1367*
Istanbul, 2/*201*, 4/424, 20/2475, 20/2476
  see also Byzantium; Constantinople
Isthmus, 5/505
Italian language, 18/2123
Italic, 20/2480–1
Italy, 11/**1312–13**, 11/*1312–13*
  Adriatic Coast, 1/36
  Borgia family, 3/370–1
  city states, 11/1311
  colonies, 1/49

(continued)

Dante Alighieri, 6/698
fascism, 8/911
Florence, 8/956, 8/*956*
Galileo Galilei, 9/1031–2
Giotto di Bondone, 9/1077–8
history, 11/**1310–12**, 11/*1310–11*
Machiavelli, Niccolò, 12/1474–5
Marconi, Guglielmo, 13/1513–14
Medici family, 13/1551–2
Michelangelo, 13/1577–8
Mussolini, Benito, 14/1693–4
Polo, Marco, 16/1970–1
Raphael, 17/2062–3
Renaissance, 17/2083–5
Romanesque architecture, 18/2125
Rome, 18/2128–9
San Marino, 18/2160–1
Titian, 20/2429–30
Venice, 21/2515–16, 21/*2515*
Verdi, Giuseppe, 21/2516
Vespucci, Amerigo, 21/2521
World War II, 22/2611–12
see also Rome, Ancient
It Happened One Night, 1/21
Iturbide, Augustín de, 5/507
Ivan I, Prince of Moscow, 18/2145
Ivan III, Grand Duke, 14/1653
Ivan IV the Terrible, Czar,
    18/2145–6, 18/*2145*
Ives, Burl, 8/973
Ivorians, 11/1314
Ivory Coast, 11/**1313–14/**, 11/*1314*
Ixtacihuatl, 13/1573, 13/1576
Izaak Walton League, 6/640
Izmir, 20/2476

Jj

Jacares, 1/103
Jackals, 11/**1315**, 11/*1315*
Jackass, 7/755
Jackass penguin, 16/1892
Jackboots, 18/2213
Jackdaws, 6/678
Jackrabbits, 17/2039–40
Jackson, Mississippee, 13/1613,
    13/*1613*
Jackson, Andrew, 1/31, 1/32, 2/245,
    6/672, 7/773, 10/1217, 11/1270,
    11/*1271*, 11/**1316–17**, 11/*1316*,
    12/1466, 16/1935, 16/1968,
    21/2507, 21/2542, 21/*2542*
    civil service under, 5/564
Jackson, Helen Hunt, 11/**1317**,
    11/*1317*
Jackson, Jesse, 3/355, 3/*356*
Jackson, Mahalia, 11/**1317–18**,
    11/*1317*, 17/*2072*
Jackson, Michael, 2/228, 21/*2558*
Jackson, Robert, 11/1316
Jackson, Thomas Jonathan
    (**'Stonewall'**), 5/567, 9/1062,
    11/**1318**, 11/*1318*, 18/2180,
    19/2337, 19/*2337*
Jackson, William S., 11/1317
Jacobins, 9/1011
Jacobites, 9/1060
Jacquard, Joseph Marie, 20/*2415*
Jacquard looms, 20/*2415*, 20/2416
Jaguar cars, 3/*274*
Jaguars, 4/488, 13/*1498*
Jaguarundi, 4/489

Jahangir, 11/1254
Jahn, Friedrich, 10/1134
Jai alai, 11/**1318–19**, 11/*1318*
Jails, 17/2006–7
Jakarta, 11/*1272*
Jamaica, 21/2569, 21/2571
James, Frank, 15/1851
James I, King of England, 3/287,
    7/837, 7/857, 8/917, 11/**1319**,
    11/*1319*, 17/2061, 18/2176,
    20/2485
James I, King of Scotland, 13/1522
James II, King of England, 2/165,
    11/**1319**, 11/*1319*, 21/2589–90
James V, King of Scotland, 13/1521
James, Jesse, 5/534, 15/1851, 15/*1851*
James, Naomi, 8/893–4
Jameson's raiders, 3/363
James River, 11/1319, 21/2532
Jamestown, 1/115, 10/1211,
    11/**1319–20**, 11/*1320*, 16/1959,
    17/1993, 18/2236, 21/2532
Jamestown Colony, 1/111
Jamoytius, 8/*941*
Jam sessions, 11/1325
Jams and jellies, 11/**1320–1★**,
    11/*1320*
Jane Eyre, 4/397
Jansky, Karl, 17/2050
Janssen, Zacharias, 5/501, 13/1583
January, 11/**1321**
    special events during, 11/1321
Janus, 11/1321
Japan, 11/**1322–4**, 11/*1322–4*
    art, 15/1846
    climate, 11/1322
    1854 Treaty, 16/1902
    emperors, 11/1369
    history, 11/1322–4
    judo, 11/1345
    land, 11/1322
    Pearl Harbor, 16/1888
    people, 11/1322
    Shinto, 18/2205
    Tokyo, 20/2432, 20/*2432*
    World War II, 22/2611, 22/2616,
        22/2618–19
Japan Current, 15/1855
Japanese crab, 6/681
Japanese giant salamander, 2/*131*
Jarvis Island, 16/1971
Jason, 11/**1324**, 11/*1324*
Jasper, 16/1990
Jasper Park, 14/1713
Jaundice, 12/1454
Java, 11/1271, *1272*
Java, 21/2541
Java Trench, 11/1260
Javelins, 7/802, 20/*2441*
Jawless fish, 8/941, 8/*943*
Jayapura, 15/1750
Jay, John, 1/128, 1/30, 10/1142
Jays, 6/678
Jazz, 4/386, 11/**1324–6**, 11/*1325–6*
    Armstrong, Louis, 2/223, 2/*223*
    Gershwin, George, 9/1072
    Handy, W.C., 10/1147
    history, 11/1324–6
    instruments, 11/1326
    Jackson, Mahalia, 11/1317–18
Jazz Singer, 14/*1658*
Jeannette, 8/981
Jefferson, Abigail, 1/31
Jefferson, Thomas, 1/30, 1/31,

    1/126, 4/416, 4/425, 6/642,
    6/652, 6/707, 6/716, 10/1142,
    11/**1326–7**, 11/*1326–7*, 12/1479,
    13/1520, 13/1616, 14/1637–8,
    16/1958, 18/2142, 18/*2142*,
    21/2488, 21/2576, 21/2582
    Lewis and Clark expedition,
        12/1420
    Library of Congress, 12/1426
    Louisiana Purchse, 12/1467
Jellyfish, 5/589–90, 5/*590*, 11/**1327–8**,
    11/*1328*
Jenne, 19/2262
Jenner, Edward, 11/**1328–9**, 11/*1329*,
    13/1553
Jenny, 7/755
Jerboa, 2/*149*, 18/*2115*
Jericho, 5/615
Jerky, 8/976
Jerome, 3/336
Jerome, Jenny, 5/549
Jersey City, 15/1754
Jersey cows, 4/494
Jerusalem, 10/1148–9, 11/**1329**,
    11/*1329*, 15/1866, 17/*2080*
    Crusades, 6/678–80
Jesuits, 17/*2082*, 18/2122, 18/2161
Jesus Christ, 5/546, 9/1030–1,
    11/1307, 11/**1330–1**, 11/*1330–1*
    Apostles, 2/182–3
    paintings of, 2/231, 2/*232*
Jet aircraft, 1/68, 3/282
Jet propulsion, 7/849–50, 11/**1332**,
    11/*1332*
Jet streams, 3/257
Jewelry, 11/**1332–4★**, 11/*133–4*
    Crown jewels, 6/676–7, 6/*677*
    gems, 9/1049–50
    silver, 18/2225
Jewish calendar, 4/434
Jewish people:
    history, 11/**1334–6**, 11/*1334–6*
    homeland, 11/1335–36
    Israel, 11/1308–10, 11/*1309–10*,
        11/1336, 13/1589
    Judaism, 11/1344–5, 11/*1344–5*
    origin of, 11/1334
    persecution, 11/1336
    promised land, 11/1335
    Passover, 16/1883
    Yiddish language, 22/**2634**
Jívaro Indians, 7/801, 11/1268–9
Jitterbugging, 6/697
Joan of Arc, 3/319, 5/514, 9/1008,
    9/*1007*, 10/1177, 10/1227,
    11/**1336–7**, 11/*1336*
Joanna, Queen of Castile, 16/1912,
    19/2301
Jobs, careers, 4/465–7
Jockeys, horse racing, 10/1208–9
Joderell Bank Observatory, 15/1813
Joeys, 11/1352
Jogging, 8/888
Johannesburg, 19/2267
John, Don, of Austria, 3/319
John, King of England, 7/814,
    7/855–6, 10/1176, 11/**1337**,
    11/*1337*, 11/1369
    Magna Carta, 12/1483, 12/*1483*
John I, King of Portugal, 5/606,
    10/1179
John of Gaunt, 17/2101
John the Good, 5/514
John Henry, 8/972

John Paul I, Pope, 16/1977
John Paul II, Pope, 16/1977, 16/*1977*
Johns Hopkins University, 5/596
Johnson, Andrew, 10/1245,
    11/**1337–8**, 11/*1338*, 17/2069
Johnson, Jack, 4/381
Johnson, Lyndon Baines, 10/1154,
    11/**1338–40**, 11/*1339*, 11/1359,
    13/1520, 21/2523, 21/2526
    civil rights, 5/563
Johnson, Samuel, 9/1044, 11/**1340**,
    11/*1340*, 16/1961
Johnston, Albert Sidney, 5/568
Johnston Atoll, 16/1971
Johnston, Joseph E., 18/2205
John XXIII, Pope, 16/1976–7,
    18/2121
Johore, Strait of, 18/226
Jokers, card game, 4/464
Joliet, Louis, 8/893, 10/1242,
    11/1296, 13/*1518*, 13/1614,
    13/1616
Joliot-Curie, Irène, 6/686
Joliot-Curie, Jean Frédéric, 6/686
Jolly Roger, 16/1934
Jolson, Al, 9/1072, 14/*1658*, 14/1662
Jonathan, Chief Leabua, 12/1418
Jones, Casey, 5/534
Jones, Jim, 10/1133
Jones, John Paul, 1/*126*, 1/128,
    11/**1340**, 11/*1340*
Jonestown, Guyana, 10/1133
Jonker diamond, 6/724
Joplin, Scott, 11/1325
Jord, 14/1695
Jordan, 11/**1340–1**, 11/*1341*, 13/1589
Jordan River, 6/703, 11/*1341*,
    12/1385, 13/1590
Jordan River (Utah), 21/2502
Jordan River Valley, 11/1308
Joséphine, Empress, 14/1701,
    14/*1702*
Joseffy, Rafael, 12/1445
Joseph, Chief, 11/**1342**, 11/*1342*,
    15/1769, 15/*1769*
Joseph of Nazareth, 11/1330
Joseph (Nez Percé Indian chief),
    11/1271
Joshua tree, 4/428
Joules, 7/845–6, 9/1019–20, 10/1170
Journalism, 11/**1342–3★**, 11/*1342–3*
    Greeley, Horace, 9/1116
    magazines, 12/1479–81
    newspapers, 15/1760–2
Journals, 6/724–5
Journeyman, 2/185, 7/803, 10/1125
Jousts, 2/223
Joyce, James, 11/1301, 16/1959
Juárez, Benito, 11/**1344**, 11/*1344*,
    13/1575–6
Juan Carlos, King of Spain, 9/1003,
    19/2299, 19/2302
Juba River, 19/2262
Judah, 11/1334–5
Judaism, 11/**1344–5**, 11/*1344–5*,
    17/2079
    Day of Atonement, 22/2635
Judea, 15/1865
Judges, 12/1401–2, 12/*1401*
    court sytem, 6/666–8
    Supreme Court, 19/2355–6
Judo, 11/**1345**, 11/*1345*
Juggling, 11/**1345–6★**
Juice, 5/555

Jujitsu, 11/1345
Juliana, Queen of the Netherlands, 14/1742
Julian calendar, 4/430, 4/434
Julius Caesar, 5/572
Julius II, Pope, 13/1577–8, 17/2062, 17/2084
July, 11/**1346–7**, 11/*1346*
special events, 11/1346
Jumping Badger, 18/2229
June, 11/**1347–8**, 11/*1348*
special events, 11/1347
Juneau, 1/87
Jung, Carl, 11/**1348**, 11/*1348*, 13/1563
Jungles, 11/**1348–50**, 11/*1349–50*
animal life, 2/150
people of, 11/1349
Junior colleges, 5/596
Junior high school, 18/2169–70
Juniper, 6/633
Junius, 11/1348
Junks, 3/362
Juno, 9/1089, 11/1347
Juntas, 19/2273
Jupiter (god), 6/702, 9/1089
Jupiter (planet), 2/250, 19/*2256*, 19/2257, 19/*2257*
basic facts, 19/2259
Jura Mountains, 20/2366
Juries, 20/2463–5
court sytem, 6/666
Justice Department, 4/425, 4/426
Justices of the peace, 6/667
Justinian Code, 4/424
Justinian, Emperor, 4/424
Jute, 18/2136
Jutes, 7/855
Jutland, 6/716
Juvenile courts, 6/667
Juvenile delinquents, 11/**1350**

Kk

K2, 10/1186
Kabaka, 20/2483
Kabalega Falls, 15/1776
Kabalega Falls National Park, 20/2482–3
Kabul, 1/42
Kaibab Plateau, 9/1099
Kaieteur Falls, 10/1133
Kalahari Desert, 1/43, 1/46, 3/376, 14/1699
Kalakaua, David, 12/1438
Kalapuia Indians, 15/1842
Kalimantan, 3/371
Kalong fruit bat, 12/1490
Kamba, 11/1363
Kamehameha I, 10/1158, 11/**1351**, 11/*1351*
Kamerun, 4/442
Kami, 18/2205
Kamikaze pilots, 22/2619
Kampala, 20/2483
Kampuchea, 11/**1351–2**, 11/*1352*, 19/2280, 21/2525, 21/2526
Kanchenjunga, 10/1186, 18/2223
Kander, John, 14/1688
Kandinsky, Vassily, 14/1621, 14/*1621*
Kanem, 15/1773
Kangaroo rat, 2/*149*, 2/150, 6/721

Kangaroos, 2/*151*, 2/152, 3/267, 3/268, 3/269, 11/**1352–3**, 11/*1353*
Kano, Jigoro, 11/1345
Kansas, 11/**1353–6**, 11/*1353–6*
climate, 11/1354–5
employment, 11/1356
history, 11/1355–6
land, 11/1353–5
map, 11/*1354*
state emblems, 11/*1354*
Kansas City, 11/1356, 13/1618
Kansas-Nebraska Act, 11/1355
Kant, Immanuel, 16/*1914*, 16/1915
Kanuri, 15/1774
Karachi, 15/1864
Karakorams, 2/239
Karakul, 1/42
Karat, 9/1090
Karate, 11/**1356**, 11/*1356*
Karats, 13/1546
Kariba, Lake, 12/*1385*, 22/*2643*
Karlsefni, Thorfinn, 21/2528
Karma, 4/402
Karmal, Babrak, 1/42
Karnali River, 14/1738
Karpov, Anatoly, 5/525
Kasaskia, 5/571
Kasavubu, Joseph, 22/2642
Kashmir, 11/1255
Kasparov, Gary, 5/525
Kata, 11/1345
Katahdin, Mount, 12/1485
Katmai, Mount, 1/87
Katmandu, 14/1738
Kauai, 10/1158
Kaufman, George S., 14/1688
Kaunda, 22/2644
Kaw Indians, 11/1355
Kayaks, 1/95, 7/868
Kaye, Danny, 15/*1839*
Kazakh, 19/2282
Kazaks, 20/*2408*
Kazan, 21/2535
Keats, John, 11/**1356–7**, 11/*1357*, 16/*1960*, 18/2203
Keels, 18/2153, 18/2210
Keeps, castles, 4/484
Keewatin, Northwest Territories, 15/1796
Keith, Benjamin F., 21/2510
Keller, Helen, 1/84, 3/270, 11/**1357–8*,** 11/*1357*
Kelley, William, 11/1303
Kellogg, 10/1237
Kellogg, Noah, 10/1237, 10/1239
Kelly, Emmett, 5/583
Kelly, Grace, 14/1627
Kelp, 1/97
Kelvin, Lord William Thomson, 20/2401
Kelvin temperature scale, 20/2401
Kemal, Mustafa, 15/1850, 15/*1850*, 20/2476
Kenai Peninsula, 1/88
Kenilworth Aquatic Gardens, 3/*373*
Kennebec River, 12/1485
Kennedy Centre for the Performing Arts, 11/1359
Kennedy International Airport, 1/77
Kennedy, Jacqueline, 11/1359, 21/2582
Kennedy, John Fitzgerald, 2/245, 4/458, 4/461, 7/813, 11/**1358–9,**

11/*1358*, 11/1365, 12/1451, 14/1709, 16/1887, 21/2526
assassination, 6/693, 11/1338, 11/1339, 11/1359
civil rights, 5/563
Cuba, 6/684–5
Kennedy, Joseph, 11/1358
Kennedy Manned Flight Center, 4/458
Kennedy, Robert Fitzgerald, 11/**1359–60**, 11/*1359*
Kentucky, 11/**1360–3**, 11/*1360–2*
climate, 11/1360
employment, 11/1362–3
history, 11/1360–2
land, 11/1360
map, 11/*1361*
state emblems, 11/*1361*
Kenya, 11/**1363–4**, 11/*1363*
Kenya, Mount, 11/1363
Kenyatta, Jomo, 11/1364
Keokuk, 11/1296
Keplerian refractor telescope, 20/2394
Kepler, Johannes, 2/250, 4/381, 11/**1364**, 11/*1364*, 15/1838, 18/2172
Kerensky, Alexander, 12/1414, 18/2149, 19/2285
Keratin, 5/571, 9/1022
Kerman, 4/473
Kerosene, 11/**1364**
Kettledrums, 16/*1897*, 16/1898
Ketzler, Johann, 13/1548
Kew Gardens, 3/374
Keyboards:
computer, 5/623
pianos, 16/1924
Key, Francis Scott, 13/1522, 16/1977, 19/2328, 19/*2329*
Keys, 12/1457–8, 12/*1457–8*
Key signatures, music, 14/1684
Khachaturian, Aram, 19/2284
Khadija, 14/1673
Khafre, 17/2033, 19/2310
Khanbalik, 16/1890, 16/1971
Khan, Jahangir, 19/2321
Khartoum, 15/1776, 19/2349
Khazars, 18/2144
Khison, 3/376
Khmer empire, 11/1352
Khmer Republic, 11/1352
Khmer Rouge, 11/1352
Khmers, 19/2280
Khomeini, Ayatollah, 11/1299
Khrushchev, Nikita, 6/685, 7/813, 10/1143, 11/1359, 11/**1364–5**, 11/*1364*, 17/*2000*, 19/2286
Khyber Pass, 1/42, 15/1864
Kiang, 7/755
Kibbutz, 11/1309
Kidd, William, 16/1935
Kidneys, 9/*1081*, 11/**1365–6**, 11/*1365*
circulatory system, 5/551
Kiel Canal, 3/299, 4/454
Kiev, 18/2144, 21/2528
Kigali, 18/2150
Kikuyu, 11/1363, 11/1364
Kilauea, 10/1158, 21/*2536*
Kilimanjaro, Mount, 20/2378
Killer bees, 3/*323*
Killer whales, 2/165, 21/2579
Kilns, 16/1987
Kilts, 18/2176, 18/*2176*

Kimberley, 6/724, 13/1601
Kindergartens, 18/2169
Kinematoscope, 14/1659
Kinescope, 22/2649
Kinetic energy, 7/844, 10/1230
Kinetoscope, 14/1659
King Abdul-Aziz airport, 1/76
King Edward VIII Falls, 10/1133
King eider duck, 16/*1965*
King George VI Falls, 10/1133
King James Bible, 3/336
King Khaled airport, 1/76
King Kong, 14/1659
King, Martin Luther, 1/84, 3/355, 3/*355*, 5/563, 5/*563*, 11/1359, 11/**1366–7**, 11/*1366*, 14/*1706*, 15/1779
King penguin, 16/*1892*
King Philip's War, 17/2099
King Ranch, 20/2411
King's College School, Cambridge, 18/*2169*
Kings Point, 21/2498
Kings and Queens, 11/**1367–9**, 11/*1367–9*
ancient civilisations, 11/1368
France, 9/1009
Great Britain 7/856
Middle Ages, 11/1368–9
modern, 11/1369
see also individuals eg Henry VIII, King of England
King, W.L. Mackenzie, 11/**1367**, 11/*1367*
Kinnaras, 9/*1083*
Kinshasa, 22/2642, 22/2643
Kioga, Lake, 15/1776
Kiowa Indians, 5/602, 11/1271
Kipling, Rudyard, 5/532, 5/534, 11/**1370**, 11/*1370*
Kiprianou, Spyros, 6/689
Kirdi, 4/442
Kirghiz, 19/2282
Kiribati, 13/1582, 15/1854, 16/1972
Kirkwood, James, 14/1688
Kirpan, 18/2223
Kirtland, 12/1396
Kisangani, 22/2642
Kissinger, Henry, 15/1779, 21/2526
Kissing gourami, 20/2465
Kitchen Cabinet, government, 17/1998
Kitchener, Lord, 3/363
Kites, 11/**1370*,** 11/*1370*
Kites (birds), 3/348
Kit fox, 8/998
Kithara, 19/2344
Kitimat, 4/394
Kittatinny Mountains, 15/1754
Kittens:
caring for, 4/485–6
characteristics, 4/486–7
choosing, 4/485
Kitti's hog-nosed bat, 8/967
Kitt Peak National Observatory, 2/*250*, 15/1813, 15/*1813*, 20/*2393*
Kitty Hawk, 15/1787
Kitwe, 22/2643
Kivas, 5/575
Kivu, Lake, 22/*2642*
Kiwi, 8/*954*, 8/954
Klamath Mountains, 15/1841
Klee, Paul, 1/19, 1/*19*, 15/1860, 15/*1861*

Klein, Calvin, 8/915
Klickitat Indians, 21/2544
Klondike, 4/448, 9/1090, 22/2639
Kneading dough, 3/292, 3/293
Knesset, 11/1309
Knickerbocker, Diedrich *see* Irving, Washington
Knighthood, 12/**1371–2**, 12/*1371–2*
Knights, 15/1780
    armor, 2/222–3, 2/*222*, 5/580
    coats of arms, 5/587
    Round Table, 2/236
Knights Hospitalers, 12/1372
Knights of Malta, 12/1372, 12/1494
Knights Templar, 12/1372
Knights of the White Camellia, 17/2071
Knitted textiles, 20/2416
Knitting, 12/**1372–3★**, 12/*1373*
Knives, 20/2368
Knobs, 11/1360
Knossos, 9/1111, 9/*1111*, 9/1114
Knots, 12/**1374**, 12/*1374*
Knotts Berry Farm, 16/*1878*
Knox, Henry, 4/425
Knox, John, 17/2015
Koalas, 2/*147*, 3/267, 3/268, 12/**1374–5**, 12/*1375*
Koboi poison-arrow frog, 16/1961
Kobolds, 7/839
Kobul Valley National Park, 14/*1711*
Koch, Robert, 13/1553
Kodiak bears, 1/*88*, 3/320
Kokomo, 11/1258
Kolwitz, Käthe, 7/*762*
Komodo dragons, 12/1455, 17/*2064*
Komsomol, 19/2285
Kon-Tiki, 10/1182
Koobi Fora, 12/1405
Koran, 2/195, 11/1307, 12/**1375–6**, 12/*1375*, 14/1673
Korea, 12/**1376–7**, 12/*1376–7*
Korean War, 1/121, 12/**1377–9**, 12/*1378*, 12/1473, 20/*2471*, 20/2472, 21/2541
Kortright, Elizabeth, 14/1638
Kosciusko, Mount, 3/263
Kosher laws, 11/1345
Kosi River, 14/1738
Kosrae, 13/1582
Kossuth, Lajos, 10/1228
Kosygin, Aleksei, 11/*1339*, 19/2286
Koto, 19/2344
Kouprey, 4/496
Kourou, 9/1006
Kowloon, 10/1199
Kpelle, 12/1422
Krakatoa, 21/2535
Kraken, 14/1625
Kraków, 16/1964
Kremlin, 12/**1379**, 12/*1379*, 14/1653, 19/*2285*
Krill, 2/170, 6/682, 13/1516, 15/1817
Krio, 18/2218
Krishna, 6/*696*, 10/1187
Kronborg Castle, 6/716
Kru, 12/1422
Kruger National Park, 19/2267
Kuala Lumpur, 12/1490
Kublai Khan, 8/892, 14/1634, 16/1890, 16/1971
Kufah, 12/*1375*
Kufic script, 12/*1375*

Ku Klux Klan, 3/354, 5/561, 17/2069, 17/2071, 20/2404
Kulikovo, battle of, 18/2145
Kuniyoshi, 15/*1847*
Kunlun, 2/239
Kuomintang, 19/2354
Kurds, 11/1300, 20/2373, 20/2476
Kush, 1/48, 2/134
Kushites, 1/48, 2/134
Kutchin Indians, 3/253
Kuwait, 2/193, 12/**1379**
Kwakiutl, 11/1263, 20/*2435*
Kwashiorkor, 8/974
Kyoto, 20/2432
Kyushu, 11/1322

Ll

Ländler, 8/969
Labor:
    child, 5/**529–30**
    division of, 5/559–60
    economics, 7/798
    Industrial Revolution, 11/1275
Laboratories, hospitals, 10/1210
Labor Day, 18/2192
Labor Department, 4/426
Labor unions, 6/704, 11/1275, 12/**1380–1**, 12/*1380–1*
    Lewis, John L., 12/1419
Laboulaye, Edouard de, 19/2332
Labrador, 4/427, 6/653, 15/1748–50
Labrador Current, 3/254, 10/1128
Labrador duck, 3/350
Labradorite, 13/1597
La Brea, 8/994
Laburnum, 18/*2187*
Labyrinthodont, 16/1965
Labyrinths, 13/1542–3, 13/*1543*
Lacandone Indians, 11/1267–8, 13/1541
Lac bug, 4/404
Lace, 12/**1381–2**, 12/*1382*
Lacewing flies, 11/*1280*
Lachesis, 8/915
Lacrosse, 12/**1382–3**, 12/*1383*
Ladder trucks, 8/935
Ladinos Indians, 5/507, 10/1123
Ladybugs, 16/1904–5
Lady's-slipper orchid, 15/1840
La Farge, John, 19/2323
Lafayette, Marquis de, 1/127, 9/1009, 12/**1383**, 12/*1383*
Lafitte, Jean, 16/1935
La Fontaine, Jean de, 8/900–1, 8/*900*, 9/1008, 12/**1384**, 12/*1384*
Lagoons, 18/2183
Lagos, 15/1774, 15/*1774*
Laissez faire, economics, 7/799
Lake Chad, 5/509
Lake dwellers, 12/**1386**, 12/*1386*
Lake Michigan, 5/526
Lakes, 12/**1384–5**, 12/*1384–5*
    pollution, 21/2554
    see individual lakes eg Mead, Lake
Lamaism, 14/1634, 20/2424
Lamarck, Jean de, 8/885–6, 8/*886*
Lamas, 3/334
Lambaréné, 9/1029, 13/1610, 18/2171
Lamb, Charles, 5/532, 6/653, 12/**1386**, 12/*1386*
Lamb, Elizabeth Searle, 16/196!

Lambeosaurus, 6/*734*
Lamb, Mary, 12/1386
Lamborghini Urraco, 3/*275*
Lambs, 2/*152*, 13/1547, 18/2201
Laminated glass, 9/1083
Laminating, plastics, 16/1956
Lammergier, 3/349
Lam Peter Church, 19/*2252*
Lamprey, 8/941, 8/*943*
Lamps, 12/1435
Lancaster, House of, 21/2543
Lances, 2/222
Lancia Theta, 3/*274*
Land rush, 15/1827, 15/*1827*
Landslides, 3/279
Landsteiner, Karl, 3/359
Lane, Burton, 14/1688
Lang, Andrew, 5/532, 8/905
Langley, Samuel, 3/281, 19/2242
Langley, USS, 1/*60*
Language arts, 12/**1386–8★**, 12/*1387*
    letter writing, 12/1418–19
    listening, 12/1387
    literacy, 12/1445–6
    reading, 12/1387
    speaking, 12/1387
    writing, 12/1387
Languages, 12/**1388–91★**, 12/*1390*
    abbreviations, 1/13–15
    African, 1/47
    alphabets, 1/105–7
    Arabic, 2/**194–5**
    Asian, 2/242–3
    capitalization, 4/460
    Chinese, 5/**541**
    computer, 12/1391
    development, 12/1388–9
    dictionaries, 6/727
    dolphins and porpoises, 7/752
    English, 7/**859–62**
    grammar, 9/**1097–8**
    Hebrew, 10/**1172**, 10/*1172*
    Homo erectus, 10/1222
    international, 12/1391
    Japanese, 11/1322
    Latin, 12/**1394–5**
    main families, 12/1390
    modern, 12/1390–1
    parts of speech, 16/1881
    pronunciation, 17/2009
    punctuation, 17/**2029–30**
    Romance, 18/**2123–4**
    Russian, 18/**2143–4**, 18/*2143*
    sign language, 10/1166, 10/*1166*, 18/2222–3, 18/*2222–3*
    speech, 19/**2307–9**
    spelling, 19/**2309**
    translation, 12/1390–1
    universal, 21/2498–9
    writing, 2/135
    written, 22/2624–5, 22/*2624*
    Yiddish, 22/**2634**
Lanolin, 21/2558
L'Anseau-Meadow, 15/1748
Lantern fish, 8/*944*
Lanzarote, 4/454
Laos, 12/**1391–2**, 12/*1391*, 21/2525, 21/2526
Lao-tse, 2/136, 16/1915
La Paz, 3/365, 15/1853
Laplace, Pierre S. de, 13/1533
Lapland, 12/**1392**, 12/*1392*
Lapps, 12/1392, 14/1656, 15/1798
    clothing, 5/578–9

Larch, 20/*2461*
Large intestine, 6/731
Lariats, 6/669
Lark buntings, 9/*1037*, 14/*1719*
Larrey, Dominique Jean, 1/109
Larvae, 2/151, 2/153
    insect, 11/1281, 13/1569
Larynx, 2/164, 19/2307
La Salle, Sieur de, 8/893, 11/1296, 12/**1392–3**, 12/*1393*, 12/1464, 13/1614
Lascaux, 1/18, 1/*19*, 4/*500*
Lasers and masers, 12/**1393–4**, 12/*1393–4*, 13/*1547*
    holograms, 10/1195–6
    surgery, 19/2358
La Spezia, 11/*1313*
Lassos, 6/669
Last Supper, 11/1331
Las Vegas, 15/1743, 15/1744, 15/*1744*
Lateran Treaty, 21/2510
Latex, 3/305, 18/2140, 18/*2141*
Latex paints, 15/1858
Lathrop, Dorothy, 4/433
Latin, 12/1389, 12/**1394–5**
    Romance languages, 18/2123–4
Latin names, animals, 2/154
Latinos *see* Hispanic Americans
Latins, 18/2129
Latitude and longitude, 12/**1395–6★**, 12/*1395*, 13/1510, 14/1726
    climate and, 5/576
Latrobe, 8/981, 14/1629
Latrobe, Benjamin, 4/461
Latter-day Saints, 12/**1396**, 12/*1396*, 17/2013
Latvia, 12/**1396–7**, 19/2282
Laughing gas, 2/143, 15/1777
Laughing hyenas, 10/1231
Laundries and dry cleaning, 12/**1397–8**, 12/*1397*
Laurentian Mountains, 15/1782, 17/2036
Laurier, Sir Wilfrid, 12/**1398**, 12/*1398*
Lava, 17/2108, 21/2535
Lava caves, 4/497
Lavalleja, Juan Antonio, 21/2502
Lavender, 9/*1000*
Lavoisier, Antoine Laurent, 12/**1398**, 12/*1398*
Law, 12/**1398–1400**, 12/*1399–1400*, 15/1851
    ancient civilizations, 2/137
    Bill of Rights, 3/340
    civil, 12/1399
    civil rights, 5/560
    community, 5/615
    constitutional, 12/1400
    court system, 6/666–8
    criminal, 6/673, 12/1399
    English common law, 12/1399
    international, 11/1289, 12/1400
    legislature, 12/1412–13
    making in Congress, 6/630–1
    military, 12/1400
    mores, 6/688
    Napoleonic Code, 12/1399–1400
    police, 16/1966–7, 16/*1966–7*
    prisons, 17/2006–7, 17/*2006–7*
    statute, 12/1399
    Supreme Court, 19/2355–6
    treaties, 20/2457–8
    trials, 20/2463–5

Law, Andrew Bonar, 15/1746
Law enforcement:
  Federal Bureau of Investigation, 8/920
  police, 16/1966–7, 16/*1966–7*
Lawns, 9/1104
Lawrence, T.E., 12/1400–1, 12/*1401*
Lawrence of Arabia, 12/**1400–1**, 12/*1401*
Lawyers, 6/674, 12/**1401–2**
Lay preachers, 8/883
Lazarus, Emma, 19/2332
Leaching, metal ores, 13/1568
Lead, 13/1567
Lead pencils, 16/1896–7, 16/*1897*
Leaf-cutter ants, 2/167
Leaf-cutter bees, 3/325
League of Nations, 6/736, 11/1309, 12/**1404**, 12/*1404*, 20/2485, 21/2592, 21/2609, 22/2611
Leagues, baseball, 3/310
League of Women Voters, 21/2600
Leakey, Louis Seymour Bazett, 10/*1223*, 12/**1405**, 12/*1405*
Leakey, Mary, 12/**1405**
Leakey, Richard, 2/*175*, 10/1220, 12/**1405**
Leaning Tower of Pisa, 9/1031, 11/*1313*, 12/**1405**, 12/*1405*
Leap years, 4/434, 8/919, 20/2428
Lear, Edward, 12/**1405–6**, 12/*1438*
Learning, 12/**1406–8**, 12/*1406–7*
  education, 7/802–4
  habits, 10/1136–7
  memory, 13/1560–1
  psychology, 17/2018
  schools, 18/2168–70
  teaching, 20/2385–6, 20/*2385*
Leather, 12/**1408–9**, 12/*1408*
  goatskin, 9/1086
Leatherback sea turtles, 20/2477
Leavening process, 3/292
Leaves, 12/**1402–4***, 12/*1402–3*
  food production, 12/1402–4
  herbivores, 10/1180
  importance of, 12/1404
  parts of, 12/1402
  plants, 16/*1938*, 16/1940–1
  shapes, 12/1402
  trees, 20/2460–2
Leaves of Grass, 21/2583
Lebanon, 8/951, 12/**1409–50**, 12/*1409*, 13/1589, 20/2373
Lebensraum, 8/911, 9/1069
Le Chatelier, Henry, 13/1597
Le Corbusier, 2/205
Lecouvreur, Adrienne, 1/27
Lecturing, public speaking, 17/2023–4
Leda, 14/1697
Lee, Henry, 12/1410
Lee, Richard Henry, 6/651, 6/707
Lee, Robert E., 1/120, 5/*566*, 5/567, 5/568, 5/569, 9/1062, 11/1318, 12/**1410**, 12/*1410*, 16/1894, 18/2180, 19/2337, 19/*2337*, 21/2533
Leeuwenhoek, Anton van, 5/501, 13/1553, 13/1583, 22/2648
Leeward Islands, 21/2569, 21/2571
Lee, William, 12/1372
Left-handedness, 10/1145
Legal tender, 14/1631
Legends, 12/**1411–12**, 12/*1411–12*, 16/1889–90

  animal, 2/160–3
  Arabian Nights, 2/194
  Atlantis, 3/255
  Beowulf, 3/331
  Bowie, James, 4/378
  Bunyan, Paul, 4/411
  fairytales, 8/904–5
  Faust, 8/917
  folklore, 8/970–2, 8/*971–2*
  King Arthur, 2/236
  maps, 13/1509–10
  mermaids, 13/1564–1, 13/*1564*
  Midas, 13/1584
  Robin Hood, 17/2106
  Tell, William, 20/2400
  see also Myths
Legion of Honor, 13/1550
Legislature, 12/**1412–13**
  Congress, 6/628–31
  parliament, 16/1878
Legs, insect, 11/1278
Le Guin, Ursula, 18/2175
Legumes, 15/1776
Leibnitz, G. W. von, 13/1533, 15/1763
Leiden, 16/1930
Leigh, Mitch, 14/1688
Leigh, Vivien, 14/*1660*
Leipzig, 15/1761
  battle of, 14/1702
Leisure, parks, 16/1878
Leitmotivs, 15/1835
Lek River, 14/1741
Lemmings, 12/**1413**, 12/*1413*, 13/1591, 13/*1592*
Lemna, 2/*189*
Lemond, Greg, 3/338
Lemons, 5/555, 5/*555*
Le Moyne, Pierre, 13/1612
Lemurs, 12/**1413**, 12/*1413*
  flying, 8/967
Lendit, 8/*902*
Lend-lease, 8/997, 18/2135
L'Enfant, Pierre Charles, 3/302, 6/741, 6/743
L'Engle, Madeleine, 5/535
Length, measurement, 13/1545, 13/1546
Leningrad, 16/1907
Lenin, Vladimir Ilich, 5/614, 12/**1414/**, 12/*1414*, 14/1653, 14/1679, 18/2149, 19/2285, 19/2286, 20/2467
Lennart, Isobel, 14/1687
Lenni-Lenape Indians, 11/1263, 15/1754, 16/1894
Lennon, John, 16/1978
Lenses, 12/**1414–16**, 12/*1415–16*, 12/*1432–3*
  eyes, 8/899
  glasses, 9/1084
  microscopes, 13/1583–4, 13/*1583–4*
Lent, 4/469
Leo I, Pope, 3/260, 16/1976
Leo III, Pope, 5/512, 10/1196, 11/1310
Leo X, Pope, 12/1471, 13/1552
Leo XIII, Pope, 16/1976
Leonardo da Vinci, 8/956, 9/1002, 12/**1416–17**, 12/*1416–17*
  inventions and technology, 3/280, 4/*377*, 10/1174, 12/1417, 16/1873, 16/1874, 16/*1900*, 16/1901

  Last Supper 2/*183–4*, 12/*1416*, 12/1417
  Mona Lisa 2/230, 12/1417, 14/*1675*
  painting, 2/232, 7/761, 12/1416–17, 17/2062, 17/2084
Leonov, Alei, 19/2291
Leopards, 4/489–90, 4/*489*
Leopard seal, 2/170
Leopold I, Emperor, 9/1004
Leopold II, King of the Belgians, 22/2612, 22/2642
Leopoldville, 22/2642
Lepanto, battle of, 3/319, 3/*319*
Lepchas, 18/2223
L'Epée, Charles Michel, 10/1165, 18/2222
Lepidodendron, 16/*1953*
Lepidoptera, 4/419
Lepidus, 18/2131
Leprechauns, 7/839
Lerner, Alan Jay, 14/1688
Lesotho, 12/**1417–18**, 12/*1418*
Lesseps, Ferdinand de, 16/1869, 19/2351, 19/*2351*
Lesser gray shrike, 3/*346*
Lesser pandas, 16/1869, 16/*1869*
Lethbridge, 1/90
Letterpress printing, 17/2003, 17/*2003*
Letters, alphabets, 1/105–7, 1/*106*
Letter writing, 12/**1418–19***
Letts, 12/1396
Leucobryum, 14/*1655*
Leukemia, 4/455
Leutze, Emanuel, 1/*126*
Levees, 8/955
Levels, surveyor's, 19/2360
Lever locks, 12/1457
Levers, 12/1475
Lewanika, 22/2644
Lewes, George Henry, 7/835, 7/836
Lewis and Clark Caverns, 14/*1640*
Lewis and Clark Expedition, 9/1024, 11/1327, 11/1342, 12/**1420–1**, 12/*1420*, 14/1642, 18/2216, 19/2278, 21/2544, 21/2576
Lewis, C.S., 5/532
Lewis, Delaware, 6/714
Lewis, John L., 12/**1419**, 12/*1419*
Lewis, Meriwether, 1/116, 5/605, 10/*1239*, 12/1420–1, 15/1842, 15/1844, 19/2278
Lewis, Sinclair, 12/**1420**, 12/*1420*, 12/1451
Lewiston, 10/1237
Lexicon and Concord, battle of, 1/116, 1/*124*, 1/125, 3/318, 17/2094
Lhasa, 20/2424
Liberal arts colleges, 5/595
Liberator, The, 1/15
Liberia, 1/49, 12/**1421–2**, 12/*1421*, 18/2237
Liberty Bell, 11/1250, 12/**1422**, 12/*1422*
Liberty Island, 19/2332
Libraries, 12/**1423–6**, 12/*1423–6*, 14/1680
  bookmobiles, 12/1425
  catalogs, 4/491, 12/1423, 12/*1424*, 12/*1425*
  classification, 12/1423–4
  early, 12/1425–6
  indexes, 11/1251

  librarians, 12/1425
  microfilm, 13/1581
  public, 12/1425, 12/1426
  reference, 12/1424–5, 17/2075–6, 17/*2076*
  specialized materials, 12/1424–5
  specialized rooms, 12/1423
Library of Congress, 12/**1426–7**, 12/*1427*, 21/2490
Librettists, Gilbert, William Schwenck, 9/1077
Libreville, 9/1028
Libya, 12/**1427–8**, 12/*1427–8*
Licensed practical nurse (LPN), 15/1808
Licensed vocational nurse (LVN), 15/1808
Lichen, 12/**1428**, 12/*1428*, 16/1939, 16/*1939*, 16/1952
  air pollution and, 1/74
Lichtenstein, Roy, 2/234
Liddell, Alice, 4/476
Liebig, Justus von, 13/1607
Liechtenstein, 12/**1428–9**, 12/*1429*
Life, 12/**1429–30**, 12/*1430*
  after death, 7/810, 17/2081–2
  origins, 12/1429–30
Lifeboats, 5/*587*
Lifeguards, 12/1430
Lifesaving, 3/252, 12/**1430–2**, 12/*1431*
  artificial respiration, 2/237
Lift, aerodynamics, 1/66–7, 1/*67*
Light, 12/**1432–4***, 12/*1432–4*
  absorption, 1/*18*
  bioluminescence, 3/343
  candles, 4/455–6
  color and, 5/599–601
  energy, 7/845
  fiber optics, 8/927, 8/*927*
  fluorescence, 8/965
  lasers, 12/1393–4, 12/*193–4*
  lens, 12/1414–16, 12/*1415–16*
  mirages, 13/1606–7
  mirrors, 13/1607–8, 13/*1606–7*
  movement, 12/1432–3
  photoelectricity, 16/1916–17
  photons, 17/2035
  radiation, 17/2043–4
  rainbows, 17/2060, 17/*2060*
  sources, 12/1433–4
  spectrum, 19/2305–7, 19/*2305–6*
  waves, 21/2557
Lighthouses, 12/**1434–5**, 12/*1435*
Lighting, 12/**1435–6**, 12/*1435–7*
  bulbs, 7/801
  electric, 7/816, 12/1435–6
  fluorescent, 12/1436
  neon, 12/1436
Lightning bugs, 3/326
Lightning and thunder, 9/1003–4, 9/*1004*, 12/**1437**, 12/*1437*
Light-years, 2/251, 19/2326
Lignite, 5/585
Lilac, 18/2217, 18/*2217*
Lilienthal, Otto, 3/281, 9/1085, 9/*1085*, 10/1147, 20/*2451*
Lilies, 4/408
Liliuokalani, Lydia Kamekeha, 10/1160, 12/**1438**, 12/*1438*
Lilongwe, 12/1489
Lily-of-the-valley, 4/408, 13/*1540*
Lima, 16/1903, 16/1936
Limbourg brothers, 13/*1603*

Limerick, 21/2528
Limericks, 12/**1438**
Limes, 5/555
Limestone, 17/*2108*, 17/2109
  caves, 4/497–8, 4/*497*
Limnologists, 9/1057
Limoges, 7/842
Limpopo River, 22/2644
Linac, 16/1881
Lincoln, Abraham, 1/120, 2/245,
  5/*561*, 10/1242, 12/**1438–41**,
  12/*1439–41*, 16/*1920*, 18/2142,
  18/*2142*
  abolition of slavery, 5/561
  assassination, 3/370, 4/461, 5/569,
    9/1042, 11/1337, 12/1441
  Cabinets, 4/426
  Civil War, 5/566–8, 8/991
  and clowns, 5/583
  early life, 12/1439–40
  Emancipation Proclamation, 7/840,
    12/1440, 18/2238
  Gettysburg Address, 9/1073,
    12/1441
  legends, 12/1411
  political career, 12/1440–1
  Reconstruction, 17/2069
  slavery, 1/16, 7/751, 7/840, 12/1440
Lincoln, Mary, 12/1439
Lincoln Memorial, 4/431
Lincoln, Sarah, 12/1439
Lincoln, Thomas, 10/1242
Lincoln, Tom, 12/1439
Lindbergh, Ann Morrow, 12/1442
Lindbergh, Charles Augustus,
  3/255, 3/282, 12/**1441–2**,
  12/*1442*, 13/1618, 19/2241
Lind, Jenny, 3/305
Lindsay, Kathleen, 12/1451
Line, definition, 9/1058–9
Linear accelerator, 16/1881
Linear motors, 12/**1442**, 12/*1442*
Line engraving, 17/*2004–5*
Line Islands, 16/1971
Linen, 5/579
Liners, ships, 18/2205, 18/*2206*
Linguistics, 12/1390
  anthropology, 2/176
Links, 9/1091
Linnaeus, Carolus, 3/375,
  12/**1442–3**, 12/*1443*, 22/2648
Linotype, 20/2481
Linsey-woolsey, 20/2416
Lion Cave, Oregon, 4/497
Lions, 4/489–90, 4/*489*, 12/**1443**,
  12/*1443*
Lippershey, Hans, 20/2393–4
Lippi, Fra Filippo, 13/1551, 17/2085
Lippizaner horses, 10/*1204*, 10/1206
Lip reading, 10/1166, 19/2304–5
Lipstick, 6/662
Liquid crystals, 12/**1444**
Liquid oxygen, 9/*1019*
Liquids, 12/**1444***, 12/*1444*, 13/1537
  absorption, 1/18
  buoyancy, 4/411–12
  fluids, 8/965
  surface tension, 19/2356–7
Liquor, prohibition, 17/2007–8,
  17/*2007*
Lisa, Manuel, 14/1642
Lisbon, 16/1982
Lisle, Rouget de, 14/1705
Lisping, 19/2308

Listening, 12/1387
Lister, Joseph, 10/1211, 12/**1445**,
  12/*1445*, 13/1553, 19/*2357*,
  19/2358
Liszt, Franz, 5/543, 12/**1445**, 12/*1445*
Literacy, 12/**1445–6**
Literary awards, 12/1451–2
Literature, 12/**1446–52**, 12/*1446–51*
  ancient civilizations, 2/136
  Caldecott Award, 4/433, 4/*433*
  censorship, 5/503–4
  children's, 5/**531–5**
  copyright, 16/1884–5
  crime fiction, 12/1450, fiction,
    12/1446–7
  diaries, 6/724–5
  dictionaries, 6/726–8
  fantasy, 12/1450
  genres, 12/1450–1
  Gothic novel, 18/2127
  horror fantasy, 12/1450
  interpretation, 12/1447–50
  literary awards, 12/1451–2
  Newbery Medal, 15/**1744–6**,
    15/*1746*
  novels, 15/1801–2, 15/*1801–2*
  O'Neill, Eugene, 15/1831–2
  poetry, 16/**1960–1**
  purposes of, 12/1446
  science fiction, 12/1450, 18/**2175**
  short stories, 18/2215–16
  symbolism, 20/2370
  themes, 12/1450
  types, 12/1446–7
  see also Children's literature;
    Writers
Lithographic printing, 17/2003,
  17/*2003*
Lithuania, 12/**1452–3**, 12/*1452*,
  18/2147, 19/2282
Litmus paper, 1/23
Little auks, 16/*1965*, 18/2181
Little Big Horn, battle of, 6/687,
  11/1271, 18/2228, 18/2229
Little Big Horn River, 14/1642
Little Dipper, 6/641, 6/*641*, 6/642,
  15/1975
Little John, 17/2106
Little League baseball, 12/**1453**,
  12/*1453*
Little Mermaid, Copenhagen, 2/140,
  2/*140*, 6/717
Little Missouri River, 15/1790
Little Rock, Arkansas, 2/218, 2/*218*
Little Tennessee River, 15/1788
Little Women, 1/94
Liu Sheng, Prince, 5/*539*
Liver, 9/1081, 12/**1453–4**, 12/*1453*
  circulatory system, 5/551
Liverpool to Manchester Railway,
  19/2333
Liverworts, 14/1655–6, 14/*1655*,
  16/1939, 16/1947
Livingstone, David, 8/*891*, 12/**1454**,
  12/*1454*, 12/1489–90, 19/2325
Livingstone Falls, 22/2642–3
Livingston, Robert, 6/707, 14/1638,
  21/2548
Livy, 18/2132
Lizards, 12/**1455–6**, 12/*1455–6*,
  17/2091, 18/2155
  molting, 14/1626
Llamas, 2/*155*, 4/440, 4/*440*, 19/*2271*

Llewellyn ap Gruffydd, 21/2539
Lloyd, Chris Evert, 19/2317, 20/*2407*
Lloyd George, David, 21/2609,
  21/*2610*
Loans, banks, 3/301
Loblolly, 6/632
Lobsters, 2/155, 6/681, 6/*681*,
  18/*2229*
Lobster trap, 8/949
Local airlines, 1/65
Local anesthetic, 2/142
Local government, 12/**1456–7**,
  12/*1456*
  counties, 6/666
  elections, 7/815
  forms, 12/1456–7
  responsibilities, 12/1457
  State government, 19/2328–9
  suburbs, 19/2347
Local radio stations, 17/2051
Loch Ness, 12/1384
  monster, 2/162
Lochs, 18/2176
Locke, John, 6/716, 10/1169,
  16/*1914*, 16/1915
Lockheed SR-71, 3/282
Locks, canal, 4/453, 4/*454*
Locks and keys, 12/**1457–8**,
  12/*1457–8*
Locomotion, 19/2333
  animals, 2/158–60, 2/*158–60*
Locomotives, 11/*1275*, 17/2055
  Stephenson, George, 19/2333
Locules, 9/1016
Locusts, 9/1104–5
  migration, 13/1594
Lodestone, 12/1483
Lodgepole, 6/632
Lodges, beavers, 2/152, 3/322, 3/*322*
Lodz, 16/1964
Loesser, Frank, 14/1687
Loewe, Frederick, 14/1688
Lofting, Hugh, 5/532, 15/1746
Logan, Mount, 4/444, 15/1782
Log cabins, 4/405–6, 4/*405*, 18/2204
Logic, mathematics, 13/1534
Loki, 14/1695
Lomax, Alan, 8/973
Lomax, John, 8/973
Lombards, 5/512, 9/1064, 11/1310
Lomé, 20/2432
Lomonosov Ridge, 2/208
Londinium, 7/855, 12/1458
London, 7/852, 7/855, 12/**1458–9**,
  12/*1458–9*
  River Thames, 20/2418, 20/*2418*
  Underground, 19/2348
  Westminster Abbey, 21/2572
London Bridge, 2/217, 4/389
London Company, 11/1319
Londonderry, 15/1793
London, Jack, 9/1091, 12/**1459**,
  12/*1459*
London School of Medicine for
  Women, 3/358
Longbows, 4/377
Long, Crawford, 2/142, 13/1553
Long-eared owl, 15/*1852*
Longfellow, Henry Wadsworth,
  10/1211, 12/**1460**, 12/*1460*,
  13/1580, 15/1746, 17/2094,
  17/2100
Long-haired cats, 4/*486*, 4/487
Long, Huey, 12/1466

Long Island, 15/1765
Longitude, 13/1510, 14/1726
Long, Jefferson, 17/*2069*
Long jump, 20/2441
Longleaf, 6/632
Longleat, 13/*1543*
Long March, 5/545, 13/1508
Long Melford, 7/*853*
Longshoremen, 10/1151
Long sighted, 8/*899*, 8/*899*
Looms, 19/2313
  carpets, 4/472–3
Loons, 21/2551
Loop knots, 12/1374
Lopez, Nancy, 19/2317
Lopez, Solano, 16/1875
LORAN, 14/1725
Lord Chamberlain's Men, 18/2197
Lorelei, 17/2096
Lorikets, 16/1880
Los Alamos, 15/1757. 15/1758
Los Angeles, 4/438, 6/722, 10/1149,
  12/**1460–1**, 12/*1460–1*
  movies, 4/439
Los Angeles International airport,
  1/77
Los Angeles Travel Century Club,
  20/2456
Loss, economics, 7/798
Lost Tribes of Israel, 11/1335
Lost wax casting, 18/2179
Lotus, 3/*373*
Loudness, hearing, 10/1165
Lou Gehrig's Disease, 9/1049
Loughs, 11/1301
Louis I the Pious, King of France,
  12/**1461**
Louis II, Emperor, 9/1065
Louis II, King of France, 12/**1461**
Louis III, King of France, 12/**1461**
Louis IV, King of France, 12/**1461**
**Louis V the Sluggard, King of
  France**, 12/**1461**
Louis VI the Fat, King of France,
  12/**1462**
Louis VII, King of France, 6/679,
  7/814, 12/**1462**
Louis VIII, King of France, 12/**1462**
**Louis IX Saint Louis, King of
  France**, 6/680, 12/**1462**, 12/*1462*,
  16/1911
**Louis X the Quarreler, King of
  France**, 12/**1462**
**Louis XI the Spider, King of
  France**, 7/805, 12/**1462**, 12/*1462*
Louis XII, King of France, 12/**1462**
Louis XIII, King of France,
  12/**1462**, 21/2520
**Louis XIV Sun King, King of
  France**, 3/296, 3/308, 3/319,
  8/996, 9/1008, 11/*1368*,
  12/**1462–3**, 12/*1462*, 15/1780
  fashion, 8/913
Louis XV, King of France, 12/**1463**
Louis XVI, King of France,
  9/1008–9, 12/1398, 12/**1463**,
  12/*1462*, 13/1514
  French Revolution, 9/1010–12
Louis XVII, King of France,
  12/**1463**
Louis XVIII, King of France,
  12/**1463**, 12/*1463*
Louisiana, 12/**1463–7**, 12/*1464–6*
  Cadillac, Antoine, 4/429

climate, 12/1464
employment, 12/1466–7
history, 12/1464–6
land, 12/1464
map, 12/*1465*
state emblems, 12/*1465*
Louisiana Maneuvers, 7/813
Louisiana Purchase, 1/116, 11/1327,
5/602, 11/1355, 12/1420,
12/1466, 12/**1467**, 12/*1467*,
13/1614, 14/1638, 14/1642
Louis, Joe, 4/381
Louis Napoleon, 9/1010
Louisville, 11/1362
Louse, 12/**1467–8**, 12/*1468*
Louvre, 12/**1468**, 12/*1468*
Lovebirds, 16/1880
Lovejoy, Elijah P., 1/15
Low Countries, 12/**1468–9**, 12/*1469*
Low Country, South Carolina,
19/2274–5
Lowell, Francis Cabot, 11/1274,
11/1275
Lowell, James Russell, 11/1347,
12/1480
Lower Peninsular, Michigan, 13/1580
Low-relief sculpture, 18/2178
Low temperatures, cryogenics, 6/682
LSD, 7/769
Luang Prabang, 12/1391
Luaus, 10/1157
Lubrication, 9/1013
Luciferin, 3/343
Lucifers, 13/1532
Luftwaffe, 22/2613
Luge, 19/2239
Lukeman, Augustus, 19/2337
Lullabies, 8/972
Lumber and lumbering,
12/**1469–70★**, 12/*1469–70*
forests, 8/987–8
lumberjacks, 4/411
national forests, 14/1706–7
Luminescence, 3/343
fluorescence, 8/965
Luminosity, stars, 19/2327
Lumumba, patrice, 22/2642
Luna moth, 4/421–2, 4/*421*
Lunar eclipses, 7/793, 14/1644
Lunar months, 14/1643
Luna spacecraft, 19/*2287*, 19/2288
Lundquist, Steven, 20/2366
Lungfish, 8/943, 8/944
Lungs, 4/387–8, 4/*388*, 17/2093
fish, 8/943
Lunula, 5/571
Luo, 11/1363
Luray Caverns, 4/431
Lusaka, 22/2643
Lusitanica, 21/2609
Luster:
metal, 13/1566
minerals, 13/1597
Lutes, 19/2344
Lutheran Church, 17/2013
Lutheranism, 12/1471, 17/2013
Luther, Martin, 4/378, 5/546, 7/803,
8/880–1, 9/1065, 9/1070,
12/**1470–1**, 12/*1471*, 17/2015,
18/2121
Luthuli, Albert John, 15/1779
Lux, 12/1433
Luxembourg, 12/1468–9, 12/**1471**,
12/*1471*

Luxembourgish, 12/1471
Luzco, 19/*2270*
Luzon, 16/1913
Lvov, Prince, 18/2149, 19/2285
Lyceum, 2/212
Lydia, 7/792, 9/1112
Lye poisons, 16/1961–2
Lymph, 6/731
Lymphatic system, 13/1565
Lymphoid tissue, 4/389
Lynxes, 4/489, 4/*489*
Lyozyme, 8/953
Lyrebird, 3/267
Lyres, 7/802, 19/2344
Lyricists, Gershwin, Ira, 9/1072
Lyric poetry, 9/1115–16, 16/1960

Mm

Macadamia nuts, 15/1810
Macadamization, 19/2342
McAdam, John Loudon, 19/2342
Macao, 12/**1472–3**, 12/*1472*, 16/1982
Macaques, 14/1636–7
Macaroni penguin, 16/*1892*
MacArthur, Arthur, 12/1473
MacArthur, Charles, 10/1162
MacArthur, Douglas, 7/813,
12/1378, 12/**1473**, 12/*1473*,
22/2616, 22/2617
Macaws, 16/1880
Maccabee, Judah, 10/1148–9
McCall, Jack, 10/1184
McCardle, Eliza, 11/1338
McCarthy, Joseph, 20/2472
McCartney, Paul, 16/1978
McClellan, George B., 5/567
McCormick, Cyrus, 8/903, 8/909,
8/*909*, 13/**1543**, 13/*1543*, 20/*2480*
McCormick, Robert, 13/1543
McCullers, Carson, 1450
Macdonald, 15/1795
MacDonald, George, 5/532
MacDonald, John A., 4/*499*, 450,
8/*894*, 8/915, 12/**1473–4**, 12/*1473*
McDonnell Douglas DC-8, 1/*64*, 1/*69*
McDowell, Irwin, 5/567
Macedonia, 9/1110, 9/1113, 12/**1474**,
12/*1474*
Macedonia, 21/2541
Macedonians, 22/2639
McEnroe, John, 19/2317, 20/*2406*
McGee, Thomas D'Arcy, 8/916
McGillivray, William, 3/261
Machel, Samora, 14/1672
McHenry, Donald F., 3/355
Machiavelli, Niccoló, 12/**1474–5**,
12/*1474*
Machicolations, 4/483
Machines, 12/**1475–6**, 12/*1475*
Industrial Revolution, 11/1274–6
inventions, 11/1292
Machu Picchu, 11/*1247*
Mackenzie, Northwest Territories,
15/1796
Mackenzie, Sir Alexander, 4/392–3,
12/**1476**, 12/*1476*, 12/1477
Mackenzie River, 12/**1476–7**,
12/*1476*, 15/1796, 15/*1797*
Mackerel, 8/*949*
McKinley, Mount, 15/1782, 21/2491
McKinley Tariff Act, 13/1544

McKinley, William, 2/245, 4/399,
13/**1543–4**, 13/*1544*, 19/2299
McKittrick County, 20/*2412*
Macleod, John, 3/303
McMath Solar Telescope, 20/*2393*
Macon, 1/79
Madagascar, 3/*353*, 12/**1477–8**,
12/*1477*
Madero, Francisco, 13/1576
Madison, 21/*2597*
Madison, Dolley, 12/1479
Madison, James, 1/31, 1/116, 6/642,
6/644, 10/1142, 12/**1478–9**,
12/*1478*, 21/2488
Madras, 11/1253, 14/*1640*
Madrid, 19/2298
Madrigals, 5/544
Maeterlinck, Maurice, 20/2370
Magarac, Joe, 8/972
Magazines, 12/**1479–81**, 12/*1479*
children's, 5/332–3
journalism, 11/1342–3
libraries, 12/1423
publishing, 12/1480–1, 17/2026
young people's, 12/1480
Magellan, Ferdinand, 1/109, 8/893,
11/1269, 12/**1481**, 12/*1481*,
13/1582, 15/1795, 15/1857,
16/1914, 16/1982
Maggots, 8/966, 13/1569
Magi, 17/2011
Magic, 12/**1481–3★**, 12/*1481–2*
Houdini, Harry, 10/1212–13
Maginot Line, 8/990
Magistrates' courts, 6/667
Magma, 17/2108, 21/2535
Magna Carta, 3/340, 7/855–6,
11/1337, 11/1369, 12/**1483**,
12/*1483*
Magnalium, 13/1568
Magnetic compass, 5/617–18
Magnetic energy, 16/1923
Magnetic filters, 8/929
Magnetic poles, 3/262
north pole, 15/1974
Magnetism, 8/983, 16/1923
Ampère, André Marie, 2/129
electric motors, 14/1664–5, 14/*1665*
Magnetite, 12/1483, 12/*1483*
Magnetometer, 13/1600
Magnetrons, 13/1584
Magnets, 12/**1483–4★**, 12/*1483–4*
electromagnets, 7/823–4, 7/*824*
Magnifying glasses, 12/1415, 12/*1415*
Magnitude, stars, 19/2326–7
Magnolias, 8/*884*, 9/*1039*, 18/2217
Magyar language, 10/1227
Magyars, 9/1065, 10/1228
Mahal, Mumtaz, 20/2377
Mahayana Budists, 4/402
Mahdi, 19/2350
Mahé, 18/*2197*
Mahican Indians, 1/100
Mahler, Gustav, 3/269, 12/**1484**
Maia, 13/1540
Maidenhair fern, 8/*923*
Maiden name, 14/1698
Maid of Orléans, 11/1337
Mail:
handling, 16/1984–5
history, 16/1985–6
international, 16/1986
Pony Express, 16/1975
postage, 16/1984

postal services, 16/1983–6
types of, 16/1983–4
Mail-order companies, 19/2338
Maine, 12/**1484–8**, 12/*1485–7*,
13/1544, 14/1729, 19/2299
climate, 12/1485
employment, 12/1487–8
history, 12/1485–7
land, 12/1484–5
map, 12/*1486*
state emblems, 12/*1486*
Maine, 1/120
Maize, 6/659, 9/1097, 9/*1097*, 16/1950
Majolica, 16/1990
Makah Indians, 21/2544
Makarios, Archbishop, 6/689
Makeup, 6/662–3, 12/**1488–9★**,
12/*1488*
theatrical, 7/*760*
Makhachkala, 4/481
Malabo, 7/865
Malacca, 19/2280
Malachite, 13/*1597*
Malaria, 6/649, 6/737, 17/2018
Malawi, 12/**1489–90**, 12/*1489*
Malay language, 4/400
Malayo-Polynesian languages, 2/243
Malaysia, 12/**1490–1**, 12/*1490–1*
Malcolm X, 3/357, 12/**1491–2**,
12/*1491*
Maldives, 12/**1492**, 12/*1492*
Malé, 12/1492
Malecite Indians, 12/1485
Male fern, 8/923
Mali, 3/352, 12/**1492–3**, 12/*1492–3*,
19/2262
Malignant tumors, 6/737–8
Malinké, 10/1126, 12/1493
Malintzin, 6/662
Mallard, 7/771
Mallarmé, Stéphane, 6/705
Malleability, metal, 13/1567
Mallee, 3/267
Malnutrition, 8/975, 15/1810, 15/1811
Malory, Sir Thomas, 2/236
Malpighi, Marcello, 22/2648
Malta, 12/**1493–4**, 12/*1493–4*
Malvinas, 8/907
Mamluks, 18/2238
Mammals, 13/**1495–8**, 13/*1495–8*
Australian, 3/268–9, 3/*268*
birth, 13/1495–6
dolphins and porpoises, 7/751–2,
7/*751–2*
evolution, 13/1495–6
extinct, 13/**1498–1501**,
13/*1499–1500*
feet, 10/1145–6, 10/*1145*, 13/1497
flying, 8/967, 8/*967*
food, 13/1496–7
hair, 10/1137–8, 10/*1137–8*,
13/1495
hearing, 10/1166
herbivores, 10/1180, 10/*1180*
hoofed animals, 10/1200
migration, 13/1591–2
skin, 13/1495
Mammary glands, 13/1495
Mammoth Hot Springs, 14/*1713*,
22/2626
Mammoths, 13/1500
Managua, 5/507, 15/1771
Manatees, 13/**1501–2**, 13/*1501*,
13/1564

Manchester, New Hampshire, 15/1751
Manchu dynasty, 5/538, 14/1634
Mandalay, 4/415
Mandarin, 5/541
Mandarin duck, 7/770
Mandolin, 19/2344
Mandrills, 14/1637
Maneater sharks, 18/2200
Manet, Edouard, 6/711, 13/**1502**★, 13/1502
  Gare Saint-Lazare, 13/1502, 13/1502
Manganese nodules, 15/1817, 15/1818–19
Manhattan, SS, 2/209, 2/210, 8/894, 15/1795
Manhattan Indians, 15/1767
Manhattan Island, 15/1765, 15/1767, 15/1767
Manigault, Joseph, 9/1025
Manila hemp, 18/2137
Manitoba, 4/450, 13/**1503–5**, 13/1503–4
  climate, 13/1503
  history, 13/1503
  land, 13/1503
  map, 13/1504
  people, 13/1503–5
  provincial flower, 13/1504
Manitou Lake, 12/1384
Manjako, 10/1126
Man-made fabrics, 5/581
Manners, 13/**1505–6**, 13/1506
Mannheim, 17/2096
Mann, Horace, 13/**1505**, 13/1505
Mann, Thomas, 8/917
Manors, 8/925
Man-o'-war bird, 18/2181
Man *see* Human beings, Human body
Manslaughter, 14/1675
Manta rays, 18/2200
Mantegna, 17/2085
Mantis shrimps, 6/681
Mantle, Earth's, 7/782
Mantles, mollusks, 14/1624, 18/2202
Manual transmisson, automobiles, 7/766
Manuel I, King of Portugal, 9/1032
Manufacturing, 13/**1506–8**, 13/1506–8, 18/2188
  automation, 3/272
Maoris, 15/1768, 15/1768, 16/1972
Mao Tse-tung, 5/538, 5/539, 5/540, 5/545, 10/1124, 13/**1508**, 13/1508, 20/2402–3
Maple sugar, 19/2351
Mapmakers, 9/1054
Maps, 13/**1509–12**★, 13/1509–11
  atlases, 3/256
  globes, 13/1511
  legends, 13/1509–10
  making, 13/1511–12
  scale, 13/1510
  surveying, 19/2360–1
  types, 13/1510–11
  see also individual countries, states, provinces etc
Maputo, 14/1672
Maquis, 10/1124
Maracaibo, Lake, 16/1909, 21/2514, 21/2514, 21/2515
Maramokotro, Mount, 12/1477

Marathon, battle of, 1/40, 3/318, 9/1112, 16/1903
Marathon races, 13/**1512**, 13/1512, 20/2441
Marat, Jean, 9/10011
Marble, 17/2035, 17/2036, 17/2108
Marbled cone, 18/2202
Marceau, Marcel, 1/27, 16/1870
March, 13/**1512–13**, 13/1512
  special events, 13/1513
Marching bands, 15/1840
Marchionesses, 15/1779–80
Marciano, Rocky, 4/380, 4/381
Marconi, Guglielmo, 5/611, 13/**1513–14**/, 13/1513, 20/2389
Marcos, Ferdinand, 6/726, 16/1914, 17/2095
Marcus Aurelius, 18/2131
Mardi Gras, 4/469
  New Orleans, 12/1466
Mardonius, 22/2628
Marduk, 3/286
Mares, 10/1203
Margaret of Anjou, 21/2543, 21/2543
Margarethe II, Queen of Denmark, 6/717
Margay, 4/488
Marianas Islands, 10/1123, 13/1582
Marianas Trench, 15/1855
Maria Theresa, Empress, 5/513, 13/1514
Marie Antoinette, Queen of France, 8/913, 9/1009, 10/1139, 12/1463, 13/**1514**/, 13/1514
Marie Louise, Empress, 13/1519, 14/1701
Marietta, 15/1824
Marignano, battle of, 9/1002
Marigolds, 9/1039
Marigot Lagoon, St Lucia, 4/467
Marijuana, 7/769
Marimba, 22/2631
Marine aquarium, 2/190
Marine Corps, 13/**1514–15**, 13/1514–15, 21/2498
Marine ecology, 13/1517
Marine life, 13/**1515–17**, 13/1515–17
  Benthos, 13/1517
  ecology, 13/1517
  nekton, 13/1516–17
  plankton, 13/1515–16
Mariner spacecraft, 19/2288, 19/2289
Marinus, 18/2161
Marionettes, 17/2031
Marion, Francis, 1/128, 13/**1517–18**, 13/1518
Maritime Administration, 13/1564, 18/2211
Mark Antony, 5/572–3, 18/2131
Marketing:
  selling, 18/2188–9
  stores and shops, 19/2337–9, 19/2337–8
  supply and demand, 19/2355
  vending machines, 21/2513–14, 21/2514
Markova, Alicia, 8/973
Marksmanship, 18/2214
Marlborough, Duke of, 2/165
Marlow, Christopher, 8/917
Marmara, Sea of, 20/2475
Marmosets, 14/1636
Marmots, 9/1120, 10/1183
Marne, battle of, 3/319

Maroon clownfish, 13/1516
Marquesas Islands, 16/1971
Marquess, 15/1779–80
Marquette, 11/1296
Marquette, Jacques, 8/893, 10/1242, 11/1296, 13/**1518**, 13/1518, 13/1580, 13/1614, 13/1616
Marrakech, 14/1648
Marrow, bone, 3/366
Marriage, 13/**1518–19**, 13/1519
Mars, 6/702, 9/1089, 10/1233, 18/2129, 19/2257, 19/2260
  basic facts, 19/2259
  geology, 9/1057
Marseille, La, 14/1705, 14/1705
Marseilles, 10/1149
Marshall, George C., 7/813, 20/2471, 22/2616
Marshall Islands, 13/1582
Marshall, John, 12/1422, 13/**1519–20**, 13/1520, 19/2356
Marshall Plan, 20/2471, 22/2619
Marshall, Thurgood, 5/563, 13/**1520**, 13/1520
Marsh crocodiles, 1/103
Marshes, 19/2361–2, 19/2361–2
Marsh hawks, 3/343, 3/349
Marsh, Othniel, 6/733
Marsupials, 2/152, 3/268–9, 3/268, 14/1496, 13/**1520–1**, 13/1520–1
  kangaroos, 11/1352–3, 11/1353
  koalas, 12/1374–5, 12/1375
  opossums, 15/1836–7, 15/1836
Martel, Charles, 3/319
Martens, 21/2560
Martial arts, 19/2318
Martinique, 21/2569, 21/2572
Martius, 13/1512
Marx Brothers, 1/28, 14/1662, 21/2510
Marx, Karl, 4/459, 5/614, 12/1414, 13/**1521**, 13/1521, 19/2249
Mary, Queen of Scots, 6/663, 9/1002, 13/**1521–2**, 13/1522, 17/2015, 18/2195, 19/2300
Mary, Virgin, 11/1330, 18/2121
Mary I, Queen of England, 7/805, 7/836, 9/1119, 13/**1522**, 13/1522, 16/1912, 17/2015, 18/2121
Mary II, Queen of England, 2/165, 7/858, 11/1319, 13/**1522**, 21/**2589–90**, 21/2589
Maryland, 13/**1522–5**, 13/1523–5
  climate, 13/1524
  employment, 13/1525
  history, 13/1524–5
  land, 13/1522–4
  map, 13/1523
  state emblems, 13/1523
Masada, 11/1335
Masai, 11/1363, 20/2378, 20/2379
Masers, 12/1393
Maseru, 12/1418
Mashad, 11/1299
Masks, 13/**1526–7**★, 13/1526
Mason bees, 3/325
Mason, Charles, 13/1527
Mason-Dixon Line, 13/**1527**, 13/1527
Mason wasps, 21/2549
Masquerades, 13/1526
Masques, 13/1526
Mass, 13/1536
Massachusetts, 13/**1527–31**, 13/1527–30

climate, 13/1528
employment, 13/1530–1
history, 13/1528–30
land, 13/1527
map, 13/1529
state emblems, 13/1529
Massachusetts Bay Colony, 1/111, 1/115, 13/1530
Massachusetts Bay Company, 17/2032
Massachusetts Institue of Technology (MIT), 13/1530
Massasoit, 13/**1531**, 13/1531, 16/1931, 20/2419
Mass media:
  communications, 5/612
  radio, 17/2051–3
Mass production, 8/985, 11/1274, 13/1507
Masteroff, Joe, 14/1688
Master's degrees, 5/596
Mastodon, 7/831, 13/1500
Masts, 18/2207
Matadi, 22/2643
Mata Hari, 19/2320
Matamoros, 17/2104
Matanuska Valley, 1/87, 1/88
Matches, 8/933, 9/1013, 13/**1531–2**, 13/1531
Matchlocks, 10/1130–1
Mathematics, 13/**1532–5**★, 13/1532–4
  algebra, 13/1534, 13/1535
  angles, 2/143, 2/143
  Archimedes, 2/200
  arithmetic, 2/212–15
  assumptions, 13/1533
  basics of, 13/1533
  binary system, 3/340
  Bowditch, Nathaniel, 4/377–8
  calculators, 4/432–3
  chance, 5/510–11
  decimal numbers, 6/706
  definitions, 13/1533–4
  Euclid, 8/875
  fractions, 9/999
  geometry, 9/1057–60, 9/158–9, 13/1534–5, 13/1533
  graphs, 9/1101–2, 9/1101–2
  history, 13/1532
  logic, 13/1534
  Newton, Sir Isaac, 15/1763
  numbers, 15/1806–8
  Pascal, Blaise, 16/1882–3
  percentages, 16/1897
  Pythagoras, 17/2034
  sets, 18/2192–3
  statistics, 19/2331–2, 19/2331
  theorems, 13/1534
  topology, 13/1535
Matilda, 19/2333
Mating calls, 2/164
Matisse, Henri, 5/509, 13/**1535–6**, 13/1536, 14/1620, 15/1861, 15/1862, 15/1863, 15/1863, 20/2380
  View of Tangiers Seen from a Window, 13/1536, 13/1536
Matoaka, 16/1959
Mattamuskeet, Lake, 15/1787
Matter, 13/**1536–7**★, 13/1537, 16/1922
  antimatter, 2/177
  atoms, 3/258–60
  chemistry of, 5/518–19

properties of, 13/1536–7
states of, 13/1537
Matterhorn, 20/2367
Matthes, F.E., 4/457
Matthews, Mitford M., 6/727
Maui, 10/1158, 11/1351
Mau Mau, 11/1364
Mauna Kea, 10/1158
Mauna Loa, 10/1158, 14/1669, 21/2535
Maunday Thursday, 7/790
Mauritania, 13/**1537–8**, 13/*1538*
Mauritius, 13/**1538–9**, 13/*1539*
Maurya dynasty, 11/1254
Maury, Matthew, 13/**1539**, 13/*1539*, 15/1817
Mausolus, 18/2193
Maximilian, Archduke, 11/1344, 13/1576
Maxim, Sir Hiram, 3/281
May, 13/**1540**, 13/*1540*
special events in, 13/1540
Mayas, 3/295, 5/506, 10/1124, 10/*1124*, 10/1199, 11/1267, 13/**1541**, 13/*1541*, 22/*2626*
art, 11/*1258*, 11/1259
calendars, 4/434
May Day, 13/1540
Mayer, Louis B., 1/21
Mayflower, 1/111, 13/1528, 13/**1541–2**, 13/*1542*, 16/1930, 20/2419
Mayflower airship, 1/79
Mayflower Compact, 13/**1542**, 13/*1542*, 16/1931
Mayflower II, 13/1542
Mayotte, 5/617
Maypoles, 13/1540
Mays, Willie, 19/2317
Mazarin, Cardinal, 12/1463
Mazes, 13/**1542–3**, 13/*1543*
Mazurka, 5/543
Mazzini, Giuseppe, 9/1043
M'Bochi, 6/626
Mbunbu, 2/144
Me-163 *Komet*, 1/66
Mead, Lake, 2/217
Mead, Margaret, 2/176
Meadows, wildflowers, 21/2586–7
Meals, cooking, 6/653–6
Mealworms, 3/326
Meanders, 17/2105, 17/*2106*
Measles, 5/528, 6/649
Measurement, 13/**1545–7**, 13/*1545–7*
area, 13/1545, 13/1546
astronomy, 2/251–2
capacity, 13/1545
dimensions, 6/732
distance, 13/1545, 13/1546
electricity, 7/820–1
energy, 7/845–6
heat, 9/1019–20, 10/1170
latitude and longitude, 12/1395–6, 12/*1395–6*
length, 13/1545, 13/1546
measuring the Earth, 7/783
metric, 13/1545, 13/1547, 13/1571
scales, 18/2167
temperature, 20/2400–1, 20/2422, 20/*2422*
time, 13/1545
volume, 13/1545, 13/1546
weight, 13/1545, 13/1546

Meat, 13/**1547–9**, 13/*1548*
beef cattle, 4/494–5
cooking, 6/655
cuts of, 13/1548, 13/*1548*
frozen, 13/1548
packing, 13/1548–9
Mecca, 2/193, 11/1307, 14/1673, 18/2166
Mechanical drawing, 13/**1549–50**, 13/*1549*
Mechanical energy, 7/844
Mechanical engineering, 7/851
Mechanical radiation, 17/2043
Mechanics, 16/1923
friction, 9/1012–13, 9/*1012–13*
gears, 9/1047–8
hydraulics, 10/1230
pumps, 17/2028–9, 17/*2028–9*
Meck, Nadezhda von, 20/2383–4
Medals and decorations, 13/**1550–1**, 13/*1550–1*
Medea, 11/1324
Medes, 11/1299, 16/1902
Medflies, 16/1904
Media, 7/792
advertising, 1/37–8
Medical caseworkers, 19/2252
Medici, Catherine de', 10/1178, 13/1552
Medici, Cosimo de', 13/1551
Medici family, 8/956, 12/1474, 13/**1551–2**, 13/*1551–2*, 16/1988
Medici, Lorenzo de', 11/*1311*, 13/1551, 13/*1551*, 13/1577
Medici, Marie dei, 12/1462, 13/1552
Medicinal plants, 13/**1552**, 13/*1552*
Medicine, 13/**1552–6**, 13/*1553–5*
acupuncture, 1/29–30, 1/*30*
advances in, 13/1554
ancient civilizations, 2/135
anesthetics, 2/142–3
antibiotics, 2/176–7
antibodies, 2/177
antigens, 2/177
antiseptics, 2/179
bacteria, 3/288–9
Banting, Sir Frederick, 3/302–3
Blackwell, Elizabeth, 3/358
body scanners, 3/363
cancer, 4/455
contagious diseases, 6/649–50
dentistry, 6/717
disease, 6/736–40
Drew, Charles, 7/763
drugs, 7/767–9, 7/*767–9*
Ehrlich, Paul, 7/811
fever, 8/926, 8/*926*
first aid, 8/938–40, 8/*939–40*
Fleming, Sir Alexander, 8/953
forensic science, 8/986
fractures, 9/999
health, 10/1163–5
Hippocrates, 10/1187
Holmes, Oliver Wendell Sr., 10/1195
homeopathic, 10/1196–7
hospitals, 10/1209–11, 10/*1209–11*
immunity, 10/1244
Jenner, Edward, 11/1328–9
Lister, Joseph, 12/1445
mental health, 13/1562–3
nursing, 15/1808–9
Pasteur, Louis, 16/1883–4
plant products, 16/1951

poisons, 16/1961–2
preventive, 13/1554
public health, 13/1554, 17/2021–2
Reed, Walter, 17/2074–5
Salk, Jonas, 18/2156
sterilization, 13/1553
surgery, 19/2357–8, 19/*2357–8*
veterinary, 21/2522
X rays, 22/2629–31
Medicine Hat, 1/90
Medicine men, 12/1481–2
Medieval times *see* Middle Ages
Medina, 11/1307, 18/2166
Meditation, 17/2080
yoga, 22/2634–5
Mediterranean Sea, 13/**1556–7**, 13/*1556*
Medium of Exchange, 14/1630–1
Medulla, 4/384
Medullosa, 16/*1952*
Medusa, 5/590, 9/1092, 11/1328, 16/1902
Megalopolis, 5/557
Megatherium, 13/1500
Meiji, Emperor, 20/2432
Meiosis, 5/502–3, 17/2087
Meir, Golda, 13/**1557**, 13/*1557*
Mekong River, 11/1351, 11/1352, 12/1391, 21/2525
Mekrou River, 3/330
Melanesia, 13/**1557–8**, 13/*1557–8*, 15/1750, 15/1854
climate, 13/1557
land, 13/1557
life in, 13/1558
people, 13/1557–8
Melanin, 10/1138, 18/2233
Melbourne, 3/266
Melcher, Frederic G., 4/433, 15/1744
Melilla, 19/2298
Mellon, Andrew, 10/1152
Melody, music, 14/1683
Melpomene, 14/1678
Melville, Herman, 12/1447, 13/**1558–9**, 13/*1559*
Membranes, 2/145
Memorial Day, 13/**1559–60**
Memory, 13/**1560–1***, 13/*1560*
Memphis, Egypt, 4/430, 7/808
Memphis, Tennesee, 20/2404
Menagerie, 5/552
Mende, 18/2218
Mendeleev, Dmitri, 7/*828*, 7/830
Mendel, Gregor, 3/375, 8/887, 9/1051, 13/**1561–2**, 13/*1561*, 16/1942
Mendelssohn, Felix, 13/**1562**, 13/*1562*
Menelik I, 7/871
Menelik II, 7/872
Menes, Pharoah, 7/808
Menhir, 2/*175*
Menkaure, 17/2033
Mennonites, 10/1139–40, 11/1356
Menominee Indians, 1/100, 13/1580
Menorah, 10/1149, 10/*1149*
Menotti, Gian-Carlo, 15/1835
Mensheviks, 19/2286
Mental diseases, 6/739
Mental health, 13/1554, 13/**1562–3**, 13/*1563*
Dix, Dorothea, 6/744
emotions, 7/841–2
Freud, Sigmund, 9/1012

see also Psychiatry; Psychoanalysis; Psychology
Mental retardation, education, 19/2304
Menuhin, Yehudi, 14/*1692*
Menus, 17/2093
Meperidine, 14/1703
Mercator, Gerardus, 3/256, 3/*256*, 13/1510, 13/1511
Mercator projection, 13/*1510*, 13/1511
Mercedes-Benz, 3/273
Mercenaries, 2/225
Merchant marine, 13/**1564**, 13/*1564*
Merchant Marine Academy, 21/2498
Merchants, guilds, 10/1124–5
Merchant ships, 18/2111, 18/2206
Mercia, 2/143
Mercury (god), 6/702, 9/1089
Mercury (planet), 19/2257, 19/2261
basic facts, 19/2259
Mercury spacecraft, 19/2291, 19/2294
Mergansers, 7/771
Meridians, 11/1288, 12/1395
Merino sheep, 18/2201
Merlin, 2/236
Mermaids, 2/160, 2/*160*, 13/**1564–5**, 13/*1564*
Merrill, Bob, 14/1687
Merrimack, 14/**1634–5**, 14/*1634*, 14/1728
Merrimack River, 15/1751
Merry-andrews, 5/583
Merton, Thomas, 14/1629
Merychippus, 10/*1204*
Mesabi Range, 13/1606
Mesa Verde National Park, 5/604, 5/574–5, 5/*574*
Mescal cactus, 4/428
Meseta, 19/2298
Mesocarp, 9/1016
Mesohippus, 10/*1204*
Mesolithic period, 19/2336
Mesopotamia, 3/286, 13/**1565**, 13/*1565*, 19/2352
kings, 11/1368
law, 2/137
pottery, 16/*1988*, 16/1989
Mesosphere, 3/257
Mesozoic era, 7/786, 17/*1996*
Messerschmidt aircraft, 9/*1067*
Messiah, 11/1344
Mestizos, 5/536, 7/837–8, 11/*1268*, 16/1875, 19/2272, 21/2515
Metabolic diseases, 6/739
Metabolism, 7/863, 13/**1565–6**
Metacomet, 11/1270
Metal, 13/**1566–9**, 13/*1566–8*
alloys, 13/1568–9
building materials, 4/407
casting, 6/728
characteristics, 13/1566–7
color, 13/1566
conductivity, 13/1567
corrosion, 6/661
dies, 6/728, 6/*728*
ductibility, 13/1567
extrusion, 6/728
fusibility, 13/1567
hardness, 13/1567
luster, 13/1566
malleability, 13/1567

(continued)

refining, 13/1567–8
silver, 18/2225
tenacity, 13/1567
see also individual metals
Metallurgical engineers, 7/851
Metallurgy, 7/851, 13/1568
Metalworking, 11/1273
Metamorphic rocks, 17/*2108*, 17/2109
Metamorphosis, 4/420, 13/**1569–70**, 13/*1569–70*, 14/1626
Metaphysics, 16/1915
Metastasis, 4/455
Metazoa, 2/158
Meteorites, 8/888, 13/1570–1
Meteoroids, 19/2260
Meteorological satellites, 18/2165
Meteorology, 9/1055, 9/1056, 21/2563
see also weather
Meteors, 3/257, 13/**1570–1**, 13/*1570–1*, 17/2036, 19/2260
Methadone, 14/1703
Methane, 14/1713
Methodist church, 17/2013
Wesley, John and Charles, 21/2568
Methodius, 18/2143
Metrical verse, 16/1960
Metric system, 6/732, 13/1545, 13/1547, 13/**1571**
decimal numbers, 6/706
Metropolitan areas, 5/556–7
Metropolitan Opera, New York, 2/140
Mexican War, 1/117, 10/1217, 13/**1571–2**, 13/*1572*, 14/1728, 16/1969
Mexico, 2/217, 5/506, 13/**1572–6**, 13/*1572–5*
Aztecs, 3/280
and California, 4/438
Cibola, 5/549
climate, 13/1573–4
Cortés, Hernando, 6/662
Hidalgo y Costilla, Miguel, 10/1184
history, 13/1575–6
Juárez, Benito, 11/1344
land, 13/1572–3
Mexico City, 13/1576–7
natural resources, 13/1574–5
people, 13/1575
Texas and, 20/2412–14
Villa, Pancho, 21/2529
Mexico City, 3/284, 8/951, 11/1259, 13/1572, 13/1573, 13/1575, 13/**1576–7**, 13/*1576*
Meyer, Debbie, 20/2366
Mezzo-sopranos, 18/2227
Miami, 8/*957*
Miami Indians, 11/1256, 15/1824, 21/2596
Mice, 17/*2065–7*, 17/*2065–6*
pet, 16/1906–7
Michael I Romanov, Csar, 18/2146
Michelangelo Buonarotti, 2/232, 2/*233*, 5/503, 7/761, 8/956, 11/*13434*, 13/1551, 13/**1577–8**, 13/*1577–8*, 17/2062, 17/2084, 18/2178,
David, 13/1577, 13/*1578*
Moses, 13/1577, 13/*1577*
Pietá, 17/*2085*
Sistine Chapel, 13/1577–8, 15/1859, 15/*1860*
Michener, James, 14/1687

Michigan, 13/**1578–81**, 13/*1578–80*
Antoine Cadillac, 4/429
climate, 13/1580
employment, 13/1581
history, 13/1580–1
land, 13/1578–80
map, 13/*1579*
state emblems, 13/*1579*
Michigan, Lake, 9/1107–8
Michigan University, 6/724
Mickey Mouse, 1/*28*
Micmac Indians, 17/2002, 17/2038
Microchips, 7/826, 7/827, 7/828
calculators, 4/432
computers, 5/*621*, 5/622
Microcomputers, 7/*803*
Microfiche, 12/1425
Microfilm, 12/1425, 13/**1581**, 13/*1581*
Micrometallography, 13/1569
Micronesia, 13/**1581–2**, 13/*1582*, 15/1854
Microprobes, 7/850–1
Microscopes, 5/501, 12/1415–16, 13/**1583–4**, 13/*1583–4*
compound, 13/1583, 13/*1583*
electron, 13/1583–4, 13/*1584*
Microwave ovens, 13/1584, 13/*1584*
Microwaves, 13/**1584**, 13/*1584*
Microwaving, 6/655
Midas, 13/**1584**, 13/*1585*
Mid-Atlantic Ridge, 3/254
Middle Ages, 13/**1585–9**, 13/*1585–9*
alchemy, 18/*2172*
arts, 13/1588–9
businesses, 13/1588
castles, 8/990, 8/*990*, 13/1586, 13/*1586*
church, 13/1585
costume, 8/912, 8/*912*
Crusades, 13/1588
education, 13/1588
end of, 13/1589
feudalism, 8/925–6, 8/*925*
flags, 8/*952*
folk song, 8/*972*
fur clothes, 9/1023
harbors, 10/1150
houses, 10/1213, 10/1214, 10/*1214*
important events, 13/1587
knights, 12/1371–2
Magna Carta, 12/1483
medicine, 13/1553
navies, 14/1727
needlework, 14/1735
prisons, 17/2006
puppets, 17/2031
Rome, 9/1025
ships, 18/2206
shoes, 18/2213
theater, 20/2420–1
towns, 13/1588
trade, 20/2444
village life, 13/1585
witchcraft, 21/2598–9
Middleby, 3/*274*
Middle distance races, 20/2440–1
Middle ear, 7/778, 7/*779*
Middle East, 8/880, 13/**1589–91**, 13/*1590–1*
Crusades, 6/678–80
history, 13/1590–1
land, 13/1590
Lawrence of Arabia, 12/1400–1
people, 13/1589

Middle English, 7/860–1
Middle Kingdom, 7/808–9
Middlemen, 18/2188
Middle names, 14/1698
Midnight sun, 2/*209*
Midocean ridges, 21/2535
Midway Island, battle of, 3/319
Midway Islands, 16/1971
Midwife toad, 2/*131*
Mies van der Rohe, Ludwig, 2/205–6
Migration, 2/151, 13/**1591–4**, 13/*1592–4*, 18/2184
birds, 13/1591, 13/*1592–4*, 14/1720
ducks, geese and swans, 7/771
fish, 13/1594
insects, 13/1594
lemmings, 12/1413
mammals, 13/1591–2
people, 10/1243
population, 16/1979
Mihrab, 14/1654, 14/*1654*
Mikkola, Heikki, 14/*1666*
Mildews, plant diseases, 16/1943
Mile race, 20/2440–1
Military Academy, 5/597, 21/2497–8
Military Airlift Command (MAC), 1/61–2
Military dictatorships, 9/1095
Military law, 12/1400
mutiny, 14/1694–5
Military parks, 14/1709
Militia, 2/226
National Guard, 14/1707–8
Militiades, 3/318
Milk, 15/1811, 15/*1811*
condensed, 6/692
dairy cows, 4/394, 6/691–2
dairy products, 6/692–3
homogenized, 6/692
pasteurized, 6/692
powdered, 6/692
skim, 6/692
sour, 6/692
Milk cheese, 5/516–17
Milking parlors, 6/692
Milking shorthorn cattle, 4/495
Milk teeth, 20/2387
Milkweed butterfly, 4/*420*
Milky Way, 13/**1594**, 13/*1595*, 19/2287, 19/2326, 19/2327
Millay, Edna St Vincent, 12/*1450*
Miller, Arthur, 7/760
Miller, Glen, 11/1325
Millet, Jean François, 17/2068
The Sower, 17/2068, 17/*2068*
Millett, Kate, 21/2601
Millikan, Robert A., 3/259
Millinery, 10/1157
Milling, 8/960
Millipedes, 5/504, 5/*504*
Milne, A.A., 5/532, 13/**1594–5**, 13/*1595*
Milosz, Czeslaw, 12/1451
Milton, John, 13/**1595**, 13/*1595*
Mimbars, 14/1654
Mime, 1/27, 16/1870
Mimicry, 17/2012
Mimosa pudica, 16/*1940*
Minarets, 11/1307
Mindanao, 16/1913
Minden, 14/1734
Minelayers, 14/1728
Mineral dyes, 7/777
Mineralogy, 9/1055

Minerals, 13/**1596–9**, 13/*1596–9*
color, 13/1597
crystal structure, 13/1598
crystals, 6/683
diet, 21/2534–5
formation, 13/1597
gemstones, 9/1049–50
geology, 9/1055–7
gold, 9/1089–90, 9/*1089–90*
harness, 13/1597
indentifying, 13/1597–8
index of refraction, 13/1598
luster, 13/1597
metallic, 13/1597
naming, 13/1597
non-metallic, 13/1597
rocks, 13/1596–7
sea, 15/1817, 15/*1818–19*
specific gravity, 13/1598
streak, 13/1598
structure, 13/1596
useful minerals, 13/159
Mineral tanning, 12/1408
Miner bees, 3/325
Mines and mining, 13/**1599–1602**, 13/*1599–1602*
coal, 5/585–6, 5/*585–6*
conserving minerals, 13/1602
gold, 9/190–1
iron ore, 11/1302
methods, 13/1600–1
ocean minerals, 15/1817, 15/*1818–19*
prospecting, 13/1599–1600
safety, 13/1601–2
Minesweepers, 14/1728
Ming dynasty, 5/538
Miniatures, 13/**1602–3***, 13/*1603*
Minibikes, 14/1667
Minibuses, 4/419
Minicycles, 14/1667
Minimum security prisons, 17/2007
Mining engineers, 7/851
Minis, 3/*275*
Miniskirt, 5/*580*
Mink, 5/559, 9/*1022*, 21/2560
Minneapolis, 13/1604, 13/*1604*
Minnesota, 13/**1603–6**, 13/*1604–6*
climate, 13/1603
employment, 13/1606
history, 13/1604–6
land, 13/1603
map, 13/*1605*
state emblems, 13/*1605*
Minoans, 1/39, 9/1111
art, 2/136–7, 9/1114–15
decline, 2/137
summary, 2/134
Minority Whip, 6/629
Minor plants, 2/246
Minos, King, 6/691, 13/1543
Minotaur, 6/691, 13/1543, 13/*1543*
Minstrels, 1/26, 4/470
Minting coins, 5/592
Minuend, 2/213
Minuit, Peter, 6/714, 15/1767
Minuteman missiles, 1/125, 21/*2560*
Miocene Epoch, 7/786
mammals, 13/1499
Miracle plays, 1/26, 7/759, 20/2420
Miraflores Locks, 16/1868
Mirages, 13/**1606–7**, 13/*1606–7*
Miró, Joan, 20/2380
Mirrors, 13/**1607–8***, 13/*1606–7*

Misdemeanours, 6/673
Miskey, John, 19/2321
Missiles, 13/**1608–9**, 13/*1608–9*
Missionaries, 13/**1610**, 13/*1610*
 Livingstone, David, 12/1454
 Schweitzer, Albert, 18/2171
 Theresa, Mother, 20/2408–9
Mississippi, 8/893, 13/**1610–14**/, 13/*1611–13*
 climate, 13/1612
 employment, 13/1613
 history, 13/1612–13
 land, 13/1610–12
 map, 13/*1611*
 state emblem, 13/*1611*
Mississippi kites, 3/348
Mississippi River, 10/1240, 11/1295, 11/1296, 11/1360, 12/1464, 13/1518, 13/1610, 13/**1614–15**, 13/*1614–15*, 16/1930, 20/2403
Missouri, 13/**1615–19**, 13/*1616–19*
 climate, 13/1616
 employment, 13/1618
 history, 13/1616–18
 land, 13/1615–16
 map, 13/*1617*
 state emblems, 13/*1617*
Missouri Compromise:, 5/571, 14/1638
Missouri River, 11/1295, 13/1614, 13/1615, 13/1640, 14/1732, 15/1790, 19/2277
Missouri, U.S.S., 12/1473
Mistletoe, 16/1876–7
Mistrals, 21/2592
Mitchell, Billy, 1/63
Mitchell, Mount, 2/183
Mithras, 18/*2120*
Mitosis, 5/502, 17/2088
Mitten, Michigan, 13/1580
Mitterand, François, 9/1010
Mixtecs, 11/*1258*
Mix, Tom, 14/1659
Mnemonic aids, 13/1561
Mnemosyne, 14/1677
Moa, 3/343
Mobile, Alabama, 1/84
Mobile Bay, battle of, 8/910
Mobile homes, 10/1215, 20/2470
Mobiles, 18/2178
Mobutu, Joseph Désiré, 22/2642
Mobutu Sese Seko, Lake, 15/1776
Moby Dick, 13/1559
Mocha, 5/591
Mockingbirds, 9/*1037*, 14/*1719*
Model making, 14/**1619★**, 14/*1619*
Model T Ford, 3/273, 3/276, 8/985
Modems, 5/624
Modern architecture, 2/201, 2/204–6
Modern art, 14/**1620–1**, 14/*1620–1*
Modern dance, 6/696
 Duncan, Isadore, 7/774
Modoc War, 1/120
Modred, Sir, 2/236
Modular construction, 6/648–9
Modular housing, 10/1214–15
Moebius strip, 13/1535
Moengo, 19/2359
Mogadishu, 19/2261
Mogollon Indians, 2/215
Moguls, India, 11/1254
Mohammed Riza Pahlavi, 11/1299
Mohave Desert, 4/436, 6/720, 14/**1622**, 14/*1622*

Mohave River, 14/1622
Mohawk Indians, 11/1304
Mohawk River, 15/1766
Mohéli, 5/617
Mohegan Indians, 6/636
Mohole Project, 7/784
Mohs's Scale, 13/*1598*
Moi, Daniel Arap, 11/1364
Moirai, 8/915
Molars, 20/2386–7
Molasses, 19/2351
Mold, 9/1020
Moldavia, 18/2126, 19/2282
Molds, 6/728, 6/*728*
 antibiotics, 2/176–7
 casting, 18/2179
 fermentation, 8/922
Molecular physics, 16/1923
Molecules, 3/258, 13/1536
 chemistry, 5/520, 5/521
Mole rats, 18/*2115*
Moles, 5/559, 14/**1622–4**, 14/*1622–3*
Molière, 9/1008
Molina, Rafael Trujillo, 21/2570
Mollusks, 2/156, 5/570, 14/**1624–6**, 14/*1624–6*, 15/1822–3
 cephalopods, 14/1625
 classification, 14/1625
 common features, 14/1624
 destructive, 14/1626
 gastrapods, 14/1625
 internal anatomy, 14/1624
 pelecypods, 14/1625
 reproduction, 14/1625
 shells, 14/1624, 18/2202
 snails, 19/2243–4, 19/*2243*
 valuable, 14/1626
Molting, 14/**1626–7**, 14/*1626*
 insect, 11/1281
Molucca Islands, 12/1481
Mombasa, 11/1363
Monaco, 14/**1627–8**, 14/*1627–8*
Monaco-Ville, 14/1627
Monarch butterfly, 4/421
Monarchs, 11/1367–8
Monarchy, republics and, 17/2091
Monastic life, 13/1585, 14/**1628–9**, 14/*1628*
Moncton, 15/1746
Mondale, Walter, 4/476, 21/*2523*
Monday, 6/702
Mondrian, Piet, 1/*19*, 14/1621
Monégasque, 14/1628
Monet, Claude, 10/1245, 10/1246, 10/*1246*, 14/**1629–30★**, 14/*1629*, 17/2085
Money, 14/**1630–3**, 14/*1630–2*
 ancient civilizations, 2/137
 banking, 3/300–2
 barter, 14/1630
 checks, 14/1631–2
 coin dies, 6/728, 6/*728*
 coins, 5/*592*, 14/1631
 counterfeiting, 6/665
 credit cards, 14/1631–2
 inflation, 7/799, 7/*799*
 interest, 11/1285–6
 medium of exchange, 14/1630–1
 paper money, 14/1631, 14/*1631*, 14/*1632*
 United States, 14/1632–3
Mongolia, 14/**1633–4**, 14/*1633*, 15/1780
 Gobi Desert, 9/1087, 9/*1087*

Mongoloids, 2/242
Mongols, 2/244, 16/1890, 18/2145
 Genghis Khan, 9/1053–4
Mongoose, 4/469
Monhegan, 12/1485
Monitor, 14/**1634–5**, 14/*1634*, 14/1728
Monkey-puzzle trees, 6/633
Monkeys, 2/*151*, 13/1497, 14/**1635–7**, 14/*1636–7*
 see also apes
Monks, 5/546, 13/1585, 14/1628–9, 18/2122
Monk seal, 13/*1497*
Monk, Thelonius, 11/1325, 11/*1325*
Monmouth, New Jersey, battle of, 15/1756
Monoa, 7/814
Monocacy River, 13/1524
Monocotyledons, 3/374, 8/964, 16/1947, 16/*1949*
Mono Indians, 4/436
Monomoy Island, 21/2585
Monoplacophora, 14/1625
Monopolies, 7/799, 17/2025
Monorails, 17/2059, 20/2453
Mono River, 3/330
Monotheism, 17/2079
Monotremes, 16/1957, 19/2315
Monotype, 20/2481
Monreale Abbey Church, 18/*2124*
Monroe Doctrine, 1/31, 14/1637, 14/1638, 14/**1639**
Monroe, James, 1/31, 11/1262, 12/1422, 12/1467, 14/**1637–9**, 14/*1638*
Monroe, Marilyn, 14/*1663*
Monrovia, 12/1421, 12/1422
Mons, battle of, 21/*2605*
Monsoon, 2/239, 4/415, 11/*1251*, 11/1252, 11/1351–2, 14/**1639–40**, 14/*1639–40*
Monsters, 2/161–2
Montagnais Indians, 1/100
Montana, 14/**1640–3**, 14/*1640–3*
 climate, 14/1640–2
 employment, 14/1643
 history, 14/1642–3
 land, 14/1640
 map, 14/*1641*
 state emblems, 14/*1641*
Montaña, Peru, 16/1903
Montcalm, Marquis de, 3/319, 4/447, 9/*1005*, 9/1006
Monte Carlo, 14/1627
Monte Carlo Grand Prix, 14/1627–8
Monte Cassino, 14/*1628*
Montenegrins, 22/2639
Monterey Canyon, 4/458
Monterey pine, 6/631
Monterrey, 13/1573
Montezuma, Emperor, 3/284, 6/662, 13/1575
Montgolfier, Jacques, 3/280, 3/297–8
Montgolfier, Joseph, 3/280, 3/297–8
Montgolfier, Marianne, 3/297
Montgomery, Alabama, 1/83, 6/625, 11/1366
Montgomery, Bernard, 22/2617
Montgomery Bus Boycott, 5/563
Months, 14/**1643–4**, 14/*1643*
 April, 2/185–6
 August, 3/260–1
 December, 6/705–6
 February, 8/919–20

January, 11/1321
July, 11/1346–7
June, 11/1347–8
March, 13/1512–13, 13/*1512*
May, 13/1540
November, 15/1802–3
October, 15/1821–2, 15/*1821*
September, 18/2191–2
Monticello, 11/1327, 11/*1327*
Montmartre, 16/1877
Montpelier, 21/2516
Montreal, 4/*451*, 14/**1644**, 14/*1644*
Mont St Michel 9/*999*
Monument Valley, 21/*2505*
Moomba Festival, 3/268
Moon, 14/**1644–8**, 14/*1645–8*
 basic facts, 19/2259
 eclipses, 7/792–3, 7/*792–3*
 flights to, 19/2290
 gravity, 14/1647
 landings, 1/94–5, 2/224, 5/597
 orbit, 14/1646, 15/1837
 origin, 14/1646
 phases, 2/249, 14/1647–8, 14/*1647*
 rock, 14/1646, 14/*1648*
 surface, 14/1646–7
 temperature, 14/1647
 tides, 20/2425
Moon jelly, 11/1328
Moon Lake, 18/*2219*
Moon landings, 9/*1057*
Moore, Clement C., 5/533
Moore, Henry, 2/*230*, 18/2178, 18/*2179*
Moors, 13/1538
 in Spain, 5/550, 19/2298, 19/2301
Moose, 6/709–10, 6/*709*
Moose Jaw, 18/2164
Mopti, 12/*1492*
Moraine, Lake, 12/*1385*
Morality plays, 1/26
Morals, fables, 8/900
Moravia, 6/689
Mordants, 7/777
Morehead Planetarium, Chapel Hill, 16/1937
Mores, 6/687
More, Sir Thomas, 10/1177, 10/1193, 14/**1648**, 14/*1648*, 16/1981, 16/*1981*, 20/2437,
Morgan, Edwin D., 2/235
Morgan, Henry, 16/1934–5
Morgan horses, 10/1206
Mormans, 10/1242, 12/1396, 12/*1396*, 15/1743, 17/2013, 21/2504–5
 Smith, Joseph, 19/2241
 Young, Brigham, 22/2636
Morning glory, 18/*2192*
Morocco, 11/1369, 14/**1648–9**, 14/*1649*, 19/2262
 Ibn Battuta, 10/1232
Moropus, 13/*1499*
Morphine, 14/1703
Morphology, plant, 3/375
Morris dancers, 8/*970*
Morrison Planetarium, San Francisco, 16/1937
Morris, Robert, 18/2138
Morristown, 15/1756
Morse Code, 14/1650, 14/**1651**, 14/*1651*, 18/2221, 20/2389
Morse, Samuel F.B., 5/611, 11/1292, 14/**1650**, 14/*1650*, 14/1651, 20/2389

Morse, Wayne, 17/2023
Morta, 8/915
Mortimer's Cross, battle of, 7/805
Morton, J. Sterling, 14/1732
Morton, William, 2/143, 13/1553
Mosaic, 14/**1651–3***, 14/*1651–2*
  Roman, 18/2120
Mosaic Code, 6/673
Moscow, 14/**1653**, 14/*1653*, 18/2145,
  21/2535
  climate, 19/2282
  Kremlin, 12/1379, 12/*1379*
  Red Square, 14/1653, 14/*1653*
  subway, 19/2349, 19/*2349*
Moscow Canal, 14/1653
Moses, 11/*1334*, 11/1335, 11/1344,
  16/1883, 17/2074
Moses, Grandma, 2/228
Moshesh I, King, 12/1418
Moshoeshoe II, King, 12/1418
Moskva River, 14/1653
Mosques, 2/*243*, 4/430, 11/*1299*,
  11/*1307*, 14/**1654**, 14/*1654*
Mosquito Coast, 15/1771
Mosquitoes, 14/**1654–5**, 14/*1655*
Mosquito Indians, 15/1771
Mosses, 14/**1655–6**, 14/*1655*,
  16/1939, 16/1947
Mote-and-bailey, 4/*483*
Motels, 10/1212
Motets, 5/544
Mother Carey's chickens, 18/2181
Mother countries, 5/598
Mother-of-pearl, 16/1888, 18/2202
Moths, 4/419–22, 4/*420*, 4/*421*
Motion, 14/**1656–7***, 14/*1656–7*
  animals, 2/158–60, 2/*158–60*
  forces and, 8/983–4, 8/*984*
  friction, 9/1012–13, 9/*1012–13*
  gravity, 9/1105–6
  gyroscopes, 10/1134–5, 10/*1135*
  laws of, 7/848
  perpetual, 16/1900–1, 16/*1900*
  relativity, 17/2078
Motion pictures, 14/**1658–64**,
  14/*1658–64*
  Academy Awards, 1/21, 14/1660–1
  acting, 1/27–8
  beginning of sound, 14/1662–3
  censorship, 5/504
  Chaplin, Charlie, 5/511
  Disney, Walt, 6/740
  documentaries, 14/1663
  early days, 14/1659
  European, 14/1662
  future, 14/1664
  Griffith, D.W., 9/1119–20
  Hollywood era, 14/1659–62
  making, 14/1658–9
  surrealism, 19/2360
  television and, 14/1663–4
Motivation:
  learning, 12/1407
  psychology, 17/2018–19
Motorboats, 3/362
Motorcycles, 14/**1666–7**, 14/*1666–7*
Motor nerves, 14/1740
Motors, 14/**1664–6**, 14/*1665*
  electric, 7/816–17, 7/*817*
Motor scooters, 14/1667
Motor vehicles:
  driving, 7/764–6
  parts of, 7/765–6
  see also Automobiles; Trucks

Mott, Lucretia, 21/2600
Mouflon, 10/*1202*, 18/*2201*
Mound Builders, 11/1295–6, 15/1824
Mounds State Park, 11/1258
Mountain beaver, 3/322
Mountain climbing, 14/**1671–2**,
  14/*1671*
  Hillary, Sir Edmund, 10/1185
Mountain gorillas, 17/2065
Mountain hares, 17/*2039*
Mountain lions, 2/*146*, 4/488
Mountains, 7/780, 14/**1668–71**,
  14/*1668–70*
  animal life, 2/150
  avalanches, 3/279–80
  cable cars, 4/426, 4/427
  climate and, 5/576
  formation, 7/782
  highest known, 14/1669
  interesting, 14/1670
  Rocky Mountains, 17/2112–13,
   17/*2112*
  skiing, 18/2230–3
  wildflowers, 21/2587
Mountbatten, Lord Louis, 22/2617
Mount Desert Island, 12/1485
Mounties, 18/2140, 18/*2140*
Mount Palomar Observatory, 15/1813
Mount Robson Park, 4/*444*
Mount Rushmore National Memo-
  rial, 14/1709
Mounts *see under individual names eg*
  Katmai, Mount
Mount Vernon house, 2/*17921/2547*,
  21/2548, 21/*2548*
Mourning dove, 16/1929, 16/*1929*
Mousht, 9/1031
Moussorgsky, Modest, 17/2103
Mouth, taste, 20/2381
Mouth organs, 10/1153
Mouths, digestion, 6/730
Mouth-to-mouth breathing, 2/237,
  2/237
Movement:
  animals, 2/158–60, 2/*158–60*
  snakes, 19/2245
Movie cameras, 4/441
Movies *see* Motion pictures
Mowhawk Indians, 8/950
Mozambique, 14/**1672–3**, 14/*1672–3*
Mozart, Leopold, 14/1673
Mozart, Maria Anna, 14/1673
Mozart, Wolfgang Amadeus, 3/269,
  5/*619*, 14/**1673**, 14/*1673*, 14/1705
Mswati III, King, 19/2362
Mubarak, Muhammad Hosni, 7/807
Mucin, 6/730
Mucous membrane, 15/1799
Mud daubers, 21/2549
Mud houses, 18/2204, 18/*2204*
Mudpuppy, 18/2155
Mud slides, 3/280
Muezzin, 11/1307, 14/1654
Mugabe, Robert, 22/2645
Muggers, 1/103
Muhammad, 2/191–2, 2/*191*,
  11/1306–7, 14/**1673–4**, 14/*1674*,
  18/2166
Muhammad II, Sultan, 15/1850
Muhammad, Elijah, 3/357, 3/*357*,
  12/1491
Mukluks, 7/868
Mulattoes, 6/684, 19/2272
Mulch, 9/*1041*

Mule deer, 6/709
Mules, 7/755
Mullens, Priscilla, 16/1931
Mulroney, Brian, 14/**1674**, 14/*1674*
Multilateral disarmament, 6/736
Multiple-arch dams, 6/694
Multiplicands, 2/214
Multiplication, 2/213–14
Multipliers, 2/214
Mumps, 5/528, 6/649
Munch, Edvard, 8/896–7, 8/*896*
Muncie, 11/1258
Munich, Cuvilliers Theater, 20/*2421*
Municipal government, 12/1457
Murchison Falls, 15/1776
Murder, 14/**1675**
  assassination, 2/245
  United States, 21/2497
Murfreesboro, 2/220
Muridae, 17/2065
Murmansk, 2/208
Murray-Darling Rivers, 14/**1675**,
  14/*1675*
Musalla, 14/1654
Muscles, 14/**1675–7**, 14/*1675–7*
  cells, 5/502
Muses, 9/1089, 14/**1677–8**, 14/*1678*
Museum beetles, 3/326
Museums, 14/**1678–80**, 14/*1678–80*
  art, 2/238
  Smithsonian Institution, 19/2241–2
Mushet, Robert F., 11/1303
Mushrooms, 9/1021, 14/**1680–1**,
  14/*1681*
  poisonous, 16/1961, 16/1963
Music, 14/**1681–7***, 14/*1681–4*
  Bach family, 2/287
  bands, 15/1838–40
  Beethoven, Ludwig van, 3/325
  Beatles, The, 16/1978
  bells, 3/329
  Bernstein, Leonard, 3/333
  Brahms, Johannes, 4/381–2
  calliope, 4/439
  choral, 5/**543–4**
  compact discs, 5/**617**
  composers, 5/**618–20**
  Copland, Aaron, 6/657–8
  Debussy, Claude, 6/704–5
  duration, 14/1682
  electronic, 7/824–5, 7/*824*
  Elgar, Edgar William, 7/834
  folk song, 8/972–3, 8/*972–3*
  Foster, Stephen, 8/995
  Gershwin, George, 9/1072
  Gilbert and Sullivan, 9/1077
  Grieg, Edvard, 9/1119
  Handel, George Frederick, 10/1144
  Handy, W.C., 10/1147
  harmony, 14/1683
  Haydn, Franz Joseph, 10/1161
  intensity, 14/1682
  jazz, 11/1324–6, 11/*1325–6*
  Liszt, Franz, 12/1445
  Mahler, Gustav, 12/1484
  melody, 14/1683
  Mendelssohn, Felix, 13/1562
  Mozart, Wolfgang Amadeus,
   14/1673
  musicians, 14, /1684, 14/1685
  notation, 14/1683–5
  opera, 15/1834–5
  operetta, 15/1835
  orchestras, 15/1838–40

  pitch, 14/1682
  popular music, 16/1977–8
  Prokofiev, Sergei, 17/2008
  Rachmaninoff, Sergei, 17/2041–2
  recordings, 17/2071–3
  Rimsky-Korsakov, Nicolai,
   17/2103
  Rococo, 17/2114
  Schubert, Franz, 18/2170–1
  Sibelius, Jean, 18/2217
  singing, 18/2226–8, 18/*2227–8*
  sound, 14/1682, 19/2264–5
  Sousa, John Philip, 19/2265–6,
   19/*2266*
  Strauss, Johann, 19/2340
  Stravinsky, Igor, 19/2340
  Tchaikovsky, Peter Ilyich,
   20/*2383–4*, 20/*2383*
  terms, 14/1685–6
  tone, 14/1682
  tone quality, 14/1682–3, 14/1689
  types, 14/1681–2
  Verdi, Giuseppe, 21/2516
  Wagner, Richard, 21/2538
  see also Musical instruments
Musical comedies, 14/**1687–8**,
  14/*1687*
Musical instruments, 14/**1688–93***,
  14/*1688–92*
  bagpipes, 3/291
  brass instruments, 4/384–6, 4/*385*
  harmonica, 10/1153
  harps, 10/1153, 10/*1153*
  organs, 15/1844–5, 15/*1844*
  percussion instruments, 16/1897–8,
   16/*1897–8*
  piano, 16/1924–5, 16/*1924–5*
  stringed instruments, 19/2343–5
  woodwind instruments, 21/2602–3,
   21/*2602–3*
  xylophones, 22/2631, 22/*2631*
Musicals, motion pictures, 14/1663
Music boxes, 14/**1693**, 14/*1693*
Musicologists, 5/620, 14/1684
Muskets, 10/1130
  manufacture, 13/1507
Muskogean Indians, 12/1464
Muskogean-speaking Indians, 6/672
Muskrats, 5/559
Muslims, 2/191–2, 3/366, 11/1306–7,
  17/*2080*
  in Africa, 1/48
  Crusades, 6/678–80
  India, 11/1254
  mosques, 14/1654, 14/*1654*
  Muhammad, 14/1673–4
  Pakistan, 15/1864
  prayer carpets, 15/1846–7, 15/*1847*
Mussolini, Benito, 8/911, 8/*911*,
  9/1095, 11/1311, 11/1312,
  13/1514, 14/**1693–4**, 14/*1694*,
  22/2611, 22/2613, 22/2617
Mustaches, 10/1139–40
Mustangs, 10/1207
Mustard gas, 5/518
Mutations, 8/887, 9/1051
Mute swans, 3/*346*, 7/772
Mutinies, 14/**1694–5**, 14/*1694*
Mutton, 13/1547, 18/2201
Mutualism, 7/795, 20/2369, 20/*2370*
Muybridge, Eadweard, 14/1659
Mwali, 5/617
Mycelium, 9/*1021*, 14/1680
Mycenae, 13/*1526*

Mycenaeans, 1/39, 9/1111
Myerson, Morris, 13/1557
My Fair Lady, 1/28, 14/1687,
    14/*1687*
Myofibril, 14/1676
Myra, 15/1772
Myron, 9/*1114*, 9/1115
Mystery plays, 1/26, 20/2420
Mystery stories, 5/534
Mythology, 12/1411, 14/**1695–7**,
    14/*1695–6*
  animal, 2/160–3
  Beowulf, 3/331
  Daedalus, 6/691
  elves and fairies, 7/839
  fairytales, 8/904–5
  Fates, 8/915
  flying, 3/280
  folktales, 8/971
  giants, 9/1075–6, 9/*1076*
  gods and godesses, 9/1087–9
  gorgons, 9/1092–3, 9/*1093*
  Greek, 10/1181
  Jason, 11/1324
  Midas, 13/1584
  muses, 14/1677–8
  Pandora, 16/1870
  sphinx, 19/2310
  see also Legends

Nn

Namgyal, Prince, 18/2224
Naber, Mark, 20/2366
Nacal, 12/1489
Nacre, 16/1888
Na-Dené languages, 3/253
Nagasaki, 20/2471, 22/2619
Nahuatl, 11/1267
Nails, 5/**571**, 5/*571*
Nairobi, 1/*49*, 11/1363, 11/*1363*
Naismith, James, 3/313, 3/315,
    19/2316
Namath, Joe, 19/2317
Names, 14/**1698–9**
  Chinese, 5/536
  gazetteer, 9/1047
Namib Desert, 1/43, 14/1699
Namibia, 14/**1699–1700**,
    14/*1699–1700*
Nanak, 18/2223
Nanna, 14/1695
Nantucket, 13/1530
Napoleon Bonaparte, 3/319, 8/914,
    8/977, 9/*1007*, 9/1009–10,
    9/1012, 10/1196, 12/1463,
    12/1494, 13/*1519*, 14/**1700–2**,
    14/*1700–2*, 14/1737, 18/2147,
    18/*2148*, 19/2302, 21/2566
  law reforms, 12/1399
  occupies Moscow, 14/1653
  in Russia, 14/*1700*, 14/1701–2
  Waterloo, 21/2553–4, 21/*2554*
Napoleonic Code, 12/1399–1400,
    14/1701
Napoleon II, Emperor, 9/1010,
    14/1701
Napoleon III, Emperor, 3/319
Nara, 15/1857
Narcotics, 1/33, 14/**1702–3**,
    14/*1703*
  drug abuse, 7/769–70

Narraganset Indians, 1/100, 17/2097,
    17/2099
Narragansett Bay, 17/2097
Narrative poetry, 16/1960
Narrative sculpture, 18/2120
Narvaez, Panfilo de, 7/868
Nashville, 20/2404
Nashville basin, 20/2403
Naskapi Indians, 1/100, 17/2038
Nassau, 15/*1785*
Nasser, Gamal Abdel, 7/807,
    14/**1703–4**, 14/*1704*, 19/2351
Nasser, Lake, 15/1776
Nast, Thomas, 4/478
Natal, 3/363, 19/2266
Natchez, Mississippee, 13/1613
Natchez Indians, 13/1612
National Aeronautics and Space Ad-
    ministration (NASA), 1/84,
    2/248, 4/458, 21/2490
National anthems, 14/**1705**, 14/*1705*,
    19/2328
National Association for the Ad-
    vancement of Colored People
    (NAACP), 3/334, 3/355, 5/562,
    14/**1705–6**, 14/*1706*
National Association of Radio and
    Television Broadcasters, 17/2051
National Audubon Society, 3/261
National Basketball Association
    (NBA), 3/315
National Broadcasting Company
    (NBC), 20/2398
National Council of Negro Women,
    3/334
National dances, 8/970
National Elk Refuge, 22/2626
National forests, 14/**1706–7**, 14/*1707*
National Foundation on the Arts and
    the Humanities, 21/2490
National Guard, 2/227, 14/**1707–8**,
    14/*1708*
National Hockey League (NHL),
    10/1235
Nationalism, 14/1704
National Labor Relations Board,
    21/2490
National monuments, 14/**1708**,
    14/*1708*
National Organization for Women
    (NOW), 21/2601
National parks, 14/**1709–13★**,
    14/*1709–13*, 21/2585
  Canadian listed, 14/1712
  US listed, 14/1710
National Park Service, 14/1708,
    14/1709, 14/1712
National Radio Observatory,
    15/1813
National Recovery Administration
    (NRA), 18/2134
National Science Foundation,
    21/2490
National security, Federal Bureau of
    Investigation, 8/920
National sovereignty, 11/1290
National Urban League, 22/2637
National Wildlife Refuges, 3/347
National Woman Suffrage Associa-
    tion, 21/2600
National Women's Political Caucus,
    21/2600
Nation, Carry A., 17/*2007*
Nation of Islam, 3/357

Nations, 14/**1704–5**, 14/*1704*
  republics, 17/2091–2
  see also individual countries
NATO *see* North Atlantic Treaty
  Organization
Natural dyes, 7/777
Natural gas, 9/1019, 9/*1019*,
    14/**1713–14**, 14/*1714*
Natural history, museums, 14/1679
Naturalists:
  Agassiz, Louis, 1/50
  Darwin, Charles, 6/699–700
  Fabre, J. Henri, 8/901
  Huxley, Sir Julian, 10/1229
  Huxley, Thomas Henry, 10/1229
  Linnaeus, Carolus, 12/1442–3
  Thoreau, Henry David, 20/2422–3
  Wallace, Alfred Russel, 21/2539–40
Naturalization, 5/554
Natural resources, 7/798,
    14/**1714–16**, 14/*1714–15*
Natural selection, 8/886, 17/2012
Nature study, 14/**1716–22★**,
    14/*1716–22*
  collections, 5/594
  walks, 14/1717
Nauru, 13/1581, 15/1854
Nauset Marsh, 19/*2361*
Nautilus, 2/209, 6/634, 8/893, 9/1020,
    15/1974, 19/2346
Nautiluses, 14/1625
Nauvoo, 10/1242, 12/1396
Navaho Indians, 2/215, 3/253, 3/*253*,
    11/*1259*, 11/1260, 11/*1267*,
    11/1271, 14/**1722–4**, 14/*1722–3*,
    15/1758
Navaho National Monument, 14/1723
Naval Academy, 5/597, 21/2498
Nave, 4/492
Navies, 14/**1726–31**, 14/*1726–31*
  mutiny, 14/1694–5
Navigation, 14/**1724–6**, 14/*1724–6*
  Bowditch, Nathaniel, 4/377–8
  compass, 5/617
  electronic, 14/1725
  Henry the Navigator, 10/1179
  Hudson, Henry, 10/1217–19
  lighthouses, 12/1434–5
  maps, 13/1509–12, 13/*1509–11*
  Maury, Matthew, 13/1539
  North Star, 15/1975
Nazis, 1/34, 9/1068–9, 22/2611–18
  Hitler, Adolf, 10/1190–1
Ndola, 22/2643
Neanderthal man, 10/*1220*, 10/*1221*,
    10/1222
  life after death, 17/2081
Neap tides, 20/2425
Nearsighted, 8/899, 8/*899*
Nebraska, 14/**1731–5**, 14/*1732–4*
  climate, 14/1732
  employment, 14/1734
  history, 14/1732–4
  land, 14/1731–2
  map, 14/*1733*
  state emblems, 14/*1733*
Nebuchadnezzar, 3/286, 20/2402
Nebuchadnezzar II, 18/2193
Nectar, 8/961, 9/1088, 19/2351
Needlepoint lace, 12/1382
Needles, 5/580
  acupuncture, 1/29–30
  conifers, 8/884
  pine, 6/632

Needlework, 14/**1735–6★**, 14/*1735–6*
  American, 14/1735–6
  ancient, 14/1735
  knitting, 12/1372–3, 12/*1373*
  lace, 12/1381–2, 12/*1382*
Nefertiti, 7/809
Negative numbers, 15/1808
Negev Desert, 11/1308, 13/1590
Negrillos, 1/47, 17/2033
Negroids, 2/242
Nehru, Jawaharlal, 9/1035, 14/**1737**,
    14/*1737*
Nehru, Motilal, 14/1737
Neighborhoods, 5/557–8
Nekton, 13/1516–17
Nelson, Horatio, 14/**1737–8**, 14/*1737*
Nematodes, 2/156, 22/2620
Neo-Classical architecture, 2/201
Neolithic period, 19/2336
Neon lighting, 12/1336, 12/*1437*
Neopilina, 14/1625
Neoplasm, 6/737–8
Nepal, 14/**1738**, 14/*1738*
Nepalese, 18/2223
Neptune, 19/2257
  basic facts, 19/2259
Nero, 3/291, 9/1084, 11/*1310*,
    14/**1739**, 14/*1739*, 18/2131
Nerva, 18/2131
Nervous system, 10/1224,
    14/**1739–41**, 14/*1740*
  diseases and disorders, 14/1741
  parts of, 14/1740–1
Nests, 2/152–3, 2/*153*, 2/*154*
  ants, 2/167
  birds, 3/345–7
Netherlands, 12/1468–9, 14/**1741–2**,
    14/*1741–2*
  American colonies, 1/110–11, 112
  Amsterdam, 2/132, 2/*132*
  art, 7/775–6, 7/*775–6*
  Boer War, 3/363–4
  colonies, 1/48–9
  Hals, Frans, 10/1141–2
  Rembrandt van Rijn, 17/2082–3
  Stuyvesant, Peter, 19/2345
  Suriname, 19/2359
  Van Gogh, Vincent, 21/2508–9
Netherlands Antilles, 21/2569
Netted slug, 19/*2243*
Network television, 20/2398
Neurobiochemistry, 1562
Neurologists, 13/1555
Neurology, 14/1741
Neurons, 14/1739
Neuroses, 7/763
Neurosurgeons, 19/2358
Neutrons, 3/259, 3/260, 7/829
Nevada, 15/**1743–4**, 15/*1743–5*
  climate, 15/1743
  employment, 15/1744
  history, 15/1743–4
  land, 15/1743
  map, 15/*1745*
  state emblems, 15/*1745*
Neve, Felipe de, 12/1460
Nevinson, C.R.W., 9/*1067*
Nevis, 21/2571
Nevsky, Alexander, 18/2145
New American Bible, 3/336
New Amsterdam, 15/1765–6, 15/1767
Newark, New Jersey, 15/1754,
    15/1756
New Bedford, 13/1530, 13/1531

Newbery, John, 15/1744
Newbery Medal, 15/**1744–6**, 15/*1746*
Newbold, Charles, 8/908
New Brunswick, 4/450, 15/**1746–8**,
    15/*1747–8*, 15/*1746*
  employment, 15/1746
  history, 15/1746–8
  land, 15/1746
  map, 15/*1747*
  provincial flower, 15/*1747*
New Caledonia, 13/1558
New Castle, Delaware, 6/715
Newcomen, Thomas, 7/848, 7/*848*
New Deal, 18/2134, 18/2135,
    20/2472, 21/2490
New Delhi, 11/*1253*
New England, 13/1542
  colonists, 1/112, 1/113
New England Courant, 9/1003
New English Bible, 3/336
Newfoundland-Labrador, 4/444, 4/446,
    5/550, 6/653, 15/**1748–50**, 15/*1749*
  history, 15/1748
  land, 15/1748
  map, 15/*1749*
  people, 15/1748–50
  provincial flower, 15/*1749*
New Guinea, 15/*1743*, 15/**1750–1**,
    15/*1750*, 15/1854, 16/1873
New Hampshire, 15/**1751–3**,
    15/*1751–3*
  employment, 15/1752
  history, 15/1751–2
  land, 15/1751
  map, 15/*1753*
  state emblems, 15/*1753*
New Harbor, Maine, 12/*1485*
New Haven, 6/636
New Ipswich, 15/1752
New Jersey, 15/**1754–6**, 15/*1754–6*
  climate, 15/1754
  employment, 15/1756
  history, 15/1754–6
  land, 15/1754
  map, 15/*1755*
  state emblems, 15/*1755*
New Jersey, USS, 14/*1730*
New Kingdom, Ancient Egypt,
    7/809–10
New Lanark, 11/*1275*
Newman, Larry, 8/893
New Mexico, 11/1355, 15/**1757–9**,
    15/*1757–9*
  climate, 15/1757
  employment, 15/1758
  history, 15/1757–8
  land, 15/1757
  map, 15/*1759*
  state emblems, 15/*1759*
New Moon, 14/1647
New Netherland, 15/1765, 16/1894,
    19/2345
New Orleans, 10/1128, 12/1463,
    12/1464, 12/1466, 12/*1466*
  battle of, 21/2542, 21/*2542*
Newport, Rhode Island, 17/2099,
    17/*2099*
Newport, Wales, 21/2539
Newport News, 5/523, 21/2533
News, journalism, 11/1342–3
News agencies, 11/1342
New Salem State Park, 10/1242
Newspapers, 15/**1760–2**, 15/*1760–2*,
    17/2026

comic strips, 5/608
  history, 15/1761
  journalism, 11/1342–3
  production, 15/1761–2
New Testament, 3/335
Newton, Sir Isaac, 2/*250*, 7/812,
    7/848, 9/1105, 11/1332, 13/1533,
    16/*1923*, 15/**1762–3**, 17/*1763*,
    17/2016, 18/2164, 18/2172,
    18/*2172*, 19/2290, 19/2305
  Laws of Motion, 14/1656–7,
    15/1763
Newts, 18/2155
New Year's Day, 15/**1763**
New Year's Eve, 6/706
New York, 15/**1763–7**, 15/*1764–6*
  climate, 15/1765
  employment, 15/1766
  history, 15/1765–6
  land, 15/1765
  map, 15/*1764*
  state emblems, 15/*1764*
New York Botanical Garden, 3/374
New York City, 10/1151, 10/*1151*,
    15/1765, 15/1766, 15/**1767–8**,
    15/*1767–8*, 19/2345
  police, 16/1966, 16/*1967*
  subway, 19/2349
New York City Ballet, 3/297
New York Infirmary, 3/358
New York State Barge Canal,
    15/1766
New York State University, 5/596
New York Stock Exchange, 19/2335
New York Times, 15/1761
New York Tribune, 9/1116, 15/1761
New Zealand, 6/653, 15/**1768–9**,
    15/*1768–9*
  Commonwealth, 5/610
New Zealand fur seal, 18/*2185*
Nez Percé Indians, 10/1239,
    11/1271, 15/**1769**, 15/*1769*,
    21/2544, 21/2546
  Chief Joseph, 11/1342
Nez Percé War, 1/120
Ngo Dinh Diem, 21/2526
Nguema, Francisco Macias, 7/865
Nguyen Van Thieu, 21/2526
Niagara Falls, 1/25, 9/1108, 9/*1108*,
    15/**1770**, 15/*1770*, 21/2553
Niagara River, 15/1770
Niamey, 15/1772
Nibelungenlied, 14/1697
Nibelungs, 7/839
Nicaragua, 5/505–7, 15/**1770–1**,
    15/*1771*
  CIA and, 5/508
  earthquakes, 5/507
Nicaragua, Lake, 15/1770–1
Nicholas I, Czar of Russia,
    15/**1771–2**, 15/*1772*, 18/2148
Nicholas II, Czar of Russia,
    12/1379, 15/**1772**, 15/*1772*,
    18/2148, 19/2285
Nicholas, Saint, 5/547, 15/**1772**,
    15/*1772*
Nickelodeons, 14/1659
Nicklaus, Jack, 19/2317
Nicknames, 14/1699
Nicolet, Jean, 21/2598
Nicotine, 19/2242, 20/2430
Nicotinic acid, 1/24
Nicot, Jean, 20/2431
Niépce, Joseph N., 16/1920

Nielson, Kurt, 9/1077
Nieuw Nickerie, 19/2359
Niger, 15/**1772–3**, 15/*1773*, 19/2262
Nigeria, 15/**1773–4**, 15/*1774*, 19/2262
Niger River, 12/1489, 15/1772,
    15/1773, 19/2262
Night, 6/701–2
Night-blooming cereus, 4/428
Night herons, 21/2551
Nightingale, Florence, 6/674,
    15/**1774–5**, 15/*1775*
Night latches, 12/1458
Nightmares, 7/762
Nijinsky, Vaslav, 3/297, 15/**1775**,
    15/*1775*, 16/1886
Nikolais Dance Theater, 6/*698*
Nile crocodile, 1/103
Nile River, 7/807, 7/*807*, 7/808,
    7/810, 9/1057, 12/1454,
    15/**1775–6**, 15/*1776*, 18/2150,
    19/2349
  Abu Simbel, 1/20–1
Niles, John Jacob, 8/973
Nilotes, 1/47
Nimbostratus clouds, 5/*582*
Nimbus clouds, 5/583
Nimbus satellite, 18/*2165*
Nimipu Indians, 15/1769
Nimitz, USS, 1/59, 1/60
Nimitz, Chester W., 22/2616,
    22/2617
Nina, 5/606
Nine-banded armadillo, 2/221
Nineteen Eighty-four, 15/1848
Nineveh, 2/246
Ninio, Pech Alonso, 3/352
Ninth Amendment, 3/340
Nirvana, 4/402
Nitrates, 8/978, 15/1776
Nitric acid, 1/23, 1/24
Nitrogen, 1/57, 15/**1776–7**, 15/*1777*
Nitroglycerine, 8/895, 8/896
Nitrous oxide, 2/143, 15/1777
Nits, 12/**1468**, 12/*1468*
Niue Island, 16/1971
Nivelle, Robert G., 21/2609
Niven, Larry, 18/2175
Nixon, Richard Milhous, 5/545,
    7/813, 8/984, 10/1245, 11/1358,
    13/1508, 14/1640, 15/**1777–8**,
    15/*1777*, 21/2523, 21/2527
Niza, Marcos de, 2/217, 7/869
Njazidja, 5/616–17
Njordhr, 14/1695
Nkrumah, Kwame, 9/1075
Nobel, Alfred, 8/896, 15/**1778**,
    15/1779
Nobel Prize, 15/**1778–9**, 15/*1778–9*
Nobile, Umberto, 2/132
Nobility, 15/**1779–80**
Noctovisor, 3/292
Noise:
  pollution, 16/1970
  sound, 19/2264–5
Nok, 15/*1173*
Nolde, Emil, 15/*1859*, 15/1860
Nomads, 1/42, 5/559, 12/1392,
    15/**1780–1**, 15/*1781*
  Africa, 1/47
  ancient civilizations, 2/133
  gypsies, 10/1134
  Iraq, 11/1300
  Mongolia, 14/1633, 15/1780–1
  tents, 20/2408, 20/*2408*

Nona, 8/915
Nones, 4/434
Nonfiction, definition, 5/534
Nonflammable substances, 8/937
Nonobjective painting, 14/1621
Non-rigid airships, 1/78
Nonsettlement colonies, 5/599
Noonan, Fred, 7/780
Nordenskjöld, Nils, 2/209
Nordic skiing, 18/2231
Norfolk and Western Railway,
    17/2053
Norfolk Island pine, 6/633
Norfolk, Virginia, 5/523
Normandy, battle of, 3/319
Normans, 7/855
Norris Dam, 17/*2024*
Norsemen *see* Vikings
Norse myths, 14/1695, 14/1696–7
North America, 15/**1781–6**,
    15/*1781–6*
  animals, 15/1785
  climate, 15/1784–5
  geography, 15/1782
  map, 15/*1783*
  nations, 15/1782
  people, 15/1785–6
  physical statistics, 6/650
  plants, 15/1785
North American Air Defense Com-
    mand (NORAD), 1/62
North American buffalo, 17/*2064*
North American X-15, 3/*282*
North Atlantic Treaty Organization
    (NATO), 7/813, 8/881,
    15/**1786–7**, 16/1889, 20/2458,
    21/2542
North Carolina, 15/**1787–90**,
    15/*1787–90*
  climate, 15/1788
  employment, 15/1790
  history, 15/1788–90
  land, 15/1787–8
  map, 15/*1789*
  state emblems, 15/*1789*
North Dakota, 15/**1790–3**, 15/*1791–2*
  climate, 15/1792
  employment, 15/1793
  history, 15/1792–3
  land, 15/1790–2
  map, 15/*1791*
  state emblems, 15/*1791*
Northeast Passage, 2/209
North Equatorial Current, 15/1855
Northern Ireland, 11/1301, 11/1302,
    15/**1793–4**, 15/*1793*, 20/*2411*,
    20/2485
Northern Rhodesia *see* Zambia
Northern seals, 18/2185
Northern Territory, 3/266
North Korea, 12/1376–7, 12/*1376*
North magnetic pole, 5/618
North Platte River, 14/1732
North Pole, 2/132, 2/207–10, 4/423,
    8/894, 10/1179–80, 15/**1794**,
    15/*1794*
  Peary, Robert, 16/1889
North River Steamboat of Clermont,
    18/*2210*
North Sea, 15/**1794–5**, 15/*1794–5*
North, Simeon, 6/637
North Star, 6/641, 6/*641*, 7/756,
    15/**1795**
North Star, The, 1/15

Northumberland, Duke of, 9/1119
Northumbria, 2/143
North West Company, 10/1219, 13/1503
Northwest Ordinance (1787), 18/2236
Northwest Passage, 2/209, 2/132, 4/392, 8/894, 15/**1795**, 15/*1795*
Northwest Territories, 15/**1796–7**, 15/*1796–7*, 15/1824
map, 15/*1797*
Provincial flower, 15/*1797*
North West Trading Company, 12/1476
North Yemen, 2/193
Norton, André, 18/2175
Norway, 8/875, 15/**1798–9**, 15/*1798*
Grieg, Edvard, 9/1119
Ibsen, Henrik, 10/1232–3
King Canute, 4/457, 4/*457*
Vikings, 21/2527–9
Norway rats, 17/2066
Norway spruce, 6/633, 20/*2461*
Norwegian language, 18/2168
Nosebleed, first aid, 8/939, 8/*939*
Noses, 15/**1799**, 15/*1799*
first aid, 8/939–40
smell, 19/2241
sneezing, 19/2246
Nostrils, 15/1799
Notation, music, 14/1683–5
Notes, money, 14/1631
Notre Dame, Paris, 9/*1094*
Notre Dame Mountains, 2/183
Notre Dame University, 17/2112
Nouakchott, 13/1538
Nouméa, 13/1558
Nouns, 16/1881
Nova Scotia, 4/450, 15/**1799–1801**, 15/*1800*
map, 15/*1800*
provincial flower, 15/*1800*
Novels, 12/1447, 15/**1801–2**, 15/*1801–2*
science fiction, 18/2175
November, 15/**1802–3**, 15/*1802*
special events, 15/1803
Novgorod, 18/2144, 18/*2145*
Novial, 21/2499
Novocain, 2/142
Nu, U, 4/415
Nubian Desert, 19/2349
Nubian goats, 9/1086
Nuclear bombs, test sites, 15/1758
Nuclear chemistry, 5/519
Nuclear energy, 7/845, 8/923, 15/**1803–5**, 15/*1804–5*
Nuclear engineers, 7/851
Nuclear explosions, test sights, 15/1743
Nuclear explosives, 8/895–6, 8/*895*
Nuclear fallout, 8/907
Nuclear fuel, 9/1019
Nuclear nonproliferation treaty, 6/736
Nuclear physics, 16/1923
Fermi, Enrico, 8/922–3
Nuclear radiation, 17/2044
geiger counters, 9/1049, 9/*1049*
radioactivity, 17/2048–9, 17/*2048–9*
Nuclear reactors, 7/*831*
electricity generation, 7/822
Nuclear Regulatory Commission, 21/2490, 21/*2490*
Nuclear shelters, 18/2204

Nuclear weapons, 6/736
Nucleic acids, 3/341
Nucleus, 5/501
atomic, 3/258, 3/*258*, 3/259, 7/829
Nuggets, gold, 9/1090
Numbers, 15/**1806–8**, 15/*1806–7*
Arabic, 2/212, 15/1807
chance, 5/510–11
fractions, 9/999
kinds of, 15/1807–8
negative, 15/1808
perfect, 9/1059
prime, 15/1808
Roman, 2/212–13, 15/1606–7
Numerators, 2/214, 9/999
Numidia, 1/100
Numismatists, 5/594
Nuns, 14/1628, 18/2122
Nureyev, Rudolf, 3/297, 8/973, 8/*973*
Nurseries, plant, 9/1040, 9/*1040*
Nursery rhymes, 8/971
Nursery schools, 18/2169
Nurses' aide, 15/1809
Nursing, 15/**1808–9**, 15/*1808–9*
Cavell, Edith Louisa, 4/500
hospitals, 10/1210
Nightingale, Florence, 15/1774–5
Nut (goddess), 21/*2499*
Nutmeg, 19/*2311*
Nutmeg State, 6/634
Nutrition, 8/974–6, 8/*974–6*, 15/**1810–11**, 15/*1811*
carbohydrates, 4/462
fats and oils, 8/916–17, 8/*917*
meat, 13/1547
protein, 17/2013
Nutritional diseases, 6/738
Nuts, 15/**1809–10**, 15/*1809–10*
Nyasaland *see* Malawi
Nylon, 8/926, 16/1955, 20/2372
rope, 18/2137
Nymphs, 9/1088
dragonfly, 7/757
insects, 11/1280, 13/1569–70
Nzwani, 5/617

Oo

Oahu, 10/1158, 10/1160, 11/1351
Oak, 8/884
Oakley, Annie, 4/404, 15/**1812**, 15/*1812*
Oak Ridge, 20/2403
Oak trees, 20/*2461*, 20/*2462*
OAO spacecraft, 19/2288
OASDHI, 19/2250
Oasis, 6/721, 18/2152
Oates, Lawrence, 18/2177
Oaths, court system, 6/666
Oats, 6/659, 9/1097
Oaxaca, 13/1575
Oberlin College, 5/596
Obesity, 10/1163
Oboes, 14/1689, 21/2603
Obote, Milton, 20/2483
Observation balloons, 3/298
Observatories, 15/**1812–14**, 15/*1813–14*
Obsidian, 9/1083, 17/*2108*
Obstetricians, 13/1555
Occult, witchcraft, 21/2598–9, 21/*2599*

Oceanic trenches, 15/1816
Ocean liners, 13/1564
Oceania, 15/1854
Oceanographic engineering, 7/851
Oceanology, 9/1055, 9/1057
Oceans, 15/**1814–21**, 15/*1814–20*
area, 15/1820
Atlantic, 3/254–5
climate and, 5/576
currents, 15/1815, 15/*1815*
depth, 15/1820
desalinization, 21/2556
exploring, 15/1817–20
floods and, 8/955–6, 8/*955–6*
floor, 15/1815
formation, 7/785
Gulf Stream, 10/1128, 10/*1128*
Indian, 11/1260–1, 11/*1260*
life, 15/1816–17
marine life, 13/1515–17, 13/*1517*
Maury, Matthew, 13/1539
merchant marine, 13/1564
movement of, 15/1814–15
Pacific, 15/1855–7, 15/*1856–7*
resources, 15/1817
seacoasts, 18/2182–3, 18/*2182–3*
tides, 15/1815, 20/2424–6, 20/*2425–6*
volume, 15/1820
water, 15/1814
water pressure, 15/1814
waves, 15/1814–15, 15/*1814*
Ocelot, 4/488–9
O'Connor, Sandra Day, 15/**1821**, 15/*1821*
Octavian, Emperor, 5/573, 18/*2129*, 18/2131
October, 15/**1821–2**, 15/*1821*
special events, 15/1822
Octopuses, 14/1625, 14/1626, 15/**1822–3**, 15/*1822*
Odd numbers, 15/1808
O'Dell, Scott, 5/535
Odessa, 3/357
Odet, Clifford, 7/760
Odin, 14/1695, 14/1696
Odoacer, 11/1310, 18/2132
Odobenus, 21/*2540*
Odometer, 13/1546
Odysseus, 14/1697, 20/2465
Odyssey, 9/1115, 10/1197
Oedipus, 17/2102, 19/2310
Oersted, Hans Christian, 2/129, 7/817, 14/1664
Office of Personnel Management, 21/2490
Officials, elections, 7/815
Offset lithography, 17/*2003*, 17/2004, 17/*2004*
Offshore drilling, 16/1909
rigs, 7/764, 7/*764*
Ogaden, 19/2262
Oglethorpe, James Edward, 9/1062
OGO spacecraft, 19/2288
O'Hara, Lorenz, 14/1688
O'Hare International Airport, 1/77, 5/526, 10/1240
O'Higgins, Bernardo, 5/536
Ohio, 15/**1823–6**, 15/*1823–5*
climate, 15/1824
employment, 15/1824–6
history, 15/1824
land, 15/1823–4
map, 15/*1824*
state emblems, 15/*1825*

Ohio River, 10/1240, 11/1255, 13/1615
Ohms, 7/821
Oil, 9/1019
drilling rigs, 7/763–4, 7/*764*
finding, 16/1909
future of, 16/1910
kerosene, 11/1364
petroleum, 16/1908–10, 16/*1908–10*
pipelines, 16/1933, 16/*1934*
refineries, 16/1909, 16/*1910*
spillage, 6/*639*
transporting, 16/1909–10, 16/1933
wells, 16/*1908*, 16/1909, 16/*1909*
Oil painting, 15/1860
Oil paints, 15/1858
Oil tankers, 18/*2211*, 18/2212, 18/*2212*
Oistrakh, David, 19/2284
Ojeda, Alonso de, 21/2514
Ojibwa Indians, 1/100, 13/1503, 13/1580, 13/1604, 13/1614, 15/**1826**, 15/*1826*
O.K. Corral, 7/780
Okeechobee, 8/883, 8/957
O'Keefe, John, 18/2165
Okefenokee Swamp, 9/1061, 19/2361, 19/2362
Okefenokee Wildlife Refuge, 9/*1062*
Oklahoma, 15/**1827–9**, 15/*1827–9*
climate, 15/1827
employment, 15/1828
history, 15/1827–8
land, 15/1827
map, 15/*1829*
state emblems, 15/*1829*
Oklahoma City, 15/1827, 15/1828, 15/*1828*
Okovango River, 3/376
Old Faithful, 9/1074, 14/*1709*, 21/2567, 22/*2634*
Old Ironsides, 17/2094
Old Kingdom, Ancient Egypt, 7/808
Oldsmobile, 3/273
Olds, Ransom E., 3/273, 6/723
Old Testament, 3/335
Olduvai Gorge, 12/1405
Oleander, 16/1963
Oleg, 18/2144
Olfactory organ, 19/2241
Oligarchies, 9/1095
Oligocene Epoch, 7/786
mammals, 13/1499
Oliver, Joe 'King', 2/223, 11/1325
Olives, 1/*53*
Olivier, Laurence, 1/27
Olmec, 11/1259
Olmsted, Frederick Law, 16/1878
Olympia, 15/1830
Statue of Zeus, 18/2193, 18/*2193*
Olympic Games, 9/1113, 15/**1830–1**, 15/*1830–1*, 15/1851, 19/2316, 20/2366, 20/2423, 20/2440
medals, 13/1550
Olympic Mountains, 21/2544
Olympus Mons, Mars, 14/1669
Olympus, Mount (Greece), 9/1087–9, 9/1110, 14/1677, 14/1695–6
Olympus, Mount (Washington), 21/2544
Omaha, 14/1732, 14/1734
Omaha Indians, 14/1731, 14/1732
Oman, 2/193
Omar Khayyam, 1/98

Omens, 17/2011
Ommatidia, 8/899
Omnibuses, 4/418
Omnivores, 4/470, 7/794, 13/1497
    digestive tracts, 6/731
Omsk, climate, 19/2282
Onager, 7/755
Onassis, Jacqueline, 21/2582
Oneida Indians, 8/950, 11/1304
O'Neill, Eugene, 7/760, 12/1451,
    15/**1831–2**, 15/*1832*
Onions, 4/408
Onondaga Indians, 8/950, 11/1304
Ontario, 4/450, 15/**1832–4**, 15/*1833*
    geography, 15/1832
    history, 15/1832
    map, 15/*1833*
    people, 15/1832–4
    provincial flower, 15/*1833*
Ontario Lake, 9/1107–8
On the Waterfront, 14/*1660*
Opals, 13/*1597*
Opaque materials, 12/1432
Opechancanoigh, 17/1993
Open-pit mines, 11/1302
Opera, 15/**1834–5**, 15/*1834–5*
    Anderson, Marian, 2/140
    Caruso, Enrico, 4/479
    Verdi, Giuseppe, 21/2516
    Wagner, Richard, 21/2538
Operation Push, 3/355
Operations, surgery, 19/2357,
    19/*2357*
Operetta, 15/1835
    Gilbert and Sullivan, 9/1077
Ophthalmologists, 13/1555
Ophthaloscope, 3/285
Opinion polls, 15/**1836**, 15/*1836*
Opium, 14/1703
Opium Wars, 5/538
Oporto, 16/1982
Opossums, 3/269, 5/559, 13/*1520*,
    13/1521, 15/**1836–7**, 15/*1836*
Oprichniki, 18/2146
Optical filter, 8/929
Optics, 16/1923
    lens, 12/1414–16
    microscopes, 13/1583–4, 13/*1583–4*
    mirages, 13/1606–7
    mirrors, 13/1607–8, 13/*1607–8*
    Newton, Sir Isaac, 15/1763
Oracles, 8/992, 17/2011, 17/*2011*
Oral surgeons, 6/718
Oral tradition, folk tales, 8/970
Orange Free State, 3/363, 19/2266
Oranges, 5/555, 5/*555*, 9/1017, 9/1018
Orangutans, 2/181–2, 2/*181*, 13/*1495*
Oratorios, 5/544, 14/1681
Orbits, 15/**1837–8**, 15/*1837–8*
    moon, 14/1646
Orbs, 6/677
Orchestras, 15/**1838–40**, 15/*1839–40*
Orchids, 15/**1840**, 15/*1840*
Order of the Garter, 13/1550
Orders:
    animals, 2/155
    awards, 13/1550
    monastic, 14/1628–9
Order of Victory, 13/*1550*
Oregon, 15/**1841–3**, 15/*1841–3*
    climate, 15/1841–2
    employment, 15/1842
    history, 15/1842
    land, 15/1841

map, 15/*1843*
    state emblems, 15/*1843*
Oregon Territory, 4/394
Oregon Trail, 1/117, 14/1732,
    15/*1841*, 15/**1842–4**, 15/*1844*
O'Reilly, Edward, 16/1890
Orellana, Francisco de, 1/108, 6/638,
    7/814
Ores, 11/1302
    mining, 13/1599–1602
Oresund, 6/717
Organelles, 5/502
Organic chemistry, 4/463, 5/519
Organization for African Unity
    (OAU), 1/49
Organization of Afro-American
    Unity, 12/1491
**Organization of American States
    (OAS)**, 15/**1845**, 15/*1845*
Organization of Central American
    States, 5/507
Organization of Oil Exporting Coun-
    tries (OPEC), 2/192
Organized crime, 6/674
Organ pipe cactus, 4/428
Organs, 15/**1844–5**, 15/*1844*
    calliope, 4/439
    human body, 10/1224
Oriental art, 15/**1845–7***, 15/*1845–7*
Orientation, ears and, 7/779
Original Dixieland Jazz band,
    11/1325
Origin of the Species, 6/699, 6/700
Orinoco River, 17/2061, 21/2514
Orioles, 3/345
Orion, 6/641, 6/642, 14/1697
Orizaba, Mount, 13/1573, 15/1782
Orkney, 18/2176
Orlando, Vittorio, 21/2609, 21/*2610*
Orléans, battle of, 3/319, 12/1466
Orlon, 20/2372
Ormazd, 16/1902
Ornithologists, 3/343
Orozco, José Clemente, 13/1576,
    20/2371
Orthodontists, 6/718
Orthodox Church, 15/**1847–8**,
    15/*1848*, 18/2121
Orthodox Jews, 11/1345
Orthographic projections, 13/*1511*
Orthopedic surgeons, 19/2358
Orthopedists, 13/1555
Orwell, George, 15/**1848**, 15/*1848*,
    18/2175
Oryx, 2/173
Oryza sativa, 17/2100
Osage Indians, 11/1355, 13/1616,
    15/1827
Osage Plains, 13/1615
Oscars, 1/21, 1/*21*, 1/29
    table, 14/1660–1
Oscar spacecraft, 19/2288
Osceola, 18/2189, 18/*2189*
Osiris, 7/810
Oslo, 11/1798
Osman, Sultan, 15/1850
OSO spacecraft, 19/2288
Ospreys, 3/349, 10/1146
Osteopathy, 5/542
Ostriches, 3/*346*, 8/954, 8/955, 8/*955*,
    10/*1146*
    eggs, 5/*501*
Ostrogoths, 1/85
Oswald, Lee Harvey, 11/1359

Otis, Elisha Graves, 7/833, 7/*833*
Oto Indians, 14/1731, 14/1732
Otolaryngologists, 13/1555
Ottawa, 4/448, 15/1832, 15/**1848–9**,
    15/*1849*
Ottawa Indians, 1/100, 11/1270,
    13/1580, 15/1824, 16/1975,
    21/2559
Ottawa River, 15/1848–9
Otters, 15/**1849–50**, 15/*1849*
    tracks, 2/*164*
Otter trawls, 8/949, 8/*949*
Otto I the Great, Emperor, 9/1065,
    10/1196, 11/1310
Ottoman Empire, 15/**1850**, 15/*1850*
    Lawrence of Arabia, 12/1400–1
Otumba, 6/662
Ouachita Mountains, 2/218, 15/1827
Oueme River, 3/330
Out of Africa, 14/*1661*
Outback, Australia, 3/263
Outcault, Richard F., 5/608
Outer ears, 7/778, 7/779
Outer Mongolia, 14/1633
Outlaws, 15/**1851**, 15/*1851*
Outpatients, 10/1209
Ova, reproduction, 17/2087, 17/2088
Oval window, ears, 7/778
Ovaries, 9/*1081*, 17/2088
    flowers, 8/961, 8/*961*
Ovenbirds, 2/*154*
Ovens, microwave, 13/1584, 13/*1584*
Overburden, 13/1600
Overhand knot, 12/*1374*
Overtures, 15/1834
Ovid, 2/136, 12/1394, 18/2132
Ovington, Mary White, 5/562
Ovipositors, 11/1280
Ovis, 18/2201–2
Owen, Robert, 11/*1275*, 19/2249,
    19/*2250*
Owens, Jesse, 3/355, 15/1831,
    15/**1851**, 15/*1851*, 20/2440
Owls, 3/344, 3/*346*, 3/348,
    15/**1851–2**, 15/*1852*
Oxen, 4/495, 7/754
Oxeye daisy, 8/962
Oxford, 20/2418
Oxford University, 5/595
Oxygen, 1/57, 15/**1852–3**, 15/*1853*,
    17/1999
    liquid fuel, 9/*1019*
    respiration, 17/2092–3, 17/*2092*
Oymyakon, 2/239
Oystercatchers, 18/*2181*
Oysters, 5/*570*, 5/*570*, 14/1626
    pearls, 16/1887–8
Ozark Plateau, 13/1615, 15/1827
Ozawa, Jisaburo, 22/2618–19
Ozocerite, 21/2558
Ozone, 15/1853
Ozone layer, 1/39

Pp

P-51 Mustang, 3/*282*
Pacheco, Francisco, 21/2513
Pacheco, Juana, 21/2513
Pachomius, 14/1629
Pachystomius, 6/708
Pacific Islands, 15/**1854–5**, 15/*1854–5*
Pacific Ocean, 15/**1855–7**, 15/*1856–7*

Pack ice, 2/208, 2/209
Pack rats, 17/2066
Paddle dolls, 7/749
Paddle steamers, 18/*2206*, 18/2208
Paddy fields, 2/243, 2/*244*, 17/2100
Padlocks, 12/1458
Paektu-san, 12/1376
Page proofs, 17/2025
Pages, 12/1371
Pagodas, 15/**1857**, 15/*1857*
Pahouin, 4/442
Paine, Thomas, 15/**1857–8**, 15/*1858*
Painkillers, 1/33, 7/767
Paint, 15/**1858**, 15/*1858*
Painted Desert, 6/720, 15/**1859**,
    15/*1859*
Painters:
    Audubon, John James, 3/260–1
    Cassaatt, Mary, 4/481–2
    Cezanne, Paul, 5/**508–9**
    Constable, John, 6/640–1
    Degas, Edgar, 6/711
    Gainsborough, Thomas, 9/1029–30
    Gauguin, Paul, 9/1046–7
    Giotto di Bondone, 9/1077–8
    El Greco, 7/834–5
    Hals, Frans, 10/1141–2
    Holbein, Hans the Younger,
        10/1192–3
    Homer, Winslow, 10/1197–8
    Lear, Edward, 12/1405–6
    Leonardo da Vinci, 12/1416–17
    Manet, Edouard, 13/1502
    Matisse, Henry, 13/1535–6
    Michelangelo, 13/1557–8
    Monet, Claude, 14/1629–30
    Morse, Samuel F.B., 14/1650
    Picasso, Pablo, 16/1925–6
    Raphael, 17/2062–3
    Rembrandt van Rijn, 17/2082–3
    Renoir, Pierre Auguste, 17/2085–6
    Reynolds, Joshua, 17/2095–6
    Rubens, Peter Paul, 18/2141–2
    Sargent, John Singer, 18/2162
    Titian, 20/2429–30
    Toulouse-Lautrec, Henri de,
        20/2436
    Turner, Joseph Mallord William,
        20/2476–7
    Van Gogh, Vincent, 21/2508–9
    Velázquez, Diego, 21/2513
    Whistler, James McNeill,
        21/2581–2
Painting, 15/**1859–63**, 15/*1859–63*
    abstract, 1/18–20, 1/*19–20*
    American Indian, 11/1260
    ancient civilizations, 2/136–7
    cave, 2/231, 2/*231*
    drawing, 7/760–2
    Expressionism, 8/896–7, 8/*896*
    Impressionism, 10/1245–6,
        10/*1245–6*
    miniatures, 13/1602–3, 13/*1603*
    modern, 14/1620–1
    perspective, 17/2083
    portraits, 16/1980–1, 16/*1981*
    primitive, 8/969
    Realism, 17/2068
    Rococo, 17/2113–14
    Roman, 18/2120, 18/*2120*
    Romanticism, 18/2127–8, 18/*2127–8*
    surrealism, 19/2360
    symbolism, 20/2370–1, 20/*2370–1*
    see also Painters

Paiute Indians, 15/1743, 21/2504
Pakistan, 2/*239*, 2/*243*, 15/**1864**, 15/*1864*
India and, 11/1255
Palaeozoic era, 7/786
Palatine Hill, 18/2129
Palau Islands, 13/1582
Paleocene Epoch, 7/786
mammals, 13/1498–9
Paleolithic period, 19/2335–6
Paleontologists, 8/994, 9/1056
Paleontology, 3/343, 15/**1865**, 15/*1865*
fossils, 8/992–5, 8/*993–5*
Paleozoic era, 17/*1996*
Palestine, 13/1590, 15/**1865–6**, 15/*1865*
Christianity, 5/546
Crusades, 6/678
refugees, 17/2077
Palestine Liberation Organization (PLO), 11/1310, 15/1866
Palette knives, 15/1860
Palindromes, 21/2603
Palisades, 8/989, 11/1304
Palisades, New Jersey, 15/1754
Pallas' cat, 4/490
Palma, 4/454
Palmer, Arnold, 19/2317
Palmer, Daniel D., 5/542
Palm reading, 8/992, 8/*992*
Palms, 15/**1866**, 15/*1866*, 16/*1943*
Palm Sunday, 7/790
Palmyra, 18/*2132*, 20/*2373*
Palmyra Island, 16/1971
Palomar Mountain, 2/*250*
Palominos, 10/*1203*, 10/1206
Palouse Indians, 21/2546
Pamir Mountains, 2/239, 19/2282
Pampas, 2/210, 17/1993, 19/2268
Pan, 9/1088–9, 13/1584
Panama, 5/505–7, 5/598, 16/**1867–8**, 16/*1867–8*
Panama Canal, 1/120–1, 4/453, 5/507, 6/694, 9/1046, 16/1867, 16/**1868–9**, 16/*1868*
Panama City, 16/1867
Pan-American Exposition (1901), 13/1544
Panamint Range, 6/704
Panchatantra, 8/900
Pancreas, 6/731, 9/1081, 9/*1081*
Pandarasannadhi, Swami, 10/1139
Pandas, 13/*1495*, 16/**1869**, 16/*1869*
Pandora, 16/**1870**
Pangaea, 6/650
Panhandle, 10/1237, 15/1827
Pantagruel, 9/1076
Pantaloon, 16/1870
Pantaloons, 5/583
Pantheon, 18/2119
Pantomimes, 3/295, 5/583, 16/**1870**, 16/*1870*
Pantotheria, 13/1498
Papago Indians, 2/215, 4/428, 11/*1259*
Papal States, 11/1312
Paper, 3/367, 16/**1870–2**, 16/*1870–1*, 16/1951
Paper dolls, 7/750
Paper money, 14/1631, 14/*1631*, 14/*1632*
Paper sculpture, 16/**1872–3***, 16/*1872–3*

Papier-Mâché, 16/1872
Papua New Guinea, 13/1558, 15/1750–1, 16/**1873**, 16/*1873*
Papyrus, 7/810, 16/1871
Parabola, 15/1838
Paracelsus, Philippus, 13/1553, 13/1556
Parachutes, 16/**1873–4**, 16/*1874*
Paraffin wax, 21/2558
Paraguay, 16/**1874–5**, 16/*1875*
Paraguay River, 16/1875, 19/2268
Parakeets, 16/1879–80, 16/*1879–80*
Paramaribo, 19/2359
Paramecium, 5/*503*
Paraná River, 16/1874–5, 19/2268
Parapsychology, 17/2020
Parasites, 7/794, 7/795, 9/1021, 16/**1875–6**, 16/*1876*
bacterial, 3/289
diseases, 6/737
louse, 12/1467–8, 12/*1468*
Parasitic plants, 16/**1876–7**, 16/*1877*, 16/*1943*
Parasitology, 3/343
Parasympathetic nerves, 14/1741
Parathyroid glands, 9/1081, 9/*1081*
Parathyroxine, 10/1201
Parcae, 8/915
Parchment, 16/1871
Paregoric, 14/1703
Parentheses, 17/2030
Parents, adoption, 1/35–6
Parícutin, 14/1668, 21/2535
Paris, 16/**1877**, 16/*1877*
Louvre, 12/1468, 12/*1468*
Treaty of (1763), 15/1746
Treaty of (1783), 1/128
Treaty of (1814), 18/2197
University of, 5/595
Paris Exposition (1889), 8/903
Paris (god), 20/2465
Parishes, 6/666
Parkas, 5/579, 7/868
Parker, Quanah, 5/*606*
Park, Mungo, 15/1773
Parks, 16/**1878**, 16/*1878*
national, 14/1709–13
Parks, Rosa, 5/563
Parliamentarians, 7/857
Parliaments, 16/**1878–9**, 16/*1879*
legislature, 12/1412–13
Parochial schools, 5/548–9
Parole, 17/2006
Parr, Catherine, 10/1177
Parris Island, 19/2274
Parrots, 16/**1879–80***, 16/*1879–80*
Parry, Sir Edmund, 8/977
Parsees, 3/365–6
Parthenogenesis, 17/2089
Parthenon, 1/26, 3/253
Particle accelerators, 16/**1880–1**, 16/*1881*, 18/*2173*
Parties, political, 16/1967–8, 21/2489
Partisans, 10/1124
Partricians, 18/2129
Partridges, 9/*1034*
Parts of speech, 16/**1881–2**
Pascal, Blaise, 4/432, 13/*1532*, 13/1534, 16/**1882–3**, *1883*
Passaic River, 15/1756
Passenger pigeons, 3/350, 16/1929–30
Passover, 16/**1883**, 17/2081
Passports, 20/2455

Pastels, 15/1860–1
Pasternak, Boris, 19/2284
Pasteurization, 16/1884
Pasteurized milk, 6/692
Pasteur, Louis, 3/289, 8/977, 10/1211, 10/*1244*, 12/1445, 13/1553, 16/**1883–4**, 16/*1883*
Pastimes:
amateur radio, 17/2047–8
collecting, 5/**593–5**, 5/*593–4*
crossword puzzles, 6/676
darts, 6/699
dominoes, 7/754–5
hobbies, 10/1191–2, 10/*1191–2*
horse riding, 10/1207–8
ice skating, 10/1236–7, 10/*1236–7*
model making, 14/1619
needlework, 14/1735–6, 14/*1735–7*
scuba diving, 18/2177–8
stamp collecting, 19/2324–5, 19/*2324*
terrariums, 20/2410
toys, 20/2437–9, 20/*2437–9*
word games, 21/2603–4
see also Sport
Pastors, 18/2121
Pastor, Tony, 21/2510
Patagonia, 2/211, 19/2268, 19/*2268*
Patapasco River, 13/1524, 13/1525
Patent leather, 12/1409
Patents, 16/**1884–5**, 16/*1884*, 20/2458
Paterson, Katherine, 5/535, 15/1746
Paterson, New Jersey, 15/1754, 15/1756
Pathans, 15/1864
Pathet Lao, 12/1392
Pathologists, 13/1555
Pathology, plant, 3/375
Patriarchs, 5/546, 15/1847
Patrick, Saint, 11/1301, 16/**1885**
Patriotism, 14/1704
Patterns, sewing, 18/2195
Patton, George S., 22/2618
Pauling, Linus, 15/1779
Paul, Saint, 5/546, 5/*546*, 16/**1885**, 16/*1885*
Paul VI, Pope, 16/1977
Pavia, battle of, 9/1002
Pavlov, 13/1501
Pavlova, Anna, 3/297, 16/**1886**, 16/*1886*
Pavlov, Ivan, 16/**1885–6**, 16/*1885*
Pawnee Indians, 5/602, 11/1355, 14/1732, 16/**1886–7**, 16/*1886*
Pawtucket, 17/2099
Pawtuxet River, 17/2097
Payton, Walter, 19/2317
Pétrusse River, 12/1471
Peabody, Sophia, 10/1161
Peace of Augsburg, 9/1065
Peace Corps, 11/1359, 16/**1887**, 16/*1887*
Peace of Westphalia, 9/1065
Peace pipe, 11/1263
Peace River, 12/1476
Peacocks, 3/344, 8/*918*
Peano, Giuseppe, 21/2499
Peanuts, 15/1809, 17/*2013*
Pearl Harbor, 1/59, 1/*118*, 1/121, 1/*121*, 10/1160, 11/1323, 16/**1888**, 16/*1888*, 22/2616
Pearlies, 4/422
Pearl oysters, 14/1626
Pearls, 9/1050, 16/**1887–8**, 16/*1887–8*

Pearson, Lester, 4/450–1, 15/1779, 16/**1888–9**, 16/*1889*, 20/2470
Peary, Robert, 2/132, 2/209, 8/*891*, 8/893, 10/1179–80, 16/**1889**, 16/*1889*
Peat, 8/*878*, 11/1301
as fuel, 9/1019
Peat bogs, 19/2361
Pecans, 15/1809
Pecos Bill, 8/972, 16/**1889–90**
Pecos River, 15/1757
Pecos Valley, 20/2412
Pectin, 9/1018, 11/1320
Pectoral fins, 8/944
Pectoral muscles, 14/*1677*
Peddlers, 19/2337
Pediatricians, 13/1555
Pediatric nurses, 15/1808
Pedodontists, 6/718
Pedro I, Emperor of Brazil, 18/2161
Pedro Miguel Locks, 16/1868
Pedunculate oak, 20/*2461*
Pegasus, 6/641, 9/1093, 14/1697
Peking, 5/*540*, 16/**1890**, 16/*1890*, 16/1971
Peking Man, 2/244
Pelée, Mont, 21/2572
Pelecypods, 14/1625
Pelias, 11/1324
Pelicans, 16/*1867*, 16/**1891**, 16/*1891*, 18/2182
Pellagra, 1/24
Pellia epiphylla, 14/*1655*
Peloponnesian War, 9/1113
Pelota, 11/1318
Pemba, 20/2378, 20/2379
Pen, swans, 7/772
Pencils, 16/**1896–7**, 16/*1897*
Pend d'Oreille Indians, 10/1239
Pend Oreille Lake, 10/1237
Pendulum clocks, 5/578, 5/*578*
Pendulums, 16/**1891–2**, 16/*1891–2*
Penguins, 2/170, 2/*171*, 3/343, 3/344, 9/1–30, 16/**1892**, 16/*1892*
Penicillin, 2/176–7, 7/768, 8/953, 9/*1021*
Penicillium, 2/176–7, 2/*176*, 9/*1021*
Penicillum notatum, 8/953
Peninsulas, 18/2183
Penitentiaries, 17/2006–7
Penmanship, 10/1146
Pennacook Indians, 12/1485, 15/1751
Pen names, 14/1699
Pennine Hills, 4/396, 7/852
Pennsylvania, 16/**1893–6**, 16/*1893–6*
climate, 16/1893–4
employment, 16/1894–6
history, 16/1894
land, 16/1893
map, 16/*1895*
state emblems, 16/*1895*
Pennsylvania Gazette, 9/1003
Pennsylvania University, 9/1003
Penn, William, 13/1527, 16/**1893**, 16/1910, 19/2252
Pennyroyal Plateau, 11/1360
Penobscot Indians, 12/1485
Pens, 16/**1896–7**, 16/*1896*
ink, 11/1276
Peony, 9/*1039*
People, 10/1220–1, 10/*1220–3*
Peoria, 10/1242
Pepin the Short, 5/512
Peppered moths, 8/*885*

Pep pills, 7/769
Pepsin, 6/731
Pepys, Samuel, 6/724
Pequot Indians, 6/636, 11/1270
Peradeniva, 19/2323
Percentages, 16/**1897***
Perception:
  psychology, 17/2018
  sight, 18/2219–20
Percheron horses, 10/1207
Perches water table, 21/2567
Percussion instruments, 14/1682,
  14/1688–9, 15/1839, 16/**1897–8***,
  16/*1897–8*
Peréz, Juan, 4/392
Peregrine falcons, 3/348, 17/2065
Perennial flowers, 9/1039
Perennial plants, 8/963
Perfect numbers, 9/1059
Perfumes, 6/662–3, 16/**1899**, 16/*1899*
Pericarp, 9/1016
Pericles, 9/1112, 9/*1112*
Perigee, 15/1838
Period, punctuation, 17/2029
Periodic table, 7/830–1, 7/*830*
Periodontics, 6/718
Peripheral nervous system, 14/1740
Periscopes, 19/2345
Peristalsis, 6/730
Perkin, William, 7/777
Permafrost, 2/207, 20/2473
Perón, Eva, 2/211, 16/**1900**, 16/*1900*
Perón, Isabel, 2/211, 16/1900
Perón, Juan, 2/211, 6/726, 16/**1900**
Perpetual motion, 16/**1900–1**,
  16/*1900*
Perrault, Charles, 5/531, 8/904–5,
  16/**1901**, 16/*1901*
Perry, Matthew, 8/929, 11/1323,
  16/**1902**, 16/1927
Perry, Oliver, 16/**1902**, 16/*1902*,
  21/2541
Persepolis, 16/1903
Perseus, 2/142, 6/641, 9/1092–3,
  16/**1902**, 16/*1902*
Pershing II missiles, 13/*1609*
Pershing, John, 13/1618, 21/2529
Pershing tanks, 20/*2377*
Persia, 16/**1902–3**, 16/*1903*
  armies, 2/224, 2/*225*
  pottery, 16/*1988*, 16/1989
  Xerxes I, 22/2628
Persians, 2/134, 11/1299
Personality:
  emotions, 7/841–2
  psychology, 17/2019
Personnel psychologists, 17/2020
Perspective, 7/761, 15/1863, 17/2083
Perspiration, 10/1226, 18/2232
Perth, 3/266
Peru, 16/**1903–4**, 16/*1903–4*
  Indians, 11/1268, 11/*1270*
Pesticides, 14/1715
Pestle and mortar, 7/767
Pests, 10/*1228*
  control, 16/**1904–5**, 16/*1904*
  insect, 11/1277
Petain, Henri, 22/2613
Petals, 8/961, 8/*961*
Peter I the Great, Emperor of Rus-
  sia, 3/331, 16/**1907–8**, 16/*1907*,
  18/2145, 18/2146–7, 18/*2146*
Peter III, Emperor of Russia, 4/493

Peter the Hermit, 6/678
Peter Pan, 3/308
Peter Rabbit, 16/1986–7
Peter, Saint, 5/546, 16/1976, 18/2121
Petioles, 12/1402, 16/1940
Petitcodiac River, 15/1746
PETN, 8/895
Petoskey, 17/2105
Petrels, 17/2065, 18/2181
Petrified forests, 15/1859, 16/**1908**,
  16/*1908*
Petrolatum, 21/2558
Petroleum, 9/1019, 16/**1908–10**,
  16/*1908–10*
  finding oil, 16/1909
  future of, 16/1910
  gasoline, 9/10466
  transportation, 16/1933
  transporting oil, 16/1909
  see also Oil
Petrology, 9/1055
Pets, 7/753, 7/754, 16/**1905–7**,
  16/*1905–7*
  cats, 4/485–8
  dogs, 6/745–8, 6/*745–8*
  gerbils, 10/1126–7, 10/*1127*
  guinea pigs, 10/1126–7
  hamsters, 10/1126–7
  tropical fish, 20/2465–6
  veterinary medicine, 21/2522
Petunias, 9/*1039*
Peul, 15/1772
Pharmacies, hospitals, 10/1210
Pharoahs, 11/1368
Pharos at Alexandria, 18/*2193*,
  18/2194
Pharynx, 15/1799
Phases of the moon, 14/1647–8,
  14/*1647*
Pheasants, 9/*1034*
  poultry, 17/1992, 17/*1992*
Pheidippides, 3/318
Phenolics, 6/1955
Phidias, 18/2193
Philadelphia, 16/1893, 16/*1894*,
  16/**1910–11**, 16/*1910*
  Franklin, Benjamin, 9/1003
  Independence Hall, 11/1250, 11/*1250*
Philadelphia, USS, 3/303
Philanthropists, 8/995–6
  Carnegie, Andrew, 4/468–9
Philatelists, 5/594
Philately, 19/2324–5, 19/*2324*
Philby, Kim, 19/2319
Philip I, King of France, 16/**1911**,
  16/*1911*
Philip I the Handsome, King of
  Spain, 16/**1912**
Philip II, King of France, 6/679,
  16/**1911**, 17/2101
Philip II, King of Macedonia, 1/96,
  12/1474
Philip II, King of Spain, 3/319,
  16/**1912**, 16/*1912*, 16/1914,
  19/2300,
  marriage, 13/1522
Philip III, King of France, 16/**1911**
Philip III, King of Spain,
  16/**1912–13**
Philip IV the Fair, King of France,
  16/**1911–12**, 16/*1911*
Philip IV, King of Spain, 16/**1913**,
  21/2513
Philip V, King of France, 16/**1912**

Philip V, King of Spain, 16/**1913**,
  19/2302
Philip VI, King of France, 9/1008,
  10/1227, 16/**1912**
Philip VI, King of Spain, 16/**1913**
Philip, King of Macedon, 2/212
Philip, Prince, Duke of Edinburgh,
  7/837
Philippines, 12/1473, 12/1481,
  13/1544, 16/**1913–14**, 16/*1913*,
  19/2299, 20/2375
Philistines, 15/1865
Phillip, Arthur, 3/265
Phillumenists, 5/594
Philosopher's stone, 1/93
Philosophy, 16/**1914–15**, 16/*1914–15*
  ancient civilizations, 2/136
  Aquinas, St Thomas, 2/190
  Aristotle, 2/211–12
  Bacon, Francis, 3/28708
  Confucius, 6/626–7
  Socrates, 19/2254
  yoga, 22/2634–5
Phloem, 3/305, 16/1939, 20/2459
Phnom Penh, 11/1352
Phoenicia, 8/889, 9/1083, 14/1649,
  15/1865, 16/**1915–16**, 16/*1916*
  alphabet, 1/105–6, 1/*106*
  Carthage, 4/477
  ships, 18/2206, 18/*2206*
  summary, 2/134
  trade, 20/2444
Phoenix Islands, 16/1971
Phoenix (mythical bird), 2/161
Phoenix, 2/216
Phonograph, 5/612, 7/801, 7/*801*
Phosphors, lighting, 12/1336
Photocopiers, 16/**1916**, 16/*1916*
Photoelectricity, 16/**1916–17**
Photoengraving, 17/2004–5
Photo-finishes, 10/*1208*
Photographic collage, 6/691
Photography, 16/**1917–20***,
  16/*1917–20*
  astronomical, 2/251
  cameras, 4/440–2, 4/*441–2*
  careers, 16/1920
  developing, 16/*1918*, 16/1919
  film cartridges, 4/482
  history, 16/1920
  holography, 10/1195–6, 10/*1195*
  printing, 16/1919–20
  taking photographs, 16/1917–19
Photomicrography, 13/1583
Photons, 13/1584, 17/2035
Photosynthesis, 4/462, 4/463,
  12/1402–4, 16/**1920–1**, 16/*1921*,
  16/1940, 19/2351
Phrygia, 13/1584
Phyfe, Duncan, 9/1027
Phyla, 2/155
Phylloclads, 6/634
Physical anthropologists, 2/175
Physical chemistry, 5/519
Physical education, 16/**1921–2**,
  16/*1922*
Physical geography, 9/1054
Physical geology, 9/1055
Physical therapists, 10/1211
Physics, 16/**1922–4**, 16/*1922–4*
  cold, 10/1168–70, 10/*1169–70*
  Einstein, Albert, 7/812
  elasticity, 7/813

  energy, 16/1922–3
Faraday, Michael, 8/908
Fermi, Enrico, 8/922–3
fiber optics, 8/927, 8/*927*
force, 8/983–4
Franklin, Benjamin, 9/1004
friction, 9/1012–13, 9/*1012–13*
Galvani, Luigi, 9/1032
gas, 9/1044–6, 9/*145–6*
heat, 10/1168–70, 10/*1169–70*
lenses, 12/1414–16, 12/*1415–16*
light, 12/1432–4, 12/*1432–4*
liquid crystals, 12/1444
liquids, 12/1444
machines, 12/1475–6, 12/*1475–6*
magnets, 12/1483–4, 12/*1483–4*
matter, 13/1536–7, 16/1922
motion, 14/1656–7, 14/*1656–7*
Planck, Max, 16/1936
power, 17/1992–3
pressure, 17/1999
quantums, 17/2035
radiation, 17/2043–4, 17/*2044*
relativity, 7/812, 17/2078
solids, 19/2261
sound, 19/2262–5, 19/*2263–5*
spectrum, 19/2305–7, 19/*2305–6*
stress, 19/2343
surface tension, 19/2356–7
vacuums, 21/2506
Physiology, 3/342, 10/1224
  plant, 3/375
Phytoplankton, 13/1515, 13/*1516*
Piano accordion, 1/21
Pianos, 16/**1924–5**, 16/*1924–5*,
  19/2345
Piazzi, Giuseppe, 2/246
Pibrochs, 3/291
Picaresque novels, 15/1801
Picasso, Pablo, 1/18, 2/234, 3/296,
  5/509, 14/1620–1, 16/**1925–6**,
  16/*1925–6*, 20/2380
  Acrobat with a Ball, 16/1926,
    16/*1926*
  Dove of Peace, 16/1926
  Guernica, 16/1926
  Paulo as Pierrot with Mask,
    16/1926, 16/*1926*
Piccard, Auguste, 15/1820
Piccard, Jacques, 8/893
Piccolo, 21/2602
Pickford, Mary, 9/1119, 14/1659
Pickled foods, 8/976
Picric acid, 8/895
Picts, 7/855
Picture books, children's, 5/533
Pieces of eight, 14/1632
Pie diagrams, 9/1102, 9/*1102*
Piedmont, 21/2532
  Delaware, 6/714
  Georgia, 9/1061–2
  New Jersey, 15/1754
Piedmont Plateau, 13/1522, 13/1524,
  15/1787, 19/2274
Pied shield bug, 4/*404*
Pierce, Benjamin, 16/1927
Pierce, Franklin, 16/**1927–8**, 16/*1927*
Pierce, Jane, 16/1927
Piero della Francesca, 17/2085
Pierre, South Dakota, 19/2278
Piers, 4/431, 18/2125
Piezo-electric crystals, 17/2071
Pigeons, 5/558, 5/*559*, 16/**1929–30**,
  16/*1929*

Pig iron, 11/1303
Pigments, 5/601, 15/1858
  albinos, 1/92
Pigs, 16/**1928–9**, 16/*1928*
Pikes Peak, 15/1782, 16/1930
Pike, Zebulon, 16/**1930**
Pilate, Pontius, 11/1331
Pilatre de Rozier, Jean-François,
  3/298
Pile, carpets, 4/472
Piles, 6/647
Pile weaves, 20/2416
Pilgrim settlers, 1/111, 1/115,
  13/1528–30, 13/1531, 13/1541–2,
  13/1588, 16/**1930–1**, 16/*1930–1*,
  20/2419
  Mayflower Compact, 13/1542
Pilgrim's Progress, 4/410–11
Pilipino, 16/1914
Pillboxes, fortifications, 8/990
Pillow lace, 12/1382
Pillow lava, 15/1816
Pilocerus, 4/428
Pilohippus, 10/*1204*
Piloting, navigation, 14/1724
Pilots, 22/2623
  Byrd, Richard E., 4/423
  Earhart, Amelia, 7/780
  Lindbergh, Charles Augustus,
    12/1441–2
  see also Flyers
Pima Indians, 2/215
Pinchback, Pinckney B.S., 3/354
Pinchot, Gifford, 6/639, 14/1707
Pincushion cactus, 10/*1215*
Pineapples, 9/1018
Pine Belt, Texas, 20/2412
Piney Woods, 13/1612
Pink orchard mantis, 4/*443*
Pinocchio, 17/2032
Pinpoint maps, 13/1512
Pins, 16/**1931**
Pinta, 5/606
Pintails, 7/770, 7/771
Pintos, 10/1203
Pin-tumbler cylinder locks, 12/1457,
  12/1458
Pinus thunbergii, 20/*2459*
Pinworms, 22/2620
Pinyin, 5/536, 5/541
Pinyon pine, 6/632
Pioneer life, 16/**1931–3**, 16/*1932–3*
  family life, 16/1932
  frontier houses, 16/1932, 16/*1932*
  hardships, 16/1933
  Westward Movement, 21/2575–8
  Wilderness Road, 21/2585–6,
    21/*2586*
Pioneer spacecraft, 19/2288, 19/2289
Pipelines, 16/**1933–4**, 16/*1934*
Pipes, music, 21/2602
Pipes, plumbing, 16/1957–8
Pipe smoking, 19/2242–3, 19/*2242*
Pipil Indians, 7/838
Pipsissewa, 13/1552
Pirates, 16/**1934–5**, 16/*1934–5*,
  19/2303
  Barbary Coast, 3/303
  Verrazano, Giovanni da, 21/2520
Pisa, 11/*1313*
  Leaning Tower, 12/1405, 12/*1405*
Piscataqua River, 15/1751, 15/1752
Piscataway Indians, 13/1525

Pisces, 6/641, 6/642
Pissarro, Camille, 10/*1245*, 10/1246
Pistachio nuts, 15/1810
Pistia, 2/*189*
Pistils, 8/961, 16/1941
Pistols, 10/1131–2
Pitcairn Island, 14/1695, 16/1971
Pitch:
  hearing, 10/1165
  music, 14/1682
  singing, 18/2227
  sound, 19/2265
  voice, 19/2307
Pitcher plant, 11/1281, 11/*1281*
Pitman Shorthand, 18/2215
Pitman, Sir Isaac, 18/2215
Pitons, 14/1671
Pits, mining, 13/1601
Pitti Palace, Florence, 4/390
Pittsburgh, 9/1005, 16/1894, 16/*1896*
Pitt, William the Elder, 9/1006
Pituitary gland, 9/1080, 9/*1081*,
  10/1202
Pius IX, Pope, 18/2121
Pius XI, Pope, 14/1648, 21/2510
Pixies, 7/839
Pizarro, Francisco, 6/637, 6/723,
  7/801, 11/1248, 16/**1935–6**,
  16/*1936*, 19/2273
Placenta, 7/840
Placental animals, 3/268–9, 13/1496,
  13/*1496*
Placer deposits, 9/1090
Plains of Abraham, battle of, 4/447
Plains Apache, 15/1827
Plains Indians, 3/356, 6/669, 6/687,
  11/1262, 11/*1263*, 11/1266,
  14/1732, 15/1781
Plainsong, 5/544
Plaintiffs, court sytem, 6/667
Planck, Max, 3/364, 16/**1936**,
  16/*1936*, 17/*2035*
Plane geometry, 9/1058
Planes, carpentry, 4/472, 4/*472*
Plane surveying, 19/2361
Plane tables, 19/2360
Planetariums, 14/1716, 16/**1936–7**,
  16/*1937*
Planetary geology, 9/1055, 9/1057,
  9/*1057*
Planets:
  atmospheres, 3/257
  Earth, 7/780–4, 7/*781–3*
  orbits, 15/1837–8
  solar system, 19/2256–7
  see also individual planets
Planing hulls, 3/361
Plankton, 2/149, 2/170, 5/590,
  13/1515–16, 13/*1516*, 15/1816
  luminescence, 3/343
Plantations, 1/54, 1/83, 1/112–13
  slavery, 18/2236
Plant breeding, 16/**1942**, 16/*1942*
  Burbank, Luther, 4/412–13
Planter, 3/354
Plant kingdom, 3/341, 16/**1946–9**,
  16/*1948–9*
Plants, 16/**1937–41★**, 16/*1938–41*
  animals and, 16/1945
  barriers to distribution, 16/1946
  botany, 3/374–5
  bulbs, 4/408–9, 4/*408*
  cactus, 4/427–8

carbohydrates, 4/462
caves, 4/499
cells, 16/1939
climate, 16/1944–5
coal forests, 16/1952, 16/*1952*
desert, 6/720–1, 6/*720*
diseases, 16/**1942–3**, 16/*1943*
distribution, 16/**1943–6**, 16/*1943–6*
drugs from, 7/768
ecology, 7/793–8
environment, 16/1943–6
evergreen trees, 8/885
evolution, 8/885–8
fats and oils, 8/916–17, 8/*917*
ferns, 8/923–4, 8/*923–4*
fertilizer, 8/925
fire and, 16/1946
flowers, 8/961–3, 8/*961–3*
food web, 8/978–9, 8/*979*
fossils, 8/992–5
fruit, 9/1016–18, 9/*1016–18*
fungus, 9/1020–2, 9/*1021–2*
garden flowers, 9/1038–9, 9/*1038–9*
gardening, 9/1040–2, 9/*1041–2*
genetics, 9/1050–3
grass, 9/1103–4, 9/*1104*
greenhouses, 9/1116–17, 9/*1117*
growth, 9/1121–2
horsetails, 10/1209
houseplants, 10/12–17, 10/*12–17*
insect-eating, 11/1281–2, 11/*1281*
kinds, 16/1939
leaves, 12/1402–4, 12/*1402–3*,
  16/*1938*, 16/1940
lichen, 12/1428, 12/*1428*
location, 16/1937–8
medicinal, 13/1552
mountain, 14/1669
nature study, 14/1720–1
nitrogen cycle, 15/1776–7
North America, 15/1785
nuts, 15/1809–10
of the past, 16/**1951–4**, 16/*1952–3*
orchids, 15/1840
parasitic, 16/1876–7, 16/*1877*,
  16/1943
photosynthesis, 16/1920–1, 16/*1921*
poisonous, 16/1962–3, 16/*1962*
pond life, 16/1973–4
products, 16/**1950–1**, 16/*1950–1*
reproduction, 16/1941, 17/2086–9
respiration, 17/2092–3
roots, 16/*1938*, 16/1939
roses, 18/2137–8, 18/*2137*
seeds and fruit, 18/2186–8, 18/*2187*
shrubs, 18/2216–17, 18/*2217*
soil, 16/1945
South American, 19/2270–1
stems, 16/*1938*, 16/1940
structure, 16/1939
trees, 20/2458–63, 20/*2458–62*
vegetables, 21/2511–12
wildflowers, 21/2586–8, 21/*2586–8*
Plasma, blood, 3/359
Plasmatron, 18/*2174*
Plasmodium, 17/*2017*
Plaster molds, 18/2179
Plastic, 16/**1954–6**, 16/*1954–6*,
  20/2372
  building materials, 4/407
  extrusion, 6/728
Plastic surgeons, 19/2358
Platelets, blood, 3/359, 3/*360*
Platen presses, 17/2004

Plates, Earth's, 7/782
Plate tectonics, 6/652, 9/1055,
  16/**1956**
Platinum, 13/*1567*
Plato, 2/136, 2/212, 2/249–50, 3/255,
  9/1113, 9/1116, 16/*1914*,
  16/**1956–7**, 16/*1956*, 19/2249
Platte River, 14/1731, 14/1732
Platypus, 13/*1497*, 16/**1957**, 16/*1957*
Playing cards, 5/538, 5/*594*
Plays, thermometers, 20/2419–22,
  20/*2420–1*
Playwrights:
  Barrie, James M., 3/308
  Chekhov, Anton, 5/517
  Eliot, T.S., 7/836
  Ibsen, Henrik, 10/1232–3
  Shakespeare, William, 18/2197–8
  Wilder, Thornton, 21/2584–5
  Williams, Tennessee, 21/2590
Plebeians, 18/2129
Plectrums, 19/2344
Pleistocene Epoch, 7/786
Pleistocene Ice Age, 10/1233
Pleven, 4/409
Plimpton, James, 18/2118
Pliny the Elder, 7/843, 7/*843*,
  18/2132, 18/2155
Pliny the Younger, 16/1973
Pliocene Epoch, 7/786
  mammals, 13/1500
Pliopithecus, 10/*1220*
Plovdiv, 4/409
Plovers, 21/2552
Plows, 8/908
Plumage, feathers, 8/918–19
Plumbing, 16/**1957–8**, 16/*1958*
Plutarch, 9/1116, 16/**1958**, 16/*1958*
Pluto, 9/1088, 19/2257, 19/*2258*
  basic facts, 19/2259
Plymouth, England, 13/1541, 19/2300
Plymouth, Mass., 1/115, 13/1530,
  13/1531, 13/1542, 16/1930–1,
  17/2032
Plymouth Colony, 16/1930–1
Plymouth Rock chicken, 17/1991
Plywood, 4/405, 12/1470
  furniture, 9/1027
Pneumatic caisson, 4/431, 4/*431*
Pneumatic hammer, 1/77
Pneumatic tires, 20/2428
Poaching, 6/655
Pocahontas, 11/1319, 16/**1959**,
  16/*1959*, 17/1993, 17/*1993*,
  21/2532
Pocket billiards, 3/339
Pocket mice, 2/150, 17/2067
Pocono Mountains, 16/1896
Podocarps, 6/633
Poe, Edgar Allan, 12/*1449*, 16/**1959**,
  16/*1959*, 18/2127, 18/2175,
  18/2216
Poetry, 12/1447, 16/**1960–1★**,
  16/*1960–1*
  children's, 5/533–4
  limericks, 12/1438
  see also Writers
Po, Fernão do, 7/865
Pogroms, 11/1336
Poine du Sable, Jean Baptiste,
  5/526
Point, definition, 9/1058
Pointe-à-Pitre, 21/2572
Pointe-Noire, 6/628

Poison frog, 17/*2012*
Poisoning, first aid, 8/939, 8/*939*
Poison ivy, 16/1962, 16/*1961*
Poison oak, 16/1962
Poisonous plants, 16/**1962–3**, 16/*1962*
Poisonous snakes, 19/2244, 19/2245–6
Poisons, 16/**1961–2**
Poison sumach, 16/1962
Poitiers, battle of, 10/1227
Poland, 16/**1963–4**, 16/*1963–4*
  World War II, 16/1963
Polar bears, 3/320, 16/*1965*
Polar climate, 5/576
Polar fronts, 21/2562
Polaris (missile), 6/641, 6/*641*
Polaris (star), 15/1795
Polar life, 16/**1964–5**, 16/*1965*
  tundra, 20/2473
Polaroid cameras, 4/*442*
Polders, 14/1742, 14/*1742*
Polecats, 21/2560
Pole vault, 20/*2439*, 20/2442
Polians, 16/1963
Police, 16/**1966–7**, 16/*1966–7*
  detectives, 6/723
  forensic science, 8/986
  history, 16/**1966**
  officers, 16/1967
  organization, 16/1966–7
  Royal Canadian Mounted, 18/2140, 18/*2140*
  work, 16/1967
Police courts, 6/667
Policies, insurance, 11/1283
Poliomyelitis, 5/528, 18/2156
Polisario Group, 14/1649
Politeness, 13/1505–6
Political geography, 9/1054
Political parties, 16/**1967–8**, 16/*1968*, 21/2489
Politicians and statesmen:
  Adams, John, 1/30–1
  Adams, John Quincy, 1/31–2
  Adams, Samuel, 1/32
  Brooke, Edward, 4/397
  Bruce, Blanche K., 4/399
  Bunche, Ralph, 4/410
  Burr, Arnold, 4/416
  Calhoun, John C., 4/435
  Castro, Fidel, 4/484–5
  Chester A. Arthur, 2/235–6
  Cromwell, Oliver, 6/675–6
  Davis, Jefferson, 6/701
  Debs, Eugene V., 6/704
  De Gaulle, Charles, 6/711
  Douglas, Stephen A., 7/755–6
  Eisenhower, Dwight David, 7/812–13
  Ford, Gerald Rudolf, 8/984–5
  Gandhi, Indira Priyadarshini, 9/1035
  Garfield, James A., 9/1042–3
  Garibaldi, Giuseppe, 9/1043
  Glenn, John, 9/1084–5
  Gorbachev, Mikhail Sergeyevich, 9/1092
  Grant, Ulysses Simpson, 9/1100–1
  Hamilton, Alexander, 10/1142
  Hancock, John, 10/1143
  Harding, Warren G., 10/1151–2
  Harrison, Benjamin, 10/1154–5
  Harrison, William Henry, 10/1155–6

Harris, Patricia Roberts, 10/1154
Hayes, Rutherford B., 10/1162–3
Henry, Patrick, 10/1179
Hitler, Adolf, 10/1190–1
Hoover, Herbert, 10/1200–1
Houston, Samuel, 10/1217
Jackson, Andrew, 11/1316–17
Jefferson, Thomas, 11/1326–7
Johnson, Andrew, 11/1337–8
Johnson, Lyndon Baines, 11/1338–40
Juárez, Benito, 11/1344
Kennedy, John Fitzgerald, 11/1358–9
Kennedy, Robert Fitzgerald, 11/1359–60
Khrushchev, Nikita, 11/1364–5
King, W.L. Mackenzie, 11/1367
Lafayette, Marquis de, 12/1383
Laurier, Sir Wilfrid, 12/1398
Lenin, Vladimir Ilich, 12/1414
Lincoln, Abraham, 12/1438–41
MacDonald, John A., 12/1473–4
Machiavelli, Niccolò, 12/1474–5
McKinley, William, 13/1543–4
Madison, James, 12/1478–9
Mao Tse-tung, 13/1508
Meir, Golda, 13/1557
Monroe, James, 14/1637–9
More, Sir Thomas, 14/1648
Mulroney, Brian, 14/1674
Mussolini, Benito, 14/1693–4
Nasser, Gamal Abdel, 14/1703–4
Nehru, Jawaharlal, 14/1737
Nixon, Richard Milhous, 15/1777–8
Pearson, Lester, 16/188–9
Perón, Eva, 16/1900
Perón, Juan, 16/1900
Pierce, Franklin, 16/1927–8
Polk, James Knox, 16/1968–9
Rankin, Jeannette, 17/2062
Reagan, Ronald, 17/2067–8
Roosevelt, Franklin D., 18/2133–5
Roosevelt, Theodore, 18/2135–6
Stalin, Joseph, 19/2324
Sun Yat-sen, 19/2354
Taft, William Howard, 20/2375
Taylor, Zachary, 20/2382–3, 20/*2383*
Teng Hsiao-p'ing, 20/2402
Thatcher, Margaret, 20/2419
Tito, 20/2430
Trudeau, Pierre, 20/2470
Truman, Harry S., 20/2470–2
Tyler, John, 20/2479–80
Van Buren, Martin, 21/2507–8
Washington, George, 21/2547–8
Webster, Daniel, 21/2564
Wilson, Woodrow, 21/2590
Young, Andrew, 22/2636
Politics:
  democracy, 6/715–16
  dictators, 6/726
  fascism, 8/910–11
  parliament, 16/1878–9
  socialism, 19/2249–50
Polkas, 6/697
Polk, James Knox, 13/1572, 16/**1968–9**, 16/*1969*
Pollen, 8/961
Pollination, 8/961–2, 16/*1941*, 16/*1941*, 16/1942, 16/*1942*, 17/*2087*

Polling, elections, 7/814–16
Polliwogs, 2/130
Pollock, Jackson, 1/19–20, 1/*20*, 2/234, 14/*1620*, 14/1621
Pollution, 6/639, 7/795, 7/797, 14/1715–16, 16/**1969–70**, 16/*1970*, 17/*2021*
  acid rain, 1/22–3
  aerosols, 1/39
  air, 1/72–5, 1/72–*5*
  detergents, 19/2248
  diseases, 6/738
  Great Lakes, 9/1108
  Industrial Revolution, 11/1275
  marine, 13/1517
  nuclear radiation, 12/1392
  trees and, 20/2462
  water, 21/2554–5, 21/*2554*
Pollution index, 1/74–5
Polo, 16/**1970**, 16/*1970*
Polo, Marco, 2/150, 8/889, 8/892, 11/1322–3, 16/1890, 16/**1970–1**, 16/*1971*, 16/1985, 20/2444
Polonaise, 5/543
Polonium, 6/686, 17/2048
Polydectes, 16/1902
Polyesters, 16/1955
  rope, 18/2137
Polyethylene, 16/1955
Polygamy, 19/2241
Polygons, 9/1059
Polyhymnia, 14/1678
Polymerization, 16/1955
Polymers, 8/926, 16/1955
Polynesia, 15/1854, 16/**1971–2**, 16/*1972*
Polynesians, 10/1158, 10/1182
Polyphemus moth, 4/422
Polyphonic music, 5/544
Polyps, 5/590
  coral, 6/658
Polystyrene, 16/1955
Polytheism, 17/2079
Pomegranates, 18/*2187*
Pomes, 9/*1017*, 18/2187
Pompeii, 2/*139*, 2/198, 14/1651, 14/*1651*, 16/**1973**, 16/*1973*, 18/2120, 21/2535
Pompey, 4/429
Pompey the Great, 18/2130
Pompidou, Georges, 9/1010
Pompilius, Numa, 8/919
Ponape, 13/1582
Ponca City, 16/*1933*
Ponca Indians, 14/1732
Ponce de León, Juan, 6/637, 8/957–8, 8/997, 16/**1973**, 16/*1973*, 17/2027
Ponderosa, 6/632
Pond life, 16/**1973–4***, 17/*1974*
Pond skater, common, 4/*404*
Pond turtles, 20/2478
Ponies, 10/1207
Pontchartrain d'Etroit, 4/429
Ponte Vecchio, Florence, 4/390, 8/956
Pontiac, 11/1270, 16/**1975**, 16/*1975*
Pontoon bridges, 4/390, 4/*390*
Pony Express, 10/1184, 16/**1975**, 16/*1975*
Pool, 3/339
Poona, 3/291
Poor Richard's Almanack, 9/1003
Poor, Salem, 3/353

Pop art, 14/1621
Popes, 5/546, 16/**1976–7**, 16/*1976–7*
  see also individual popes
Popocatépetl, 13/1573
Poppaea, 14/1739
Poppies, 21/*2588*
Popular music, 14/1686, 16/**1977–8**, 16/*1977–8*
  Dylan, Bob, 7/777
  Foster, Stephen, 8/995
  Gershwin, George, 9/1072
  Gershwin, Ira, 9/1072
  Handy, W.C., 10/1147
  musicals, 14/1687–8
Population, 16/*1978*, 16/**1979–80***, 16/*1979*
Porcelain, 16/1988
Porcupine fish, 8/*942*
Porcupines, 16/**1980**, 16/*1980*, 18/2115
Porifera, 2/156, 19/2315
Po River, 11/1312
Pork, 13/1547
Porpoises, 7/751–2, 7/*751–2*
Porsche, 20/*2451*
Port, sailing, 18/2153
Port authorities, 10/1151
Port Elizabeth, 19/2267
Porter, Cole, 11/1255, 14/1687
Porter, Sydney *see* Henry, O.
Portinari, Beatrice, 6/698
Port Jackson, 3/265, 20/2369
Portland, Maine, 12/1485
Port Louis, 13/1538
Port Moresby, 13/1558, 16/1873
Port-of-Spain, 21/2571
Portraits, 16/**1980–1**, 16/*1981*
Port Royal, 16/1934
Ports, 10/1149–51, 10/*1149–51*
Port Said, 10/1149
Portsmouth, New Hampshire, 15/1751
Portsmouth, Rhode Island, 17/2099
Portsmouth, Virginia, 21/2533
Port Stanley, 8/907, 8/*907*
Portugal, 8/*878*, 16/**1981–3**, 16/*1982–3*
  American colonies, 8/893
  Brazil and, 4/386, 4/387, 17/2104, 18/2161
  colonies, 1/48–9, 2/144
  flag, 8/951
  folk dancing, 8/*970*
  Gamo, Vasco da, 9/1032–3
  Guinea-Bissau, 10/1126
  Macao, 12/1472–3
  Magellan, Ferdinand, 12/1481
  Mozambique, 14/1672
  São Tomé and Príncipe, 18/2161–2
Portuguese East Africa *see* Mozambique
Portuguese Guinea *see* Guinea-Bissau
Portuguese language, 18/2123
Portuguese man-of-war, 11/1328, 11/*1328*
Portuguese West Africa (Angola), 2/144
Poseidon, 2/142, 7/751, 9/1088
Postage stamps, collecting, 19/2324–5, 19/*2324*
Postal services, 16/**1983–6***, 16/*1983–6*
  handling, 16/1984–5
  history, 16/1985–6

international, 16/1986
Pony Express, 16/1975, 16/*1975*
postage, 16/1984
types of, 16/1983–4
Poster paint, 15/1860
Post-Impressionists, 5/509
Post-mark, 16/1984
Postulates, 13/1533
Posture, 10/1163, 16/**1986***
Potaro River, 10/1133
Potatoes, 4/408, 4/*408*, 4/413,
16/1946
Potato pickers, 8/*910*
Potato prints, 9/1103
Potato Salad, 6/654–5
Potawatomi Indians, 11/1270,
13/1580, 21/2559
Potential energy, 7/844
Potlatches, 20/2430
Potomac River, 13/1524
Potter, Beatrix, 5/533, 16/**1986–7**,
16/*1987*
Potter's wheel, 16/1989, 16/*1990*
Potter wasps, 2/*154*, 21/2549
Pottery, 5/572, 16/**1987–90***,
16/*1988–90*
American Indian, 11/1259, 11/*1260*
Pottowatomie Creek, 11/1355
Pouched mammals, 3/268–9
Poultry, 17/**1991–2**, 17/*1991–2*
Pound, Ezra, 7/836
Powahatan, 21/2532
Powder down feathers, 8/918
Powdered milk, 6/692
Powell, John Wesley, 9/1099
Powell, Lake, 12/1385
Power, 17/**1992–3**
democracy, 6/715–16
dictators, 6/726
hydroelectricity, 10/1230, 10/*1230*
solar energy, 19/2256, 19/*2256*
Powerboats, 3/362
Power lines, 7/823
Powers, Francis Gary, 19/2320
Power stations, nuclear, 15/1803–5
Powhatan, 16/1959, 17/**1993**, 17/*1993*
Powhatan Confederacy, 17/1993
Powhatan Indians, 1/100, 11/1270
Praia, 4/459
Prairie chickens, 9/1034
Prairie dogs, 2/153–4, 9/1120,
9/1121, 17/**1994–5**, 17/*1995*,
17/2063
Prairies, 17/**1993–4**, 17/*1993–4*
animal life, 2/150
wildflowers, 21/2587
Prairie wolf, 21/2599
Praslin, 18/2197
Pravda, 15/1761
Prawns, 6/681
Praxiteles, 2/231, 2/*232*
Prayer, 17/**1995**, 17/2080
Precession, 10/1135
Precincts, 16/1966
Precious stones, 9/1049–50
Precipitation, 21/2553
rain and snow, 17/2059–60
Precott, Samuel, 1/125, 1/*125*
Prefabricated houses, 6/648
Prehistoric animals, mammals,
13/1498
Prehistory, 17/**1996**, 17/*1996*
Premature babies, incubators,
11/1249, 11/*1249*

Premiums, insurance, 11/1283
Premolars, 20/2386
Prepositions, 16/1882
Pre-Raphaelite Brotherhood, 18/2127
Presbyterian church, 17/2013
Prescott, 17/2094
Preservatives, bread, 3/293
Presidency, 17/**1996–9**, 17/*1998*
Cabinet, 4/425–6
campaigns, 16/*1968*
clubs, 5/584–5
Congress, 6/628–30
constitution, 6/642, 6/644
elections, 7/815
impeachment, 6/630, 10/1244–5,
11/1337–8
list of, 17/1997
Senate and, 6/630
spoils system, 11/1317
veto power, 6/631
see also Presidents; Vice-Presidents
Presidential Medal of Freedom,
13/1550
President pro tempore, 6/630
Presidents:
Adams, John, 1/30–1
Adams, John Quincy, 1/31–2
Buchan, James, 4/400–1
Carter, James Earl, 4/476
Cleveland, Grover, 5/**573–4**
Coolidge, Calvin, 6/656
Eisenhower, Dwight David,
7/812–13
Fillmore, Millard, 8/928–9
Ford, Gerald Rudolf, 8/984–5
Garfield, James A., 9/1042–3
Grant, Ulysses Simpson, 9/1100–1
Harding, Warren G., 10/1151–2
Harrison, Benjamin, 10/1154–5
Harrison, William Henry,
10/1155–6
Hayes, Rutherford B., 10/1162–3
Hoover, Herbert, 10/1200–1
Jackson, Andrew, 11/1316–17
Jefferson, Thomas, 11/1326–7
Johnson, Andrew, 11/1337–8
Johnson, Lyndon Baines,
11/1338–40
Kennedy, John Fitzgerald,
11/1358–9
Lincoln, Abraham, 12/1438–41
McKinley, William, 13/1543–4
Madison, James, 12/1478–9
Monroe, James, 14/1637–9
Nixon, Richard Milhous,
15/1777–8
Pierce, Franklin, 16/1927–8
Polk, James Knox, 16/1968–9
Reagan, Ronald, 17/2067–8
Roosevelt, Franklin D., 18/2133–5
Roosevelt, Theodore, 18/2135–6
Taft, William Howard, 20/2375
Taylor, Zachary, 20/2382–3,
20/*2383*
Truman, Harry S., 20/2470–2
Tyler, John, 20/2479–80
Van Buren, Martin, 21/2507–8
Washington, George, 21/2547–8
Wilson, Woodrow, 21/2590–2
Presidium, 19/2285
Presley, Elvis, 16/1978, 17/**1999**,
17/*1999*
Presses, printing, 3/367, 17/2004
Pressure, 17/**1999**, 17/*1999*

barometers, 3/306
gases, 9/1045–6
Prestressed concrete, 6/625
Pretoria, 19/2267
Prevailing winds, 21/2592
Preventive medicine, 13/1554
Príncipe, 18/2161–2, 18/*2162*
Priam, 20/2465
Pribilof Islands, 1/95, 13/1591
Prickly pear, 4/428, 4/*429*
Pride of lions, 12/1443
Priesthood, 17/2080–1
Priestley, Joseph, 17/**1999–2000**,
17/*2000*, 18/2141
Primary colors, 5/601
Primary elections, 7/815
Primates:
apes, 2/180–2, 2/*180–2*
lemurs, 12/1413, 12/*1413*
monkeys, 14/1635–7, 14/*136–7*
Prime meridian, 11/1288
Prime ministers, 16/1879, 17/**2000**,
17/*2000*
Prime numbers, 15/1808
Prince Albert National Park, 18/2164
Prince Edward Island, 4/450,
17/**2000–2**, 17/*2001*
Princeton, N.J., 1/127
Princeton University, 5/574, 5/595
Pring, Martin, 15/1752
Printing, 3/367, 9/1102, 17/**2002–6***,
17/*2002–5*
communication, 5/611
Gutenberg, Johannes, 10/1132
ink, 11/1276
kinds of, 17/17/2003–4
photocopiers, 16/1916, 16/*1916*
photoengraving, 17/2004
presses, 17/2004
typesetting, 20/2480–1
Prints, 9/1102
engraving, 7/870, 7/870–1, 7/*870*
etching, 7/869–70, 7/*869–70*
Japan, 15/1846, 15/*1847*
Prisms, 5/600, 12/1433, 12/**1434–5**,
12/*1435*, 19/2305
Prisons, 17/**2006–7**, 17/*2006–7*
Privateers, 16/1934–5
see also Pirates
Private investigators, 6/723
Private schools, 18/2169
Prizefights, 4/380
Probability, 5/**510–11**
Probate courts, 6/668
Probation officers, 11/1350
Proboscis, 4/419
Processed foods, 8/976–8, 8/*976–8*,
15/1810
Proclamation of Neutrality, 21/2548
Producer gas, 9/1019
Producers, 18/2188
Production, economics, 7/798
Products, mathematics, 2/214
Profile lake, 15/1751
Profit, 1/22, 7/798
Progesterone, 10/1201
Programmed learning, 12/1408
Programs, computer, 5/623, 5/*623*,
5/624
Prohibition, 17/**2007–8**, 17/*2007*
Prokofiev, Sergei, 17/**2008**, 17/*2008*,
19/2284
Prometheus, 9/1075, 16/1870,
17/**2008–9**

Promotory Point, 21/2578
Prone float, 20/2364
Prone glide, 20/2365
Pronghorn, 2/*173*, 2/174, 10/1202
Pronouns, 16/1881
Pronunciation, 17/**2009**
Proofreading, 3/368, 17/2025
Propaganda, 17/**2009–10**, 17/*2010*
Propagation, houseplants, 10/1216–17
Propelling pencils, 16/*1897*
Properties of matter, 5/519
Property taxes, 20/2382
Prophets, 17/**2010–11**, 17/*2011*
Prophet's Town, 20/2386
Prosceniums, 20/2421
Prosecution, 20/2464
Prosecutors, 6/674
Prospecting, 13/1599–1600
Prospectors, 9/1090
Prosthodontists, 6/718
Protection:
insulation, 11/1282–3
insurance, 11/1283–4
masks, 13/1527
shelters, 18/2203–5
Protective coloring, 17/**2011–13**,
17/*2012*
Protein, 8/917, 13/1565, 15/1776,
15/1810, 17/**2013**, 17/*2013*
diet, 15/1811, 15/*1811*
fish, 8/948
Protestant churches, 8/881,
17/**2013–14**, 17/*2014*
evangelists, 8/883
leading US groups, 17/2014
Protestant Reformation, 5/546–7,
9/1065, 12/1470–1, 17/2013,
17/**2015–16**, 17/*2015–16*
begins, 17/2015
early stirrings, 17/2015
last years, 17/2015–16
Protest songs, 7/777
Prothallus, 8/924
Prothrombin, 12/1454
Protist Kingdom, 3/342
Protists, 2/158, 17/**2016–17**, 17/*2016*
Protons, 3/259, 7/810, 7/829
Proton synchrotons, 16/1881
Protoplasm, 5/501, 12/1429, 17/2013,
17/2017
Prototype Fast Reactor (PFR), 15/*1805*
Protozoans, 2/156, 2/158, 5/501,
6/737, 13/1516, 16/1973–4,
17/2016, 17/**2017–18**, 17/*2017–18*
Provençal, 18/2123
Provesi, Franco, 21/2516
Providence Plantations, 17/2097
Providence River, 17/2097
Provincetown, 13/1541
Proxima Centauri, 19/2327
Prudhoe Bay, 1/88
Pruning, 9/1017
Prussia, 9/1065–8
Bismarck, Otto von, 3/350–1
Przewalski's horse, 7/*754*, 10/1207
Psaltry, 19/2344
Psaronius, 16/*1953*
Pseudonyms, 14/1699
Pseudopods, 2/129
Psusennes, 18/*2225*
Psychiatric caseworkers, 19/2252
Psychiatric nurses, 15/1808
Psychiatrists, 11/1350, 13/1555,
17/2020

Psychiatry, 13/1562
Psychoanalysis, 7/763, 13/1563, 17/2021
  Freud, Sigmund, 9/1012
  Jung, Carl, 11/1348
Psychodelic drugs, 7/769
Psychology, 17/**2018–21**, 17/*2019–20*
  branches of, 17/2019–20
  emotions, 7/841–2
  extrasensory perception, 8/897–8
  Freud, Sigmund, 9/1012
  habits, 10/1136–7
  history, 17/2020–1
  intelligence, 11/1284–5
  Jung, Carl, 11/1348
  learning, 12/1406–8, 12/*1406–7*, 17/2108
  mental health, 13/1562–3
  mind and behavior, 17/2018–19
  motivation, 17/2018–19
  Pavlov, Ivan, 16/1885–6
  perception, 17/2018
  personality, 17/2019
Psychosis, 13/1563
Psychosomatic illnesses, 13/1563
Psychotherapy, 13/1562
Ptarmigans, 17/*2012*
Pteraspis, 8/*941*
Pteridophytes, 16/1947, 16/*1948*
Ptolemy, 7/810, 8/875, 9/1116
Ptolemy, Claudius, 2/250
Ptolemy dynasty, 5/572
Ptolemy V, 18/2138
Ptyalin, 6/730
Puberty, 1/34
Public Broadcasting Service (PBS), 20/2398
Public health, 13/1554, 17/**2021–2★**, 17/*2021–2*
  sanitation, 18/2159–60
  Social security, 19/2250
Publick Occurences, 15/1761
Public relations, 17/**2022–3★**, 17/*2022*
Public schools, 7/803–4, 18/2168–9
Public speaking, 17/**2023–4★**, 17/*2023*
Public utilities, 17/**2024–5**, 17/*2024*
Public Works Administration (PWA), 18/2134
Publishing, 3/367–8, 11/1343, 17/**2025–6★**, 17/*2025–6*
  copyright, 16/1884–5
  magazines, 12/1479–81
Puddle butterfly, 4/421
Puddle ducks, 7/771
Pudu, 6/710
Pueblo Indians, 2/215, 11/1263, 11/1266, 14/1722, 15/1757–8, 17/**2026**, 17/*2026*
Pueblos, 2/215, 5/575, 5/604
Puerto Rico, 10/1189, 13/1544, 16/1973, 17/**2027–8**, 17/*2027–8*, 19/2299, 21/2569, 21/2570
Puerto Rico trench, 3/254–5
Puerto Vallarta, 13/1573
Puffins, 18/2181, 18/*2181*
Pugachev, Emelyan, 18/2147
Puget Sound, 21/2543, 21/2546
Pulaski, 17/2069
Pulcinella, 17/2031
Pulitzer, Jospeh, 12/1451
Pulitzer Prize, 12/1451
Pullets, 17/1991

Pulleys, 12/1476
Pulp, wood, 12/1470
Pulsars, 3/356, 19/2327
Pulse, 5/550
Pulvilli, 8/966
Pumas, 2/*146*, 4/488
Pumpkins, 21/*2495*
  Halloween, 8/971, 8/*971*
Pumps, 17/**2028–9★**, 17/*2028–9*
  irrigation, 11/1305
  vacuum, 21/2506, 21/*2506*
Punch and Judy, 17/2032
Punctuation, 17/**2029–30**
Punic Wars, 4/477, 18/2130
Puns, 17/2102
Punta del Este, 21/2502
Pupas, 2/167, 4/421, 13/1569
  insect, 11/1281
Pupils, eyes, 8/898
Puppets, 17/**2030–2★**, 17/*2030–1*
Puppies, 6/747–8
  care, 6/747–8
  selection, 6/747
  training, 6/748
Pup tents, 20/2408
Pure science, 18/2174
Puritans, 1/111, 1/115, 7/857, 8/913, 8/*913*, 13/1541–2, 17/**2032–4**, 17/*2032*, 17/2099
  children's literature, 5/531
Purple gallinules, 6/671
Purple Heart, 13/*1550*
Purple tigers, 3/325
Purse seine net, 8/*949*
Pusan, 12/*1377*, 12/1378
Pushkin, Alexander, 15/1772
Putnam, George, 7/780
Putrefaction, 8/922
Putt, 9/1091
Putters, 9/1092
Puyallup Indians, 21/2544
Puya raymondii, 8/*961*
Puzzles:
  crosswords, 6/676
  riddles, 17/2102
  word games, 21/2603–4
Pygmies, 1/47, 4/417, 4/442, 9/1028, 17/**2033**, 17/*2033*, 18/2150
Pygmy gliding possum, 8/967
Pygmy pine, 6/634
Pygmy seahorse, 18/2183
Pygmy shrews, 14/1623
Pyjama cardinalfish, 13/*1516*
Pyongyang, 12/1376
Pyramids, 7/808, 7/810, 17/**2033–4**, 17/*2034*, 18/2193, 18/*2193*
Pyramid tents, 20/2408
Pyrenees, 2/141, 4/499, 19/2297
Pythagoras, 2/249, 17/**2034**, 17/*2034*
Pytheas, 2/209
Pythons, 19/2244, 19/2245

Qq

Qadhafi, Muammar, 12/1428
Qatar, 2/193
Quagga, 22/2644
Quails, 3/344, 3/345, 9/1034
Quakers, 1/112, 16/1910, 17/2013, 19/2252, 19/*2252*
  Penn, William, 16/1893
  Underground Railroad, 20/2483

Quaking grass, common, 9/*1104*
Quant, Mary, 5/*580*
Quantum, 3/364, 16/1936, 17/**2035**, 17/*2035*
Quarantine, 6/650
Quarks, 16/1881
Quarrie, Don, 15/*1831*
Quarrying, 17/**2035–6**, 17/*2036*
Quarter horses, 10/1206, 10/*1207*
Quartering Act, 1/124
Quartz, 13/*1596*, 13/1597, 18/2158
Quartz crystal watches, 5/578
Quasars, 2/252, 17/2050
Quebec, 4/447, 4/448, 4/*449*, 4/450, 4/452, 5/510, 17/**2036–8**, 17/*2037–8*
  battle of, 3/319, 9/*1005*, 9/1006
  climate, 17/2038
  history, 17/2038
  industry, 17/2038
  land, 17/2036–8
  map, 17/*2037*
  provincial flower, 17/*2037*
Quechua, 7/800, 11/1268, 12/1389
Quechua Indians, 3/365, 16/1904
Queen Anne's War, 15/1746
Queen ants, 2/166–7
Queensberry, Marquis of, 4/380
Quesada, Jiminez, 6/638
Question marks, 17/2030
Questionnaires, 15/1836
Quests, 12/1372
Quetzal, 10/1123
Quetzalcoatl, 14/1697
Quezon, Manuel, 16/1914
Quicksands, 17/**2038**
Quills, 8/918, 16/1896, 16/1980
Quinary system, 15/1807
Quinault Indians, 21/2544
Quinine, 7/768, 10/1196, 16/*1950*
Quintilis, 11/1347
Quipus, 11/1248, 15/1806
Quisling, Vidkun, 20/2456
Quito, 7/800–1
Quivers, 2/199
Qumran Valley, 6/703
Quotas, international trade, 11/1292
Quotation marks, 17/2030
Quotient, 2/214
Quraish, 14/1673
Qureishites, 19/2262

Rr

R-101 airship, 1/79
Ra, 7/809, 21/*2499*
Rabat, 14/1648
Rabaul, 13/*1558*
Rabbis, 5/573, 11/1344
Rabbits, 2/*160*, 5/559, 7/797, 13/*1497*, 17/**2039–40**, 17/*2040*
  pet, 16/*1905*, 16/1907
  tracks, 2/163, 2/*164*
Rabelais, François, 9/1076
Rabies, 17/**2040–1**, 17/*2040*
Raccoons, 5/559, 8/*884*, 17/**2041★**, 17/*2041*
  pet, 16/*1907*
Races:
  athletics, 20/2439–43
  human, 10/1223–4
  marathons, 13/1512, 13/*1512*

Rachmaninoff, Sergei, 17/**2041–2**, 17/*2042*
Racial discrimination, 3/266
Racial relations, civil rights, 5/**561–4**
Racing cars, 3/278, 3/*278*
Racing horses, 10/1208–9, 10/*1208*
Racism, 6/736, 6/*736*
Rackham, Arthur, 5/533
Racquetball, 17/**2042**, 17/*2042*
Radar, 17/**2042–3**, 17/*2042–3*
  air traffic control, 1/80–1, 1/*81*
  navigation, 14/1725
Radial symmetry, 20/2371
Radial tires, 20/*2429*
Radiant energy, 7/845
Radiation, 17/**2043–4**, 17/*2044*
  fallout, 8/907
  glass protection, 9/1083
  heat, 10/1170
  microwaves, 13/1584
  radioactivity, 17/2048–9
  radio astronomy, 17/2050–1
Radiation belt, 17/**2044–5**, 17/*2045*
Radio, 17/**2045–7**, 17/*2045–7*
  acting, 1/28
  amateur, 17/**2047–8**
  Citizens Band (CB), 17/2048, 17/*2048*
  commercials, 1/38
  communication, 5/611, 5/*612*
  journalism, 11/1342–3
  Marconi, Guglielmo, 13/1513–14
  Morse Code, 14/1651
  navigation, 14/1725
  radar, 17/2042–3, 17/*2042–3*
  waves, 21/2557
Radioactive pollution, 12/1392
Radioactivity, 7/784, 17/**2048–9**, 17/*2048–9*
  Curie, Marie and Pierre, 6/686
  fallout, 8/907
  geiger counters, 9/1049, 9/*1049*
Radio astronomy, 17/**2050–1**, 17/*2050–1*
Radio beacons, 12/1434
Radio broadcasting, 17/**2051–3**, 17/*2051–2*
  entertainment, 17/2051
  frequencies, 17/2051–2
  industry, 17/2052–3
Radiocarbon, 4/463–4
Radio communications, 20/2388, 20/2389–90
Radiolarian, 17/*2018*
Radiologists, 13/1555
Radiometers, 15/1813, 17/2050
Radiosonde, 21/2563
Radio telescopes, 2/251, 2/*252*, 15/1813–14, 18/*2165*
Radio waves, 17/2043–4
  masers, 12/1393
  microwaves, 13/1584
Radisson, Pierre, 10/1218
Radium, 6/686, 17/2048
Radons, 17/2048
Radula, mollusks, 14/1624
Raffles, Sir Thomas Stamford, 18/2226
Rag dolls, 7/749
Ragged Dick, 1/99
Raggedy Andy, 7/750
Raggedy Ann, 7/750
Ragtime, 11/1325
Ra II, 8/*889*, 10/1182

Railroads, 17/**2053–9**, 17/*2053–9*,
  20/2449–50, 20/2453
  American history, 1/120
  cars, 17/2054–5
  classification yards, 17/2053
  control, 17/2053–4
  early, 17/2055–8
  future, 17/2059
  gauges, 17/2055
  locomotives, 17/2054–5
  model, 5/*594*
  signals, 17/2053–4
  Soviet Union, 19/2281
  Stephenson, George, 19/2333
  subways, 19/2348–9, 19/*2348–9*
  tunnels, 20/2474–5
Rails, birds, 6/670, 6/671
Railways, cable, 4/427
Rain, 17/**2059–60**, 17/*2060*, 21/2553,
  21/2562
  acid, 1/22–3
  artificial, 5/583
  clouds and, 5/582–3
  drought, 7/767
  erosion, 7/866
  famines, 8/907–8
  floods, 8/955–6, 8/*955–6*
  monsoon, 14/1639–40, 14/*1639–
    40*
  water supply, 21/2555
Rainbow Bridge, Utah, 14/1708
Rainbows, 17/**2060***, 17/*2060*,
  19/2305
Rainfall, plants and, 16/1944
Rain forests, 11/1348, 16/1945
Rainier III, Prince, 14/1627, 14/1628
Rainier, Mount, 20/2484, 21/2544
Rain-in-the-Face, 18/2228
Rainy, Joseph, 17/*2069*
Raleigh, Sir Walter, 1/*111*, 7/814,
  8/893, 8/*912*, 15/1788,
  17/**2060–1**, 17/*2061*, 20/2431,
  20/2437
Raleigh, Wat, 17/2061
RAM, 5/623
Rama, 10/1187
Ramadan, 11/1307
Ramapithecus, 10/1220, 10/*1220*
Rambouillet, 18/2202
Ramjets, 11/*1332*
Ramparts, 8/989
Rams, sheep, 18/2201
Ramsay, Sir William, 12/1336
Ramses II, Pharoah, 1/20, 7/809
Ran, 14/1695
Ranavallo III, Queen, 3/*353*
Rance River, 7/*846*
Ranches, 1/54
  cowboys, 6/668–9, 6/*668*
Ranching, 17/**2061–2**, 17/*2061*
Randolph, A. Phillip, 5/562
Randolph, Edmund, 4/425
Randori, 11/1345
Rangers:
  forest, 14/1707
  park, 14/1709
Ranger spacecraft, 19/2288
Rangoon, 4/415
Rankin, Jeanette, 17/**2062**, 17/*2062*
Raphael, 2/232, 6/*732*, 17/**2062–3**,
  17/*2062*, 17/2084, 17/*2085*
  Holy Family, 17/2062–3, 17/*2062*
Rapid Eye movement (REM),
  19/2240

Rapids, 21/2553
Rapid transit, 17/2054
Rapiers, 20/2368
Rare animals, 17/**2063–5**, 17/*2063–5*
Ras al Khaimah, 2/193
Ras Dashan, 7/871
Rasputin, 15/1772
Ratnapura, 19/2322
Rats, 17/**2065–7**, 17/*2066*
  in cities, 5/58, 5/*559*
Ravel, Maurice, 3/296
Ravens, 6/678, 21/2529
Ray fish, 8/943, 8/944, 18/2199–2200,
  18/*2200*
Ray, James Earl, 11/1367
Raymond, Henry J., 15/1761
Raynham Hall, Norfolk, 9/*1075*
Rayon, 20/2372
Razdan River, 19/*2281*
Razorbills, 16/*1965*
RDX, 8/895
Reactors, nuclear, 15/1803–5,
  15/*1804–5*
Reading, 12/1387
  dyslexia, 18/2168
  literacy, 12/1445–6
Reading, Pennsylvania, 16/1894
Reading lists, bibliography, 3/337
Reagan, Ronald Wilson, 2/245,
  4/476, 9/1092, 9/*1096*, 15/1771,
  17/**2067–8**, 17/*2067*
Realism, 17/**2068**, 17/*2068*
Reapers, 8/909, 8/*909*
  McCormick, Cyrus, 13/1543
Reber, Grote, 17/2050
Rebus, 17/2102
Recessive characteristics, 9/1051
Reciprocating engines, 7/848
Reciprocating pumps, 17/2028,
  17/*2028*
Recitative, 15/1834
Recollection, 13/1560
Reconstruction, 3/354, 17/**2068–71**,
  17/*2069–70*
  Freedmen's Bureau, 17/2070,
    17/*2070*
  legacy of war, 17/2069–70
  white power restored, 17/2070–1
Reconstruction Finance Corporation
  (RFC), 21/2491
Recording, 17/**2071–3**, 17/*2071–3*
  analog, 17/2073
  cassettes, 4/482
  compact discs, 5/**617**, 17/2073
  digital, 17/2073
  operation, 17/2071–2
  records, 17/2072–3
  tape recordings, 17/2072
  video, 21/2524–5
Recreation:
  areas, 14/1711
  parks, 16/1878
  Soviet Union, 19/2284
  see also Dance, Music, Pastimes,
    Sport
Rectifiers, 20/2448
Rectum, 6/731
Red bats, 3/317
Red blood cells, 3/359, 3/*360*,
  5/502
Red Brigades, 11/1313
Red cedar, 6/633
Red Cloud, 11/*1264*
Red Crescent, 17/*2073*

Red Cross, 8/907, 17/**2073–4**,
  17/*2073*
  Barton, Clara, 3/309
Red Deer, 1/90
Red Eagle, 11/*1271*
Redford, Robert, 14/*1661*
Red foxes, 8/997, 8/998
Red Guards, 13/1508
Redheads, 7/771
Red kangaroos, 11/1352–3
Red long-hair cat, 4/*486*
Rednecks, 17/2070–1
Red poll cattle, 4/495
Red River, 12/1464, 13/1603
Red River Expedition, 11/*1262*
Red River, Vietnam, 21/2525
Red Sea, 17/**2074**, 17/*2074*
Red shifts, 21/2500
Red Shirts, 9/1043, 17/2071
Red-spotted newts, 18/2156
Red spruce, 6/633
Red squirrel, 19/*2322*
Red stars, 2/172
Red Stick Indians, 6/672
Redstone rockets, 17/2111
Red-throated pipits, 13/*1593*
Reedbuck, 2/174
Reed instruments, 21/2603
Reed, Walter, 17/**2074–5**, 17/*2075*
Reefs:
  coral, 6/658–9
  Great Barrier Reef, 9/1106–7,
    9/*1107*
Reeve, Christopher, 14/*1662*
Reeves, 16/1966
Reference books, 17/**2075–6**,
  17/*2075–6*
Refineries, oil, 16/1909, 16/*19010*
Refining, metal ores, 13/1567–8
Reflecting telescopes, 15/1813,
  20/2394
Reflex actions, 14/1676, 14/1740,
  16/1886
Reformation, 5/546–7, 8/881, 9/1065,
  17/2013, 17/2015–16,
  17/*2015–16*, 18/2121
Reform Jews, 11/1345
Refracting telescopes, 15/1813,
  15/*1814*, 20/2394, 20/*2394*
Refraction of light, 12/1432
Refrigeration, 17/**2076**, 17/*2076*
Refrigerator cars, 17/2054
Refrigerators, 7/818
Refrigerator trucks, 20/2470
Refugees, 17/**2077**, 17/*2077*
Regattas, 18/2139
Regeneration, 17/**2077**, 17/*2077*
Regina, Saskatchewan, 18/*2163*,
  18/2164
Registered mail, 16/1984
Registered nurses (RN), 15/1808
Regulators, 15/1788
Rehabilitation, 19/2303
  prisoners, 17/2007
Reichstag, 9/1068
Reign of Terror, 9/1011
Reincarnation, 4/402, 10/1187
Reindeer, 6/*709*, 6/710, 12/1392
Reindeer moss, 12/1428
Reinforced concrete, 4/407
  building materials, 6/646
Relativity, 7/812, 17/**2078**, 17/*2078*,
  18/2172, 20/2428
Relay races, 20/*2440*, 20/2441

Relief maps, 13/1511–12
Relief sculpture, 18/2178
Religion, 17/**2078–82**, 17/*2079–82*
  Africa, 1/47–8
  American Colonies, 1/114
  Asia, 2/243
  Aztecs, 3/284
  Babylonians, 3/287
  Bible, 3/334–7
  Buddhism, 4/401–2
  carols, 4/470
  Christianity, 5/**546–7**
  Christian Science, 5/**547**
  civil rights and, 5/560
  Crusades, 6/678–80
  dance, 6/696
  diets and, 8/975
  Easter, 7/790
  evangelists, 8/883
  Hinduism, 10/1186–7, 10/*1186*
  Islam, 11/1306–7
  Judaism, 11/1344–5
  Koran, 12/1375–6, 12/*1375*
  major, 17/2079
  missionaries, 13/1610
  Orthodox Church, 15/1847–8,
    15/*1848*
  prayer, 17/1995, 17/2080
  priesthood, 17/2080–1
  prophets, 17/2011
  rites and rituals, 17/2081–2
  sacred writings, 17/2080
  sacrifice, 17/2080
  saints, 18/2154–5, 18/*2154–5*
  Shinto, 18/2205
  Sikhism, 18/2223
  Taoism, 20/2379
  temples, 20/2402
  Zoroastrianism, 16/1902
Religous music, 5/543–4
Rembrandt van Rijn, 2/132, 2/232,
  7/775, 7/*775*, 7/870, 7/*870*,
  13/*1553*, 17/**2082–3***, 17/*2082–3*
  Girl with a Broom, 17/2082–3,
    17/*2083*
Remond, Charles Lenox, 1/15, 1/*15*
Remus, 18/2128, 18/2129, 18/*2129*
Renaissance, 8/880, 8/956, 11/1311,
  17/**2083–5**, 17/*2083–5*
  architecture, 2/201, 2/203
  art, 2/232
  ships, 18/2206
  theater, 20/2421
Reno, 15/1743, 15/1744
Renoir, Pierre Auguste, 2/228,
  2/229, 15/1861, 15/1862,
  15/*1862*, 15/1863, 17/**2085–6***,
  17/*2086*
  Dancing at the Moulin de la Galette,
    17/2085–6, 17/*2086*
  Girl with a Straw Hat, 17/2086,
    17/*2086*
Repeating rifles, 10/1131
Reporters, 11/1342–3
Representative democracy, 9/1094
Repression, 17/2021
Reproduction, 17/**2086–9**, 17/*2087–9*
  asexual, 17/2086–7
  eggs, 7/806
  embryos, 7/840–1, 7/*840*
  evolution, 8/885–8
  fish, 8/945

(continued)

flies, 8/966
flowers, 8/962–3
fungi, 9/1021
mollusks, 14/1625
moss, 14/1655–6
plants, 16/1941
sexual, 17/2087–9
Reptiles, 5/559, 17/**2089–91**, 17/*2090–1*
eggs, 7/*806*
hearing, 10/1166
lizards, 12/1445–6, 12/*145–6*
snakes, 19/2244–6, 19/*2244–6*
turtles, 20/2477–8
Republics, 16/1968, 17/**2091–2**, 17/*2092*, 21/2489
Rescue, coast guards, 5/586–7
Reservations, 2/217, 11/1270
aborigine, 1/17, 3/268
Reservoirs, 21/2556
lakes, 12/1385
Residential hotels, 10/1212
Residential suburbs, 19/2347
Resins, 1/108, 3/305, 20/2372
Resistance:
electrical, 7/821
underground, 10/1124
Resistance wires, 7/816
Resolution, 6/653
Resonance, 19/2265
musical instruments, 14/1689
Resort hotels, 10/1212
Resources, natural, 14/1714–16
Respiration, 4/387–9, 4/*388*, 13/1565, 17/**2092–3**, 17/*2092*
mollusks, 14/1624
Restaurants, 17/**2093–4**, 17/*2093–4*
Retailing, stores and shops, 18/2188, 19/2337–8
Retina, eyes, 8/899
Retton, Mary Lou, 10/*1123*
Revels, Hiram R., 3/354, 5/561, 17/*2069*
Revenue marine, 5/587
Revere, Paul, 1/116, 1/125, 3/373, 17/**2094**, 17/*2094*, 18/2220
Reversing Falls, 15/1746
Revivalists, 8/883
Revolutions, 17/**2094–5**, 17/*2095*
Revolvers, 10/1132
Reykjavík, 10/1235
Reynard the Fox, 8/900
Reynolds, Joshua, 2/232, 17/**2095–6**, 17/*2095–6*
George Hare, 17/2095–6, 17/*2095*
Rhea, 8/954–5
Rhee, Syngman, 12/1377
Rheims Cathedral, 9/1093
Rhetoric, 7/803
Rhine, J.B., 8/897
Rhine-Main-Danube Canal, 4/454
Rhine River, 9/*1071*, 17/**2096**, 17/*2096*
Rhinoceroses, 2/*145*, 10/*1145*, 17/**2096–7**, 17/*2097*
Rhinocoris iracundra, 4/*404*
Rhizoids, 14/1655
Rhode Island, 17/2032, 17/**2097–2100**, 17/*2097–9*, 21/2590
climate, 17/2097
employment, 17/2099–2100
history, 17/2097–9
land, 17/2097

map, 17/*2098*
state emblems, 17/*2098*
Rhode Island reds, 17/2099
Rhodes, Colossus, 18/*2193*, 18/2194
Rhodes, Cecil, 17/**2100**, 17/*2100*, 22/2644, 22/2645
Rhodesia *see* Zimbabwe
Rhododendrons, 18/2217
Rhodope Mountains, 4/409, 4/*409*
Rhyme, 16/1960
Rhythm, poetry, 16/1960
Río de la Plata, 16/1875, 19/2268
Río Muni, 7/864–5
Rialto Bridge, Venice, 4/392
Rias, 18/2183
Ribbon Fall, 22/2635
Ribbon worms, 22/2620
Rice, 2/243, 2/*244*, 9/1097, 9/*1097*, 17/**2100–1**, 17/*2100–1*
flour making, 8/960
Rice, Dan, 5/583
Rice, Timothy, 14/1688
Richard I Lion Heart, King of England, 6/677, 6/679, 7/814, 10/1176, 11/1337, 17/**2101**, 17/*2101*
Richard II, King of England, 10/1176, 17/**2101–2**, 17/*2101*
Richard III, King of England, 5/587, 7/857, 10/1177, 17/**2102**, 17/*2102*, 21/2543
Richard Plantagenet, Duke of York, 21/2543
Richardson, Samuel, 15/1801
Richardson, William, 4/438
Richelieu, Cardinal, 12/1462
Richmond, Virginia, 6/626
Richter Scale, 7/*789*
Rickenbacker, Eddie, 21/*2606*
Ricketts, John, 5/553
Ricmond, Virginia, 21/*2530*
Riddles, 8/971, 17/**2102**
Rideau Canal, 15/1849
Rideau River, 15/1849
Ridgway, Matthew, 12/1378
Riding:
equestrianism, 7/865–6, 7/*865*
horses, 10/1207–8, 10/*1207–8*
rodeos, 18/2116–17, 18/*2116–17*
Riel, Louis, 13/1503
Riel Rebellion, 4/450
Rifles, 10/1129–32, 10/*1131*
Riga, 12/1396
Rigging, 18/2154, 18/2206
Right-handedness, 10/1145
Rigid airships, 1/78
Riley, James Whitcomb, 11/1255, 17/**2102–3**, 17/*2102*
Rimsky-Korsakov, Nicolai, 17/**2103**, 17/*2103*, 19/2340
Ringed seal, 16/*1965*, 18/2185
Ringling Brothers, 3/305, 5/553
Ringling Brothers and Barnum & Bailey, 5/553, 5/583
Ring-necked pheasant, 9/1034
Rings, jewelry, 11/*1334*
Ring-tailed lemurs, 12/*1413*
Rio de Janeiro, 4/387, 17/**2103–4**, 17/*2103*
Rio Grande, 13/1572, 15/1757, 17/**2104★**, 17/*2104*
Rio Grande Plain, 20/2412
Riot control, 2/227
Ripcords, 16/1874

Ripple Rock, 8/896
Rites, religious, 17/2081–2
Rituals, religious, 17/2081–2
Rivera, Diego, 13/1576, 13/1581
The Flower Vendor, 20/*2370*, 20/2371
Rivera, Hernando, 13/1573
Rivers, 17/**2104–6**, 17/*2104–6*
dams, 6/693–5, 6/*694–5*
floods, 8/955–6, 8/*955–6*
longest, 17/2105
pollution, 21/2554–5
waterfalls, 21/2553
see under individual river eg, Nile River
Rivière des Lacs, 15/1790
Riza Shah Pahlavi, 11/1299
Rizzio, David, 13/1522
RNA, 3/341
Road maps, 13/1509
Roadrunners, 15/1757
Roads, 19/2340–3, 19/*2341–2*
Roman, 18/2133, 20/2449
signs, 7/766, 7/*766*
traffic planning, 20/2445–6
tunnels, 20/2474–5
Roanoke Indians, 15/1788
Roanoke Island, 15/1788, 15/1790, 17/2060, 17/2061
Roans, 10/1203
Roasting, 6/655
Robards, Rachel, 11/1316
Robert, Duke of Burgundy, 10/1177
Roberts, Lord, 3/363
Robespierre, Maximilien, 9/1011, 9/*10011*
Robin Hood, 5/533–4, 10/1124, 17/**2106**
Robins, 14/*1719*
Robinson, Bill 'Bo-jangles', 21/2510
Robinson Crusoe, 6/710
Robinson, Jackie, 17/**2106**, 17/*2106*
Robots, 3/272, 13/*1508*, 17/**2107–8**, 17/*2107*
Robson, Mount, 4/*444*
Rochambeau, Count, 1/128
Roche L'Eveque, 4/499
Rochester, N.Y., 4/446
Rock-and-roll, 16/1978, 17/1999
Rock crab, 6/681
Rockefeller, John D., 8/995
Rocket, 19/2333, 19/*2333*, 20/*2450*
Rockets, 17/**2109–12**, 17/*2109–11*
Cape Canaveral, 4/458–9
engines, 7/849–50
Goddard, Robert H., 9/1087
Von Braun, Wernher, 21/2537
Rockford, 10/1242
Rock fowl, 17/*2064*
Rock hounds, 5/594
Rock lobsters, 6/681
Rockne, Knute, 17/**2112**, 17/*2112*
Rock 'n' roll, 6/697
Rocks, 17/**2108–9★**, 17/*2108–9*
avalanches, 3/279
geology, 9/1055
granite, 9/1099–1100, 9/*1099*
igneous, 17/2108
metamorphic, 17/*2108*, 17/2109
quarrying, 17/2035–6
sand, 18/2158
sedimentary, 17/2109
Rock salt, 18/2156
Rockwell, Norman, 5/609

Rocky Mountain goats, 9/1086, 9/*1086*, 18/2202
Rocky Mountain National Park, 5/604
Rocky Mountains, 4/444, 5/601–2, 5/*601*, 14/1640, 14/1671, 15/1782, 17/**2112–13**, 17/*2112*, 20/2460, 22/2625
continental divide, 6/652
Rococo art, 17/**2113–14**, 17/*2113–14*
Rodents, 18/**2115–16**, 18/*2115–16*
beavers, 3/321–2
gerbils, 10/1126–7, 10/*1127*
groundhogs, 9/1120
guinea pigs, 10/1126–7
hamsters, 10/1126–7
lemmings, 12/1413, 12/*1413*
mice, 17/2065–7
rats, 17/2065–7
squirrels, 19/2322, 19/*2322*
Rodeo Cowboys Association, 18/2116
Rodeos, 6/669, 18/**2116–17**, 18/*2116–17*, 21/2495, 22/2625
clowns, 5/584
Rodgers, Richard, 14/1687, 14/*1687*, 14/1688
Rodin, Auguste, 7/864, 18/**2117–18**, 18/*2117*
The Kiss, 18/2117, 18/*2117*
The Thinker, 18/2117, 18/*2117*
Rod puppets, 17/2031
Roebling, John, 4/392
Roe deer, 10/*1202*
Roentgen, Wilhelm Conrad, 13/1554, 22/2629, 22/2631
Rogers, Ginger, 14/1663
Rogers, Will, 15/1828, 18/**2118**, 18/*2118*, 21/2510
Rogers, William, 15/*1777*
Rolfe, John, 11/1319, 16/1959, 17/1993, 21/2532
Roller-derbies, 18/2119
Roller-hockey, 18/2119
Roller-skating, 18/**2118–19**, 18/*2118*
dancing, 6/698
Rolling-stock, railroads, 17/2054–5
Rollo, 21/2527–8
Rolls Royce Corniche, 3/275
ROM, 5/623
Roman candles, 8/938
Roman Catholic Church, 5/546–7, 8/880–1, 18/**2120–3**, 18/*2121–2*
American colonies, 10/1188
clergy, 5/573
faith, 18/2122–3
French Revolution, 9/1011
missionaries, 13/1610
organization, 18/2121–2
Popes, 16/1976–7
Protestant Reformation, 9/1065, 12/1470–1, 17/2015–16
sacraments, 18/2123
Vatican City, 21/2509–10
Romance languages, 12/1390, 12/1394, 18/**2123–4**
Romance novels, 12/1451
Romanesque architecture, 2/201
Romanesque art, 18/**2124–5**, 18/*2124–5*
Romania, 18/**2126**, 18/*2126*
Roman numerals, 2/212, 15/1806–7
Romanov, Fyodor, 18/2146
Romansch, 20/2367

Roman snail, 19/*2244*
Romanticism, 18/2127–8, 18/*2127–8*
Romantic period, 18/**2127–8**, 18/*2127–8*
Roman type, 20/2480–1
Romany, 10/1134
Romberg, Sigmund, 14/1687, 15/*1835*
Rome, 2/*201*, 8/*879*, 11/1312, 18/**2128–9**, 18/*2129*
St Peters, 13/*1577*, 13/1578
Santa Prassede, 14/*1652*
Rome, Ancient, 8/880, 18/**2129–33**, 18/*2129–32*
abacus, 1/13
Adriatic Sea, 1/36
aqueducts, 21/*2556*
architecture, 2/201
army, 5/587
art, 2/137, 18/**2119–20**, 18/*2119–20*
in Britain, 7/855
Byzantine Empire, 4/424
calendars, 4/434
Carthage and, 4/477
catacombs, 4/490
Christianity, 5/546
circuses, 5/553
cities, 5/556
Cleopatra and, 5/572–3
clothing, 5/*579*, 5/580
coins, 5/*592*
colonizes Spain, 19/2300–1, 19/*2300*
cosmetics, 6/663
education, 7/802–3
empire, 18/2131
Etruria and, 7/872
exploration, 8/892
fashion, 8/912, 8/*912*
Fates, 8/915
furniture, 9/1025
gladiators, 9/*1080*
gods, 9/1088
Goths attack, 1/85
Hannibal, 10/1147–8
harbors, 10/1150
heating systems, 10/1171, 10/*1171*
Hun invasions, 3/260
interior decoration, 11/1286
Italian history, 11/1310
jewelry, 11/1333
Jews, 11/1335
Julius Caesar, 4/429
key dates, 18/2130
Latin, 12/1394–5
law, 2/137
legends, 18/2129
libraries, 12/1425
literature, 2/136
masks, 13/1526
mosaics, 14/1651, 14/1652
myths, 14/1696
Nero, 14/1739
people, 18/2132–3
Pompeii, 16/*1973*, 16/*1973*
postal services, 16/1985
republic, 17/2091–2, 18/2129–31
roads, 19/2341, 19/*2342*, 20/2449
Rome, 18/2128
ships, 18/2206
slavery, 18/2235
Spartacus, 19/2303
temples, 20/2402
theater, 1/26, 20/2420
trade, 20/2444
Rommel, Erwin, 22/2613

Romulus, 18/2128, 18/2129, 18/*2129*
Romulus Augustulus, 11/1310, 18/2132
Ronan, 14/*1642*
Roof rats, 17/2066
Rookeries, 18/2180, 18/2184
Rooks, 6/678
Rooney, Pat, 21/2510
Roosevelt, Alice Lee, 18/2136
Roosevelt, Edith, 18/2136
Roosevelt, Eleanor, 18/**2133**, 18/*2133*
Roosevelt, Franklin D., 2/245, 7/813, 8/997, 10/1201, 12/1473, 14/1639, 18/**2133–5**, 18/*2133–4*, 20/2470, 20/2485, 21/2523
civil rights, 5/562
hobbies, 10/1192
World War II, 22/2616, 22/*2619*
Roosevelt, Theodore, 1/120, 2/245, 6/639, 6/700, 15/1779, 16/*1968*, 18/**2135–6**, 18/*2135*, 18/2142, 18/*2142*, 19/2299, 19/*2299*, 20/2375
Roots, plants, 16/*1938*, 16/1939
Rope, 18/**2136–17**, 18/*2136*
knots, 12/1374, 12/*1374*
Rosaries, 17/1995
Roseate spoonbill, 21/2551
Rosenberg, Ethel, 20/2456, 20/*2456*
Rosenberg, Julius, 20/2456, 20/*2456*
Roses, 18/**2137–8**, 18/*2137*
Rosetta River, 15/1776
Rosetta Stone, 7/810, 10/1185, 18/**2138**, 18/*2138*
Rosh Hashanah, 11/1344, 15/1763
Rosin, 19/2343
Ross, Betsy, 8/952, 18/**2138**, 18/*2138*
Rossini, Gioacchino, 20/2400
Ross, John, 18/2138
Ross, Nellie Tayloe, 22/2626
Rostock, 5/*557*
Rostov-Suzdal, 18/2144
Rostropovich, Mstislav, 19/2284
Rotary engines, 7/*850*
Rotary presses, 17/2004
Rotary pumps, 17/*2028*, 17/2029
Rotation, agriculture, 1/55
Rothko, Mark, 2/234, 14/1621, 14/*1621*
Rotterdam, 10/1151, 10/*1150*, 14/1741
Rotifers, 18/**2138–9**, 18/*2139*
Rough meadow grass, 9/*1104*
Rough Riders, 18/2136, 19/2299, 19/*2299*
Roundheads, 6/675, 7/857, 17/2032
Round Table, 2/236
Roundworms, 22/2620
Rousseau, Jean Jacques, 5/531, 8/913
Roustabouts, 5/552
Rowboats, 3/362, 3/*363*
Row houses, 10/1215
Rowing, 18/**2139–40**, 18/*2139*
Royal antelopes, 2/173
Royal Ballet, 3/297
Royal Botanic Gardens, Kew, 3/374
Royal Canadian Mounted Police, 1/90, 18/**2140**, 18/*2140*
Royal Flying Doctor, 13/*1555*
Royalists, 7/857
Royal jelly, 3/324
Royal Navy, Nelson, Horatio, 14/1737

Royalty, 11/1368
Ruanda-Urundi, 18/2150
Rub'al Khali, 18/2166
Rubber, 3/305, 16/1951, 18/**2140–1**, 18/*2141*
elasticity, 7/813
synthetic, 18/2141
Rubbings, 7/762
Rube clown, 5/583
Rubella, 5/528, 6/738
Rubens, Peter Paul, 3/307, 3/*308*, 18/**2141–2**, 18/*2141–2*, 21/2513
Saint Paul, 18/*2141*, 18/2142
Rubies, 9/1050, 13/*1600*
Rubislaw, 9/*1099*
Ruby, Jack, 11/1359
Ruby-throated hummingbirds, 10/1227
Ruffed grouse, 9/1033
Rugby football, 8/979, 8/980
Rugs, 4/*472–4*, 4/*473*
Rum, 1/93
Rumba, 6/697
Rumford, Count, 10/1169
Ruminants, 10/1180
antelopes, 2/173
cattle, 4/493–6
Runes, 20/*2363*, 21/2527
Running, marathon races, 13/1512, 13/*1512*
Running pine, 5/584
Running stitch, 18/2194
Runways, 1/75
Rupert's land, 13/1503
Rurik, 18/2144, 21/2528
Ruse, 4/409
Rush-Bagot treaty, 4/450
Rushmore, Mount, 18/**2142–3**, 18/*2142*, 19/2277, 19/*2277*
Russell, Bertrand, 13/1533, 13/*1533*
Russia (before 1917):
ballet, 3/296
Catherine the Great, 4/493
Crimean War, 6/674–5
history, 18/**2144–9**, 18/*2144–9*
Napoleon in, 14/*1700*, 14/1701–2
Pavlova, Anna, 16/1886
Pavlov, Ivan, 16/1885–6
Peter the Great, 16/1907–8
Prokofiev, Sergei, 17/2008
Rachmaninoff, Sergei, 17/2041–2
revolution, 5/614
Rimsky-Korsakov, Nicolai, 17/2103
Russian America (Alaska), 1/88
Stravinsky, Igor, 19/2340
Tchaikovsky, Peter Ilyich, 20/2383–4, 20/*2383*
Tolstoy, Leo, 20/2433
World War I, 21/2608, 21/2609
Zworykin, Vladimir Kosma, 22/2649
see also Soviet Union (after 1917)
Russian blue cat, 4/*486*
Russian Five, 17/2103
Russian language, 18/**2143–4***, 18/*2143*
Russian Revolution, 17/2095
Rust, 6/661, 6/*661*
Rusts, plant diseases, 16/1943
Ruth, Babe, 18/**2150**, 18/*2150*
Rutherford, Ernest, 18/*2173*
Rutledge, Ann, 12/1439
Ruwenzori Mountains, 20/2482

Ruwenzori National Park, 20/2482
Rwanda, 18/**2151**, 18/*2150*
Rwanda-Urundi, 4/418
Rye, 6/659, 9/1097
flour making, 8/960
Ryskind, Morris, 14/1688
Ryumin, Valeri, 19/2289

Ss

Saaremaa, 7/869
Saarinen, Eero, 8/932
Saarinen, Eliel, 8/932
Sabbath, 11/1344
Sabbats, 21/2599
Sabers, 20/2368
fencing, 8/921–2, 8/*912–2*
Saber-toothed tiger, 13/1500
Sabin, Albert B., 18/2156
Sabines, 18/2129
Sable, 2/173
Sacagawea, 12/1420, 18/2216
SACEUR, 15/1787
Sachems, 8/951, 11/1304
SACLANT, 15/1787
Saclay, 20/2401
Sacramento Mountains, 15/1757
Sacramento River, 4/436
Sacraments, Roman Catholic Church, 18/2123
Sacrifice, religions, 17/2080
Sadat, Anwar, 7/807, 15/1779
Saddle bronc riding, 18/2116
see also Rodeos
Saddles, 10/1207–8
Sadlers Wells Ballet, 3/297
Safaris, 11/1363, 20/2378
Safety, 18/**2151–2**, 18/*2151–2*
at home, 18/2152
at play, 18/2151–2
first aid, 8/938–40, 8/*939–40*
lifesaving, 12/1430–2, 12/*1431*
lighthouses, 12/1434–5
masks, 13/1527
mining, 13/1601–2
toys, 20/2438–9
Safety glass, 9/1083
Safety matches, 13/1532
Safety pins, 16/1931
Sagas, 14/1696
Saguaro cactus, 8/963, 16/1943
Sahaptian Indians, 21/2544
Sahara Desert, 1/43, 1/99, 5/509, 6/719–20, 6/*721*, 12/1427, 13/1537, 15/1772, 18/**2152–3**, 18/*2153*, 19/2349
Sahel, 1/*10*, 18/**2153**
Saidy, Fred, 14/1688
Saiga antelope, 2/*173*
Saigon, 21/2525
Sailfish, 8/941
Sailing, 18/**2153–4**, 18/*2153–4*
boats, 3/360–2
wind surfing, 21/2593
Sailing ships, 18/2206–8
Sailors:
Drake, Sir Francis, 7/757–8
Farragut, David, 8/910
Jones, John Paul, 11/1340
Nelson, Horatio, 14 /1737–8

(continued)

Perry, Matthew, 16/1902
Perry, Oliver, 16/1902
pirates, 16/1934–5, 16/*1934–5*
Vespucci, Amerigo, 21/2521
see also Explorers
Sailplanes, 3/*283*, 9/1085
Sails, 18/2207
St Augustine, Florida, 8/959
St Basil's Cathedral, Moscow, 4/*493*
St Blasius Cathedral Brunswick, 18/*2124*, 18/2125
St Christopher, 21/2571
St Croix, 21/2572
St Croix River, 12/1485
Ste Genevieve, 13/1616
St Helena, 14/1702, 14/*1702*
St Helens, Mount, 21/2535
St John, 21/2572
Saint John, New Brunswick, 15/1746
St John's River, 15/1746
St Kitts-Nevis, 21/2571–2
St Lawrence River, 6/653, 17/2036
St. Lawrence Seaway, 4/454, 5/526, 9/1108, 11/1258, 15/1766, 19/**2334**, 19/*2334*
St Louis, 5/571, 9/1023, 13/1615, 13/1618
St Lucia, 21/2571
St Martin, 21/2569
Saint Mary's Island, 9/1033
Saint Marys, Maryland, 13/1525
St Paul, Minnesota, 13/1604
Saintpaulia, 10/*1216*
St Paul's Cathedral, 12/*1458*
St Peters, Rome, 2/203–4, 3/307, 3/*307*, 4/491, 13/1577, 13/1578, 18/*2122*, 18/*2129*, 21/2509
St Petersburg, 14/1653, 16/1907, 18/2147, 18/2148, 19/2285
see also Leningrad
St Petersburg Conservatory, 17/2103
Saint-Pierre, 21/2572
Saints, 18/**2154–5**, 18/*2154–5*
Aquinas, Thomas, 2/190
Becket, Thomas á, 3/322–3
Francis of Assisi, 9/1002
Joan of Arc, 11/1336–7
More, Sir Thomas, 14/1648
Nicholas, 15/1772
Patrick, 16/1885
Paul, 16/1885
Saint-Saëns, Camille, 12/1445
Saint-Simon, Comte de, 19/2249
Saint Sophia, Istanbul, 4/424
St Stephens, Alabama, 1/83
St Stephen's crown, 6/677, 6/*677*
Saint, Thomas, 18/2196
St Thomas, 21/2572
St Vincent, 21/2571
St Vincent's Archabbey, 14/1629
Saskatoon, 18/2164
Sakharov, Andrei, 15/1779
Sakonnet River, 17/2097
Saladin, 4/430, 6/679, 6/*680*
Salamanders, 2/130, 2/*131*, 2/163, 8/910, 17/2077, 18/**2155–6**, 18/*2155*
Salamis, battle of, 1/41, 3/319, 9/1112, 22/2628
Salazar, António, 16/1983
Salazar, Juan de, 16/1875
Salem, 1/111
Salem, Peter, 3/353
Salerno, 5/595

Salespeople, 18/2188–9
Sales tax, 20/2382
Salinger, J.D., 12/*1449*, 12/1450, 15/1801
Salisbury Cathedral, 15/*1844*
Saliva, 6/730
Salivary glands, 9/1081
Salk, Jonas, 18/**2156**, 18/*2156*
Salmon, migration, 13/1594
Salmonella, 3/*288*
Salmon River, 10/1239
Salmon River Mountains, 10/1239
Salt, 18/**2156–7**, 18/*2156*
seawater, 15/1814
Salt Cathedral, 5/598
Salt ceramic, 5/572
Salted foods, 8/976
Salt Lake City, 21/*2503*
SALT treaties, 20/2458
Salvarsan, 7/811
Salvation Army, 18/**2157**, 18/*2157*
Samarra, 14/*1654*
Samba, 6/697
Samhain, 10/1141
Samoset, 13/1531
Sampans, 3/362
San Andreas Fault, 18/2159
San Antonio, 1/84–5, 20/2414
San Blas archipelago, 16/1867
San Blas Indians, 11/1268, 16/1867
Sanctions, 11/1289, 18/**2157**
Sand, 18/**2158**, 18/*2158*
quicksand, 17/2038
Sandblasting, 1/17
Sandburg, Carl, 6/658, 18/**2158**, 18/*2158*
Sand Creek Massacre, 5/602
Sandhill cranes, 6/670
Sand Hills, Nebraska, 14/1732, 14/1734, 14/*1734*
Sandhills, North Carolina, 15/1787
San Diego, 4/438
Sandinista guerillas, 15/1771
Sandpaper, 1/17, 4/472
Sandpipers, 21/2552
Sand sharks, 18/2200
Sandwich Islands, 10/1158
San Fernando, 12/1460
San Francisco, 9/1090, 18/**2159**, 18/*2159*
cable cars, 4/426–7, 4/*427*
California, 4/438
history, 4/438
San Francisco Peaks, 2/215
Sanger, Margaret, 18/**2159**, 18/*2159*
Sanger, William, 18/2159
Sangha, 6/626
Sangre de Cristo Range, 15/1757
Sanitary engineering, 7/851
Sanitation, 18/**2159–60***, 18/*2160*
San Jacinto, 20/2414
San Joaquin River, 4/436
San José, 6/*663*, 6/664
San Juan, 17/2027, 17/2028
San Juan Hill, battle of, 18/2136, 19/2299, 19/*2299*
San Juan Mountains, 17/2104
San Marino, 18/**2160–1**, 18/*2160*
San Martin, José de, 5/536, 2/211
San Salvador, 5/606, 7/838, 7/*838*
Sans serif type, 20/2480–1
Sans Souci, 17/2114
Santa Ana, 7/838
Santa Ana wind, 21/2592

Santa Anna, 14/1727
Santa Anna, Antonio López de, 13/1572, 20/2414
Santa Anna, General, 1/84–5, 4/378, 11/1344, 13/1575
Santa Barbara, California, 4/438
Santa Claus, 5/547, 5/*548*, 15/1772
Santa Fe, 15/1757, 18/2161
Santa Fe Trail, 18/**2161**, 21/2577
Santa Gertrudis cattle, 4/495, 20/2411
Santa Isabel, Bioko, 7/865
Santa Maria, 1/115, 5/*605*, 5/606, 8/*891*, 18/2207
Santa Sophia, Istanbul, 2/*201*
Santee Indians, 18/2228
Santiago, 5/535, 5/536, 19/2299
Santo Domingo, 21/2570
Santorini, 9/1111, 21/2535
Santos-Dumont, Alberto, 1/78
Sanuinetti, Julio, 21/2502
São Paulo, 4/387, 18/**2161**, 18/*2161*
São Tiago, 4/459
São Tomé, 18/**2161–2**, 18/*2162*
Sapphires, 9/1050
Sappho, 9/1116, 16/*1960*
Saprophytes, 3/289, 9/1021
Saqqara, 17/2033
Sarai, 18/2145
Saratoga, 21/2542
Saratoga, Battle of, 1/127, 3/318, 3/319
Sarcee Indians, 1/90
Sardines, 8/*949*, 8/950
Sargent family, 8/969, 8/*969*
Sargent, John Singer, 18/**2162**, 18/*2162*
Street in Venice, 18/2162, 18/2162
Sargon, 19/2352
Sari, 5/*579*
Saroyan, William, 8/901
Saskatchewan, 4/450, 18/**2162–4**, 18/*2163*
history, 18/2164
map, 18/*2163*
people, 18/2164
provincial flower, 18/*2163*
Satellites, 18/**2164–6**, 18/*2164–6*, 19/2260
communication, 5/**612–13**, 18/2165
moon, 14/1644–8, 14/*1645–8*
navigation, 14/1725
orbits, 15/1837
planetary, 19/2257
unmanned, 19/2288
weather, 18/2165
Satin weaves, 20/2415
Saturated solutions, 6/683
Saturday, 6/702
Saturn, 2/*252*, 6/702, 19/2257, 19/*2257*
basic facts, 19/2259
Saturn V rockets, 1/84, 17/2110, 17/*2110*, 17/2111
Satyrs, 2/160
Sauaro, 4/428, 4/429
Saud, Ibn, 18/2167
Saudi Arabia, 2/192–3, 18/**2166–7**, 18/*2166–7*
Sauk Indians, 11/1296, 13/1616, 21/2596
Sausages, 13/1549
Savannah, 9/1061
Savannah (city), 9/1061, 9/1062
Savannah Indians, 9/1061

Savannah River, 9/1061, 19/2276
Savannas, 5/505, 14/1672
Africa, 1/43
animal life, 2/151
Savings, 18/**2167**
Savings accounts, 3/301
Savings banks, 3/302
Savonerrie carpets, 4/474
Sawgrass, 8/883–4
Sawmills, 12/1469
Saws, 4/471–2, 4/*472*
Sawtooth Mountains, 10/1239, 10/1240
Saxons, 7/855, 9/1064
Saxophones, 21/2603
Saybrook, 6/636
Scalawags, 17/2070
Scaled quail, 9/1034
Scales, 18/**2167**, 18/*2167*
fish, 8/942
Scale trees, 16/1952
Scallops, 14/1626
Scaly anteaters, 2/172
Scanderberg, 1/89
Scandinavia, 18/**2167–8**, 18/*2168*
Denmark, 6/716–17, 6/*716–17*
Finland, 8/931–2, 8/*931*
giant myths, 9/1075
Iceland, 10/1235–6, 10/*1235–6*
languages, 18/**2168**, 18/*2168*
Lapland, 12/1392
Norway, 15/1798–9, 15/*1798*
Vikings, 21/2527–9, 21/*2527–9*
Scanning, hospitals, 10/1210
Scaphopoda, 14/1625
Scarab beetles, 3/*327*
Scarlatti, Domenico, 17/2114
Scarlet fever, 5/528
Scarlet ibis, 21/*2551*
Scat singing, 2/223
Scaup, 7/771
Scavengers, 10/1231
jackals, 11/1315, 11/*1315*
Scent, perfume, 16/1899, 16/*1899*
Scepters, 6/677
Scheele, Karl Wilhelm, 17/1999
Scheherazade, 2/194, 2/*194*
Schiller, Friedrich von, 20/2400
Schirra, Walter M., 2/248
Schleiden, Mathias, 5/501
Schlesinger and Meyer Department Store, 2/204, 2/*205*
Schlieffen Plan, 21/2605, 21/2608
Schmitt, Harrison, 2/248, 9/*1057*
Schönberg, Arnold, 3/269
Scholastica, Saint, 14/1628
Schollander, Don, 20/2366
Schools, 18/**2168–70**, 18/*2169–70*
abroad, 18/2169
American Colonies, 1/114
learning, 12/1406–8
education, 7/802–4
elementary, 18/2169–70
holidays, 6/687
industrial arts, 11/1272–4, 11/*1273*
kindergartens, 18/2169
Mann, Horace, 13/1505
nursery, 18/2169
parochial, 5/548–9
physical education, 16/1921–2
secondary, 18/2169–70
segregation, 5/563
social studies, 19/2250–1
teaching, 20/2385–6, 20/*2385*

Schooners, 18/2207
Schrieffer, John, 3/304
Schubert, Franz, 3/269, 18/**2170**, 18/*2170*
Schulz, Charles, 5/*608*
Schumann, Clara, 4/382
Schumann, Robert, 3/282, 18/**2170–1**, 18/*2171*
Schuylkill River, 16/1910
Schwann, Theodore, 5/501
Schwartz, Lillian, 12/1417
Schweitzer, Albert, 9/1029, 13/1610, 13/*1610*, 18/**2171**, 18/*2171*
Schwitters, Kurt, 6/690
Science, 18/**2171–5***, 18/*2172–4*
  ancient civilizations, 2/135
  applied, 18/2174
  becoming a scientist, 18/2174
  history of, 18/2171–2
  museums, 14/1679–80
  nature study, 14/1716–22
  Newton, Sir Isaac, 15/1762–3
  pure, 18/2174
  scientific method, 18/2173
Science fiction (SF), 12/1450, 18/*2115*, 18/**2175**, 18/*2175*
Scientific method, 18/2173
Scientists:
  Ampère, André Marie, 2/129
  Archimedes, 2/200
  Bacon, Roger, 3/288
  Bardeen, John, 3/304
  Bohr, Niels Henrik David, 3/364
  Carver, George Washington, 4/479
  Darwin, Charles, 6/699–700
  Einstein, Albert, 7/812
  Faraday, Michael, 8/908
  Fermi, Enrico, 8/922–3
  Fleming, Sir Alexander, 8/953
  forensic, 6/723
  Galileo Galilei, 9/1031–2
  Humboldt, Alexander von, 10/1225
  Huxley, Thomas Henry, 10/1229
  Lavoisier, Antoine Laurent, 12/1398
  Newton, Sir Isaac, 15/1762–3
  Pasteur, Louis, 16/1883–4
  Plank, Max, 16/1936
  Priestley, Joseph, 17/1999–2000
Scimitars, 20/2368
Scintillation meter, 13/1600
Scioto River, 15/1823
Scipio, 3/319
Scissors kick, 20/2365
Scituate Reservoir, 17/2097
Score comunication satellite, 18/2165
Scorpio, 6/*641*
Scorpius, 2/172
Scoter, 7/771
Scotland, 4/396, 18/**2176**, 18/*2176*, 20/2485
  crown jewels, 6/677
  names, 14/1699
  Robert Bruce, 4/399
  union with England, 7/858
Scots, 18/2176
Scott, David, 2/224
Scott, Dred, 18/2237
Scottish Dove, 15/*1760*
Scottish reel, 8/970
Scott Lake, 21/*2494*
Scott Motorcycle Company, 14/*1666*
Scott, Robert, 2/132, 2/171, 8/893, 18/**2176–7**, 18/*2177*

Scotts Bluff National Monument, 14/1734
Scott, Sir Walter, 6/677, 6/724, 12/*1449*, 18/**2177**, 18/*2177*
Scott, Winfield, 5/567, 13/1572, 16/1927
Scouts, 22/2637–8
Scramasax, 20/2368
Scranton, 16/1894
Screen printing, textiles, 20/2416
Screwdrivers, 4/472, 4/*472*
Screws, 12/1476
Scripts, handwriting, 10/1146
Script type, 20/2480–1
Scriptures, Bible, 3/334–7
Scrovegni frescos, 9/1078
Scuba diving, 6/668, 18/**2177–8**, 18/*2178*
Sculling, 18/2139
Sculpture, 18/**2178–80**, 18/*2178–90*
  abstract, 1/18–20, 1/*19–20*
  ancient civilizations, 2/136–7
  carving, 4/480
  Epstein, Sir Jacob, 7/863–4, 7/*863*
  fountains, 8/996, 8/*996–7*
  Greek, 9/1115, 9/*1115*
  oriental, 15/1846
  paper, 16/1872–3, 16/*1872–3*
  Rodin, Auguste, 18/2117–18
  Roman, 18/2119–20, 18/*2119*
  Romanesque, 18/2125
  Stone Mountain, 19/2337
Scurvy, 5/555
Sélibaby, 13/*1538*
Sèvre, 16/*1990*
Sea anemones, 5/589, 5/590, 13/*1517*
Sea arches, 18/2182
Seabirds, 18/**2180–2**, 18/*2180–2*
Sea caves, 4/497
Seacoasts, 18/**2182–3**, 18/*2182–3*
Sea cows, 13/1501
Sea cucumbers, 2/*145*, 7/791, 7/792
Sea fan, 6/658
Seafarming, 15/1817
Seafood, mollusks, 14/1624–6
Sea of Galilee, 9/1030–1, 9/*1031*
Sea gooseberry, 5/607
Seagram Building, New York, 2/205–6
Seahorses, 8/*944*, 18/**2183–4**, 18/*2184*
Sealab, 15/1821
Sealab III, 19/2347
Sea life, Echinoderms, 7/791–2, 7/*791–2*
Sea lily, 7/791
Sea lions, 18/2184–5
Seal point siamese cat, 4/*486*
Seals, 2/*145*, 9/1022, 9/*1022*, 13/1497, 13/1591, 18/**2184–5**, 18/*2184–5*
Seal trees, 16/1952
Seamounts, 15/1816
Sea nettle, 11/1328
Sea otters, 15/*1849*, 15/1850, 17/*2064*, 17/2065
Sears Tower, Chicago, 2/*206*
Seas, 15/**1814–21**, 15/*1814–20*
  area, 15/1820
  Atlantic Ocean, 3/254–5
  Baltic, 3/299
  Caspian, 4/481
  Coral Sea, 6/659
  currents, 15/1815, 15/*1815*

Dead Sea, 6/702–3
  depth, 15/1820
  English Channel, 7/853–4
  exploring, 15/1817–20
  floor, 15/1815
  Galilee, 9/1030–1, 9/*1031*
  Gulf of Mexico, 10/1127–8, 10/*1128*
  Gulf Stream, 10/1128, 10/*1128*
  harbors and ports, 10/1149–51, 10/*1149–51*
  Hudson Bay, 10/1218
  islands, 11/1307–8, 11/*1307–8*
  life, 15/1816–17
  lighthouses, 12/1434–5, 12/*1435*
  marine life, 13/1515–17, 13/*1515–17*
  Mediterranean, 13/1556–7, 13/*1556*
  merchant marine, 13/1564
  movement of, 15/1814–15
  North Sea, 15/1794–5, 15/*1794–5*
  pirates, 16/1934–5, 16/*1934–5*
  Red Sea, 17/2074
  resources, 15/1817
  scuba diving, 18/2177–8
  surfing, 19/2357, 19/*2357*
  tides, 15/1815, 20/2424–6, 20/*2425–6*
  volume, 15/1820
  water, 15/1814
  waves, 15/1814–15, 15/*1814*
Sea serpents, 2/162
Sea slugs, 10/2244
Seasonal forests, 11/1349–50
Seasoning lumber, 4/406, 12/1469
Seasons, 18/**2185–6**, 18/*2186*
  autumn, 3/279
  spring, 19/2318–19, 19/*2319*
  summer, 19/2352–3, 19/*2352*
  winter, 21/2595, 21/*2595*
Seasprite, 3/*283*
SEATO, 20/2458
Seaton, Fred E., 19/*2330*
Sea turtle, 2/*160*
Sea urchin, 7/791, 7/792
Seawalls, 8/955
Sea walnut, 5/607
Seawater aquarium, 2/190
Seaweeds, 1/97
Sea worms, 22/2621
Sebaceous glands, 13/1495
Sebago, 12/*1847*
Sebum, 18/2232
Second Amendment, 3/340
Secondary colors, 5/601
Secondary school, 18/2169–70
Second Continental Congress, 1/126, 6/651–2, 6/707
Second Vatican Council, 18/2121
Secretaries, 5/585
Secretary birds, 3/348
Secretion, glands, 9/1080–1, 9/*1081*
Secret Service, 5/508, 16/1966
  codes and ciphers, 5/**589**
Securities and Exchange Commission, 6/661, 21/2490
Security Council, 20/2485–6
Security systems, computerized, 5/*624*
Sedan, battle of, 3/319
Seder, 16/1883
Sediment, oceanic, 15/1816
Sedimentary rocks, 17/2109
Seed ferns, 16/1953

Seedless fruit, 9/1017
Seeds, 18/**2186–8**, 18/*2187*
  flowers, 8/963
  fruit, 9/1016–18, 9/*1016–18*
  nuts, 15/1810
Seeger, Pete, 8/973
Seeing, eyes, 8/898–9, 8/*988–9*
Segovia, 19/*2300*
Seiche, 9/1108
Seine River, 16/1877
Seismogram, 7/789
Seismograph, 7/789, 13/1599–1600
Seismology, 9/1055
Selandia, 18/*2210*
Selective Service System, 21/2490
Self-defense, judo, 11/1345
Self-pollination, 8/961
Seljuk Turks, 15/1850
Selkirk, Alexander, 12/*1446*
Sellers, Coleman, 14/1659
Selling, 18/**2188–9**, 18/*2188*
  stores and shops, 19/2337–8
  vending machines, 21/2513–14, 21/*2514*
Semaphore, 18/2220–1, 18/*2221*
Semicircular canals, 7/779
Semicolon, 17/2029
Semiconductors, 7/825, 7/827–8, 18/**2189**, 18/*2189*, 18/2224, 20/2447
Seminarians, 5/573
Seminole Indians, 8/959, 11/1316, 15/1827, 18/**2189–90**, 18/*2189*
Seminole War, 11/1270
Semiprecious stones, 9/1050
Semitic languages, 2/195
Semmelweiss, Ignaz, 10/1211
Senate, 6/628, 6/630, 6/*630*
  Roman, 18/2129
Senators, 6/630
Sendak, Maurice, 5/533
Seneca Indians, 8/950, 11/1304
Senegabia, Confederation of, 9/1033
Senegal, 9/1033, 18/**2190**, 18/*2190*
Senegal River, 12/1493, 13/1538
Sengambia, 18/2190
Senghor, Léopold Sédar, 18/2190
Senglea, 12/*1943*
Senior high school, 18/2170
Sennacherib, King, 2/246
Sense organs, 18/**2190–1**
  eyes, 8/898–9, 8/*988–9*
  fish, 8/944–5
  hearing, 7/778–9, 7/*779*, 10/1165–7, 10/*1165–7*
  perception, 17/2018
  sight, 18/2219–20, 18/*2219–20*
  smell, 19/2241
  taste, 20/2381
  touch, 20/2435
Sensory nerves, 14/1740
Sentences, grammar, 9/1097–8
Seoul, 12/1376, 12/1378
Sepals, 8/*961*
Separation of powers, 21/2488–9
September, 18/**2191–2**, 18/*2192*
  special events, 18/2191
Septuagint, 3/336
Septum, 15/1799
Sequoia National Park, 14/1709
Sequoias, 6/*632*, 18/2192, 20/2458
Sequoya, 18/**2192**, 18/*2192*
Sequoya (Cherokee Indian), 5/523, 15/1828

Serapis, 1/*126*, 1/128, 11/1340
Serbs, 22/2639
Serengeti National Park, 20/2378
Serfs, 8/925, 13/1585, 18/2235
Serials, movies, 14/1662
Serra, Junípero, 4/438, 12/1460, 13/1610, 14/1629
Servants, 10/1214
Service academies, 21/2497–8
Service Medal, 13/*1551*
Service, Robert, 9/1091
Services, selling, 18/2188–9
Sets, 13/1533, 18/**2192–3**
Settlers, pioneer life, 16/1931–3, 16/*1932–3*
Seurat, Georges, 1/18
Seuss Geisel, Theodore, 5/533
Seven Cities of Cibola, 5/**549**, 6/637, 6/660, 7/869
Seventh Amendment, 3/340
Seven Wonders of the World, 18/**2193–4**, 18/*2193*
Seven Years' War, 9/1005
Severn River (Maryland), 13/1524
Sevier, John, 20/2403, 20/2404, 21/2576
Seville, 19/2298
Sewage, 18/2159–60
    pollution, 21/2554
    treatment plants, 21/2556
Seward, William H., 1/88
Sewellel, 3/322
Sewing, 5/579, 18/**2194–6**, 18/*2195*
    buttons, 4/422
    cutting, 18/2195
    fabric, 18/2195
    finishing, 18/2196
    fitting, 18/2196
    hand stitching, 18/2194–5
    needlework, 14/1735–6, 14/*1735–6*
    patterns, 18/2195
Sewing machines, 18/*2194*, 18/**2196**, 18/*2196*
Sex glands, 9/1081
Sextants, 14/1724–5, 14/*1725*
Sextilis, 3/261
Seychelles, 11/*1260*, 11/1261, 18/**2196–7**, 18/*2197*
Seymour, Jane, 10/1177
Seymour Narrows, 8/896
SF *see* Science fiction
Shading, 7/*761*, 7/762
Shadow puppets, 17/2031
Shafts, drilling rigs, 7/763–4
Shah Jahan, 11/*1247*, 11/1254, 20/2377
Shakers, furniture, 2/228, 2/*228*, 9/1027
Shakespeare, Hamnet, 18/2197
Shakespeare, John, 18/2197
Shakespeare, Judith, 18/2197
Shakespeare, Susanna, 18/2197
Shakespeare, William, 1/27, 5/532, 7/759, 7/839, 7/852, 9/1044, 12/*1446*, 18/**2197–8**, 18/*2197–8*
    England of, 18/2198
    life, 18/2197
    today, 18/2198
    works, 18/2198
Shakti, 10/1187
Shamanism, 12/1377
Shamans, 12/1481–2, 17/2010–11, 17/2080, 21/2599
Shang Dynasty, 5/538, 15/*1845*, 15/1846

Shanghai, 18/**2198–9**, 22/2632
Shannon River, 11/1301
Shantungosaurus, 14/*1678*
Sharecropping, 13/1613, 13/1618
Shares, 4/459
    corporations, 6/661
Sharjah, 2/193
Sharks, 8/943, 18/**2199–2200**, 18/*2199*
Sharp, music, 14/1684
Sharpsburg, 13/1525
Sharp-shinned hawks, 3/349
Sharpshooters, 18/2214
Shasta daisy, 4/413
Shatt al Arab, 20/2427
Shaw, George Bernard, 1/*28*, 11/1301, 7/861, 11/1336, 14/1687, 17/2009, 18/**2200**, 18/*2200*
Shawnee Indians, 11/1256, 11/1270, 11/1362, 15/1824, 20/2386, 21/2559, 21/2574
Shearwaters, 18/2181, 18/*2181*
Sheathbills, 16/*1965*
Sheba, Queen of, 7/871
Shebelle River, 19/2262
Sheep, 10/*1145*, 18/**2201–2**, 18/*2201–2*
    wool, 5/580
Sheepdogs, 7/*753*
Sheepshank, 12/*1374*
Sheet bend, 12/1374, 12/*1374*
Sheet lightning, 12/1437
Sheets, sailing, 18/2153
Sheiks, 2/194, 11/1300
Shelby, Evan, 20/2404
Sheldrakes, 7/771
Shelley, Mary, 18/2175, 18/2203
Shelley, Percy, 11/1357, 18/**2203**, 18/*2203*
Shellfish, 8/948
Shell parakeet, 16/1880
Shells, 5/570, 18/**2202–3**, 18/*2202–3*
    coral, 6/658–9
    mollusks, 14/1624
    molting, 14/1626
    snails, 19/2243
Shelters, 18/**2203–5**, 18/*2204–5*
    nuclear, 18/2204–5
    tents, 20/2408, 20/*2408*
Shenandoah, 1/79
Shenandoah Valley, 21/2532
Shepard, Alan, 2/248, 4/458, 19/2291
Shepard, Ernest H., 5/533
Sheraton, Thomas, 9/1027
Sheridan, Philip H., 5/567, 5/569
Sheriffs, 16/1966
Sherman, Roger, 6/707
Sherman, William T., 5/567, 5/569, 18/**2205**, 18/*2205*, 18/*2238*
Sherpas, 14/1738
Sherwood Forest, 17/2106
Shetland, 18/2176
Shetland ponies, 10/1207
Shields, 2/222, 2/223
    coats of arms, 5/588
Shih-Huangdi, Emperor of China, 5/*538*
Shiite Muslims, 11/*1307*
Shikoku, 11/1322
Shiloh, 5/568
Shiloh, battle of, 18/2205
Shinto, 2/243, 11/1322, 17/2079, 18/**2205**

Ships and shipping, 18/**2205–12**, 18/*2206–12*
    aircraft carriers, 1/58–60, 1/*59–60*
    canals, 4/453–4, 4/*453–4*
    crossing the equator, 19/*2355*
    diesel engines, 6/729, 6/*729*
    engine-powered, 18/2208
    flags, 8/953
    Fulton, Robert, 9/1020
    gyroscopes, 10/1135
    harbours and ports, 10/1149–51, 10/*1149–51*
    history, 18/2206–10
    lighthouses, 12/1434–5, 12/*1435*
    merchant marine, 13/1564
    modern, 20/2452
    mutiny, 14/1694–5
    navies, 14/1726–31
    navigation, 14/1724–6, 14/*174–6*
    pirates, 16/1934–5, 16/*1934–5*
    sailing, 18/2206
    shipbuilding, 18/2206–7
    shipping, 18/211–12
Shipton, Eric, 1/*16*
Shipworms, 14/1626
Shipyards, 18/2210
Shire horses, 10/1207
Shiva, 10/1187
Shock, first aid, 8/938, 8/*939*
Shockley, William, 3/304, 20/2447, 20/*2447*
Shoes, 18/**2212–14**, 18/*2213–14*
Shoho, 22/*2615*
Sholokov, Mikhail, 19/2284
Shooting, 18/**2214**, 18/*2214*
    game birds, 9/1033–4
Shooting stars, 13/1570, 19/2260
Shoplifting, 19/2339
Shops, 19/2337–9, 19/*2337–8*
    selling, 18/2188–9
    signs, 5/609
Short-eared owl, 15/*1852*
Short-haired cats, 4/*486*, 4/487
Shorthand, 18/**2214–15**★, 18/*2215*
Shorthorn cattle, 4/495
Short stories, 12/1447, 18/**2215–16**, 18/*2216*
Short-tailed shaerwater, 13/*1593*
Shoshone Indians, 10/1239, 12/1421, 15/1743, 18/**2216**, 18/*2216*, 21/2504
Shostakovich, Dmitri, 19/2284
Shotguns, 10/1132
Shot putting, 20/*2441*, 20/2442
Shovelers, 7/770, 7/771
Shrews, 5/559, 14/1622–3, 14/*1623*
Shrimps, 6/681
Shrubs, 18/**2216–17**, 18/*2217*
Shu, 21/*2499*
Siamese fighting fish, 20/*2466*
Siam *see* Thailand
Sibelius, Jean, 8/932, 14/1705, 18/**2217**, 18/*2217*
Siberia, 18/2147
Siberian Plain, 19/2282
Siberian tigers, 20/2426
Siberian willow warblers, 13/*1593*
Sibyls, 17/2011
Siddhartha Gautama, 4/401–2
Siddons, Sarah, 1/27
Side effects, drugs, 7/768–9
Sidereal months, 14/1643
Sidereal period, 14/1646
Sideshows, 5/552

Side-striped jackal, 11/1315
Sidestroke, 20/2365
Sidewinders, 19/2245
    tracks, 2/*164*
Sidney, Nova Scotia, 15/1801
Sidon, 16/1916
Siegel, Jerry, 5/608
Siege weapons, 8/990, 21/2559
Sierra Club, 6/640
Sierra Leone, 18/**2217–18**, 18/*2218*
Sierra Madre Occidental mountains, 13/1573
Sierra Nevada, 4/436, 14/1668, 15/1743, 18/**2218–19**, 18/*2219*
Sight, 18/**2219–20**, 18/*2219–20*
    eyes, 8/898–9, 8/*988–9*
    glasses, 9/1084
Signal Hill, St John's, 15/1748
Signals, 18/**2220–2**★, 18/*2221–2*
    flags, 8/953
    railroads, 17/2053–4
    telecommunications, 14/1651
Signatures, 10/1146
    autographs, 3/270–1
Sign language, 10/1166, 10/*1166*, 18/**2222–3**★, 18/*2222–3*
Sika deer, 6/*710*
Sikhism, 18/**2223**, 18/*2223*
Sikhs, 10/1140, 18/2223
Sikkim, 11/1369, 18/**2223–4**, 18/*2224*
Sikorsky, Igor, 10/1174
Silhouette, Seychelles, 18/2197
Silica, 18/2224
Silicon, 18/**2224**
    chips, 3/304, 7/826, 7/827, 7/828
    sand, 18/2158
Silicones, 16/1955
Silk, 5/579, 5/580, 18/**2224–5**, 18/*2224*
Silkworms, 13/1569, 18/2224–5, 18/*2224*
Silky anteaters, 2/173
Silver, 13/1567, 18/**2225**, 18/*2225*
    coins, 5/592
    mines, 15/1743–4
Silverfish, 11/*1279*
Silver fox, 8/998
Silver work, American Indians, 11/1259
Silvisaurus, 6/*734*
Simmering, 6/655
Simplon tunnel, 1/107
Simpson, James Young, 2/143
Simpson, O.J., 19/2317
Simpson, Sir James, 13/1553
Simpson, Wallis Warfield, 7/805
Simulators, 2/248
Sind, 15/1864
Singapore, 18/**2225–6**, 18/*2226*
Singer, Isaac Bashevis, 12/1451, 18/2196, 18/*2196*
Singhalese, 19/2323
Singing, 18/**2226–8**, 18/*2227–8*
    Anderson, Marian, 2/140
    carols, 4/470
    Caruso, Enrico, 4/479
    Dylan, Bob, 7/777
    Jackson, Mahalia, 11/1317–18
    voice and vocals, 18/2226–7
Single-arch dams, 6/694
Single lens reflex (SLR) cameras, 4/441, 16/1917, 16/*1917*
Sinkers, fishing, 8/946
Sinkhole lakes, 12/1385

Sinks, river, 15/1743
Sinn Féin, 11/1302
Sinoite, 13/1597
Sioux Indians, 1/120, 6/687, 11/*1264*,
  11/1271, 11/1296, 13/1604,
  14/1732, 14/1734, 18/**2228–9**,
  18/*2228–9*, 19/2277, 19/2278
Sioux War, 1/120
Siqueiros, David, 20/2371
Sirenia, 13/1501
Sirens, 2/160
Sirhan, Sirhan Bishara, 11/1360
Sirius, 18/*2210*
Sirius (star), 3/261, 6/642, 19/2327
Sirocco, 21/2593
Sisal, 18/2137
Sisters, nuns, 14/1628
Sistine Chapel, 2/232, 2/*233*,
  13/1577–8, 15/1859, 15/*1860*,
  17/2084
Siswati, 19/2362
Sitar, 19/2344
Sitting Bull, 4/404, 4/*404*, 6/687,
  11/*1264*, 11/1271, 18/2228,
  18/**2229**, 18/*2229*
Sitting position, 16/1986
Six-Day War, 11/1310, 14/1704
Six Nations, 8/951
Sixth Amendment, 3/340
Skalds, 14/1696
Skate, 2/209
Skateboarding, 18/2119
Skates, fish, 8/944, 18/2200
Skating:
  ice skating, 10/1236–7, 10/*1236–7*
  roller-skating, 18/2118–19,
  18/*2118*
Skeet shooting, 18/2214
Skeletal muscles, 14/1676
Skeleton keys, 12/1458
Skeletons, 3/366, 3/*366*, 18/**2229–30**,
  18/*2229–30*
  broken bones, 9/999
Skiing, 18/**2230–2**, 18/*2230–2*,
  19/*2318*
Ski lifts, 4/427
Skim milk, 6/692
Skin, 10/1224, 18/**2232–3**, 18/*2232–3*
  care of, 18/2233
  color, 18/2233
  cosmetics, 6/662–3
  fingerprints, 8/930–1, 8/*930*
  fur, 9/1022–4, 9/*1022–4*
  hair, 10/1137–8, 10/*1137–8*
  horns, 10/102
  leather, 12/1408–9
  mammals, 13/1495
  molting, 14/1626–7
  tattoos, 18/2233
  touch, 20/2435
Skin diving, 15/1820, 18/2178
Skinks, 12/1456
Skins, clothing, 5/578–9
Skirl, 3/291
Skulls, 10/1220, 10/1221, 12/1405
Skunks, 5/559, 18/**2233–4**, 18/*2234*,
  21/2560–1
Skuta, 18/2206
Sky, 18/**2234**, 18/*2234*
  atmosphere, 3/257
  colour, 3/257
Sky diving, 16/1874
Skylab, 19/2289, 19/2292, 19/2294
Skyrockets, 8/938

Skyscrapers, 2/204, *206*, 4/407,
  4/*407*, 6/723, 14/*1644*
  building, 6/647–8
  elevators, 7/833
  Empire State Building, 7/842
Slag, 11/1303
Slaloms, 18/2231, 18/*2231*
Slapjack, 4/464
Slater, Samuel, 17/2099
Slave River, 12/1476
Slavery, 1/112, 1/117, 1/*117*, 2/220,
  4/398, 4/400–1, 13/1613,
  18/**2234–8**, 18/*2235–8*
  abolition, 1/15–16, 5/561, 5/*561*,
  5/564–6, 5/569
  agriculture, 1/55
  America, 3/352–3
  Civil War and, 5/564–6
  Davis, Jefferson, 6/701
  Douglass, Frederick, 7/756
  Douglas, Stephen A., 7/755
  Emancipation Proclamation, 7/840
  freedmen, 17/2069–701
  Fugitive Slave Act, 8/928
  Georgia, 9/1062
  gladiators, 9/1080
  Jefferson, Thomas, 11/1326–7
  Lincoln, Abraham, 12/1440
  Mozambique, 14/1672
  Pierce, Franklin, 16/1927
  Reconstruction, 17/2069
  Spartacus, 19/2303
  spirituals, 2/229
  Truth, Sojourner, 20/2472
  Tubman, Harriet, 20/2472–3
  Turner, Nat, 20/2477
  Underground Railroad, 20/2483–4
  United States, 18/2235–8
Slavs, 16/1963, 18/2144, 19/2282
Slayton, Donald K., 2/248
Sleds and sledges, 4/474, 19/**2239**,
  19/*2239*, 20/*2448*, 20/2449
Slee, Noah H., 18/2159
Sleep, 10/1163, 19/**2239–40**, 19/*2240*
  dreams, 7/762–3
'Sleeping Beauty', 8/904
Sleigh bells, 3/329
Slime molds, 9/1021
Sloat, John D., 4/438
Sloops, 18/2207
Sloth bears, 3/*320*, 3/321
Sloths, 19/**2240–1**, 19/*2240*
Slovakia, 6/689
Slovaks, 6/689
Slovenes, 22/2639
Slugs, 19/2243–4, 19/*2244*
Sluter, Claus, 17/2083
Small Business Administration,
  21/2490
Small intestine, 6/731
Small-leaved lime, 20/*2461*
Smallpox, 6/649–50, 6/671, 11/1328–9
Smalls, Robert, 3/354
Smell, 19/**2241**, 19/*2241*
  nose, 15/1799, 15/*1799*
Smelting, 11/1302–3, 13/1568
Smetana, Bedrich, 12/1445
Smet, Pierre Jean de, 14/1642
Smith, Captain John, 8/893
Smith, John, 11/1319, 11/*1320*,
  13/1542, 15/1752, 16/1959,
  17/*1993*
Smith, Joseph, 10/1242, 12/1396,
  19/**2241**, 19/*2241*, 21/2505

Smith, Robert Angus, 1/22
Smithsonian Institution, 19/**2241–2**
Smithson, James, 19/2242
Smog, 1/72–5, 12/1461, 14/1715
Smoke, 1/39
  air pollution, 1/72–5, 1/*72–5*
Smoked foods, 8/976
Smokey the Bear, 3/321
Smoking, 19/**2242–3**, 19/*2242–3*
Smoothing planes, 4/472
Smooth muscles, 14/1676
Smooth newt, 2/*131*
Smuts, General, 3/363
Smuts, plant diseases, 16/1943
Smyrna, 20/2476
Snails, 14/1625, 14/1626, 19/**2243–4**,
  19/*2243*
Snake charmers, 19/*2245*
Snake River, 10/1237, 10/1239,
  22/2625
Snakes, 17/2091, 19/**2244–6**,
  19/*2244–6*
  bites, 10/*1244*
  in cities, 5/559
  molting, 14/1626
Snapping turtles, 20/2478
Sneezes, 19/**2246**
Snekkas, 18/2206
Snooker, 3/339
Snorkels, 18/2178
  submarines, 19/2346
Snow, 17/2059–60
  avalanches, 3/279–80
  glaciers, 9/1079–80, 9/*1079–80*
  skiing, 18/2230–3
  sleds, 19/2239
Snow goose, 13/*1592*, 13/*1593*
Snow houses, igloos, 7/867, 7/868
Snow leopard, 4/*489*, 4/490
Snowmobiles, 19/**2247**, 19/*2247*
Snowy egret, 21/2551
Snowy owl, 15/*1852*
Soap operas, 1/28
Soaps, 19/**2247–8**, 19/*2247–8*
Sobhuza II, King, 19/2362
Soccer, 19/**2248–9**, 19/*2248–9*
Socialism, 19/**2249–50**, 19/*2249–50*
  Debs, Eugene V., 6/704
Social planners, 19/2252
Social psychologists, 17/2020
Social security, 19/**2250**
Social Security Administration,
  19/2250
Social studies, 19/**2250–1**
Social wasps, 21/2549
Social work, 19/**2251–2**, 19/*2251*
Societies, 5/**584–5**
Society of Friends, 16/1910,
  19/**2252**, 19/*2252*
Society Islands, 16/1971
Society of Jesus *see* Jesuits
Society for Psychical Research,
  9/1075
Sociologists, 19/2253
Sociology, 19/**2253–4**, 19/*2253–4*
  juvenile delinquency, 11/1350
Socorro, 17/2050
Socrates, 2/136, 16/1956, 19/**2254**,
  19/*2254*
Sod busters, 11/1296
Sodium chloride, 18/2156–7
Sofia, 4/409
Softball, 3/313
Soft coal, 5/586

Software, 5/623, 5/624
Soft water, 21/2550
Softwood lumber, 12/1470, 21/2601
Soil, 19/**2254–5**, 19/*2255*
  formation, 19/2255
  plants and, 16/1945
  pollution, 16/1970
  prairie, 17/*1993*
Sokemen, 8/925
Solar eclipses, 7/792, 7/*792–3*,
  14/1644
Solar energy, 19/**2256**, 19/*2256*
Solar furnaces, 7/847
Solar heaters, 10/1172, 10/*1172*
Solar power, 7/847
Solar system, 19/**2256–61**,
  19/*2256–60*
  asteroids, 2/246–7
  Copernicus, Nicolaus, 6/657
  orbits, 15/1837–8
  sun, 19/2353
Solar winds, 17/2044, 17/*2045*
Solar years, 4/433
Soldier fly, 8/*966*
Soldiers:
  Alexander the Great, 1/96
  armies, 2/224–7, 2/*225–7*
  armor, 2/221–3
  Bowie, James, 4/378
  camouflage, 4/443
  Caesar, Julius, 4/429–30
  Cromwell, Oliver, 6/675–6
  Crusades, 6/678
  Custer, George, 6/687
  Davis, Benjamin Oliver, 6/700
  Davis, Benjamin Oliver Jr.,
    6/700–1
  De Gaulle, Charles, 6/711–12
  Eisenhower, Dwight David,
    7/812–13
  Ethan Allen, 1/100–1
  Garibaldi, Giuseppe, 9/1043
  Grant, Ulysses Simpson, 9/1100–1
  Hale, Nathan, 10/1140
  Hannibal, 10/1147–8
  Houston, Samuel, 10/1217
  insignia, 2/227
  Jackson, Thomas Jonathan
    ('Stonewall'), 11/1318
  Lafayette, Marquis de, 12/1383
  Lawrence, T.E., 12/1400–1
  Lee, Robert E., 12/1410
  MacArthur, Douglas, 12/1473
  Marion, Francis, 13/1517–18
  Pike, Zebulon, 16/1930
  Raleigh, Sir Walter, 17/2060–1
  Roman, 18/2132–3
  Sherman, William T., 18/2205
  Taylor, Zachary, 20/2382–3,
    20/*2838*
  Tomb of the Unknowns, 20/2433,
    20/*2433*
  US Army, 2/226–7
  Washington, George, 21/2547–8
  Wayne, Anthony, 21/2558–9
Solicitors, 12/1401
Solids, 13/1537, 19/**2261**
Solid-state physics, 16/1923
Solis, Juan Diaz de, 2/211
Solomon Islands, 13/1558, 15/1854
Solomon, King, 7/871, 11/1329,
  11/1335
  Temple of, 20/2402
Solutions, crystals and, 6/683

Solzhenitsyn, Aleksandr, 19/2284
Somalia, 19/**2261–2**, 19/*2261–2*
Somalis, 6/745
Somoza Debayle, Anastasio, 15/1771
Somoza family, 15/1771
Songhai Empire, 3/352, 12/1493, 15/1773, 19/**2262**
Songs:
  carols, 4/470
  Foster, Stephen, 8/995
  Handy, W.C., 10/1147
  see also Singing
Sonoma, 4/438
Sonora, 18/2225
Soon Mei-ling, 5/525
Sophocles, 2/136, 9/1116
Sopranos, 18/2227
Sopwith Camel, 3/*281*
Sorbonne, 16/1877
Sostenuto, 16/1925
Soufrière, La, 21/2572
Souhegan River, 15/1752
Sound, 19/**2262–5***, 19/*2263–5*
  echoes, 19/2264, 19/*2264*
  energy, 7/845
  hearing, 10/1165–7, 10/*1165–7*
  insulation, 11/1282
  intensity levels, 19/2265
  movement of, 19/2263–4
  music, 19/2264–5
  noise, 19/2264–5
  speed of, 19/2264
Sound recordings, 17/2071–3
  analog, 17/2073
  compact discs, 17/2073
  digital, 17/2073
  operation, 17/2071–2
  records, 17/2072–3
  tape recordings, 17/2072
Souphanouvong, 12/1392
Sousa, John Philip, 4/385, 15/1840, 19/**2265–6**, 19/*2266*
Sousaphone, 4/386, 19/2265
South Africa, 19/**2266–7**, 19/*2266–7*
  apartheid, 19/2267
  Boer War, 3/363–4
  Namibia, 14/1700
  Rhodes, Cecil, 17/2100
  sanctions against, 14/2157
South America, 19/**2267–73**, 19/*2268–73*
  Andes Mountains, 2/140–1
  animals, 19/2270–1
  Bolívar, Simón, 3/364
  climate, 19/2268–70
  geography, 19/2268
  history, 19/2272–3
  map, 19/*2269*
  nations, 19/2268
  natural resources, 19/2270
  people, 19/2271–2
  physical statistics, 6/650
  plants, 19/2270–1
South Bend, 11/1258
South Carolina, 19/**2274–7**, 19/*2274–6*
  climate, 19/2274
  employment, 19/2276–7
  history, 19/2274–6
  land, 19/2274
  map, 19/*2275*
  state emblem, 19/*2275*
South Dakota, 19/**2277–9**, 19/*2277–9*
  climate, 19/2277

  employment, 19/2278
  history, 19/2277–8
  land, 19/2277
  map, 19/2279
  state emblems, 19/2279
Southeast Asia, 19/**2280–1**, 19/*2280*
Southeast Asia Treaty Organization (SEATO), 20/2458
Southern Christian Leadership Conference (SCLC), 3/355, 11/1366
Southern Cross, 6/641
South Georgia Island, 8/907
South Korea, 12/1376–7, 12/*1377*
South Pole, 2/132, 2/171, 4/423
  Scott, Robert, 18/2176–7
South Sandwich Island, 8/907
South Yemen, 2/193
Sovereignty, 9/1094
Soviets, 9/1095
Soviet Union (after 1917), 19/**2281–6**, 19/*2281–6*
  Afghanistan and, 1/42
  ballet, 3/297
  beginnings, 18/2149
  Berlin Blockade, 9/1069
  Black Sea, 3/357
  climate, 19/2282
  Communism, 5/614
  Cuba, 6/684–5
  Cuban missile crisis, 11/1359, 11/1365
  Czechoslovakia, 6/689
  education, 19/2284
  Estonia, 7/869
  Finland, 8/932
  flag, 8/951
  Gagarin, Yuri, 9/1029
  Gorbachev, Mikhail Sergeyevich, 9/1092
  government, 19/2284–5
  history, 19/2285–6
  Khrushchev, Nikita, 11/1364–5
  Korean War, 12/1377–8
  Kremlin, 12/1379, 12/*1379*
  land, 19/2281–2
  Lenin, Vladimir Ilich, 12/1414
  Lithuania, 12/1452–3
  map, 19/*2283*
  Moscow, 13/1653
  people, 19/2282–4
  recreation, 19/2284
  republics of, 19/2282
  Russian language, 18/2143–4, 18/*2143*
  Stalin, Joseph, 19/2324
  Trotsky, Leon, 20/2467
  Ural Mountains, 21/2501
  Volga River, 21/2535
  World War II, 22/2611–18
  see also Russia (before 1917)
Soya, 19/**2287**
Space, 19/**2287**, 19/*2287*
  aerospace, 1/40
  exploration, 8/889, 8/894
Space balloons, 3/298
Space biology, 3/343
Spacecraft, 1/40
  navigation, 14/1725
  rockets, 17/2109–12, 17/*2110–11*
Space flight, satellites, 18/2164–6, 18/*2164–6*
Spacelab, 19/2292
Spacelab, 8/889
Space probes, 19/2288, 19/2289–90

Space research, 19/**2287–90**, 19/*2287–90*
  Collins, Michael, 5/**597**
  Von Braun, Wernher, 21/2537
Space Shuttle, 2/248, 2/*248*, 3/282, 8/889, 17/*2110*, 19/2292, 19/2296
  communications satellites, 5/614
Space travel, 19/**2290–7**, 19/*2291–6*, 20/2454
  Apollo program, 19/2291–2
  Cape Canaveral, 4/458–9
  future of, 19/2296–7
  Gagarin, Yuri, 9/1029
  history, 19/2290–1
  manned, 19/2292–5
  people, 19/2295–6
  planning, 19/2296
  unidentified flying objects, 20/2484, 20/*2484*
Space weapons, 19/**2297**, 19/*2297*
Spain, 8/880, 19/**2297–9**, 19/*2298*
  American colonies, 1/110, 2/217, 4/438, 8/893, 10/1188–9, 11/1355
  Argentina and, 2/211
  Canary Islands, 4/454–5
  Central American conquests, 5/507
  Colombia, 5/598
  Columbus, Christopher, 5/**605–6**
  colonies, 1/49
  Colorado, 5/602
  conquers the Aztecs, 3/284, 6/662
  conquistadors, 6/637–8, 6/*637–8*
  Cuba, 6/684
  De Soto, Hernando, 6/723
  El Cid, 5/550
  El Greco, 7/834–5
  El Salvador, 7/838
  explorers, 3/294
  fascism, 8/911
  Florida, 8/957–9
  Franco, Francisco, 9/1002–3
  Gibraltar, 9/1076
  Guam, 10/1123
  history, 19/**2300–2**, 19/*2300–2*
  Incas, 11/1248–9
  introduction of farming to America, 1/53–4
  Jivaro Indians, 11/1268
  Maya, 13/1541
  Mexico, 13/1575, 20/2412
  modern, 19/2302
  New Mexico, 15/1758
  Nicaragua, 15/1771
  Panama and, 16/1868
  Paraguay, 16/1875
  pirate raids, 16/1934
  Pizarro, Francisco, 16/1935–6
  Ponce de León, Juan, 16/1973
  Pueblo Indians, 17/2026
  Puerto Rico, 17/2027
  South America, 19/2273
  South American colonies, 3/364
  Velázquez, Diego, 21/2513
Spanish-American War, 1/120, 13/1544, 13/*1544*, 14/1729, 19/**2299**, 19/*2299*
Spanish Armada, 3/319, 7/757–8, 7/837, 7/854, 14/1727, 19/**2300**, 19/*2300*
Spanish eagles, 17/*2064*
Spanish Inquisition, 11/1336
Spanish language, 18/2123
Spanish lynx, 17/*2064*
Spanish Main, 19/**2302–3**

Spanish Succession, war of, 19/2302
Spark plugs, 7/849
  automobiles, 3/276
Sparrow hawks, 3/348, 3/*348*
Sparta, 9/1112, 9/1113
Spartacus, 9/1080, 19/**2303**, 19/*2303*
Spawn, fish, 8/945
Speakeasies, 17/2008
Speaker of the House, 6/629
Speakers' Corner, London, 6/*715*
Speaking, 12/1387
  public, 17/2023–4
  singing and, 18/2228
Special Astrophysical Observatory, 15/1813
Special education, 19/**2303–5**, 19/*2303–4*
Species, animals, 2/154–5
Specific gravity, minerals, 13/1598
Spectacled bear, 3/320, 3/321
Spectographs, 2/251
Spectroscope, 19/2306
  astronomy, 15/1813
Spectrum, 3/364, 5/599–7, 12/1433, 19/**2305–7**, 19/*2305–6*
Speech, 5/610–11, 19/**2307–9***, 19/*2307–8*
  defects, 19/2308–9
Speed, animals, 2/158
Speedboats, 3/362
Speed of sound, 19/2264
Speedway racing, 14/*1667*
Speedwriting, 18/2215, 18/*2215*
Speke, John, 20/2483
Spelling, 19/**2309**
Spells, 21/2599
Spelunking, 4/498, 19/**2310**, 19/*2310*
Spencer, Herbert, 19/2253
Sperm, 17/2087, 17/*2087*
Spermaceti, 21/2579, 21/2580
Spermatophytes, 16/1947, 16/*1949*
Spermatozoon, 7/840
Sperm whales, 21/2579–80
Spewack, Bella, 14/1687
Spewack, Sam, 14/1687
Sphagnum moss, 14/1656
Sphenophyllum, 16/*1952*
Spherical geometry, 9/1060
Sphinx, 2/*137*, 17/2102, 19/**2310**, 19/*2310*
Spice Islands, 11/1272
Spices, 19/**2310–11***, 19/*2311*
Spider monkeys, 14/1636
Spiders, 2/153, 19/**2312**, 19/*2312*
Spies, 19/**2319–20**, 19/*2320*
  CIA, 5/508
  Hale, Nathan, 10/1140
  treason, 20/2456–7, 20/*2456*
Spiked loosestrife, 8/962
Spillways, 6/695
Spin casting, fishing, 8/946
Spinneret, 4/420
Spinning, 5/580, 19/**2313–14***, 19/*2313*
Spinning jenny, 19/2313, 19/*2313*
Spiny anteater, 2/172, 3/269, 19/**2315**, 19/*2315*
Spiracles, 4/419, 11/1280
Spiral galaxies, 13/1594
Spirilla, 3/288
Spirit of St Louis, 12/1441–2, 12/*1442*, 14/*1679*, 19/2241
Spirituals, 2/229, 8/972
  Jackson, Mahalia, 11/1317–18

Spitfires, 3/*282*
Spits, 18/2183
Spitz, Mark, 20/2366
Split, 22/2638, 22/2639
Spoilers, 9/1085
  aircraft, 1/*69*
Spokane, 21/2544
Sponges, 2/158, 19/**2315–16**,
  19/*2315–16*, 20/2372
Sponsors, radio, 17/2052
Spontaneous combustion, 8/937
Sporangia, 9/1021
Spores, 16/1941, 16/1952, 17/2086
Sporting dogs, 6/746
Sports, 19/**2316–18**, 19/*2316–18*
  Australia, 3/267–8
  badminton, 3/290–1
  balls, 3/295
  baseball, 3/310–13
  basketball, 3/313–15
  bowling, 4/378–9, 4/*379*
  cattle and, 4/495
  cricket, 6/672–3, 6/*672*
  curling, 6/686–7, 6/*686*
  cycling, 3/338
  diving, 6/743–4, 6/*743–4*
  equestrianism, 7/865–6, 7/*865*
  exercise, 8/888
  falconry, 8/906, 8/*906*
  fencing, 8/921–2, 8/*912–2*
  field hockey, 8/927–8, 8/*927–8*
  fishing, 8/945–7, 8/*946–7*
  football, 8/979–83, 8/*980–2*
  games, 9/1035
  gladiators, 9/1080
  golf, 9/1091–2, 9/*1091–2*
  gymnastics, 10/1133–4, 10/*1134*
  handball, 10/1143–4, 10/*1143*
  hang gliding, 10/1147, 10/*1147*
  ice hockey, 10/1235, 10/*1235*
  ice skating, 10/1236–7, 10/*1236–7*
  jai alai, 11/1318, 11/*1318*
  judo, 11/1345, 11/*1345*
  karate, 11/1356, 11/*1356*
  lacrosse, 12/1382–3, 12/*1383*
  Little League baseball, 12/1453,
    12/*1453*
  marathon races, 13/1512, 13/*1512*
  medals, 13/1550
  mountain climbing, 14/1671–2,
    14/*1671*
  Olympic Games, 15/1830–1,
    15/*1830–1*
  Owens, Jesse, 15/1851
  parachuting, 16/1874
  physical education, 16/1921–2,
    16/*1922*
  polo, 16/1970
  racquetball, 17/2042, 17/*2042*
  rodeos, 18/2116–17, 18/*2116–17*
  roller-skating, 18/2118–19, 18/*2118*
  rowing, 18/2139–40, 18/*2139*
  sailing, 18/2153–4, 18/*2153–4*
  scuba diving, 18/2177–8, 18/*2178*
  shooting, 18/2214
  skiing, 18/2230–2, 18/*2230–2*
  sledding, 19/2239
  soccer, 19/2248–9, 19/*2248–9*
  softball, 3/313
  spelunking, 19/2310
  squash, 19/2321, 19/*2321*
  surfing, 19/2357, 19/*2357*
  swimming, 20/2364–6, 20/*2364–6*
  table tennis, 20/2374–5, 20/*2375*

  tennis, 20/2406–7, 20/*2406–7*
  volleyball, 21/2536–7, 21/*2537*
  waterskiing, 21/2555
  weight lifting, 21/2565–6, 21/*2566*
  wind surfing, 21/2593
  wrestling, 22/2621–2, 22/*2621–1*
  see also Games
Sports car racing, 3/278
Sportsmanship, 19/2317
Spotted hyenas, 10/1231
Spotted Tail, 11/*1264*
Spring, 19/**2318–19**, 19/*2319*
Springbok, 2/174
Springfield, Mass., 13/1528
Springs, 21/2566–7
Spring tides, 20/2425
Sprinklers, irrigation, 11/1305
Spruce, 6/633
Spruce Knob, 21/2574
Spurs, 18/2116
Sputniks, 18/*2164*, 18/2165, 19/2288
Spyri, Johanna, 5/534, 19/**2320**
Squabs, 16/1929
Square dancing, 6/697, 6/698,
  19/**2320–1**, 19/*2321*
Square knot, 12/1374, 12/*1374*
Squash, 19/**2321**, 19/*2321*
Squash bug, 4/404
Squids, 14/1625, 14/*1625*, 15/1822–3,
  15/*1823*
Squires, 12/1371
Squirrel monkeys, 14/*1637*
Squirrels, 5/558, 5/*558*, 13/*1498*,
  18/*2115*, 19/**2322**, 19/*2322*
  flying, 8/967, 8/*967*
Sri Lanka, 19/**2322–3**, 19/*2322–3*
  S.S. troops, 22/2612
Stabiae, 16/1973, 21/2535
Staff, musical notation, 14/1683
Stagecoaches, 4/475
Stage makeup, 12/1488
Stage names, 14/1699
Stags, 6/709
Stag's-horn club moss, 5/*584*
Stained glass, 19/**2323**, 19/*2323*
Stainless steel, 11/1303
Stairs, escalators, 7/834, 7/*834*
Stalactites, 4/498, 4/*499*
Stalagmites, 4/498, 4/*499*, 4/500
Stalingrad, 22/2613
Stalin, Joseph, 6/726, 11/1365,
  12/1379, 18/2135, 19/2286,
  19/**2324**, 19/*2324*, 20/2467,
  22/2612, 22/*2619*
Stalin, Svetlana, 19/2324
Stallions, 10/1203
Stamens, 8/961, 8/*961*
Stammering, 19/2308–9
Stamps, 16/*1983*, 16/1984
  collecting, 5/593, 5/*593*, 5/594,
    19/**2324–5***, 19/*2324*
Stampedes, 6/669
Standardbred horses, 10/1206
Standard time zones, 20/2428
Standish, Miles, 16/1931
Stanislavski, Konstantin, 1/28
Stanley, Sir Henry Morton,
  12/1454, 19/**2325**, 19/*2325*
Stanley Steamer, 3/273
Stanleyville, 22/2642
Stanley, Wendell M., 21/2533
Stanton, Edwin M., 10/1245, 12/1441
Stanton, Elizabeth, 19/**2325–6**,
  19/*2325*, 21/2600

Stanton, Henry, 19/2325
Stapes, 18/2230
Starboard, sailing, 18/2153
Starfish, 7/791, 7/*791–2*, 9/1106–7
  regeneration, 17/2077, 17/*2077*
Starley, J.K., 3/338
Starlings, 15/1785
Starr, Helen, 1/33
Starr, Ringo, 16/1978
Stars, 19/**2326–7**, 19/*2326–7*, 21/*2501*
  Antares, 2/172
  astrology, 2/247
  astronomy, 2/248–52
  black holes, 3/356–7
  constellations, 6/641–2
  double, 10/1182
  life of, 19/2327
  luminosity, 19/2327
  magnitude, 19/2326–7
  make-up of, 19/2326
  Milky Way, 13/1594
  North Star, 15/1795
  observatories, 15/1812–14,
    15/*1813–14*
  planetariums, 16/1936–7, 16/*1937*
  solar system, 19/2256–61,
    19/*2256–60*
  starlight, 19/2326–7
  Sun, 19/2353
Stars, movie, 1/27–8
Star-spangled banner, 14/1705,
  16/1977, 19/**2328**, 19/*2328*
Stars and Stripes, 8/952, 8/*952*,
  18/2138
Star Trek, 18/*2175*
Star Wars, 14/*1664*
State, Church and, 5/546–7
State Court system, 6/667–8
State Department, 4/425, 4/426
State government, 19/**2328–9**,
  19/*2328*, 21/2487
Statehood, 19/**2329–30**, 19/*2330*
  order of, 19/2329
Staten Island, 15/1765, 15/1767
Statesmen *see* Politicians and states-
  men; Presidents
States' rights, 19/**2330–1**
Static electricity, 7/819
Statistics, 19/**2331–2***, 19/*2331*
Statue of Liberty, 14/1708,
  19/**2332–3**, 19/*2332*
Statute law, 12/1399
Steam, geysers, 9/1073–4, 9/*1074*
Steam cars, 3/272–3, 3/*272*
Steam engines, 7/847–9, 7/*847–8*
  plows, 8/*909*
  Watt, James, 21/2557
Steaming, 6/655
Steam locomotives, 11/*1275*, 17/2055,
  17/*2056*, 17/2057
Steam organs, 4/439
Steam ships, 18/2208–10
Steam turbines, 7/848, 7/*848*
Steel, 11/1303–4, 11/*1302–4*, 13/1568
  alloys, 1/104
  building materials, 6/646
  furnaces, 13/*1506*
Steel bands, 15/1840
  drums, 16/1898
Steeplechases, 10/1208, 20/2441
Stegosaurus, 6/733, 6/*734*
Steichen, Lillian, 18/2158
Steinbeck, John, 12/*1449*, 12/1451,
  15/1802

Steinem, Gloria, 21/2601
Stein, Joseph, 14/1688
Stems, plants, 16/*1938*, 16/1940
Stenographers, 18/2214
Stentor, 17/*2017*
Step-down transformers, 7/823
Stephen, King of England, 10/1176,
  19/**2333**, 19/*2333*
Stephen II, Pope, 18/2121
Stephens, Alexander Hamilton, 6/626
Stephenson, George, 17/2055,
  19/**2333–4**, 19/*2333*, 20/2449,
  20/*2250*
Stephenson, Robert, 19/2334
Stepovich, Michael A., 19/*2330*
Steppes, 14/1633, 15/1780–1,
  17/1994, 18/2144, 19/2282
  animal life, 2/150
Step-up transformers, 7/822–3
Stereographic projections, 13/*1511*
Stereoplanigraphs, 13/*1511*
Stereoscopic vision, 18/2220
Sternum, 18/2230
Steroids, 7/768
Steuben, Baron von, 1/127
Stevedores, 10/1151
Stevenson, Robert Louis, 5/532,
  19/**2334**, 19/*2334*
Stewart Island, 15/1768
Stewart, Michael, 14/1687
Stewing, 6/655
Stheno, 9/1092
Stick puppets, 17/2031
Stieglitz, Alfred, 6/690
Stigma, 8/961, 8/*961*
Stiletto, 20/2368
Still, Andrew T., 542
Stimulants, 1/33
Stinging coral, 6/659
Stingless bees, 3/324–5
Stingrays, 18/2200, 18/*2200*
Stings:
  bee, 3/*323*, 3/324, 3/*325*
  first aid, 8/940
Stink bug, 4/404
Stitches, 18/2194
Stoats, 21/2560
Stock car racing, 3/278
Stock farming, 1/52
Stockhausen, Karlheinz, 5/*619*
Stockholm, 20/2363
Stock markets, 18/2223
Stocks, punishment, 17/2032
Stocks and bonds, 19/**2334–5**,
  19/*2335*
  corporations, 6/661
  interest, 11/1285–6
Stock tickers, 7/801
Stockton-Darlington Railway,
  17/2055
Stockton Plateau, 20/2412
Stolas, 8/912, 18/2132
Stolons, 17/*2087*
Stomachs, digestion, 6/730–1
Stomata, 16/1941
Stone:
  building materials, 4/406–7, 6/646
  carving, 4/480
  granite, 9/1099–1100, 9/*1099*
  quarrying, 17/2035–6, 17/*2036*
Stone Age, 19/**2335–6**, 19/*2335–6*
  weapons, 21/2559, 21/*2559*
Stonehenge, 7/854, 7/*854*, 19/**2336**,
  19/*2336*

Stone, Lucy, 21/2600
Stone Mountain, 9/*1061*, 9/1062, 18/2180, 19/**2337**, 19/*2337*
Stones, gems, 9/1049–50
Stoneware, 16/1988
Stony Point, battle of, 21/2558
Stores, 19/**2337–9**, 19/*2337–8*
Stories, composition, 5/620–1
Storks, 19/**2339**, 19/*2339*, 21/2551
Storm petrels, 18/2181
Storms:
   hurricanes, 10/1228–9
   thunder and lightning, 12/1437
Stoves, 10/1171
Stowe, Calvin Ellis, 19/2339
Stowe, Harriet Beecher, 1/15, 19/**2339–40**, 19/*2339*
Stradivari family, 19/2344
Strain, 19/2343
Straits of Mackinac, 13/1578
Strata, 9/1057
   archaeology, 2/197
Strategic Air Command (SAC), 1/62
Strategic Defense Initiative (SDI), 6/736, 19/2297
Stratford, Ontario, 15/1832
Stratford-upon-Avon, 18/2197, 18/*2198*
Stratocumulus clouds, 5/*582*
Stratosphere, 3/257
Stratus clouds, 5/*582*, 5/583
Strauss, Eduard, 19/2340
Strauss family, 3/269
Strauss, Johann, 19/**2340**, 19/*2340*
Strauss, Johann the Elder, 19/2340
Strauss, Josef, 19/2340
Stravinsky, Igor, 3/296, 5/544, 15/1775, 19/**2340**, 19/*2340*
Streep, Meryl, 14/*1661*, 14/*1663*
Streetcars, 4/426–7
Streets, 19/**2340–3**, 19/*2341–2*
   traffic planning, 20/2445–6
Stress, 19/**2343**
Strikes, 12/1381
Stringed instruments, 14/1682, 14/1688, 19/**2343–5**, 19/*2343–5*
   blown instruments, 19/2345
   bowed instruments, 19/2343–4
   hammered instruments, 19/2345
   plucked instruments, 19/2344
Striped hyenas, 10/1231
Strip-mining, 13/1601, 21/2574
Stroessner, Alfredo, 16/1875
Strokes, swimming, 20/2365–6
Strong, John, 8/907
Structural geology, 9/1055
Structural psychologists, 17/2020
Stuart, J.E.B., 5/567
Studios, recording, 17/*2071*
Stump dolls, 7/749
Stuntmen, 14/*1663*
Stupa, 4/*402*
Sturluson, Snorri, 14/1696
Stuttering, 19/2308–9
Stuyvesant, Peter, 19/**2345**, 19/*2345*
Style:
   fashion, 8/912–15, 8/*912–15*
   flowers, 8/961
Styne, Jule, 14/1687
Subaqueous tunnels, 20/2475
Subarctic climate, 5/576
Subatomic particles, 3/258, 16/1180–1
Sublimation, 13/1537
Submarine canyons, 15/1816

Submarines, 14/1728, 19/**2345–7**, 19/*2345–7*
Submersibles, 19/2347
Substitution codes, 5/589
Subtitles, motion pictures, 14/1662
Subtraction, 2/213
Subtrahend, 2/213
Subtropical climate, 5/576
Suburbs, 5/556, 19/**2347**, 19/*2347*
Subways, 19/**2348–9**, 19/*2348–9*
Succor Creek Canyon, 15/*1842*
Succulent houseplants, 10/1216
Sucre, Antonio José de, 7/801
Sucrose, 4/462, 19/2351
Sudan, 12/1493, 19/**2349–50**, 19/*2349–50*
Sudbury, Massachusetts, 10/1211
Sudd, 15/1776
Suez Canal, 4/453, 4/*453*, 4/454, 7/807, 13/1556–7, 19/**2350–1**, 19/*2350–1*
   1956 crisis, 14/1703–4, 16/1889, 19/2351
Suffolk punch horses, 10/1207
Suffragists, 21/2600
Sugar, 19/**2351**, 19/*2351*
   candy, 4/456
Sugar beet, 19/2351
Sugarcane, 19/2351
Sugar Loaf Mountain, 17/2103
Suharto, General, 11/1272
Suits, card game, 4/464
Sukarno, Achmed, 11/1272
Sukuma, 20/2379
Suleiman the Magnificent, 2/239, 15/1850, 15/*1850*
Sulfur butterfly, 4/*420*
Sulfur dioxide, 6/661
   bleaching, 3/358
Sulfuric acid, 1/23, 1/24
Sulkies, 10/1206
Sullivan, Anne, 11/1357
Sullivan, Sir Arthur, 9/1077, 15/*1834*
Sullivan, Louis, 2/204, 2/*205*, 22/2622
Sumatra, 11/1271
Sumer, 19/**2352**, 19/*2352*
Sumerians, 2/133, 3/286, 2/*133*, 13/1565
   calendars, 4/433
   kings, 11/1368
   summary, 2/134
   writing, 2/135
Summa Theologica, 2/190
Summer, 19/**2352–3**, 19/*2352*
Summer solstice, 18/2186
Sumo wrestling, 22/*2621*, 22/2622
Sun, 10/*1169*, 19/**2353**, 19/*2353*
   eclipses, 7/792–3, 7/*792–3*
   seasons, 18/2186–9
   solar energy, 19/2256
   time and, 20/2427
   weather, 21/2561
Sun bears, 3/*320*, 3/321
Sun compass, 4/423
Sundance Kid, 15/1851
Sunday, 6/702
Sundews, 11/1281, 11/*1281*
Sundials, 5/577, 5/*577*, 20/*2427*
Sunflowers, 9/*1039*
Sung dynasty, 5/538, 11/1254, 16/*1989*
Sunlight, 12/1432
   plants and, 16/1944

Sunna, 14/1673
Sunnis, 11/*1307*
Sunspots, 3/262
Sun Yat-sen, 5/525, 5/538, 5/540, 13/1508, 17/2095, 19/**2354**, 19/*2354*
Super Bowl, 8/989
Superconductivity, 3/304, 6/682
Superego, 9/1012
Superfluidity, 6/682, 8/965
Superior, Lake, 9/1107–8, 12/1384
Supermarkets, 19/2338
Supernovas, 4/381, 19/2327
Super Saber, 3/282
Superstitions, 6/688, 19/**2354–5**, 19/*2355*
   folklore, 8/971
Supertankers, 18/*2211*, 18/2212, 18/*2212*
Suppé, Franz von, 15/1835
Supplemental airlines, 1/65
Supply and demand, 7/798, 19/**2355**
Supreme Court, 6/667, 6/*667*, 19/**2355–6**, 19/*2355*, 21/2488
   appointment, 17/1998
   constitution, 6/642, 6/645
   Marshall, John, 13/1519–20
   Marshall, Thurgood, 13/1520
   O'Connor, Sandra Day, 15/1821
   Taft, William Howard, 20/2375
Supreme soviet, 19/2285
Surahs, 12/1375
Surface tension, 19/**2356–7***, 19/*2356*
Surface-to-air missiles (SAM), 13/1609
Surface-to-surface missiles (SSM), 13/1609
Surfboards, surfing, 19/2356
Surf casting, fishing, 8/947
Surfing, 19/**2357**, 19/*2357*
   windsurfing, 21/2593
Surgeons, 13/1555
Surgery, 19/**2357–8**, 19/*2357–8*
   antiseptics, 12/1445
   history of, 19/2358
   lasers, 12/1394
   Lister, John, 12/1445
Surgical nurses, 15/1808
Suriname, 19/**2358–9**, 19/*2359*
Surnames, 14/1698
Surrealism, 6/691, 19/**2359–60**, 19/*2359–60*
Surtsey, 11/*1308*
Surveying, 19/**2360–1**, 19/*2360*
Surveyor spacecraft, 19/2288
Survival of the fittest, 8/886
Susa, 16/1903
Susan Constant, 11/1319
Suspension bridges, 4/390, 4/*390*
Susquehanna Indians, 13/1525
Susquehanna River, 13/1524, 16/1893
Susu, 10/1125
Sutherland, Graham, 20/2379
Sutherland, Joan, 18/*2227*
Sutter, John A., 9/1090
Sutter's Mill, California, 4/438
Sutton Hoo burial ship, 7/855
Suva, 13/1558
Swaanedael, 6/714
Swahili, 1/47
Swallows, 13/*1593*
Swallowtail butterfly, 4/*420*, 4/421
Swallow-tailed kites, 3/348

Swamps, 19/**2361–2**, 19/*2361–2*
   wildflowers, 21/2587
Swans, 3/*346*, 7/*772*, 7/772
Swansea, 21/2539
Swaziland, 19/**2362**, 19/*2362*
Sweat, 18/2232
   glands, 9/1081, 13/1495, 18/2232
Sweden, 20/**2363**, 20/*2363*
   American colonies, 1/110–11
   Finland, 8/932
   Hammarskjöld, Dag, 10/1142–3
   Linnaeus, Carolus, 12/1442–3
   Vikings, 21/2527–9
Swedish language, 18/2168, 20/2363
Sweetbreads, 13/1547
Sweeteners, 19/2351
Sweet peas, 9/*1039*
Swift Bear, 11/*1264*
Swift, Jonathan, 5/531, 6/724, 9/1076, 20/**2364**, 20/*2364*
Swifts, 10/*1146*
Swimming, 19/2316, 20/**2364–6**, 20/*2364–6*
   diving, 6/743–4, 6/*743–4*
   English Channel, 954
   fish, 8/942, 8/943–4
   history, 20/2366
   learning, 20/2364–6
   lifesaving, 12/1430–2, 12/*1431*
   safety, 12/1431–2
   scuba diving, 18/2177–8
   strokes, 20/2365–6
Swine, 16/1928
Swing, 11/1325
Swing bridges, 4/390, 4/*390*
Switchblades, 20/2368
Switchboards, 20/2392
Switchmen, 19/2348
Switzerland, 8/877, 20/**2366–8**, 20/*2367*
   Spyri, Johanna, 19/2320
   Tell, William, 20/2400
Sword of Damocles, 6/695
Swords, 20/**2368**, 20/*2368*
   fencing, 8/921–2, 8/*912–2*
Sycamore, 20/*2461*
Sydney, 3/265, 3/266, 20/**2369**, 20/*2369*
Sydney Opera House, 2/*201*
Syllabary, 22/2624
Symbiosis, 20/**2369–70**, 20/*2370*
Symbolism, 20/**2370–1**, 20/*2370–1*
Symbols:
   alphabets, 1/105–7, 1/*106*
   flags, 8/951–3
Symmetry, 20/**2371***
Sympathetic nerves, 14/1741
Symphony orchestras, 15/1838–9
Symptoms, diseases, 6/736–7
Synagogues, 11/1344, 11/*1344*
Synapse, 14/1739
Syncopation, 11/1325
Synodic period, 14/1646
Syntax, 9/1098
Synthesizers, music, 7/824, 14/1692, 14/*1692*
Synthetic, 20/**2371–2**, 20/*2371–2*
Synthetic dyes, 7/777, 7/*777*
Synthetic fabrics, 5/581
Synthetic fibers, 8/926–7
Synthetic gemstones, 9/1050
Synthetoceras, 21/*1499*
Syon House, 11/*1286*
Syphilis, 7/811

Syracuse, Damocles, 6/695
Syracuse (N.Y.), 4/446
Syracuse (Sicily), 4/490, 8/881
Syr Darya, 2/195
Syria, 13/1589, 20/**2372–3**, 20/2372–3

Tt

Tabby cats, 4/488
Table tennis, 20/**2374–5**, 20/2375
Tachina flies, 8/967
Tack, horse riding, 10/1207–8
Tacks, sailing, 18/2153, 18/2153
Taconic Mountains, 21/2518
Taconite, 11/1302
Tactical Air Command (TAC), 1/63
Tadpoles, 2/130, 2/131, 2/152,
    9/1013, 9/1013, 13/1570. 14/1721
Tadzhik, 19/2282
Taft, Robert Alphonso, 20/2375
Taft, Robert Alphonso Jr., 20/2375
Taft, William Howard, 16/1914,
    16/1968, 18/2136, 19/2355,
    20/**2375–6**, 20/2375
Tagalog, 16/1914
Tagus River, 16/1982
Tahiti, 6/653
    Gauguin, Paul, 9/1047
Taiga, 2/150, 19/2282
Tailors, 5/580
Tails, monkeys, 14/1635
Taipa, 12/1472
T'ai Tsung, 5/538
Taiwan, 5/540, 13/1508, 20/**2376–7**,
    20/2376
    Chiang Kai–shek, 5/**525–6**
    Sun Yat–sen, 19/2354
Taj Mahal, 11/1247, 11/1254,
    20/**2377**, 20/2377
Tajumulco, 10/1123
Takahe, 8/954
Talc, 13/1597
Tallahatchie River, 13/1610
Talleyrand, 1/30
Tallinn, 7/869
Tallow, 8/917
Tallow candles, 4/456
Tall tales, 8/972
Tallulah Gorge, 1/25
Talmud, 11/1344, 11/1345
Tamandua, 2/172
Tamayo, Rufino, 15/1861, 15/1862,
    15/1862, 15/1863
Tamerlane, 11/1254
Tamils, 19/2323
Tampico, 13/1573
Tana, Lake, 15/1776
Tanganyika, 20/2378
Tanganyika, Lake, 1/43, 20/2378
Tang Dynasty, 16/1988
Tangerines, 5/555
Tangier, 14/1648
Tanglewood, 13/1528
Tanguy, Eves, At Four O'Clock in
    Spring, the Hope, 19/2359,
    19/2360
Tank cars, 17/2054
Tankers, 13/1564
    ships, 18/2206
    trucks, 20/2469, 20/2470
Tanks, aquarium, 2/186–90
Tanks, military, 20/**2377–8**, 20/2377

Tanning, 12/1408
Tanzania, 20/**2378–9**, 20/2378
Taoism, 2/243, 17/2079, 20/**2379**
Taos, 4/476
Tape recordings, 17/2072, 17/2072
    cassettes, 4/482
Tapestry, 20/**2379–80**, 20/2380
    history, 20/2380
Tapeworm, 16/1876
Tapirs, 20/**2380–1**, 20/2381
Taproots, 16/1939
Tara, 11/1301
Tarantella, 8/970
Target shooting, 18/2214, 18/2214
Tariffs, 5/574, 11/1292, 20/2382,
    20/2445
Tarkington, Booth, 11/1255
Tarnishing, 6/661
Tarquinius Superbus, 18/2129
Tartans, 18/2176
Tartars, 18/2145
Tarzan, 4/417, 4/417
Tasman, Abel, 3/265
Tasmania, 3/265
Tasmanian wolves, 3/268, 17/2064,
    17/2065
Taste, 20/**2381**★, 20/2381
Tattoos, 18/2233
Taxco, 13/1573, 15/1784
Tax Court, 6/667
Taxes, 20/**2381–2**, 20/2382
Taxonomists, 3/342
Taxonomy, plant, 3/375
Taylor, Claudia, 11/1339
Taylor, Elizabeth, 1/27
Taylor, Richard, 20/2382
Taylor, Sarah, 6/701, 20/2382
Taylor, Zachary, 6/701, 8/928,
    13/1572, 20/**2382–3**, 20/2383
Tbilisi, 19/2284
Tchaikovsky, Peter Ilyich, 17/2041,
    20/**2383–4**, 20/2383
Tea, 2/244, 11/1252, 20/**2384–5**,
    20/2384
Teach, Edward (Blackbeard),
    16/1935, 16/1935
Teaching, 20/**2385–6**, 20/2385
Teal, 7/771
Teale, Edwin Way, 19/2318
Technology:
    aerospace, 1/40
    agriculture, 1/55–6
    inventions, 11/1292–5, 11/1292–5
    patents, 16/1884–5
Tecumseh, 10/1155–6, 11/1256,
    20/**2386**, 20/2386, 21/2541
Teenagers, adolescence, 1/34–5
Tees, 9/1091
Teeth, 20/**2386–8**, 20/2386–7
    care of, 20/2387–8
    chewing, 6/730
    dentistry, 6/717–18, 6/716–18
    fillings, 9/1090
    kinds of, 20/2386–7
    milk teeth, 20/2387
    rodents, 18/2115
    snails, 19/2243
    structure, 20/2387
Tektite II, 15/1821
Tel Aviv, 11/1309
Telecommunications, 20/**2388**,
    20/2388
    Morse Code, 14/1651
Teleconferencing, 20/2392

Telegraph, 5/611, 20/**2388–90**,
    20/2389
    Marconi, Guglielmo, 13/1513–14
    Morse, Samuel F.B., 14/1650
Telepathy, 8/897
Telephones, 1/117, 5/611, 5/612,
    7/801, 7/817, 20/2388, 20/2388,
    20/**2390–3**★, 20/2390–2
    Bell, Alexander Graham, 3/329
    communication satellites, 5/612,
        5/614
    modems, 5/624
    special services, 20/2392–3
Teleprinters, 20/2388, 20/2389
Telescopes, 2/250, 2/250, 12/1416,
    15/1763, 15/1763, 20/**2393–5**★,
    20/2393–4
    observatories, 15/1813–14,
        15/1813–14
    radio astronomy, 17/2050–1,
        17/2050–1
    radio telescopes, 2/251
Teletype, 14/1651
Television, 20/2388, 20/**2395–8**,
    20/2395–7
    acting, 1/28
    Baird, John Logie, 3/291–2
    broadcasting, 20/**2398–2400**,
        20/2398–2400
    cameras, 4/442, 7/825
    color, 20/2396–7
    commercials, 1/38
    communication satellites, 5/612–13
    control rooms, 20/2399
    effect on motion pictures, 14/1663
    journalism, 11/1342–3
    makeup, 12/1488
    news broadcasts, 20/2399
    receivers, 7/825
    video, 21/2524–5
    videotape rooms, 20/2399
    Zworykin, Vladimir Kosma,
        22/2649
Tell, William, 12/1411, 20/**2400**,
    20/2400
Telstar spacecraft, 19/2288
Tema, 9/1074
Temminck's cat, 4/490
Temne, 18/2218
Tempera, 15/1860
Temperate grasslands, animal life,
    2/150
Temperate marine climate, 5/576
Temperate zones, 21/2562
Temperature:
    cold, 10/1168–70
    cryogenics, 6/682
    fever, 8/926
    heat, 10/1168–70
    thermometers, 20/2422
Temperature scale, 20/**2400–1**,
    20/2401
    conversion table, 20/2401
Temple of Neptune, 2/201
Temples, 20/**2402**, 20/2402
    pagodas, 15/1857, 15/1857
    Roman, 18/2119
Temple, Shirley, 1/28, 7/750,
    14/1663
Tena, Lake, 7/871
Ten Commandments, 6/673, 11/1344,
    12/1399
Tendons, 14/1676
Tendrils, 12/1404

Tenerife, 4/454
Teng Hsiao-p'ing, 5/540, 13/1508,
    20/**2402–3**, 20/2403
Tengmalm's owl, 15/1852
Tennessee, 20/**2403–5**, 20/2404–5
    climate, 20/2404
    employment, 20/2404
    history, 20/2404
    land, 20/2403–4
    map, 20/2405
    state emblems, 20/2405
Tennessee Hills, 13/1612
Tennessee River, 6/694, 20/2403
Tennessee-Tombigbee Waterway,
    4/454
Tennessee Valley Authority (TVA),
    6/694, 17/2024, 17/2024,
    18/2134, 19/2249, 20/2403,
    21/2490
Tennessee walking horses, 10/1206
Tenniel, Sir John, 5/533, 12/1447
Tennis, 20/**2406–7**, 20/2406–7
    Gibson, Althea, 9/1076–7, 9/1077
Tennyson, Alfred, 6/675, 20/**2407**,
    20/2407
Tenochtitlán, 3/284, 6/662, 11/1267,
    13/1575
Tenors, 18/2227
Ten pin bowling, 4/378–9, 4/379
Tentacles, 15/1822, 15/1822
Tenth Amendment, 3/340
Tents, 18/2204, 20/**2408**, 20/2408
Tenzing Norkay, 8/892, 8/893,
    10/1185, 14/1672
Teotihuacán, 11/1259, 17/2034
Teresa, Mother, 15/1779,
    20/**2408–9**, 20/2409
Tereshkova, Valentina, 2/248
Termites, 1/11, 11/1279, 20/**2409**,
    20/2409
Terns, 10/1129, 10/1129, 18/2181,
    18/2182
Terpsichore, 14/1678
Terrain, climate and, 5/576
Terramycin, 7/768
Terra Nova, 14/1713
Terrapins, 20/2478
Terrariums, 20/**2410**★, 20/2410
Terrell, Mary Church, 5/563
Terriers, 6/747
Terrorism, 20/**2411**, 20/2411
Tesserae, mosaics, 14/1651–2
Testa, 18/2187
Testes, 9/1081
Testimonies, court system, 6/666
Test matches, 6/672
Testosterone, 10/1201
Tests, psychological, 17/2019
Teton Indians, 18/2228
Teton Mountains, 22/2626
Tetracycline, 2/177
Tetzel, Johann, 12/1470
Tewkesbury, battle of, 21/2543
Texas, 1/117, 16/1969, 20/**2411–15**,
    20/2411–14
    Alamo, 1/84–5
    climate, 20/2412
    Dallas, 6/693
    employment, 20/2414
    history, 20/2412–14
    land, 20/2411–12
    map, 20/2413
    state emblems, 20/2413
Textbooks, 3/368

Textiles, 13/1506, 20/**2415–16**, 20/*2415–16*
  dyes, 7/*776–7*
  fibers, 8/*926–7*
  Industrial Revolution, 11/1274
  plant fibers, 16/*1950–1*
  silk, 18/2224–5, 18/*2224*
  spinning and weaving, 19/2313–14
Textured paints, 15/1858
TGV, 9/*1001*
Thackeray, William Makepeace, 20/**2416–17**, 20/*2416*
Thailand, 12/1302, 20/**2417**, 20/*2417*
Thales, 7/792, 7/828
Thalia, 14/1677
Thalli, 12/1428
Thallophytes, 16/1947, 16/*1948*
Thames River, 7/795, 12/1458, 20/**2418**, 20/*2418*
Thanksgiving, 20/**2418–19**, 20/*2419*
  meals, 6/*653*
Thant, U, 4/415
Thatcher, Denis, 20/2419
Thatcher, Margaret, 20/**2419**, 20/*2419*
Thaxted, 2/*204*
Theater, 20/**2419–22**, 20/*2420–1*
  acting, 1/26–9, 1/*27–9*
  Ancient Greek, 20/2420, 20/*2420*
  drama, 7/758–60
  English, 20/2421
  pantomime, 16/1870
  Renaissance, 20/2421
  Roman, 20/2420, 20/*2420*
  stage makeup, 12/1488
  United States, 20/2421–2
  vaudeville, 21/2510–11, 21/*2510–11*
  see also Actors; Playwrights
Theater of the Absurd, 7/760
Thebes, 7/808
Theodore Roosevelt National Park, 15/1793
Theodosius, Emperor, 15/1830
Theological seminaries, 5/573, 5/595
Theophrastus, 3/374
Theorems, mathematics, 13/1534
Thera, 3/*255*, 9/1111, 21/2535
Therapists, hospitals, 10/1211
Therapsids, 17/2090
Therapy, handicapped people, 19/2303–5
Theravada Buddhists, 4/402
Thermagraphs, 10/*1169*
Thermals, 9/1085
Thermocouples, 18/*2174*
Thermodynamics, 16/1923
Thermometers, 20/2400–1, 20/**2422**, 20/*2422*
Thermoplastics, 16/1954
Thermopylae, 9/1112
  battle of, 22/2628
Thermosetting plastics, 16/1954–5
Thermostats, 10/1171–2
Thesaurus, 17/2075
Theseus, 14/*1695*
Thessalonika, 12/1474
Thessaly, 9/1110
Thiassi, 14/1695
Thimmonnier, Barthélemy, 18/2196
Third Amendment, 3/340
Third Continental Congress, 6/652
Thirteenth Amendment, 3/354, 3/355, 7/840, 17/2069, 18/2238
Thirty-three Immortals, 21/2502

Thirty Years' War, 9/1065, 17/2016
Thistles, 8/*965*, 21/2587
Tho, Le Duc, 15/1779
Thomas, Dylan, 7/777
Thompson, Daley, 20/*2440*
Thompson, David, 5/605
Thompson, Dorothy, 12/*1420*
Thompson, Polly, 11/1357
Thor, 5/548, 14/1695
Thorax, 4/419
Thoreau, Henry David, 10/1161, 20/**2422–3**, 20/*2423*
Thornback ray, 18/*2200*
Thornton, William, 4/460
Thoroughbred horses, 10/1206
Thorpe, Jim, 20/**2423**, 20/*2423*
Thrace, 12/1474
Thracian Plain, 4/409
Three-banded armadillo, 2/221
3-D movies, 14/1663
Three Mile Island, 15/1805
Three Musketeers, 7/773, 7/*773*
Three Rivers, battle of, 21/2558
Three Stooges, 21/2510
Three-toed sloth, 13/1497, 19/*2240*, 19/2241
Threshing, 8/909, 9/1097
Through the Looking Glass, 4/476
Thrushes, 3/344
Thrust, aerodynamics, 1/67
Thuidium tamariscinum, 14/*1655*
Thunderhead Mountain, 18/2143
Thunderstorms, clouds, 5/582, 5/583, 12/1437
Thurber, James, 8/901, 20/**2423–4**, 20/*2424*
Thurmond, Strom, 19/2230
Thursday, 6/702
Thutmose II, 7/809
Thylacine, 3/268, 17/*2064*, 17/2065
Thymus, 9/*1081*
Thyroid gland, 9/1081, 9/*1081*, 10/1202
Thyroxin, 10/1201, 10/1202
Tiberias, Lake, 9/1031
Tiberius, Emperor, 18/2131
Tiber River, 18/2128
Tibet, 20/**2424**, 20/*2424*
Ticos, 6/664
Tidal power, 7/846, 10/1230
Tidal races, 20/2425
Tidal waves, 7/789, 15/1815, 21/2557
Tides, 15/1815, 20/**2424–6**, 20/*2425–6*
Tien Shan, 2/239
Tiepolo, Giambattista, 3/307, 3/*307*, 17/2113
  Nobility and Virtue, 17/2113, 17/*2113*
Tierra del Fuego, 5/535, 5/*535*, 11/1269, 12/1481
Tiffany, Louis Comfort, 19/2323
Tiger cowrie, 18/*2202*
Tigers, 4/469, 4/489–90, 4/*489*, 20/**2426**, 20/*2426*
Tiger shrikes, 13/*1593*
Tiger tanks, 20/2377
Tightrope walkers, 1/24, 1/25
Tigris River, 20/**2426–7**, 20/*2427*
Tikal, 11/1259
Tilden, Samuel, 10/1162, 17/2071
Tillamook Indians, 15/1842
Till Plains, 14/1732, 15/1823
Timber:
  lumbering, 12/1469–70, 12/*1469–70*

  trees, 20/2458–63, 20/*2458–62*
  wood, 21/2601–2, 21/*2601*
Timbre, music, 14/1689
Timbuktu, 19/2262
Time, 20/**2427–8**, 20/*2427–8*
  day and night, 6/701–2
  days of the week, 6/702
  geologic time, 7/788
  International Date Line, 11/1288–9, 11/*1288*
  measurement, 13/1546
  measuring a year, 20/2428
  space and, 20/2428
  standard time, 20/2427–8
Time-lapse photography, 4/441
Time locks, 12/1458
Time signature, music, 14/1684
Timpani, 16/*1897*, 16/1898
Timucua Indians, 8/957
Tin, 13/1567
Tin-enamel ware, 16/1990
Tin Pan Alley, 16/1977
Tintagel, 2/236
Tintoretto, 2/230, 17/2085
Tints, 5/601
Tintypes, 16/1920
Tipis, 11/1262–3
Tippecanoe, battle of, 10/1155–6
Tippecanoe River, 20/2386
Tires, 20/**2428–9**, 20/*2429*
Tiro, Marcus Tullius, 18/2214–15
Tiros satellites, 18/2165, 19/2288
Tissue, 10/1224
Titan II rockets, 17/2111
Titanic, 10/1234, 14/1650
Titano, Mount, 18/2161
Titans, 9/1075, 9/1089, 14/1696, 17/2008, 18/2165
Tithes, 17/2081
Titian, 17/2085, 20/**2429–30**, 20/*2429*
  Portrait of a Man with a Blue Sleeve, 20/*2429*
  Ranuccio Farnese, 20/2429, 20/*2429*
Titicaca, Lake, 3/365, 12/1384, 12/*1384*, 16/*1950*, 19/2268
Titled people, 15/1779–80
Tito, 20/**2430**, 20/*2430*, 22/2639
Titus, Emperor, 11/1329
Titusville, 16/1909
Tiv, 15/1774
Tlingit Indians, 1/88, 3/253, 11/1263, 20/**2430**, 20/*2430*
TNT, 8/895, 8/896
Toñlé Sap, 11/1352
Toads, 2/130–1, 2/*130–1*, 9/1013–14, 9/*1014*, 13/1570
Toadstool Geological Park, 14/*1732*
Toadstools, 9/1022
  mushrooms, 14/1680–1, 14/*1681*
Tobacco, 20/**2430–1**, 20/*2431*
  smoking, 19/2242–3, 19/*2242–3*
Tobago, 21/2569, 21/2571
Toboggans, 19/2239
Todd, Mary, 12/1439
Togas, 5/*579*, 5/580, 8/912, 18/2132
Toggenburg goats, 9/1086
Togo, 20/**2431–2**, 20/*2431*
Togoland, 9/1074
Togo Mountains, 20/2431
Tokyo, 2/245, 5/558, 5/*615*, 11/1322, 20/**2432**, 20/*2432*
Tolbert, William R. Jr., 12/1422

Toledo, 15/1826
Tolkien, J.R.R., 5/532, 7/839
Toll roads, 19/2341
Tolstoy, Leo, 15/1772, 15/1802, 20/**2433**; 20/*2433*
Tomb of the Unknowns, 20/**2433**, 20/*2433*
Tombs, 4/413–14
Tone, music, 14/1682–3, 14/1689
Tonga, 15/1854, 16/1971, 16/1972
Tonkin, 21/2525
Tony awards, 1/29
Tools, carpenter's, 4/471–2, 4/*472*
Toothed whales, 21/2579–80
Toothpaste, 1/18
Tooth shells, 14/1625, 18/2203
Topeka, 11/*1355*, 11/1356
Topographic surveys, 19/2361
Topology, 13/1535
Torah, 10/1172, 11/1344, 11/1345
Tornadoes, 20/**2434**, 20/*2434*
Toronto, 4/450, 20/**2434–5**, 20/*2434*
Torpedoes, 19/2346
Torres, Luis de, 11/1335, 15/1750
Torres Strait, 15/1750
Torricelli, Evangelista, 3/306, 16/1882
Tortillas, 3/284
Tortoises, 2/155, 15/2477–8, 20/*2478*
Tortoiseshell butterflies, 4/*420*
Tortoiseshell short–hair cat, 4/*486*
Totalitarianism, 8/911, 9/1094
Totem poles, 11/1259
Totems, 20/**2435**, 20/*2435*
Totness, Suriname, 19/2359
Toubou, 15/1772
Touch, 20/**2435***, 20/*2435*
Toulouse geese, 7/772
Toulouse-Lautrec, Henri de, 20/**2436**, 20/*2436*
Tour de France, 3/338
Touré, Sékou, 10/1126
Tourism, 20/2455
Tournaments, 12/1371, 12/*1371*, 12/1372
Tours, 5/515, 9/1007
  battle of, 3/319
Toussaint l'Ouverture, Pierre Dominique, 18/2237
Tower of London, 6/677, 12/1459, 20/**2436–7**, 20/*2437*
Town government, 12/1456
Town houses, 10/1215
Towns, 19/2347
  communities, 5/615
  medieval, 13/1588
  prairie dogs, 17/1995, 17/*1995*
  streets, 19/2340–3
  suburbs, 19/2347
  traffic planning, 20/2445–6
Townsville, 6/659
Tow trucks, 20/2470
Toxic substances, 16/1961–2
Toy dogs, 6/747
Toys, 20/**2437–9***, 20/*2437–9*
  antique, 2/*179*
  balls, 3/295
  children and, 20/2437–8
  dolls, 7/749, 7/*749–50*
  history, 20/2437–8
  making, 20/2439
  safety, 20/2438–9
Trace minerals, diet, 8/974
Tracery, 9/1093

Trachea, 4/387
Track and field, 20/**2439–43**, 20/*2439–43*
  marathons, 13/1512, 13/*1512*
Track races, auto racing, 3/278
Tracks, animal, 2/163–4
Tractors, 8/908–9
Trade, 20/**2443–5***, 20/*2443–5*
  economics, 7/798–9
  international, 11/1291–2, 11/*1291*
  medieval, 13/1588
  Middle Ages, 20/2444
  modern, 20/2444–5
  old trade routes, 20/2443–4
  selling, 18/2188–9, 18/*2188*
Trade winds, 21/2561, 21/2592
Trafalgar, battle of, 14/1737, 14/*1738*, 19/2302
Traffic, cities, 5/557, 5/*557*
Traffic planning, 20/**2445–6**, 20/*2445–6*
Traffic signals, 18/*2222*, 20/*2445*, 20/*2446*
Tragedies, 7/759
Trail bikes, 14/1667
Trailer homes, 10/1215
Trailer vacations, 20/*2456*
Trail of Tears, 15/1827
Trains, 11/*1275*
  subways, 19/2348–9, 19/*2348–9*
Traitors, 20/2456
Trajan, 18/2131, 19/2301
Trampolines, 1/*25*
Tramp ships, 18/2212
Tranquillizers, **abuse**, 7/769
Trans-Am races, 3/278
Trans-Canada Pipeline, 16/1933
Transepts, 4/492
Transformers, 7/820, 7/822–3
Transient hotels, 10/1212
Transistors, 3/304, 5/622, 7/825, 7/828, 20/**2447–8**, 20/*2447*
Transits, 19/2360
Transkei, 19/2266
Translation, 12/1390–1
Transluscent materials, 12/1432
Trans-Mediterranean Pipeline, 16/1933–4
Transmission, automobiles, 3/276
Transparent materials, 12/1432
Transparent objects, 5/601
Trans-Pecos, 20/2412
Transpiration, 21/2553–3
Transportation, 20/**2448–54**, 20/*2448–54*
  airplanes, 1/*281–3*
  American Colonies, 1/113–14
  automobiles, 1/*274–5*
  buses, 4/418–19
  cable cars, 4/427
  canals, 4/453–4, 4/*453–4*
  chariots, 5/511–12
  cities, 5/557
  helicopters, 10/1173–4, 10/*1173–4*
  kinds, 20/2449–52
  milestones in, 20/2450
  railroads, 17/2053–9, 17/*2053–9*
  ships, 18/2205–12
  snowmobiles, 19/2247
  subways, 19/2348–9, 19/*2348–9*
  tomorrow's, 20/2452–4
  trucks, 20/2468–70, 20/*2468–70*
  uses, 20/2448–9
Transportation Department, 4/426

Transposition code, 5/589
Transuranium elements, 7/830
Transvaal, 3/363, 17/2100
Transverse flute, 21/2602
Transylvania, 18/2126
Transylvanian Mountains, 18/2126
Trapdoor spiders, 19/2312
Trapezes, 1/25
Traprock, 17/2036
Trap shooting, 18/2214
Travel, 20/**2454–6**, 20/*2454–6*
  hotels, 10/1211–12
  people on the move, 20/2455–6
  reasons for, 20/2454–5
  travel industry, 20/2455
Traverse Boards, 14/*1724*
Travers, P.L., 5/532
Travis, Joseph, 20/2477
Travis, William B., 1/84, 4/378
Trawlers, 8/949
Treason, 5/554, 6/673, 20/**2456–7**, 20/*2456*
Treaties, 20/**2457–8**
  commercial, 20/2458
  important, 20/2457
  international law, 11/1289
  legal, 20/2458
  see under place eg Paris, Treaty of (1783)
Treatment, diseases, 6/739
Tree ducks, 7/772
Tree-ferns, 8/923, 16/1952, 16/*1953*
Tree frogs, 2/*131*
Tree kangaroo, 11/1352
Trees, 20/**2458–63**, 20/*2458–62*
  anatomy, 20/2458–9
  annual rings, 21/*2601*
  bark, 3/304–5
  conifers, 6/624, 6/631–4, 6/*631–3*
  cross section, 20/*2459*
  ecology, 20/2462
  evergreen, 8/884–5
  forest fires, 8/986–7, 8/*986–7*
  forest regions, 20/2459–60
  forestry, 8/987–8, 8/*987–8*
  fruit, 9/1016–17
  garden, 9/1040
  growth, 20/2458–9
  identification, 20/2460–2
  leaves, 12/1402–4, 12/*1402–3*
  lumbering, 12/1469–70, 12/*1469–70*
  national forests, 14/1706–7
  palms, 15/1866
  Petrified Forest, 16/1908, 16/*1908*
  record, 16/1947
  wood, 21/260–12, 21/*2601*
Trent, Council of, 17/2015–16, 17/*2015*
Trenton, New Jersey, 1/127, 15/1754
  battle of, 15/1756
Trepang, 7/792
Trevithick, Richard, 17/2055, 17/*2058*
Trials, 20/**2463–5**, 20/*2463–4*
  bringing a case to trial, 20/2463
  courts, 6/667
  lawyers and judges, 12/1401–2
  procedure, 20/2463–5
Triangles, 9/1059
Tributaries, 17/2104
Triceratops, 6/733, 6/*734*
Trick-or-treating, 10/1141
Trieste, 15/1814
Trimarans, 3/361

Trinidad and Tobago, 21/2571
Trinity, 18/2122
Trinity River, 6/693
Tripe, 13/1547
Triplanes, 1/68
Triple Divide Peak, 14/1640
Triple jump, 20/2441
Tripoli, 3/303, 12/1427
Triremes, 14/1726–7, 18/2139, 18/2206
Triton, 19/2346
Trojan War, 9/1111, 20/**2465**, 20/*2465*
Trolley cars, 4/418
Trolling, fishing, 8/947
Trolls, 7/839
Trombone, 4/385, 4/*385*
Tropical climate, 5/576
Tropical fish, 20/**2465–6**, 20/*2466*
  aquarium, 2/186–90
Tropical rain forests, 11/1350, 16/1945
  animal life, 2/150
Tropics, 20/**2466–7**, 20/*2467*
Tropism, 16/1940
Troposphere, 3/257
Trotsky, Leon, 18/2149, 20/**2467**, 20/*2467*
Troubadours, 1/26, 10/1153, 12/1446
Troy, 2/*197*, 20/2465
Troyes, 9/*1008*
Troy Female Seminary, 21/2588
Trucial States, 2/193
Truck farming, 20/**2467–8**
Trucks and trucking, 20/2453, 20/2454, 20/**2468–70**, 20/*2468–70*
  driving, 20/2469
  modern, 20/2469–70
  types, 20/2468–9
Tructrain service, 17/2054
Trudeau, Pierre, 20/**2470**, 20/*2470*
Truk, 13/1582
Truman Doctrine, 20/2471
Truman, Harry S., 2/245, 12/1378, 12/1473, 13/1618, 20/**2470–2**, 20/*2471*, 21/2523
  civil rights, 5/562
  World War II, 22/2619
Trumpeter swans, 7/772
Trumpets, 4/385, 4/*385*, 14/*1692*
Trunk airlines, 1/65
Trunks, elephants, 7/831
Truss bridges, 4/390, 4/*390*
Trust departments, banks, 3/302
Trusteeship Council, 20/2486
Truth, Sojourner, 20/**2472**, 21/2600
Trypanosoma, 17/*2017*, 17/2018
Trypan red, 7/811
Tsangpo River, 20/2424
Tsavo National Park, 16/*1878*
Tshombe, Moise, 22/2642
Tsiolkovsky, Konstantin, 9/1087, 17/2111
Tsunami, 7/789, 15/1815, 21/2535, 21/2557
Tuamotu Archipelago, 16/1971
Tuareg, 5/559, 12/1493, 15/1772
Tuatara, 15/*1769*, 17/2065, 17/2089
Tuba, 4/385–6, 4/*385*
Tuberculosis, 7/811
Tubers, 4/408
  garden flowers, 9/1039
Tubman, Harriet, 3/353, 20/**2472–3**, 20/*2472*, 20/2484

Tubual Islands, 16/1971
Tubulidentata, 1/11
Tucker, Sophie, 21/2510
Tudor, Edmund, Earl of Richmond, 10/1177
Tuesday, 6/702
Tugboats, 3/362
Tukulor, 18/2190
Tulsa, 15/1828
Tumbler locks, 12/1457
Tumbler pigeons, 16/1929
Tumors, 4/455, 6/737
Tumwater, 21/2544
Tuna, 8/949
Tundra, 16/1945, 16/1965, 19/2282, 20/**2473**, 20/*2473*
Tunican Indians, 12/1464
Tunics, 8/912
Tunis, 20/2473
Tunisia, 20/**2473–4**, 20/*2473–4*
Tunnels, 20/**2474–5**, 20/*2474–5*
  longest, 20/2475
  subways, 19/2349
  wind tunnels, 21/2593–4, 21/*2594*
Tunney, Gene, 4/381
Tupamaros, 21/2502
Tupeks, 7/868
Tupi Indians, 4/386
Tupper, Sir Charles, 8/916
Turbans, 18/2223, 18/*2223*
Turbines:
  gas, 7/849
  hydroelectricity, 10/1230
  jet engines, 11/1332
  steam, 7/848, 7/*848*
Turbofan jet engines, 11/*1332*
Turbojets, 11/*1332*
Turboprop aircraft, 1/68
Turboprop engines, 11/*1332*
Turf grasses, 9/1104
Turgenev, Ivan, 15/1772
Turkana, Lake, 11/1363
Turkey, 13/1589, 13/*1591*, 20/**2475–6**, 20/*2475*
  Black Sea, 3/357
  captures Constantinople, 4/424
  carpets, 15/1846, 15/*1847*
  Crusades, 6/678–80
  Cyprus, 6/688–9
  folk dancing, 8/970
  Ottoman Empire, 15/1850
Turkey buzzard, 4/423
Turkey oak, 20/*2461*
Turkeys, 3/345, 9/1034
  poultry, 17/1991–2, 17/*1992*
Turkey vultures, 3/349
Turko-Tatars, 19/2282
Turner, Benjamin, 17/*2069*
Turner, Joseph Mallord William, 2/232, 15/1860, 15/*1860*, 18/2127, 18/*2127*, 20/**2476–7**, 20/*2477*
Turner, Nat, 5/561, 18/2237, 20/**2477**
Turnpikes, 19/2341
Turnstone, 3/345
Turtle, 19/2346
Turtle Mountains, 9/1041
Turtles, 17/2090, 17/*2090*, 20/**2477–8**, 20/*2478*
  pets, 16/*1905*
Tuscaloosa, Alabama, 1/83
Tuscarora Indians, 8/951, 15/1788, 21/2574

Tusi, 4/417, 4/418
Tuskegge Institute, 1/83
Tusks, 10/1202
Tusk shell, 14/1625
Tussand, Madame, wax museum, 21/2558
Tussaud, Marie, 21/2558
Tutankhamen, 5/*511*, 7/809, 18/*2178*
Tutsis, 18/2150
Tuvalu, 13/1582, 15/1854
TV *see* Television
Twain, Mark, 5/532, 9/1091, 12/1450, 13/1614, 13/1618, 18/*2216*, 20/**2478–9**, 20/*2479*
Twa people, 4/417
Twelfth Night, 11/1321
Twenty-fifth Amendment, 17/1998
Twenty-first Amendment, 17/2008
Twenty-sixth Amendment, 7/815
Twill weave, 20/2415
Twine, 18/2136
Twins, 9/*1051*, 17/2089
Twist (dance), 6/697
Two half hitches, 12/1374, 12/*1374*
Two-toed anteaters, 2/173
Tyler, John, 10/1155, 20/**2479–80**, 20/*2479–80*, 21/2523
Typesetting, 20/**2480–1**, 20/*2480–1*
Typhoons, 8/955, 10/1228
Typhus fever, 12/1467
Tyr, 14/1695
Tyrannosaurus rex, 6/733, 6/*734*, 8/992
Tyre, 16/1916
Tyrrhenia, 7/872
T'zu Hsi, Empress of China, 5/*539*

Uu

Ubangi–Shari, 5/505
Udders, 4/494, 6/692
Uemura, Naomi, 8/894
UFOs *see* Unidentified flying objects
Uganda, 20/**2482–3**, 20/*2482–3*
Ugli fruit, 16/1942
UHURU, 18/2165
Uinta Mountains, 13/1499, 21/2504
Uintatherium, 13/1499
Ukelele, 19/2344
Ukraine, 19/2282
Ulan Bator, 14/1634
Ulle, 14/1695
Ulster, 15/1793
Ultrasound, 10/*1209*
Ulyanov, Aleksandre, 12/1414
Ulysses, 14/1697
Umbilical cords, 13/1496
Umbra, 7/792
Umbrella tents, 20/2408
Umiaks, 1/95, 7/868
Umm al Qawain, 2/193
Unau, 19/2240
Uncertainty principle, 18/2172
Uncle Remus, 10/1153–4
Uncle Sam, 20/**2483**, 20/*2483*
Uncle Tom's Cabin, 1/15, 19/2339–40
Unconscious thoughts, 9/1012
Underground fortifications, 8/990–1
Underground (guerillas), 10/1124
Underground Railroad, 1/15, 5/561, 18/2238, 20/2473, 20/**2483–4**
Underground railways, 19/2348–9, 19/*2348–9*

Undertakers, 4/413
Undertow, 20/2425–6
Underwater archeology, 2/197, 2/*197*
Underwater-to-surface missiles (USM), 13/1609
Underworld, organized crime, 6/674
Ungulates *see* Hoofed animals
Unicorns, 2/160–1
Unidentified flying objects, 20/**2484**, 20/*2484*
Union Jack, 8/951–1, 8/*953*
Union Pacific Railroad, 14/1734, 17/2058, 21/2578
Unions *see* Labor unions
Unisex clothes, 5/581, 8/914
Unit crystals, 6/682–3
United Arab Emirates, 2/193
United Artists Corporation, 9/1119
United Church of Canada, 17/2014
United Church of Christ, 17/2013, 17/2014
United Empire Loyalists, 4/447
United Kingdom, 4/395, 6/688–9, 20/**2484–5**, 20/*2484–5*
American colonies, 1/110–12, 1/115
American Revolution, 1/122–8, 5/570–1
Anglo-Saxons, 2/143
Boer War, 3/363–4
Canada and, 4/447–52
colonies, 1/48–9
Commonwealth of Nations, 5/**610**
Crimean War, 6/674–5
Cromwell, Oliver, 6/675–6
crown jewels, 6/677, 6/*677*
Cuba, 6/684
Falkland Islands, 8/906–7
French and Indian Wars, 9/1005–6, 9/*1005*
furniture, 9/126
Gibraltar, 9/1076
Guyana, 10/1133
Hong Kong, 10/1199
Hundred Years War, 10/1227
India, 11/1254–5
Industrial Revolution, 11/1274–6, 11/*1274–5*
Ireland, 11/1302
Kenya, 11/1364
London, 12/1458–9, 12/*1458–9*
Malta, 12/1494
New Zealand, 15/1768–9
Northern Ireland, 15/1793–4
Parliament, 16/1878–9
Sudan, 19/2350
theaters, 20/2421
Union Jack, 8/951–2, 8/*953*
US Declaration of Independence, 6/707
War of 1812, 21/2541
Winston Churchill, 5/**549**
World War I, 21/2604–10
World War II, 22/2611–20, 22/*2611–20*
United Mine Workers of America (UMW), 12/1419
United Nations (UN), 1/121, 5/554, 11/1289, 11/1291, 12/1404, 16/1889, 18/2135, 20/2368, 20/**2485–6**, 20/*2485–6*
children's rights, 5/560
Cyprus, 6/688–9
Economic and Social Council, 20/2486

General Assembly, 11/*1289*, 20/*2485*, 20/2486
Hammarskjöld, Dag, 10/1142–3
Korean War, 12/1377–8
Namibia, 14/1700
Peacekeeping Force, 2/227, 11/*1289*
Secretariat, 20/2486
Security Council, 20/2485–6
United Nations Building, New York, 2/205
United Nations Children's Fund (UNICEF), 20/2486
United Nations Educational, Scientific and Cultural Organization (UNESCO), 2/228
United Press International (UPI), 11/1342–3
United States, U.S.S., 21/2541
United States of America, 21/**2491–7**, 21/*2492–7*
capital, 21/2497
cities, 21/2497
climate, 21/2492–4
industry, 21/2496–7
land, 21/2491–4
people, 21/2494–5
resources, 21/2495–6
United States government, 21/**2487–9**, 21/*2487–9*
Constitution, 6/642–5, 21/24888
Federal government, 21/2487–8
party system, 21/2489
separation of powers, 21/2488–9
state government, 21/2487–8
United States government agencies, 21/**2489–91**, 21/*2490–1*
independent agencies, 21/2490
United States Mint, 14/1632
United States service academies, 21/**2497–8**, 21/*2498*
Univalves, 18/2203
mollusks, 14/1625
Universal Declaration of Human Rights, 5/560
Universal language, 21/**2498–9**
Universal Negro Improvement Association, 3/355, 5/562
Universal Postal Union, 16/1986
Universe, 2/251–2, 21/**2499–2501**, 21/*2499–2501*
Universities, 5/**595–7**, 7/804
see under place eg Michigan University
Untouchables, 10/1187
Up Country, South Carolina, 19/2274–6
Upland, Pennsylvania, 16/1894
Upper Peninsula, Michigan, 13/1578–80
Upper Volta *see* Burkina Faso
Ur, 19/2352
Ural Mountains, 8/875, 19/2281, 21/**2501**
Ural River, 4/481
Urania, 14/1678
Uranium, 13/1567, 15/1803–4
Uranus, 10/1181, 10/*1182*, 19/*2257*, 19/2257
basic facts, 19/2259
Urban areas, 5/556
Urban guerrillas, 10/1124
Urban League, 3/355, 5/562
Urea plastics, 16/1955

Urologists, 13/1555
Ursa Minor, 6/642
Uruguay, 19/2268, 21/**2501–2**, 21/*2502*
Urushiol, 16/1962
US Air Force, 1/**61–4**, 1/*62–4*
combat commands, 61–3
history, 63–4
US Army, 2/226–7
camouflage, 4/443
insignia, 2/227
National Guard, 14/1707–8
US Cabinet, 4/425–6, 4/*425*
US Constitution *see* Constitution (US)
US Government, White House, 21/2582, 21/*2582*
US Information Agency (USIA), 8/985
Usk, River, 21/2539
US Marine Corps, 13/1514–15, 13/*1514–15*
US Marine Corps Women's Reserve, 13/1515
US Naval Research Laboratory, 5/578
US Navy:
aircraft carriers, 1/58–60, 1/*59–60*
history, 14/1728–31
Marine Corps, 13/1514–15
Navy Department, 14/1729
Operating Forces, 14/1729
Shore Establishment, 14/1729
World War I, 14/1729
World War II, 14/1729
US Peace Corps, 11/1359
US Secret Service, 6/665
Ussher, Archbishop, 9/1057
US Virgin Islands, 21/2572
Utah, 21/**2502–5**, 21/*2503–5*
climate, 21/2504
employment, 21/2505
history, 21/2504–5
land, 21/2504
map, 21/*2503*
state emblem, 21/*2503*
Ute Indians, 4/476, 21/2504
Utopia, 14/1648
Uzbek, 19/2282

Vv

V-2 rockets, 17/2111, 21/2537
Vaca, Cabeza de, 12/1464
Vacations, travel, 20/2454–6
Vaccinations, 3/289, 5/528, 6/737, 6/*739*, 21/2534
immunity, 2/177, 10/1244
Jenner, Edward, 11/1328–9
Vacuum, 1/77, 21/**2506**, 21/*2506*
Vacuum cleaners, 7/*818*
Vakhsh River, 6/695
Valdivia, Pedro de, 5/536
Valencia, 19/2298
Valentine, Saint, 21/2507
Valentine cards, 9/1118
Valentine's Day, 8/919–20, 21/**2507**, 21/*2507*
Valentine tanks, 20/2377
Valentino, Rudolf, 14/1659, 14/*1662*
Valhalla, 14/1696
Valkyries, 14/1696

Valletta, 12/1943
Valley Forge, 1/127, 1/*127*, 21/2548, 21/2558
Valley Forge State Park, 16/1896
Valley glaciers, 9/1079–80, 9/*1079–80*
Valley of Ten Thousand Smokes, 1/87
Vallisneria, 2/*189*
Valois dynasty, 9/1008
Valor, decorations, 13/1550
Valparaiso, 5/535
Vampire bats, 3/317
Van Allen belts, 17/2044–5, 17/*2045*, 19/2289
Van Allen, James, 17/2044, 18/2165
Van Buren, Martin, 21/**2507–8**, 21/*2507*
Vancouver, 4/394
Vancouver, George, 4/392, 21/2544
Vandals, 9/1064
Van de Graaff generator, 7/*749*
Van Diemen's Land, 3/265
Van Eyck, Jan, 13/*1519*, 17/2083–4
Van Gogh, Theo, 21/2508
Van Gogh, Vincent, 8/896, 8/*896*, 9/1047, 14/1620, 20/*2436*, 21/**2508–9**, 21/*2508–9*
  Painter on the Road to Tarascon, 21/2508, 21/*2508*
  Road with Cypresses, 21/2508, 21/*2509*
Vanguard spacecraft, 18/2165, 19/2288
Vanity Fair, 20/2416
Van Lew, Elizabeth, 19/2319
Van Loon, Hendrik, 15/1744
Vanuatu, 13/1558, 15/1854
Vaqueros, 6/668
Varanasi, 9/1036, 11/*1253*
Variation, evolution, 8/886
Variometers, 9/1085
Varna, 4/409
Vasily III, 18/2145
Vasopressin, 10/1201
Vassals, 8/925
Vatican City, 11/1312, 16/1976, 18/2128, 21/**2509–10**, 21/*2509–10*
Vatican Council, Second, 18/2121
Vaudeville, 21/**2510–11**, 21/*2510–11*
  George M. Cohan, 5/*591*
Vaults, 18/2124
Vaux, Calvert, 16/1878
VDUs, 5/624
Veal, 13/1547
Vega, 18/2165
Vegans, 21/2512
Vega spacecraft, 19/2288
Vegetables, 21/**2511–12**, 21/*2511–12*
  diet, 15/1811, 15/*1811*
  gardening, 9/1040–1
  truck farming, 20/2467–8
Vegetable tanning, 12/1408
Vegetarians, 21/**2512–13**
Vegetative, 17/2086–7
Veins, 5/550–1
Velázquez, Diego, 6/662, 13/1502, 16/1913, 17/2085, 21/**2513**, 21/*2513*
  The Prince on Horseback, 21/2513, 21/*2513*
Veld, 17/1994, 19/2266
Velocity, 14/1657
Velvet, antlers, 10/1202
Venda, 19/2266

Vending machines, 21/**2513–14**, 21/*2514*
Venera spacecraft, 19/2288, 19/*2290*
Venezuela, 21/**2514–15**, 21/*2514–15*
Venice, 4/392, 11/*1311*, 20/2444, 21/**2515–16**, 21/*2515*
  Crusades, 6/679
  Florida, 5/553
  glass, 9/1084
Venom, 19/2245–6
Venus, 6/702, 19/2257, 19/*2260*
  basic facts, 19/2259
Venus-fly trap, 11/1281
Venus's girdle, 5/607
Veracruz, 13/1572, 13/1573
Veraguas, 11/1259
Verbs, 16/1881
Verdicts, 20/2464
Verdi, Giuseppe, 7/774, 15/1835, 21/**2516**, 21/*2516*
Verdun, 21/2608–9
Verdun, Treaty of, 514
Vermeer, Jan, 2/232, 2/*233*, 7/776
Vermont, 1/101, 21/**2516–19**, 21/*2517–19*
  climate, 21/*2518*
  employment, 21/2519
  history, 21/2518–19
  land, 21/2516–18
  map, 21/*2517*
  state emblems, 21/*2517*
Vernal equinox, 13/1512, 18/**2186–8***, 18/*2187–8*
Verne, Jules, 18/2175, 21/**2519**, 21/*2519*
Vernon, Mount, 21/2547, 21/2548, 21/*2548*
Veronese, 17/2085
Verrazano, Giovanni da, 8/893, 12/1485, 15/1746, 15/1754, 17/2097, 21/**2520**
Verrazano-Narrows Bridge, 21/2520
Verrocchio, Andrea del, 12/1416, 17/2084
Versailles, 3/296, 3/308, 12/*1436*, 12/1463, 13/1514, 21/**2520**, 21/*2520*
  Treaty of, 9/1010, 9/1068, 9/1069, 21/2609, 21/*2610*
Verse, poetry, 16/1960–1
Vertebrae, 18/2230
Vertebrates, 2/155, 21/**2520–1**, 21/*2521*
Vesalius, Andreas, 2/133, 2/*133*, 13/1553, 22/2648
Vesey, Denmark, 18/2237
Vespasian, 18/2131
Vespucci, Amerigo, 1/109, 6/637, 21/**2521**, 21/*2521*
Vesta (asteroid), 19/2260
Vesuvius, Mount, 2/*139*, 2/198, 14/1651, 16/1973, 16/*1973*, 18/2120, 19/2303, 21/2535
Veterans Administration, 21/2490
Veterans Day, 21/**2521–2**
Veterinary medicine, 21/**2522**, 21/*2522*
  training, 21/2522
Veto power, 6/631
Vibraphone, 22/2631
Vice-Presidents, 21/**2523**, 21/*2523*
  elections, 7/815
Viceroy butterfly, 4/421
Vichy, 22/2613

Vicksburg, 5/568, 17/*2070*
Victor Emmanuel II, King of Italy, 9/1043
Victor Emmanuel III, King of Italy, 11/1311, 11/*1311*, 14/1694
Victoria, British Columbia, 4/394
Victoria Cross, 13/1550, 13/*1551*
Victoria Falls, 1/46, 12/1454, 21/2553
Victoria Island, 15/1796
Victoria, Lake, 20/2378, 20/2482
Victoria, Queen of England, 2/143, 6/677, 6/724, 7/*859*, 20/2407, 21/**2524**, 21/*2524*
Victoria, Seychelles, 18/2197
Vicuña, 4/440
Video, 20/2399, 20/2400, 21/**2524–5**, 21/*2524*
  cameras, 4/441–2
  cassettes, 4/482
Video cassette recorders (VCRs), movies and, 14/1664
Videodiscs, 21/2524
Video signals, 7/825–6
Videotapes, 21/2524–5
Vienna, 3/269, 15/1850, 17/*2093*
  Congress of (1815), 9/1065
Vientiane, 12/1391
Vieta, Francois, 1/98
Vietminh, 21/2526
Vietnam, 11/1352, 19/2280, 21/**2525–6**, 21/*2525*
Vietnam War, 1/*121*, 1/122, 15/1778, 21/**2526–7**, 21/*2526*, 21/2541
  chemical weapons, 5/518
Vigils, 12/1371
Vikings, 1/109, 6/716, 7/855, 8/892, 13/*1585*, 13/*1588*, 21/**2527–9**, 21/*2527–9*
  burials, 4/413
  Canada, 4/446
  discovery of America, 15/1748, 15/1786
  dress, 5/*579*
  jewelry, 11/*1333*
  myths, 14/1695, 14/1696–7
  Norwegian, 15/1798
  Russia, 18/2144
  ships, 14/1727, 18/2206, 18/*2206*
Viking spacecraft, 8/894, 9/1057, 19/2288, 19/2289, 19/*2289*
Vila, 13/1558
Villages:
  formation, 1/51, 1/*52*
  medieval, 13/1585
Villa, Pancho, 21/**2529**
Villard, Oswald Garrison, 5/562
Villeins, 8/*925*
Villi, 6/731, 6/*731*
Vilna, 12/1452
Viloas, 19/2343–4
Vincennes, 11/1256
Vineyards, 21/2594
Vintage wine, 21/2594
Vinyls, 16/1955
Violence, terrorism, 20/2411
Violets, 8/920
Violins, 19/2343–4
Viper fish, 8/*944*
Vipers, 19/2246
Virgil, 2/136, 6/698, 12/1394, 18/2132, 21/**2530**, 21/*2530*
Virginia, 21/**2530–3**, 21/*2530–2*
  climate, 21/2532

  employment, 21/2533
  history, 21/2532–3
  land, 21/2530–2
  map, 21/*2531*
  state emblems, 21/*2531*
Virginia City, Montana, 14/1680
Virginia City, Nevada, 15/1743, 15/*1744*
Virginia Colony, 1/115
Virginia reel, 8/970
Virginia University, 11/1327
Virgin Islands, 21/2572
Viruses, 16/1876, 18/2156, 21/**2533–4**, 21/*2533*
  AIDS, 21/2533
  antibodies, 2/177
  diseases, 6/737
  fever, 8/926
  plant diseases, 16/1943
Visas, 20/2456
Viscosity, 8/965
Viscounts, 15/1780
Vishnu, 10/1187
Visigoths, 1/85, 18/2132, 19/2301
Vision, 18/2219–20, 18/*2219–20*
  eyes, 8/898–9, 8/*988–9*
VISTA, 16/1887
Vistula River, 16/1963
Visual handicapped, education, 19/2305
Vitamin A, 8/917, 8/948, 8/974, 12/1454, 13/1547
Vitamin B, 8/974, 12/1454, 13/1547
Vitamin C, 8/974
Vitamin D, 8/917, 8/948, 8/974, 12/1454, 13/1547
Vitamins, 8/974, 13/1554, 21/2512, 21/**2534–5**
  citrus fruit, 5/555
Vithar, 14/1695
Vivar, Rodrigo Díaz de, 5/550, 5/*550*
Vladimir, 18/2144
Vladimir I, Grand Prince, 18/2144
Vocal cords, 2/164–5, 18/2226–7
Vocal sound, 18/2226–7
Vocational high schools, industrial arts, 11/1272–4, 11/*1273*
Voice of America, 21/*2491*
Voice box, 19/2307
Voices:
  animal, 2/164–5
  singing, 18/2226–8, 18/*2227–8*
  speech, 19/2307–9, 19/*2307–8*
Volapük, 21/2499
Volcanic belts, 21/2535
Volcano del Fuego, 15/*1786*
Volcanoes, 7/784, 9/1083, 10/1157–8, 21/**2535–6**, 21/*2534–6*
  crater lakes, 12/1385
  mountain formation, 14/1668
Volcanology, 9/1055
Voles, 17/2067
Volga-Baltic Canal, 4/454
Volga-Don Canal, 14/1653
Volga River, 4/481, 8/878, 19/2281, 21/**2536**
Volgograd, 21/2535
Volkswagen Beetles, 3/275
Volleyball, 21/**2536–7**, 21/*2537*
Volsunga Saga, 14/1697
Volta Bureau, 3/329
Voltage, 7/820–1
Voltaic, 12/1493
Volta Laboratory, 3/329

Volta River, 9/1032, 9/1074
Volume, measurement, 13/1545, 13/1546
Voluntary hospitals, 10/1209
Volunteers of America, 18/2157
Von Braun, Wernher, 21/2537, *21/2537*
Voodoo, 21/2599
Voragine, Jacobus de, 12/1411
Voskhod spacecraft, 19/2291
Vostok spacecraft, 9/1029, *19/2291*
Voting machines, 5/554
Voting Rights Act, 3/354
Voyager spacecraft, *2/252*, 8/894, 19/2256, 19/2289
Vries, Hugo de, 8/887
VTOL aicraft, 20/2454
Vulcan, 9/1089
Vulcanization, 11/1294, 18/2141, 20/2428
Vulgar Latin, 18/2123
Vulgate, 3/3367
Vultures, 3/349, 4/423

Ww

Wabash River, 10/1240, 11/1255
Waddington, Mount, 4/392
Waddy, 1/17
Wagner, Richard, 5/543, 7/839, 12/1445, 14/1697, 15/1835, 21/2538, *21/2538*
Wahunsonacock, 16/1959, 17/1993
Waimangu, 9/1074
Wai, Mount, 10/1158
Waiters, 17/2093
Wake Islands, 13/1582
Walachia, 18/2126
Walalenda, Karl, 1/25
Walden, 20/2422–3
Waldo, Peter, 17/2015
Waldseemüller, Martin, 21/2521
Wales, 4/396, 20/2485, 21/2539, *21/2539*
  union with England, 7/858
Walker family, 20/2457
Walker, John, 13/1531
Walker, Thomas, 11/1362
Walking, 20/2449
  races, 20/2441
Walking perch, 8/944
Walking stick insect, *11/1279*
Walking trucks, 20/2470
Wallabies, 11/1352
Wallace, Alfred Russel, *6/700,* 8/886, 21/2539–40, *21/2540*
Wallace, Henry, 20/2472
Walla Walla Council, 21/2546
Walled fortifications, 8/989–90, *8/989–90*
Walloons, 3/327
Walls:
  houses, 6/648
  skyscrapers, 6/648
Walls, Josiah, 17/2069
Wall Street, 19/2335
Walnuts, 15/1810
Walpole, Dorothy, *9/1075*
Walpole, Sir Robert, 9/1060, *9/1075,* 17/2000
Walruses, 13/1497, 18/*2184,* 21/2540, *21/2540*

Walsh, Donald, 8/893
Walsh, Richard J., 4/401
Walter, Bruno, 3/333
Walter, Thomas, 4/461
Waltham, 11/1276
Waltham, Mass., 13/1530
Walton, Ernest, 16/*1881*
Waltzes, 6/697
  Strauss, Johann, 19/2340
Wampanoag Indians, 13/1530, 13/1531, 17/2097, 17/2099
Wampum, 5/570, 11/1260
Wandering albatross, 13/*1593,* 18/2180
Wankel engines, 7/*850*
Wankel, Felix, 7/*850*
Wapiti, 6/710
War of Austrian Succession, 9/1005
War Department, 4/425, 4/426
Ward locks, 12/1457
Wards, castles, 4/484
Warfare:
  explosives, 8/895–6
  guerilla, 10/1124
  missiles, 13/1608–9, 13/*1608–9*
  see also Arms and armor
War Hawks, 21/2541
Warlocks, 21/2598
Warm-blooded animals, 13/1495
Warm fronts, 21/2562
War of 1812, 16/1902, 21/2541–2, *21/2542*
Warps, 19/2313
  carpets, 4/472
Warren, John, 2/143
Wars, 21/2540–1
  Boer War, 3/363–4
  Crimean, 6/674–5
  decorations, 13/1550
  famous battles, 3/318, 3/319
  knights, 12/1371–2
  Korean War, 12/13377–9, 12/*1378*
  major wars, 21/2541
  Tomb of the Unknowns, 20/2433, 20/*2433*
  Vietnam War, 21/2526–7
  War of 1812, 11/1316, 21/2541–2, *21/2542*
  Wars of the Roses, 21/2543
  World War I, 21/2604–10, 21/*2604–10*
  World World II, 22/2611–20
Warsaw, 16/1964, 16/*1964*
Warsaw Pact, 20/2458, 21/2542
Warships, submarines, 19/2345–7, 19/*2345–7*
Warspite, 17/2061
Wars of the Roses, 7/805, 7/857, 10/1177, 17/2102, 21/2543, 21/*2543*
Warwick, Rhode Island, 17/2099
Warwick, Earl of, 21/2543
Wasatch Mountains, 21/2504
Washakie, 18/*2216*
Washing, soaps and detergents, 19/2247–8
Washington, 21/2543–6, 21/*2544–6*
  climate, 21/2544
  employment, 21/2546
  history, 21/2544–6
  land, 21/2543–4
  map, 21/*2545*
  state emblems, 21/*2545*

Washington and Lee University, 12/1410
Washington, Booker T., 1/83, 3/354, 5/562, 21/2546–7, 21/*2547*
Washington, D.C., 3/302, 6/741–3, 13/1525
Washington, George, 1/30, 1/31, 1/*117,* 2/226, 3/302, 4/460, 5/553, 6/644, 9/1009, 10/1142, 15/1857, 18/2138, 18/2142, 18/*2142,* 21/2547–8, 21/*2547–8*
  American Revolution, 1/126, 1/*126,* 1/127, 1/128
  builds Washington D.C., 6/741–2
  cherry trees, 3/341, 12/1411
  Continental Navy, 14/1728
  French and Indian Wars, 9/1005–6
  hobbies, 10/1192
  house, 2/*179*
  portrait, 12/1479
  President, 4/425
  teeth, 6/717
Washington, Lawrence, 21/2547
Washington, Mount, 15/1751
Washington-on-the-Brazos, 20/2412
Washoe Indians, 15/1743
Wasps, 16/1870, 21/2548–9, 21/*2548–9*
  nests, 2/153, 2/*154*
Wasserman, Dale, 14/1688
Waste, sanitation, 18/2159–60
Watches, 2/*178,* 5/577–8, 5/*578*
Water, 7/781, 21/2549–50, 21/*2549–50*
  dams, 6/693–5, 6/*694–5*
  desalinization, 21/2556
  drought, 7/767
  erosion, 7/866, 7/*866*
  floods, 8/955–6, 8/*955–6*
  fountains, 8/996, 8/*996–7*
  geysers, 9/1073–4, 9/*1074*
  irrigation, 11/1305, 11/*1305*
  lakes, 12/1384–5, 12/*1384–5*
  lifesaving, 12/1430–2, 12/*1431*
  marshes, 19/2361–2
  oceans, 15/1814–21, 15/*1814–20*
  plumbing, 16/1957–8, 16/*1958*
  pollution, 16/1969–70, 17/*2021*
  pond life, 16/1973–4
  pressure, 15/1814
  safety, 18/2152
  scuba diving, 18/2177–8
  springs, 21/2566–7
  swamps, 19/2361–2
  swimming, 20/2364–6
  waves, 21/2557
  weather, 21/2562
  wells, 21/2566–7, 21/2567
Water birds, 7/770–2. 7/*770–2,* 21/2550–2, 21/*2551–2*
  swimmers, 21/2550–1
  waders, 21/2551–2
Water boatman, 4/*404,* 4/405
Water buffalo, 4/403, 4/495
Water clocks, 5/577, 20/*2427*
Watercolors, 15/1860
Water cycle, 21/2552–3*, 21/*2552*
Waterdogs, 18/2155
Waterfalls, 21/2553, 21/*2553*
  see also individual waterfalls e.g.
    Niagara Falls
Waterford, 21/2528
Watergate affair, 8/984, 15/1778
Water lettuce, 2/*189*

Waterloo, battle of, 3/319, 14/1702, 21/2553–4, 21/*2554*
Waterman, Lewis E., 16/*1896*
Watermarks, 16/1871
Watermills, 7/847
Water ouzel, 3/344
Water pollution, 21/2554–5, 21/*2554*
Waterproof fabrics, 20/2416
Water rails, 6/*670*
Water scorpion, 4/*404,* 4/405
Watershed, 6/652
Waterskiing, 21/2555, 21/*2555*
Water spiders, 19/2312
Waterspouts, 20/2434
Water strider, 4/405
Water supply, 18/*2160,* 21/2555–6, 21/*2556*
  springs, 21/2566–7
  treatment, 21/2556
  wells, 21/2566–7, 21/*2567*
Waterton Lakes National Park, 14/1640, 14/*1707*
Water transport, 20/2452
Water vapour:
  clouds, 5/582
  humidity, 10/1225–6
Waterwheels, 11/1294
Wats, 20/2417
Watson, James D., 9/1052, 9/*1052*
Watson, Thomas, 3/329, 20/2390
Watson, Tom, 19/2317
Watteau, Jean Antoine, 17/*2113,* 17/2114
Watt, James, 11/1274, 11/1292, 21/2556–7, 21/*2557*
Watts, 7/821
Wave caves, 4/497, 4/*498*
Wave-cut terraces, 18/2182
Wavelengths:
  light, 5/600
  radio, 17/2047
  sound, 19/2265
Waverley novels, 18/2177
WAVES, 14/1731
Waves, 18/2182, 21/2557–8, 21/*2557*
  radiation, 17/2043–4
  radio, 17/2045–6, 17/*2046*
  sea, 15/1814–15, 15/*1814*
  seismic, 7/789, 7/*789*
  sound, 19/*2263,* 19/2264
  tsunamis, 7/789
Wax, 21/2558, 21/*2558*
  ears, 7/778
Wayne, Anthony, 1/128, 15/1824, 21/2558–9, 21/*2559,* 21/2576
Wayne, John, 14/*1662*
Wayne State University, 6/723
Wayside Inn, 10/1211, 12/1460
Weapons, 21/2559–60, 21/*2559–60*
  chemical, 5/518
  disarmament, 6/736
  explosives, 8/895–6
  guns, 10/1129–32, 10/*1129–31*
  knives, 20/2368
  missiles, 13/1608–9, 13/*1608–9*
  space, 19/2297
  swords, 20/2368, 20/*2368*
  tanks, 20/2377–8, 20/*2377*
Weare, 15/1752
Weasels, 2/*146,* 5/559, 21/2560–1, 21/*2560–1*
Weather, 5/575–7, 21/2561–4, 21/*2561–3*
  air, 21/2561

atmosphere, 3/257
barometers, 3/306
clouds, 5/**581–3**
droughts, 7/767
fog, 8/967–8
frosts, 9/1015, 9/*1015*
hail, 10/1137, 10/*1137*
humidity, 10/1225–6
hurricanes, 10/1228–9, 10/*1228*
kites, 11/1370
lightning, 12/1437
local conditions, 21/2563
meteorology, 21/2563
monsoon, 14/1639–40, 14/*1639–40*
rain, 17/2059–60, 17/*2060*
rainbows, 17/2060, 17/*2060*
snow, 17/2059–60
sun, 21/2561
thunder, 12/1437
tornadoes, 20/2434, 20/*2434*
water, 21/2562
water cycle, 21/2552–3
weather patterns, 21/2562–3
winds, 21/2561, 21/2592–3
Weatherford, William, 11/*1271*
Weather satellites, 18/2165
Weather vanes, 21/2563
Weaver ants, 2/*166*
Weaver, Robert, 5/563
Weaving, 5/579–80, 19/2313–14,
    19/*2313–14*
  tapestry, 20/2379–80, 20/*2380*
  textiles, 20/2415–16
Webber, Andrew Lloyd, 14/1688
Webb, Matthew, 7/854
Web presses, 17/2004
Webster, Daniel, 15/1751, 21/**2564**,
    21/*2564*
Webster, Noah, 21/**2564–5**, 21/*2564*
Weddell seals, 18/2185
Weddings, 13/1518
  anniversaries, 2/166
Wedges, 12/1476
Wedges (golf), 9/1092
Wedgwood, Josiah, 16/1990
Wednesday, 6/702
Weems, Parson, 3/341
Weevils, 3/326, 3/*326*
Weft, 19/2313
  carpets, 4/473
Wegener, Alfred, 6/652
Weight, 21/**2565**, 21/*2565*
  measurement, 13/1545, 13/1546
  scales, 18/2167
Weight lifting, 21/**2565–6**, 21/*2566*
Weightlessness, 19/2295
Weimar Republic, 9/1068
Weine, Robert, 14/1662
Weiskopf, Tom, 19/2317
Weismann, August, 8/887
Weissmuller, Johnny, 4/*417*
Weka, 8/*954*
Welding, 11/1273
Welland Canal, 15/1770
Wellesley, Arthur *see* Wellington,
    Duke of
Welles, Orson, 1/28
Wellington, 15/1768, 15/1769
Wellington, Duke of, 21/2553,
    21/**2566**, 21/*2566*
Wells and springs, 21/**2566–7**,
    21/*2567*
Wells, H.G., 18/2175, 21/**2566**,
    21/*2566*

Wells, Horace, 2/143
Welsh ponies, 10/1207
Wenceslaus, St, 6/689
Werewolves, 2/162
Wesley, Charles, 21/**2568**, 21/*2568*
Wesley, John, 8/*883*, 21/**2568**,
    21/*2568*
Wesley, Robert, 14/*1723*
Wesminster Abbey, 21/**2572**,
    21/*2572*
Wessex, 2/143, 10/1153
Westbrook, Harriet, 18/2203
Westerlies, 21/2561
Western culture, 6/685
Western Ghats, 11/1252
Westerns, fiction, 12/1451
Western saddles, 10/1207
Western Samoa, 15/1854, 15/*1857*,
    16/1971, 16/1972
West Germany, 9/1064
  Adenauer, Konrad, 1/34, 1/*34*
  formation, 9/1069
  geography, 9/1070–1
  see also Germany (before 1945)
West Indies, 21/**2568–72**, 21/*2569–
    72*
  climate, 21/2569
  nations, 21/2570–2
  people, 21/2570
  resources, 21/2569–70
Westo Indians, 19/2274
Westphalia, Peace of, 9/1065
West Point, 21/2498
West Virginia, 6/626, 21/**2572–5**,
    21/*2573–5*
  climate, 21/2574
  employment, 21/2575
  history, 21/2574–5
  land, 21/2574
  map, 21/*2573*
  state emblems, 21/*2573*
Westward Movement, 21/**2575–8**,
    21/*2576–8*
  Greeley, Horace, 9/1116
  Lewis and Clark expedition,
    12/1420–1
  Santa Fe Trail, 18/2161
Wet continental climate, 5/576
Wethersfield, 6/636
Wet subtropical climate, 5/576
Wet suits, 18/217
Whales, 9/1022, 17/2063,
    21/**2578–80**, 21/*2578–80*
  baleen whales, 21/2579
  toothed whales, 21/2579–80
  whaling, 21/2580
Whale sharks, 18/2199, 18/*2199*,
    18/2200
Wheat, 6/659, 9/1097, 9/*1097*,
    11/1356, 21/**2580–1**, 21/*2580–1*
  flour making, 8/960
Wheatears, 13/*1593*
Wheat germ, diet, 15/1811
Wheatstone, Sir Charles, 1/21,
    10/1153, 12/1442
Wheeler Park, 6/631
Wheel-lock pistols, 10/*1131*
Wheels, 11/1294, 12/1475, 20/2449,
    20/*2450*
  potter's, 16/1989, 16/*1990*
  tires, 20/2428–9, 20/*2429*
Whip kick, 20/2366
Whirligigs, 3/326
Whiskey, 1/93, 9/1097

Whistler, James McNeill, 12/1468,
    21/**2581–2**, 21/*2581*
  Miss Cicely Alexander, 21/2581–2,
    21/*2581*
Whistling swan, 7/772
White animals, 1/92
White beluga whales, 13/1592
White blood cells, 3/359, 3/*360*
White Cliffs of Dover, 4/431
White dwarfs, 19/2327
White, E.B., 5/532
White, Edward, 8/*894*, 19/2291,
    19/2292, 19/*2292*
White-footed mice, 17/2067
White-fronted goose, 7/*771*
Whitehead, Albert North, 13/1533
White House, 1/116, 2/235, 6/743,
    12/1479, 21/**2582**, 21/*2582*
  Cabinet Room, 4/*425*
White ibis, 21/2551
White, John, 15/*1787*, 15/1788
White leghorns, 17/1991
White long-hair cat, 4/*486*
White Mountains, 2/183, 15/1751,
    15/1752, 12/1485, 21/2518
White Nile, 15/1775, 19/2349,
    20/2482
White pelicans, 16/1891
White, Peregrine, 16/1931
White pine, 6/632
White River, 11/1255
White spruce, 6/633
White storks, 19/2339, 19/*2339*
White, Susanna, 16/1931
Whitetail deer, 6/709, 6/*709*
White-tailed kites, 3/348
White-toothed pygmy shrews,
    14/1623
White, Walter Francis, 14/1706
Whitman, Walt, 21/**2582–3**, 21/*2583*
Whitney, Eli, 6/636–7, 6/*664*, 6/665,
    11/1294, 13/1507, 21/2559,
    21/**2583**, 21/*2583*
Whitney, Mount, 4/436, 15/1782,
    21/2491
Whittier, John Greenleaf,
    21/**2583–4**, 21/*2583*
Whitworth, Kathy, 19/2317
Wholesalers, 18/2188
Whole wheat flour, 8/960
Whooping cough, 5/528
Whooping cranes, 3/343, 3/344,
    3/*346*, 6/670–1, 6/*670*, 17/2065,
    21/2552
Wichita Indians, 11/1355, 11/1356,
    15/1827
Wickiup, 2/179, 11/1263
Wicks, candles, 4/455–6
Widgeon, 3/347, 7/770, 7/771
Wieliczka, 18/2157
Wie, Rabbi Stephen, 5/562
Wiggin, Kate Douglas, 21/**2584**,
    21/*2584*
Wightman Cup, 20/2407
Wigs, 10/1139
Wigwams, 10/*1214*, 11/1263,
    13/1604, 15/1826
Wildcats, 4/*488*, 4/489, 4/*489*
Wild cherry, 20/*2461*
Wild dogs, 6/669–70
Wildebeest, 2/174, 13/*1592*
Wilde, Oscar, 11/1301
Wilder, Almanzo, 21/2584

Wilder, Laura Ingalls, 21/**2584**,
    21/*2584*
Wilderness areas, 21/2585, 21/*2585*
Wilderness Road, 2/184, 3/370,
    21/2576, 21/**2585–6**, 21/*2586*
Wilder, Thornton, 14/1688,
    21/**2584–5**, 21/*2584*
Wildflowers, 21/**2586–8***, 21/*2586–8*
  desert, 21/2587
  enjoying, 21/2588
  garden flowers, 21/2587–8
  meadow, 21/2586–7
  mountain, 21/2587
  prairie, 21/2587
  swamp, 21/2587
  water, 21/2587
  woodland, 21/2586
Wildlife, in cities, 5/558–9, 5/*558–9*
Wilhelm I, King of Prussia, 9/1005,
    9/1065–8
Wilhelm II, Kaiser, 3/351, 9/1086,
    21/2605, 21/2609, 21/*2610*
Wilkes, Charles, 2/171
Wilkins, Hubert, 2/171
Wilkins, Roy, 14/1706, 14/*1706*
Willamette River, 15/1841
Willamette Valley, 15/1842
Willard, Emma, 21/**2588**, 21/*2588*
Willard, John, 21/2588
**William I the Conqueror, King of
    England**, 3/319, 7/805–6, 7/854,
    7/855, 10/1177, 12/1459,
    20/2436, 21/2528, 21/**2588–9**,
    21/*2589*
William II, King of England, 2/165,
    10/1176, 21/**2589**, 21/*2589*
William III, King of England, 7/858,
    11/1319, 21/**2589–90**
William IV, King of England,
    21/**2589**
William and Mary College, 5/595
Williamsburg, 11/1320, 14/1680,
    20/2419, 21/2530
Williams, Roger, 17/2032, 17/2099,
    21/**2590**, 21/*2590*
Williams, Tennessee, 7/760,
    21/**2590**, 21/*2590*
Williamsport, 12/1453
Williston Basin, 15/1793
Willow, Alaska, 1/87
Willow ptarmigan, 9/1034, 9/*1034*
Willson, Meredith, 14/1687
Wilmington, 6/*712*, 6/714, 6/715,
    15/1787
Wilson, Allen B., 18/2196
Wilson, Sam, 20/2483
Wilson, Woodrow, 1/121, 10/1200,
    12/1404, 12/1438, 15/1779,
    16/*1968*, 16/1977, 18/2136,
    20/2376, 21/**2590–2**, 21/*2591*,
    21/2609, 21/*2610*
Wilton carpets, 4/473
Wimbledon, 9/1077, 20/2407
Winchester carbines, 10/*1131*
Wind, 21/**2561–2**, 21/**2592–3***,
    21/*2592–3*
  Beaufort scale, 21/2593
  erosion, 7/866, 7/*866*
  instruments, 14/1682, 14/1689
  monsoon, 14/1639–40, 14/*1639–40*
  plants and, 16/1945
  tornadoes, 20/2434, 20/*2434*
Wind caves, 4/497
Windhoek, 14/1699, 14/*1700*

Wind in the Willows, 9/1096
Windmills, 7/847, 9/*1048*, 11/1294, 17/*2029*
Window Rock, 14/1724
Windows, stained glass, 19/2323, 19/*2323*
Windsor, Ontario, 15/1832
Windsor, Duke of, 7/805
Wind surfing, 21/**2593**, 21/*2593*
Wind tunnels, 7/*851*, 21/**2593–4**, 21/*2594*
Windward Islands, 21/2571
Wines and wine making, 1/23, 1/93, 21/**2594–5**, 21/*2594*
Wings, 1/21
    insect, 11/1278–80
    mammals, 13/1497
Winnebago Indians, 11/1296, 21/2596
Winnie-the-Pooh, 13/1594–5
Winnipeg, 13/1503, 13/*1504*, 13/1505
Winnipeg, Lake, 13/1503
Winslow, Edward, 16/1931
Winston-Salem, 15/1790
Winter, 21/**2595**, 21/*2595*
    December, 6/705–6
Wintergreen, 13/1552
Winter Olympics, 15/1830
Winter solstice, 18/2186
Winthrop, John, 13/1530
Wireless *see* Radio
Wire rope, 18/2137
Wisconsin, 21/**2595–8**, 21/*2596–8*
    climate, 21/2596
    employment, 21/2598
    history, 21/2596–8
    land, 21/2596
    map, 21/*2597*
    state emblems, 21/*2597*
Wisent, 3/351
Wisteria, 8/*961*
Witchcraft, 21/**2598–9**, 21/*2599*
Withdrawal symptoms, 7/769
    drug addiction, 1/33
Witwatersrand, 3/363
Wiyot Indians, 4/436
Wizards, 21/2598
Wladyslaw II, King of Poland, 12/1452
Woden, 6/702
Wolfe, James, 3/319, 4/447, 9/*1005*, 9/1006, 17/2038
Wolfe, Thomas, 15/1788
Wolffia, 8/*961*
Wolof, 18/2190
Wolsey, Cadinal, 10/1177
Wolverines, 21/2560
Wolves, 21/**2599–600**, 21/*2599*
Wombats, 3/268, 3/*268*
Women:
    Arab, 2/193–4
    priesthood, 17/2016
Women Appointed for Voluntary Emergency Service (WAVES), 14/1731
Women's Army Corps (WAC), 2/226–7
Women's rights, 21/**2600–1**, 21/*2600*
    Rankin, Jeannette, 17/2062
    Stanton, Elizabeth, 19/2325–6
Wonderful Wizard of Oz, 3/318
Wood, 16/1950, 21/**2601–2**, 21/*2601*
    building materials, 6/646
    carving, 4/480
    fuel, 9/1018

furniture, 9/1024–7
    lumbering, 12/1469–70, 12/*1469–70*
    paper, 16/1871–2
Wood anemone, 8/*962*
Wood Buffalo, 1/92, 14/1713
Woodchucks, 5/559, 8/920, 9/1120, 10/1183, 10/*1183*
Wood duck, 7/771
Wooden buildings, 4/405–6, 4/*405–6*
Wooden horse of Troy, 20/2465, 20/*2465*
Wood fern, 8/923
Wood ibis, 21/2551
Woodlands, wildflowers, 21/2586
Woodpeckers, 10/*1146*
Wood pulp, 12/1470
Wood rats, 17/2066
Woods (golf), 9/1092
Wood sorrel, 8/*962*
Wood storks, 19/2339
Wood thrush, 9/*1037*, 14/*1719*
Woodwind instruments, 14/1689, 21/**2602–3**, 21/*2602–3*
Woodwork, carpentry, 4/470–2
Woof, carpets, 4/473
Wool:
    knitting, 12/1372–3
    spinning and weaving, 19/2313–14
Woolly mammoths, 7/831
Woomera, 1/17
Worcester, Mass., 13/1528
Word games, 21/**2603–4**
Word hunt, 21/2604
Words:
    dictionaries, 6/726–8
    grammar, 9/1097–8
Wordsworth, William, 21/**2604**, 21/*2604*
Work, careers, 4/465–7
Workers:
    Industrial Revolution, 11/1275
    labor unions, 12/1380–1
Working dogs, 6/746
Work songs, 8/972
Works Progress Administration (WPA), 18/2134
World Council of Churches, 17/2014
World Driver's Championship, 3/278
World fairs, 8/902–3, 8/*903*
World Health Organization (WHO), 6/649, 20/2486
World's Columbian Exposition (1893), 8/903
World's Fair, Brussels, 8/903
World War I, 1/*118*, 1/121, 8/881, 9/1068, 21/2541, 21/**2604–10**, 21/*2604–10*
    Canada, 4/450
    causes, 21/2605–8
    Cavell, Edith Louisa, 4/500
    chemical weapons, 5/518
    chronology, 21/2606
    fighting, 21/2608–10
    outcome, 21/2610
    participants, 21/2604–5
    US Navy, 14/1729
World War II, 1/*118*, 1/121, 9/1069, 11/1323, 18/2135, 20/2471, 21/2541, 22/**2611–20**, 22/*2611–20*
    Canada, 4/450
    Churchill, Winston, 5/549
    events leading to, 22/2611–12
    fighting, 22/2612–19
    Hitler, Adolf, 10/1190–1

MacArthur, Douglas, 12/1473
    major events, 22/2615
    Normandy landings, 7/813
    peace terms, 22/2619
    Pearl Harbor, 16/1888
    US Navy, 14/1729
World Wildlife Fund, 17/2065
Worm gears, 9/1048
Worms, 2/148, 22/**2620–1**, 22/*2620–1*
    earthworms, 7/789–90, 7/*790*
Worship, freedom of, 5/548–9
Wounded Knee Creek, 11/1271, 18/2228
Wrangell, Mount, 16/*1934*
Wrenches, 4/472
Wren, Sir Christopher, 12/145, 17/2085
Wrestling, 22/**2621–2**, 22/*2621–2*
Wright Brothers, 1/63, 1/66, 1/*117*, 3/281, 3/*281*, 15/1787, 20/2452, 22/**2623**, 22/*2623*
Wright, Frank Lloyd, 14/*1680*, 22/**2622**, 22/*2622*
Wright, Joseph, 16/*1937*
Wright, Richard, 22/**2622–3**, 22/*2623*
Writers:
    Aeschylus, 1/40–1
    Aesop, 1/41
    Alcott, Louisa May, 1/94
    Alger, Horatio, 1/99
    Andersen, Hans Christian, 2/139–40
    Austen, Jane, 3/262–3
    Baldwin, James, 3/294–5
    Barrie, James M., 3/308
    Baum, Frank L., 3/318
    Bellow, Saul, 3/**330**, 3/*330*
    Blume, Judy, 3/360
    Brontë family, 4/397
    Brooks, Gwendolyn, 4/397–8
    Browning, Elizabeth Barrett, 4/398–9
    Browning, Robert, 4/398–9
    Buck, Pearl, 4/401
    Bunyan, John, 4/410–11
    Burnett, Frances Hodgson, 4/415–16
    Burns, Robert, 4/416
    Burroughs, Edgar Rice, 4/417
    Byron, George Gordon, 4/423–4
    Carroll, Lewis, 4/475–6
    Chekhov, Anton, 5/517
    Conrad, Joseph, 6/638
    Cooper, James Fennimore, 6/656–7
    Crane, Stephen, 6/671
    Dante Alighieri, 6/698
    Defoe, Daniel, 6/710
    Dickens, Charles, 6/725–6
    Dickinson, Emily, 6/726
    Doyle, Sir Arthur Conan, 7/756
    Dumas, Alexandre, 7/773–4
    Dumas, Alexandre the Younger, 7/773–4
    Eliot, George, 7/835–6
    Eliot, T.S., 7/836
    Emerson, Ralph Waldo, 7/841
    Frost, Robert, 9/1015–16
    Grahame, Kenneth, 9/1096
    Grimm brothers, 9/1120
    Hardy, Thomas, 10/1152–3
    Harris, Joel Chandler, 10/1153–4
    Hawthorne, Nathaniel, 10/1161
    Hemingway, Ernest, 10/1175
    Henry, O., 10/1178

Holmes, Oliver Wendell Sr., 10/1195
Homer, 10/1197
Hughes, James Langston, 10/1219
Hugo, Victor Marie, 10/1219
Huxley, Aldous, 10/1229
Ibsen, Henrik, 10/1232–3
Irving, Washington, 11/1306
Jackson, Helen Hunt, 11/1317
Johnson, Samuel, 11/1340
Keats, John, 11/1356–7
Kipling, Rudyard, 11/1370
La Fontaine, Jean de, 12/1384
Lamb, Charles, 12/1386
Lawrence, T.E., 12/1400–1
Lear, Edward, 12/1405–6
Lewis, Sinclair, 12/1420
London, Jack, 12/1459
Longfellow, Henry Wadsworth, 12/1460
Machiavelli, Niccolò, 12/1474–5
Melville, Hemann, 13/1558–9
Milne, A.A., 13/1594–5
Milton, John, 13/1595
Orwell, George, 15/1848
Paine, Thomas, 15/1857–8
Perrault, Charles, 16/1901
Plutarch, 16/1958
Poe, Edgar Allan, 16/1959
Potter, Beatrix, 16/1986–7, 16/*1987*
Riley, James Whitcomb, 17/2102–3
Sandburg, Carl, 18/2158
Scott, Sir Walter, 18/2177
Shakespeare, William, 18/2197–8
Shaw, George Bernard, 18/2200
Shelley, Mary, 18/2203
Shelley, Percy, 18/2203
Spyri, Johanna, 19/2320
Stephenson, Robert Louis, 19/2334
Stowe, Harriet Beecher, 19/2339–40
Swift, Jonathan, 20/2364
Tennyson, Alfred, 20/2407
Thackeray, William Makepeace, 20/2416–17
Thoreau, Henry David, 20/2422–3
Thurber, James, 20/2423–4
Tolstoy, Leo, 20/2433
Twain, Mark, 20/2478
Verne, Jules, 21/2519
Virgil, 21/2530
Webster, Noah, 21/2564–5
Wells, H.G., 21/2566
Whitman, Walt, 21/2582–3
Whittier, John Greenleaf, 21/2583–4
Wiggin, Kate Douglas, 21/2584
Wilder, Laura Ingalls, 21/2584
Wilder, Thornton, 21/2584–5
Williams, Tennessee, 21/2590
Wordsworth, William, 21/2604
Wright, Richard, 22/2622–3
see also Literature
Written communication, 5/611
Written language, 12/1387, 22/**2624–5**, 22/*2624*
    ancient civilizations, 2/133–5
    Arabic, 2/194–5, 2/*195*
    braille, 4/382, 4/*382*
    composition, 5/**620–1**
    cuneiform, 19/2352
    diaries, 6/724–5
    dictionaries, 6/726–8
    handwriting, 10/1146
    hieroglyphics, 10/1184–5, 10/*1184*

ink, 11/1276
Japanese, 11/1322
letters, 12/1418–19
pencils, 16/1896–7
pens, 16/1896
poetry, 16/1960–1
punctuation, 17/2029–30
runes, 20/*2363*
shorthand, 18/2214–15, 18/*2215*
spelling, 19/2309
see also Language; Literature
Wrought iron, 11/1303
Wu-han, 22/2632
Wuthering Heights, 4/397
Wyandotte Indians, 11/1362
Wycliffe, John, 3/336, 17/2015
Wye Mills, 16/1878
Wye, River, 21/2539
Wyeth, Andrew, 14/1620
Wyeth family, 2/228
Wylie, Lake, 19/2276
Wyoming, 22/**2625-7**, 22/*2625–7*
climate, 22/2625
employment, 22/2626
history, 22/2625–6
land, 22/2625
map, 22/2627
state emblems, 22/2627
Wythe House, 1/*113*

Xx

Xavier, Saint Francis, 11/1323
Xerxes I, King of Persia, 22/**2628**, 22/*2628*
Xhoison, 14/1700
Xochimilco, 13/1576
X rays, 13/1554, 18/*2166*, 22/**2629-31**, 22/*2629–31*
body scanners, 3/363
hospital departments, 10/1210
X-ray tubes, 7/827
Xylem, 20/2459
Xylophones, 22/**2631**, 22/*2631*
XYZ Affair, 1/30

Yy

Yachts, 18/2153–4, 18/*2154*
Yakima River, 21/2546

Yaks, 4/495–6, 4/*496*, 14/*1738*
Yale, Linus, 12/1457
Yale locks, 12/1457–8, 12/*1458*
Yale University, 5/595
Yalta, 22/*2619*
Yalu River, 12/1376
Yamacraw Bluff, 9/1062
Yam Kinneret, 9/1031
Yangtze River, 5/536, 18/2199, 22/**2632**, 22/*2632*
Yankton Indians, 18/2228
Yaoundé, 4/442
Yap, 13/1582
Yarn, spinning and weaving, 19/2313–14
Yazoo River, 13/1610
Year, measuring, 20/2428
Yeast, 3/292, 9/1020, 9/1021, 22/**2633**★
fermentation, 8/922
Yeats, William Butler, 11/1301
Yellow-bellied parrot, 16/*1880*
Yellow fever, 17/2074
Yellow jacket, 21/2549
Yellowknife, 15/1796, 22/*2640*
Yellowknife Indians, 3/253
Yellow River, 5/536, 22/**2633**, 22/*2633*
Yellow serpentine, 13/*1597*
Yellowstone Park, 3/320, 6/710, 14/1709, 14/*1709*, 14/*1712*, 14/*1713*, 22/2626, 22/*2626*, 22/**2633-4**, 22/*2634*
Yellowstone River, 14/1642, 14/*1713*, 17/*2104*
Yemen, 2/*192*, 2/193, 18/*2235*, 19/2262
coffee, 5/591
Yenisei River, 19/2282
Yerkes Observatory, 15/1813, 15/*1814*, 20/2395
Yeti, 1/16, *1/16*
Yevtushenko, Yevgeny, 19/2284
Yews, 6/633
Yiddish language, 22/**2634**
YMCA, 22/**2638**
Yoga, 10/1187, 22/**2634-5**, 22/*2635*
Yogurt, 6/692
Yom Kippur, 11/1344, 22/**2635**, 22/*2635*
York, 7/85
York, House of, 21/2543
Yorktown, 1/*117*, 1/128
Yoruba, 6/684, 15/1774, 21/*2601*

Yosemite Falls, 21/2553, 22/2635–6
Yosemite National Park, 14/1709, 22/2635–6, 22/*2636*
Yosemite Valley, 4/436, 22/**2635-6**, 22/*2636*
Young, Andrew, 3/355, 22/**2636**, 22/*2636*
Young, Brigham, 12/1396, 21/2505, 22/**2636**, 22/*2636*
Young, Chic, 5/608
Young, John, 19/*2296*
Young Men's Christian Association (YMCA), 22/2638
Young People's Associations, 22/**2637-8**, 22/*2637–8*
Young, Thomas, 18/2138
Young, Whitney Moore Jr., 22/**2637**, 22/*2637*
Young Women's Christian Association (YWCA), 22/2638
Youth hostels, 3/338
Ypres, 4/*448*
Ysleta, 20/2412
Yucatán Indians, 6/661–2
Yucatán Peninsula, 13/1541, 13/1573
Yucatec Indians, 13/1541
Yucca Flat, 15/1743
Yucca House, 14/1708
Yugoslavia, 22/**2638-9**, 22/*2638–9*
Tito, 20/2430
Yukon gold rush, 9/1090–1
Yukon River, 22/2639, 22/*2640*
Yukon Territory, 22/**2639-40**, 22/*2640*
map, 22/*2640*
Yule log, 5/548
Yuma Indians, 2/215, 4/438
Yung Lo Ta Tien, 7/843
Yurok Indians, 4/436
Yurts, 14/1633, 14/*1633*, 20/*2408*
YWCA, 22/**2638**

Zz

Zagreb, 22/2639
Zahir Shah, 1/42
Zaire, 22/**2641-5**, 22/*2641–5*
Zaire River (Congo River), 6/627, 22/**2642-3**, 22/*2642*
Zama, battle of, 3/319
Zambezi River, 22/2644
Zambia, 17/2100, 22/**2643-4**, 22/*2643*

Zamenhof, Lazarus Ludwig, 21/2498
Zamma, battle of, 10/1148, 10/*1148*
Zanzibar, 20/2378, 20/2379
Zapata, Emiliano, 21/2529
Zarathustra, 16/1902
Zealand, 6/717
Zebras, 1/46, 22/**2644**, 22/*2644*
Zebu cattle, 4/495
Zelenchukskaya, 15/1813, 20/2394
Zemsky Sobor, 18/2146
Zenobia, Queen, 20/*2373*
Zeppelin, Count von, 1/78
Zeppelins, 1/78
Zeuglodon, 13/1499
Zeus, 6/641, 8/879, 9/1088, 9/*1088*, 14/1677, 14/1696, 14/1697, 15/1830, 16/1870, 16/1902, 17/2008
statue at Olympia, 18/2193, 18/*2193*
Ziggurats, 3/286
Zimbabwe, 17/2100, 22/**2644-5**, 22/*2644–5*
Zimmermann family, 17/2113
Zinc, 13/1567
Zinjanthropus, 12/1405
Ziolkowski, Korczak, 18/2143
Zionism, 11/1336
ZIP codes, 16/1984
Zither, 19/2344
Zodiac, 2/247, 2/*247*, 6/642
Zodiacal light, 19/2260
Zond spacecraft, 19/2288
Zoology, 22/**2647-9**★, 22/*2647–9*
career, 22/2649
history of, 22/2468–9
see also Animals
Zooplankton, 6/682, 13/1515
Zoos, 14/1716, 22/**2645-7**★, 22/*2645–7*
feeding, 22/2646–7
healthy animals, 22/2646
obtaining animals, 22/2647
Zoroaster, 16/1902
Zoroastrianism, 3/366, 16/1902
Zoser, Pharaoh, 17/2033
Zuider Zee, 14/1741
Zulus, 1/*48*, 19/2267
Zuni Indians, 2/179, 5/575, 6/660, 15/1757
Zwingli, Ulrich, 17/2015
Zworykin, Vladimir Kosma, 3/292, 21/2533, 22/**2649**, 22/*2649*
Zygotes, 17/2087